THE APPLICATION OF FOREIGN LAW IN THE BRITISH AND GERMAN COURTS

This book explores the application of foreign law in civil proceedings in the British and German courts. It focuses on how domestic procedural law impacts on the application of choice of law rules in domestic courts. It engages with questions involved in the investigation and determination of foreign law as they affect the law of England and Wales, Scotland, and Germany. Although the relevant jurisdictions are the focus, the comparative analysis extends to explore examples from other jurisdictions, including relevant international and European conventions. Ambitious in scope, it expertly tracks the development of the law and looks at possible future reforms.

Volume 34 in the series Studies in Private International Law

Studies in Private International Law

Recent titles in the series

Forum (Non) Conveniens in England: Past, Present, and Future
Ardavan Arzandeh

Commercial Issues in Private International Law: A Common Law Perspective
Edited by Vivienne Bath, Andrew Dickinson, Michael Douglas and Mary Keyes

Jurisdiction and Cross-Border Collective Redress: A European Private International Law Perspective
Alexia Pato

Rethinking Judicial Jurisdiction in Private International Law
Milana Karayanidi

Economic Sanctions in EU Private International Law
Tamás Szabados

Clawback Law in the Context of Succession
Jayne Holliday

Place of Performance: A Comparative Analysis
Chukwuma Okoli

Private International Law in Nigeria
Chukwuma Okoli and Richard Oppong

Planning the Future of Cross Border Families: A Path Through Coordination
Edited by Ilaria Viarengo and Francesca Villata

The Private International Law of Authentic Instruments
Jonathan Fitchen

The Hague Judgments Convention and Commonwealth Model Law: A Pragmatic Perspective
Abubakri Yekini

A Guide to Global Private International Law
Edited by Paul Beaumont and Jayne Holliday

Parental Child Abduction to Islamic Law Countries
Nazia Yaqub

The Application of Foreign Law in the British and German Courts
Alexander D J Critchley

The Application of Foreign Law in the British and German Courts

Alexander D J Critchley

•HART•
OXFORD • LONDON • NEW YORK • NEW DELHI • SYDNEY

HART PUBLISHING
Bloomsbury Publishing Plc
Kemp House, Chawley Park, Cumnor Hill, Oxford, OX2 9PH, UK
1385 Broadway, New York, NY 10018, USA
29 Earlsfort Terrace, Dublin 2, Ireland

HART PUBLISHING, the Hart/Stag logo, BLOOMSBURY and the Diana logo are trademarks of Bloomsbury Publishing Plc

First published in Great Britain 2022

A catalogue record for this book is available from the British Library.

A catalogue record for this book is available from the Library of Congress.

ISBN: HB: 978-1-50995-958-7
ePDF: 978-1-50995-960-0
ePub: 978-1-50995-959-4

Typeset by Compuscript Ltd, Shannon

SERIES EDITOR'S PREFACE

I thoroughly enjoyed reading an earlier version of this book when it was submitted to me by the author as a possible book in the Hart Studies in Private International Law Series. It is an excellent addition to the Series. The Series did not have a book on application of foreign law so this volume fills a significant gap. A lot of original research has gone into the preparation of the book, particularly the strong historical work on application of foreign law in cross-border cases, not only in the large legal systems of Germany and England and Wales, but especially in Scotland – the homeland of both the author and me.

The original version of the book was written when the UK was still part of the EU or at least still in the transition period on the way out of the EU. The final version of the book is a fully up to date and thorough comparative and historical account of the application of foreign law in Germany and the two main legal systems in the UK (England and Wales, and Scotland). The final version of the book takes proper account of the efforts that were made at the global level in the Hague Conference on Private International Law (HCCH) in the early part of this millennium to consider whether any progress could be made on the progressive unification of the rules of private international law in this field. The author takes the opportunity to consider whether those stalled efforts could be revived and therefore help to bring about some small steps to greater unity for the law on application of foreign law in Great Britain and Germany in the future. In particular, the model provided by Articles 8(f), 14 and 15 of the Hague Child Abduction Convention 1980 and the discussion of that model in the explanatory report on that Convention, the leading works on the Child Abduction Convention and the case law on it are properly evaluated as a model for future instruments with appropriate adaptations.

The author has taken full account of the unanimous judgment of the UK Supreme Court by Lord Leggatt in *FS Cairo* [2021] UKSC on the 'default rule' (in cases where foreign law is not pleaded before an English court when the relevant English applicable law rule indicates that, in principle, a foreign law is applicable to the claim) and the 'presumption of similarity rule' (in cases where foreign law is pleaded by a party but evidence is not led about the content of the foreign law). This judgment has clarified that in England and Wales the operation of foreign law is not mandatory when English applicable law rules indicate the application of foreign law to a claim because in those cases the 'default rule' applies whereby the law of the forum (English law) is applicable to the claim (see paras 113–118). However, if a party does plead foreign law but then does not lead evidence, or does not lead evidence on a particular relevant aspect of foreign law, as to the content of that foreign law an English judge may use the 'presumption of similarity' – a rule of the law of evidence in England and Wales. The circumstances when it would be appropriate for an English judge to rule that the foreign law, or the particular relevant aspect of foreign law, is presumed to be materially similar to the English law on the matter in question are significantly clarified by Lord Leggatt in the *FS Cairo* judgment (see paras 143–153). In the course of giving guidance on when the presumption of similarity can be used by English courts, Lord Leggatt gives some interesting *obiter* observations on whether foreign law has to be proved by expert evidence:

> 148. I would add that it should not be assumed that the only alternative to relying on the presumption of similarity is necessarily to tender evidence from an expert in the foreign system of law. The old notion that foreign legal materials can only ever be brought before the court as part of the evidence of an expert witness is outdated. Whether the court will require evidence from an expert witness should depend on the nature of the issue and of the relevant foreign law. In an age when so much information is readily available through the internet, there may be no need to consult a foreign lawyer in order to find the text of a relevant foreign law. On some occasions the text may require skilled exegesis of a kind which only a lawyer expert in the foreign system of law can provide. But in other cases it may be sufficient to know what the text says.

It may be worth remembering that Lord Leggatt was dealing with a case where proof of foreign law is relevant to determining jurisdiction in England and it may be primarily in that preliminary context (where it is enough to show that there is a 'serious issue to be tried' – see para 99) that it might be safe for lawyers to lead evidence based on the text of a foreign law without leading expert evidence on the meaning of that text. If the foreign law is being considered when the merits of the case are being determined it seems much less likely that it would be wise or appropriate for counsel to plead the foreign law based on the text of the foreign law without leading expert evidence.

The author correctly identifies that this area of the law is one where domestic law reform in Great Britain should be seriously considered and he suggests a role for a joint study into the matter by the Law Commission and Scottish Law Commission. This is a very good idea. If this were to happen any recommended legislation emerging from a joint Report of the Law Commissions could be passed by the UK Parliament. Of course, such UK wide legislation would require the consent of the Scottish Parliament and of whatever bodies are functioning in Northern Ireland to represent that legal system's interests. Any such Great Britain or UK wide legislation should only occur after a collaborative exercise between appropriate experts in Scotland, Northern Ireland, and England and Wales. So it would make sense for the Law Commission and the Scottish Law Commission to work with the relevant law reform body in Northern Ireland. It would also be appropriate for the various law reform bodies to set up advisory groups, including private international law and civil procedure experts in each of the legal systems in the UK, encompassing appropriate judges, legal practitioners (solicitors and advocates/barristers) and legal academics, before getting to the stage of drafting a consultation document and again before drafting their final Report.

If the law reform bodies in the UK and the relevant Government departments at UK and devolved levels do take up the challenge of considering law reform in the field of the application of foreign law, and/or if work on these matters is resumed at the HCCH, there is no doubt at all that they will find this book invaluable in laying a foundation for those reforms. Excellent law reform is invariably built on the foundation of outstanding historical and comparative law research. This book lays a significant part of the necessary foundations.

Professor Paul Beaumont FRSE
Professor of Private International Law
University of Stirling

ACKNOWLEDGEMENTS

This work is a revised and updated version of my doctoral thesis, which was accepted by the University of Tübingen in April 2021 (D21). I am profoundly indebted to Professor Martin Gebauer for his excellent supervision during my doctorate, as well as during my LLM and my time as a research assistant in his department – this work was only made possible with his support, encouragement, and guidance. I also give my sincere thanks to Professor Stefan Huber for being an additional supervisor during my doctorate and for his valuable input.

I am sincerely grateful to the series editor, Professor Paul Beaumont, for accepting this work into the Hart Studies in Private International Law series and for providing comprehensive feedback on the drafts. I also give my thanks to Professor Beaumont for first stimulating my interest in private international law during my undergraduate studies in Aberdeen.

My appreciation also goes to the German Academic Exchange Service (DAAD) for awarding me a generous scholarship in order that I could spend a further period of time in Tübingen writing my doctoral thesis.

Significant parts of this work were researched and written during my time as a solicitor at the Scottish law firms Morton Fraser and Turcan Connell. Thanks are due to my former colleagues at both firms for their kind support and companionship. This work was significantly enriched through the professional experience I acquired at these excellent firms.

I am sincerely grateful to Patrick Layden KC, former Scottish Law Commissioner, who very kindly commented on my initial drafts, as well as all my former colleagues in Tübingen, particularly Dr Felix Berner, Dr Philip-René Retzbach, and Leonard Wagner.

A special thanks is also due to the team at Hart Publishing, particularly Joanne Choulerton for her excellent input as copy editor.

Writing this book was a very significant personal endeavour. I give my heartfelt thanks to my family and friends for their patience and support. It is, of course, my mother, Dr Christine West, to whom I give the greatest thanks and to whom this book is dedicated. I am sure that my father, Professor Julian Critchley, who is sadly no longer with us, would have been delighted that I have reached this stage in my academic and professional life.

Alexander D J Critchley
Edinburgh, September 2022

CONTENTS

ABBREVIATIONS

AC	Appeal Cases
A-G	Advocate General of the Court of Justice of the European Union
AG	Amtsgericht (Local Court)
AGO	Allgemeine Gerichtsordnung für die Preußischen Staaten (Prussian Code of Civil Procedure)
ALI	American Law Institute
Amb	Ambler's Chancery Reports
App Cas	Appeal Cases
ArbGG	Arbeitsgerichtsgesetz (Employment Courts Act)
AuRAG	Gesetz zur Ausführung des Europäischen Übereinkommens betreffend Auskünfte über ausländisches Recht und seines Zusatzprotokolls (Act implementing the European Convention on Information on Foreign Law)
BAG	Bundesarbeitsgericht (Federal Labour Court)
Beavan	Beavan's Reports
BGB	Bürgerliches Gesetzbuch (German Civil Code)
BGH	Bundesgerichtshof (Federal Court of Justice)
BGHZ	Entscheidungen des Bundesgerichtshofes in Zivilsachen (Decisions of the Federal Court of Justice in Civil Matters)
Brown	Brown's Cases in Parliament
BVerfG	Bundesverfassungsgericht (Federal Constitutional Court)
BVerfGG	Bundesverfassungsgerichtsgesetz (Act on the Federal Constitutional Court)
Campbell	Campbell's Nisi Prius Cases
CAT	Competition Appeal Tribunal (Neutral Citation)
Ch	Law Reports, Chancery Division

CISG	United Nations Convention on Contracts for the International Sale of Goods
CJEU	Court of Justice of the European Union
CJQ	Civil Justice Quarterly
Cl & Fin	Clark and Finnelly's Reports
CLC	Commercial Law Cases
CLJ	Cambridge Law Journal
CLR	Commonwealth Law Reports
Costs LO	Costs Law Reports
Cowper	Cowper's Reports, King's Bench
CPIL	Centre for Private International Law (University of Aberdeen)
CPO	Code of Civil Procedure (Civilprozessordnung)
CPR	Civil Procedure Rules 1998
Cr App R	Criminal Appeal Reports
CSIH	Court of Session, Inner House (Neutral Citation)
CSOH	Court of Session, Outer House (Neutral Citation)
Curteis	Curteis' Ecclesiastical Reports
D	Dunlop, Bell & Murray's Reports
DCFR	Draft Common Frame of Reference
De G, J & S	De Gex, Jones & Smith's Chancery Reports
Dowl & Ry NP	Dowling and Ryland's Nisi Prius Cases
Drew & Sm	Drewry and Smale's Vice Chancellor's Reports
East	East's Term Reports, King's Bench
ECR	European Court Reports
EGBGB	Einführungsgesetz zum Bürgerlichen Gesetzbuch (Introductory Act to the German Civil Code)
EJN	European Judicial Network in civil and commercial matters
Eq Ca Abr	Equity Cases Abridged
ER	English Reports

Espinasse	Espinasse's English Nisi Prius Reports
EU	European Union
EWCA Civ	Court of Appeal (Civil Division) (Neutral Citation)
EWFC	England & Wales Family Court (Neutral Citation)
EWHC	England & Wales High Court (Neutral Citation)
Exch	Exchequer Reports
F	Federal Reporter
F	Fraser's Court of Session Cases
Fam	Law Reports, Family Division
FamFG	Gesetz über das Verfahren in Familiensachen und in den Angelegenheiten der freiwilligen Gerichtsbarkeit (Act on Proceedings in Family Matters and in Matters of Non-Contentious Jurisdiction)
FCR	Butterworths Family Court Reports
FLR	Family Law Reports
FSR	Fleet Street Reports
GG	Grundgesetz für die Bundesrepublik Deutschland (German Constitution)
GVG	Gerichtsverfassungsgesetz (Judicature Act)
H & N	Hurlstone and Norman's Exchecquer Reports
Hagg (Consist)	Haggard's Consistorial Reports
Hailes	Hailes' Decisions of the Court of Session
HCCH	Hague Conference on Private International Law
HGB	Handelsgesetzbuch (German Commercial Code)
ICLQ	International & Comparative Law Quarterly
IntFamRVG	Gesetz zur Aus- und Durchführung bestimmter Rechtsinstrumente auf dem Gebiet des internationalen Familienrechts (Act to Implement Certain Legal Instruments in the Field of International Family Law)
JC	Session Cases, Justiciary
KB	King's Bench Law Reports

KG	Kammergericht
LAG	Landesarbeitsgericht (Higher Labour Court)
LG	Landgericht (District Court)
Lloyd's Rep	Lloyd's Law Reports
LQR	Law Quarterly Review
LT	Law Times Reports
M	Macpherson's Session Cases
Mor	Morison's Dictionary
NSWCA	New South Wales Court of Appeal (Neutral Citation)
N W	North Western Reporter
NY	New York Reports
NZA	Neue Zeitschrift für Arbeitsrecht
NZLR	New Zealand Law Reports
OAG	Oberappellationsgericht (Court of Appeal)
OCR	Act of Sederunt (Sheriff Court Ordinary Cause Rules) 1993
OLG	Oberlandesgericht (Court of Appeal)
P	Probate Law Reports
P Wms	Peere-Williams' Chancery & King's Bench Cases
Paton	Paton's Appeals from Scotland, House of Lords
PD	Probate, Divorce & Admiralty Division Law Reports
Peake	Peake's Nisi Prius Reports
PECL	Principles of European Contract Law
Prec Ch	Finch's Precedents in Chancery
QB	Queen's Bench Law Reports
R	Rettie, Crawford & Melville, Session Cases
RCS	Court of Session Rules
RG	Reichsgericht (Imperial Court of Justice)
RGZ	Entscheidungen des Reichsgerichts in Zivilsachen (Decisions of the Imperial Court of Justice in Civil Matters)

Robertson	Robertson's Scotch Appeal Cases
S	Shaw's Session Cases
SAC (Civ)	Sheriff Appeal Court (Civil) (Neutral Citation)
SC	Session Cases
SC EDIN	Sheriff Court, Edinburgh (Neutral Citation)
SC (HL)	Session Cases (House of Lords)
SC (UKSC)	Session Cases (Supreme Court of the United Kingdom)
SCC	Supreme Court of Canada (Neutral Citation)
S Ct	Supreme Court Reporter
Sol Jo	Solicitors Journal
SKQB	Saskatchewan Court of Queen's Bench (Neutral Citation)
SLT	Scots Law Times
StGB	Strafgesetzbuch (German Criminal Code)
Strathprints	The University of Strathclyde institutional repository
TEU	Consolidated version of the Treaty on European Union
TFEU	Consolidated version of the Treaty on the Functioning of the European Union
UK	United Kingdom of Great Britain and Northern Ireland
UKHL	United Kingdom, House of Lords (Neutral Citation)
UKSC	United Kingdom, Supreme Court (Neutral Citation)
Vern	Vernon's Chancery Reports
W Bl	William Blackstone's King's Bench Reports
WL	Westlaw
WLR	Weekly Law Reports
WLUK	Westlaw, United Kingdom
ZPO	Zivilprozessordnung (Code of Civil Procedure)
ZPOEG	Gesetz, betreffend die Einführung der Zivilprozeßordnung (Introductory Act to the Code of Civil Procedure)
ZRHO	Rechtshilfeordnung für Zivilsachen (Mutual Assistance Regulation in Civil Matters)

TABLE OF CASES

Germany

Israel

New Zealand

Scotland

UK House of Lords / Supreme Court

United States

Introduction

This work is about the application of foreign law in civil proceedings in the British and German courts. Its focus is on three jurisdictions: England and Wales, Scotland, and Germany. These jurisdictions are collectively referred to as the relevant jurisdictions. The relevant jurisdictions have the important characteristics of having different legal traditions, while nonetheless sharing many important choice of law rules. The relevant jurisdictions accordingly provide a strong platform from which to undertake a comparative analysis. In addition, no relevant jurisdiction has carried out substantive recent reform of the way in which foreign law is investigated, determined, and applied by its courts. This is particularly notable in the context of the recent substantial changes made to the applicable choice of law rules in the relevant jurisdictions, driven by developments in EU private international law;[1] not to mention recent rapid advances in the way information is accessed and exchanged in the internet age.

The UK's constitutional arrangements are complicated but important in the context of this work. For the purposes of private international law, England and Scotland have been described as 'independent foreign countries, unconnected with each other.'[2] Since the Treaty of Union of 1707,[3] this distinction has generally been respected by both English and Scottish courts, although matters have not been without difficulty. An example of difficulty was the case of *X (A Child) and Y (A Child)* (2016), in which it was noted by the Family Division of the English High Court that despite the fact that a number of English courts had been making orders purporting to have direct effect in Scotland, such orders, in the absence

[1] A myriad of choice of law rules has been introduced by the EU since the entering into force of the Treaty of Amsterdam in 1999, not all of which apply throughout the relevant jurisdictions. These rules, together with the impact of Brexit on them, are considered in more detail in due course. To understand the changes that were made to the competence of the EU in private international law, see PE McEleavy, 'The Evolution of European Private International Law' (2008) 57 *ICLQ* 969, 973. A recent study of the competence of the EU in private international law can be found in J von Hein, 'EU Competence to Legislate in the Area of Private International Law and Law Reforms at the EU Level' in PR Beaumont and others (eds), *Cross-Border Litigation in Europe* (Hart Publishing, 2017).

[2] *Stuart v Moore* (1861) 23 D 902, 904. In German, the term *Mehrrechtsstaat* is used to describe such an arrangement. See J Kropholler, *Internationales Privatrecht*, 6th edn (Mohr Siebeck, 2006), 201.

[3] For a more detailed analysis of the role of private international law within the UK from the Scottish perspective, see PR Beaumont and PE McEleavy, *Anton's Private International Law*, 3rd edn (W Green, 2011), para 1.20ff. A dedicated study has also been undertaken by Kirsty J Hood KC. See K Hood, *Conflict of Laws within the UK* (Oxford University Press, 2007). See L Collins (Lord Collins of Mapesbury) and J Harris (eds), *Dicey, Morris & Collins on the Conflict of Laws*, 15th edn & 5th supp (Sweet & Maxwell, 2018), para 1-071, for a description of what is 'foreign' in terms of English law.

of further legislation, had no effect in Scotland,[4] an analysis with which the Scottish Court of Session subsequently agreed.[5] As English[6] and Scots law cover the entirety of the island of Great Britain,[7] and demonstrate a great similarity of approach towards private international law,[8] this work often refers to Great Britain and to British law. Differences between English and Scots law are highlighted, as appropriate. There are no uniform 'federal rules' of procedure governing civil litigation within Great Britain,[9] although the UK Supreme Court does have separate rules regulating litigation in that court.[10]

The law of Northern Ireland, which forms one of the three jurisdictions[11] of the UK, is not discussed here. Neither is the law of Ireland, which, of course, constitutes a separate legal system entirely. It is understood that these jurisdictions take a similar approach[12] to the application of foreign law as is taken in Great Britain, but there are too few relevant cases and materials emanating from either of them to justify an independent study. On the other hand, Scottish decisions and writers have made a sufficiently substantial, independent contribution to the field of

[4] *Re X (A Child) and Y (A Child) (Jurisdiction: Secure Accommodation)* [2016] EWHC 2271 (Fam), [67]. See also *Re X (A Child)* [2017] EWHC 158 (Fam), where an order was made by the English court giving equivalent effect to an order of the Scottish court.

[5] See *Cumbria County Council v X* 2017 SC 451.

[6] The jurisdiction comprises both England and Wales. For the sake of brevity, this work refers to England and English law. No disrespect is intended to Wales in this regard. The same approach is taken in Collins (Lord Collins of Mapesbury) and Harris (eds) (n 3), para 1-073, as well as in some English cases such as *Rahmatullah v Ministry of Defence* [2019] EWHC 3172 (QB), although not all; see for example, *Moreno v The Motor Insurers' Bureau* [2015] EWHC 1002 (QB), where 'English/Welsh' appears on a number of occasions.

[7] Great Britain is described in Collins (Lord Collins of Mapesbury) and Harris (eds) (n 3), para 1-074, and this definition is adopted in this work. Thus, it includes England, Wales, and Scotland, but not the Isle of Man and the Channel Islands.

[8] Hood (n 3), para 4.04: 'the field of conflict of laws is one of a number of areas where there has been a particular cross-fertilization between Scots law and English Common Law.' For example, despite substantial differences in the laws of succession between England and Scotland, their private international law rules in the area show 'surprisingly little, if any' conflict. PR Beaumont and P Bremner, 'Inter-regional conflicts within the United Kingdom relating to Private International Law of Succession – The development of the applicable law rule' (2010) 54 *Revista Valenciana d'Estudis Autonòmics* 238.

[9] Most civil litigation in England is governed by the Civil Procedure Rules. In Scotland, the Ordinary Cause Rules (OCR) govern most civil litigation in the sheriff courts, and the Rules of the Court of Session (RCS) govern civil litigation in the Court of Session. This means that quite different court rules are in force throughout the various Scottish courts.

[10] The Supreme Court Rules 2009. See also W Arnold, 'The Supreme Court of the United Kingdom (UKSC), an Exploration of the Roles of Judicial Officers and Court Administrators and how the Relationship between them may be improved and enhanced: a Case Study' (2014) 6 *International Journal for Court Administration* 19.

[11] *Re X (A Child) and Y (A Child) (Jurisdiction: Secure Accommodation)* [2016] EWHC 2271 (Fam), [10].

[12] In relation to Ireland, Kennedy states in TP Kennedy, 'Ireland' in C Esplugues, JL Iglesias and G Palao (eds), *Application of Foreign Law* (Sellier. European Law Publishers, 2011), 231: 'as there are relatively few decided Irish cases, there has been very little written on this subject. Therefore, regarding the issue of foreign law by judicial authorities in Ireland we fully refer to the Chapter on the United Kingdom in this book.'

private international law generally and to this topic specifically, both in Great Britain and further afield, to justify analysis of Scots law.[13]

Germany, unlike the UK, is for the purposes of civil law and procedure essentially a single jurisdiction.[14] Thus, the German Civil Code (BGB)[15] and Code of Civil Procedure (ZPO)[16] apply to an equal extent throughout the 16 States (*Bundesländer*) that now comprise Germany, with limited residual competence in civil matters for the 16 States.[17] However, this is not to suggest that questions of internal private international law (*interlokales Privatrecht*)[18] have never caused difficulty since Germany unified in 1871.[19] Two examples of such difficulty are, first, the period during the late nineteenth century following German unification but prior to the introduction of the uniform German Civil Code at the turn of the twentieth century,[20] and, second, the period following reunification of Germany in 1990. Complex transitional arrangements were required to deal with the absorption of the German Democratic Republic (East Germany) into the Federal Republic of Germany (West Germany).[21]

The principle underpinning the British approach to the application of foreign law is that foreign law is not law properly so-called but a question of fact, which must be proven and pleaded as any other fact in the case, albeit foreign law is rather obscurely thought to be fact of 'a peculiar kind'.[22] In practice, this means

[13] Joseph Story made numerous references to early Scottish decisions in his seminal work J Story, *Commentaries on the Conflict of Laws*, 3rd edn (Maxwell and Son, 1846), for example, at 329, 456, 608 and 680. This point is also observed in SC Symeonides, *Choice of Law* (Oxford University Press, 2016), 52. It is notable that, while the UK must be the signatory state, there is precedent for instruments of the Hague Conference on Private International Law (HCCH) applying only to Scotland; see the Declaration of the United Kingdom in respect of the Convention of 13 January 2000 on the International Protection of Adults at HCCH, 'Convention of 13 January 2000 on the International Protection of Adults: Status Table', www.hcch.net/en/instruments/conventions/status-table/?cid=71.

[14] Kropholler (n 2), 204ff.

[15] The BGB is a codification regulating substantive matters of German private law. See, for example, A Stadler, *Allgemeiner Teil des BGB*, 20th edn (CH Beck, 2020), § 1 para 6ff.

[16] The ZPO is the German Code of Civil Procedure, which regulates procedure in the ordinary German civil courts. Parts of it also regulate other civil proceedings. Its extent is outlined by the introductory statute at § 3 ZPOEG.

[17] Art 74 of the German Constitution (GG) regulates those matters which are subject to concurrent competence (*konkurrierende Gesetzgebung*). In essence, there are numerous matters which may be legislated for at the federal level, but, failing the existence of relevant federal legislation, may be regulated at the State level. Once there exists federal legislation in respect of a matter, the State has no competence. For an explanation, see H Maurer, *Staatsrecht I*, 6th edn (CH Beck, 2010), § 17 para 30.

[18] Kropholler (n 2), 199. The term *interlokales Privatrecht* is also applicable to problems of private international law throughout the constituent parts of the UK (and to its overseas territories, eg Gibraltar, and its Crown dependencies, eg Jersey).

[19] For an understanding of the events leading up to German unification see, for example, G Mann, *Deutsche Geschichte des 19. und 20. Jahrhunderts*, 13th edn (Fischer Taschenbuch Verlag, 2011), 316ff.

[20] G Kegel and K Schurig, *Internationales Privatrecht*, 9th edn (CH Beck, 2004), 26–27.

[21] Kropholler (n 2), 204ff; Kegel and Schurig (n 20), 27ff.

[22] *Parkasho v Singh* [1968] P 233, 250. This statement was made when considering whether the English appeal court is entitled to review the findings of a lower instance court as to the content of a foreign law. The matter is considered in more detail in due course.

that no judicial notice[23] may usually be taken of foreign law,[24] and expert evidence must normally be led by parties to prove its content.[25] This approach, which has been described in the literature as the fact doctrine,[26] but also as the fact theory,[27] is the current fundamental basis for the treatment of foreign law in Great Britain. In this work, the treatment of foreign law as a question of fact is referred to as the fact approach. Whilst seeking to avoid a semantic discussion, the word 'doctrine' has connotations which fit uneasily with the way in which the fact approach developed, and the word 'theory' tends too much towards the abstract.

The implications of the British approach to the application of foreign law can be briefly summarised as follows: where the parties either choose not to plead foreign law or do so but, nonetheless, fail to prove the content of the relevant rule of foreign law to the necessary standard of proof,[28] the British court will decide the case on the basis of (or presume similarity with) the *lex fori*, ie English or Scots law. It has been said by the English High Court that:

> Evidence of expert witnesses is necessary for the court to find that foreign law is different from English law. In the absence of such evidence, or if the judge is unpersuaded by

[23] The meaning of judicial notice in the context of this work is explored in more depth in due course. A detailed discussion of judicial notice in terms of English law is contained in H Malek, J Auburn and R Bagshaw (eds), *Phipson on Evidence*, 20th edn (Sweet & Maxwell, 2021) ch 3.

[24] *McGowan v Summit at Lloyds* 2002 SC 638, 644; Malek, Auburn and Bagshaw (eds) (n 23) para 3-07.

[25] *Allen v Depuy International Limited* [2015] EWHC 926 (QB), [11]; *Dexia Crediop SpA v Comune di Prato* [2015] EWHC 1746 (Comm), [129]; *Bianco v Bennett* [2015] EWHC 626 (QB), [11]; *Roberts v Soldiers, Sailors, Airmen and Families Association* [2020] EWHC 994 (QB), [187], although this matter is now in a state of flux in England. See the comments of Lord Leggett in *FS Cairo (Nile Plaza) LLC v Lady Brownlie* [2021] UKSC 45, [148] and Lord Justice Warby in *Soriano v Forensic News LLC* [2021] EWCA Civ 1952, [62].

[26] See, for example, R Fentiman, *Foreign Law in English Courts: Pleading, Proof and Choice of Law* (Oxford University Press, 1998), 311. It has been referred to in such terms in the German literature: see R Hübner, *Ausländisches Recht vor deutschen Gerichten* (Mohr Siebeck, 2014), 79. Professor Richard Fentiman's 1998 text remains the leading text addressing the application of foreign law in the English courts. It has been said in the Australian literature, in this context, that any 'Writer touching on English law owes a very great debt to Richard Fentiman.' J McComish, 'Pleading and Proving Foreign Law in Australia' (2007) 31 *Melbourne University Law Review* 400. The text is heavily cited in the most recent edition of JJ Fawcett and P Torremans (eds), *Cheshire, North & Fawcett: Private International Law*, 15th edn (Oxford University Press, 2017), 105ff, and in C Trautmann, *Europäisches Kollisionsrecht und ausländisches Recht im nationalen Zivilverfahren* (Mohr Siebeck, 2011). It is cited as a leading text in Collins (Lord Collins of Mapesbury) and Harris (eds) (n 3) and in EB Crawford and JM Carruthers, *International Private Law: A Scots Perspective*, 4th edn (W Green, 2015), 245. It has also been recently cited by the English courts, eg in *Strickland v Kier Limited*, UKEAT, 23 September 2015, 2017 WL 5760129, [13], as well as less recently in other important English cases addressing foreign law, eg *MCC Proceeds Inc v Bishopsgate Investment Trust plc* [1999] CLC 417, 423, and *Shaker v Al-Bedrawi* [2003] Ch 350, 371.

[27] The term is common in the US literature. See A Nussbaum, 'The Problem of Proving Foreign Law' (1941) 50 *Yale Law Journal* 1018; AR Miller, 'Federal Rule 44.1 and the Fact Approach to Determining Foreign Law: Death Knell for a Die-Hard Doctrine' (1967) 65 *Michigan Law Review* 613, 618; B Busch and OC Sommerich, 'Expert Witness and the Proof of Foreign Law' (1952–1953) 38 *Cornell Law Quarterly* 125.

[28] See, regarding the standard of proof in British civil proceedings generally, A Zuckerman, *Zuckerman on Civil Procedure: Principles of Practice*, 4th edn (Sweet & Maxwell, 2021), para 22.54–22.55. See,

> it, then he must resolve the issue by reference to English law, even if according to the rules of private international law the issue is governed by the foreign law.[29]

This approach has been recently affirmed in several English cases and is long-standing.[30] The position is essentially the same in Scotland.[31]

The legal provision underpinning the application of foreign law in German civil proceedings is § 293 of the German Code of Civil Procedure (ZPO), which paragraph applies throughout the entire German system of civil procedure including in arbitration, employment, and family matters.[32] The terms of § 293 – the English translation[33] of which is headed 'foreign law; customary law and statutes'[34] – have been described as terse (*knapp*):[35]

> The laws applicable in another state, customary laws, and statutes must be proven only insofar as the court is not aware of them. In making inquiries as regards these rules of law, the court is not restricted to the proof produced by the parties in the form of supporting documents; it has the authority to use other sources of reference as well, and to issue the required orders for such use.[36]

§ 293 is found in the section of the Code of Civil Procedure addressing proceedings before courts of first instance. The preceding paragraphs, §§ 288–292, address evidential requirements as to facts pleaded by parties.[37] § 291 resonates with the British concept of judicial notice in so far that both address the court's deemed knowledge of notorious matters of fact:[38]

> Facts that are common knowledge with the court need not be substantiated by evidence.[39]

regarding the application of the test to the proof of foreign law: *Roberts v Soldiers, Sailors, Airmen and Families Association* [2020] EWHC 994 (QB), [187]. This point is considered in more detail in Chapter three.

[29] *MCC Proceeds Inc v Bishopsgate Investment Trust plc* [1999] CLC 417, 421.

[30] *PT Pan Indonesia Bank Limited TBK v Marconi Communications International Limited* [2005] EWCA Civ 422, [70]; *Sharp v Ministry of Defence* [2007] EWHC 224 (QB), [11]; *Iranian Offshore Engineering and Construction Co v Dean Investment Holdings SA* [2019] 1 WLR 82, 84–85; *Roberts v Soldiers, Sailors, Airmen and Families Association* [2020] EWHC 994 (QB), [187]; *FS Cairo (Nile Plaza) LLC v Lady Brownlie* [2021] UKSC 45, [119].

[31] *McGowan v Summit at Lloyds* 2002 SC 638, 644. The presumption applies equally in relation to the application of English law in the Scottish courts. See also *Rodden v Whatlings Limited* 1961 SC 132, 133.

[32] H Prütting, '§ 293' in W Krüger and T Rauscher (eds), *Münchener Kommentar zur Zivilprozessordnung: Band 1 (§§ 1–354)*, 6th edn (CH Beck, 2020), para 15.

[33] C von Schöning, 'Translation of the German Code of Civil Procedure', www.gesetze-im-internet.de/englisch_zpo/englisch_zpo.html. This translation is used in this book when referring to any provisions of the German Code of Civil Procedure.

[34] While § 293 also refers to customary law and statutes, it has been said, in the context of the scope of potential application of § 293, that only foreign law is of practical relevance today: Prütting, '§ 293' (n 32), para 11.

[35] E Huzel, 'Zur Zulässigkeit eines "Auflagenbeschlusses" im Rahmen des § 293 ZPO' (1990) *Praxis des Internationalen Privat- und Verfahrensrechts* 77. Junker describes its wording as '*unklar*' (unclear). A Junker, *Internationales Privatrecht*, 4th edn (CH Beck, 2021), § 11 para 4.

[36] Von Schöning (n 33), § 293.

[37] Prütting, '§ 293' (n 32), para 1.

[38] See Malek, Auburn and Bagshaw (eds) (n 23) para 3-02, which also notes that judicial notice applies to matters other than notorious matters of fact.

If either a systematic approach, ie where § 293 is placed within the Code of Civil Procedure, or a literal approach is taken to the interpretation of § 293, it would be reasonable to think that German law also treats foreign law as a matter of fact. However, in Germany, the argument that foreign law should be considered a question of fact has been firmly rejected,[40] and the German court plays a pronounced role in its introduction, investigation, and determination. It is for this reason that § 293 has itself been described by an academic commentator as being foreign in its place in the Code of Civil Procedure.[41]

As will be explored in significantly more detail in due course, although many of the difficulties that the British and German courts face in respect of the application of foreign law are the same, there are also many important differences in approach, including the court's role in the introduction and application of choice of law rules; the roles of the court and the parties in investigating and determining the content of foreign law; and the nature of appeals.

In terms of the structure of this work, in Chapter one, some fundamental matters are addressed. In addition to addressing several other preliminary matters, the application of foreign law by means of choice of law rules in the private international law context is distinguished from the use of foreign law as a means of comparison with domestic law, and the scene is set for the subsequent substantive discussion. Thereafter, the prerequisites for the application of foreign law by means of choice of law rules are set out.

Chapter two identifies the key source of the current approach taken by each relevant jurisdiction to foreign law from a historical perspective. Thereafter follows consideration of the mechanisms through which foreign law was proven in early cases. The focus is not on any particular epoch, eg the eighteenth century, but rather is on attempting to establish when and how the current approach taken in each of the relevant jurisdictions developed.

In Chapter three, the processes underlying the application of foreign law by means of choice of law rules in the British and German courts are critically examined by way of a detailed comparative analysis. The distinct but interconnected issues of, first, the introduction and application of choice of law rules and, second, the investigation and determination of the content of foreign law are considered

[39] Von Schöning (n 33), § 291. See H Prütting, '§ 291' in W Krüger and T Rauscher (eds), *Münchener Kommentar zur Zivilprozessordnung: Band 1 (§§ 1–354)*, 6th edn (CH Beck, 2020).

[40] This has been recently reaffirmed judicially in the *Decision of the Federal Labour Court from 7 May 2020* (BAG, II. Senat) 2 AZR 692/19, NZA 2021, 225, 231. See also Prütting, '§ 293' (n 32), para 1; H Schack, *Internationales Zivilverfahrensrecht*, 8th edn (CH Beck, 2021), para 755; O Remien, 'Die Anwendung und Ermittlung ausländischen Rechts im System des Europäischen Internationalen Privatrechts' (2016) 115 *Zeitschrift für vergleichende Rechtswissenschaft* 570, 573; Trautmann (n 26), 165; G Otto, 'Der verunglückte § 293 ZPO und die Ermittlung ausländischen Rechts durch "Beweiserhebung"' (1995) *Praxis des Internationalen Privat- und Verfahrensrechts* 299, 301; R Geimer, *Internationales Zivilprozessrecht*, 8th edn (Otto Schmidt, 2020), para 2579; Kropholler (n 2), 212; I Saenger, *Zivilprozessordnung*, 9th edn (Nomos, 2021), § 293 para 9.

[41] Prütting, '§ 293' (n 32), para 1.

as they apply to the principal actors in the process, ie the court, the parties, and the experts. The objective is to draw out the differences and similarities in the approaches taken in the relevant jurisdictions, and to assess whether the processes underlying the application of foreign law in the relevant jurisdictions are effective.

In Chapter four, a glance is cast into the future by considering possible domestic and multilateral reform to both the processes underlying and the mechanisms available to facilitate the application of foreign law.

1

Fundamentals

I. Preliminary Matters

A. Putting the Application of Foreign Law into Context

In the following, the concepts which underpin the application of foreign law through the conduit of choice of law rules in the private international law context are introduced,[1] and the scene is set for the subsequent substantive discussion. In the first instance, however, it should be noted that foreign law can be drawn on by domestic courts as a means of comparison falling short of application.[2]

It has been concisely argued by the Dutch judge and academic Thijmen Koopmans that there are two main uses for comparative law by national courts.[3] A court may draw comparisons with other legal systems, first, to assist it to find an answer to a problem it is presented with or, second, to justify an answer found by it.[4] The field of comparative law benefits from enthusiastic judicial proponents[5] and abundant literature.[6]

[1] The term 'conduit pipe' was used by the UK Supreme Court in *R (Miller) v Secretary of State for Exiting the European Union* [2017] UKSC 5, [65], to describe the role of the European Communities Act 1972 in providing a means through which to apply EU law. The case concerned the necessity for an Act of the UK Parliament to initiate the Article 50 EU withdrawal process, in terms of the Consolidated version of the Treaty on the Functioning of the European Union of 26 October 2012 [2012] OJ C 326/47 (TFEU). The term 'conduit' (with or without 'pipe') is relevant and useful to describe the process through which foreign law is applied in the context of choice of law rules.

[2] The distinction has occasionally given rise to confusion. In *Roy v MR Pearlman Ltd* 1999 SC 459, 469, Lord Hamilton rejected the suggestion that French expert evidence was required for the Scottish court to make comparative reference to French law and practice in the interpretation of a European directive. Such reference was considered 'more in the nature of a comparative law exercise, for the purposes of which a Scottish court is entitled to have direct regard to sources of foreign law.'

[3] T Koopmans, 'Comparative Law and the Courts' (1996) 45 *ICLQ* 545, 550.

[4] ibid, 550.

[5] A Barak, 'A Judge on Judging: The Role of a Supreme Court in a Democracy' (2002) 116 *Harvard Law Review* 19, 110; TH Bingham, '"There is a world elsewhere": The Changing Perspectives of English Law' (1992) 41 *ICLQ* 513; C L'Heureux-Dube, 'The Importance of Dialogue: Globalization and the International Impact of the Rehnquist Court' (1998) 34 *Tulsa Law Journal* 15.

[6] See, for example, K Zweigert and H Kötz, *Einführung in die Rechtsvergleichung: auf dem Gebiete des Privatrechts*, 3rd edn (JCB Mohr (Paul Siebeck), 1996); JM Smits (ed), *Elgar Encyclopedia of Comparative Law*, 2nd edn (Edward Elgar, 2012); U Kischel, *Rechtsvergleichung* (CH Beck, 2015); E Genzmer, 'A Civil Lawyer's Critical Views on Comparative Legal History' (1966) 15 *The American Journal of Comparative Law* 87; CM Lawson, 'The Family Affinities of Common-Law and Civil-Law Legal Systems' (1982) 6 *Hastings International and Comparative Law Review* 85; DS Clark, 'The Use

A pertinent example of how foreign law can be drawn on by domestic courts is to allow them to properly interpret incorporated international treaties and conventions. The justification for a comparative approach in this context is particularly strong, as it ensures the uniform application of treaties in force in different legal jurisdictions consistent with the signatory states' international obligations.

For example, the Convention for the Unification of Certain Rules for International Carriage by Air of 1999, known as the Montreal Convention, is binding[7] in both the UK and in Germany.[8] Relevant cases in which domestic courts have carried out a comparative analysis, albeit in relation to its predecessor, the Warsaw Convention,[9] include the question of the meaning of place of business (*Geschäftsstelle*) in questions of jurisdiction,[10] whether it covers cases of psychiatric, as well as physical bodily harm,[11] and the meaning of damage, with specific discussion of the importance of the preparatory works (*travaux préparatoires*).[12]

of Comparative Law by American Courts (I)' (1994) 42 *The American Journal of Comparative Law Supplement* 23; BS Markesinis, *Comparative Law in the Courtroom and Classroom: The Story of the Last Thirty-Five Years* (Hart Publishing, 2004); AA Levasseur, 'The Use of Comparative Law by Courts (II)' (1994) 42 *The American Journal of Comparative Law Supplement* 41; DC Miller, 'Sibling Mixed Systems: Reviewing South African/Scottish Comparative Law' (2016) 20 *Edinburgh Law Review* 257; U Drobnig, 'Rechtsvergleichung in der deutschen Rechtsprechung' (1986) 50 *Rabels Zeitschrift für Ausländisches und Internationales Privatrecht* 610.

[7] Both the UK and Germany require the implementation (*Transformation*) of international treaties into domestic law by way of implementing legislation. On this point, see, in respect of Germany, M Herdegen, *Völkerrecht*, 20th edn (CH Beck, 2021), § 22 para 17ff, citing Art 59(2) of the German Constitution. In respect of the UK, see P Kunig, 'Völkerrecht und staatliches Recht' in W Vitzthum and A Proelß (eds), *Völkerrecht*, 7th edn (De Gruyter, 2016), para 48, and note the dicta of Lord Templeman in *JH Rayner (Mincing Lane) Ltd v Department of Trade and Industry* [1990] 2 AC 418, 476–77, who said: 'Except to the extent that a treaty becomes incorporated into the laws of the United Kingdom by statute, the courts of the United Kingdom have no power to enforce treaty rights and obligations at the behest of a sovereign government or at the behest of a private individual.' See also a House of Commons Library Briefing Paper authored by A Lang, 'Briefing Paper Number 5855: Parliament's role in ratifying treaties' (2017) *House of Commons Library*, researchbriefings.parliament.uk/ResearchBriefing/Summary/SN05855.

[8] In the UK, the implementing legislation of the Montreal Convention is the Carriage by Air Act 1961, and, in Germany, the Law on the Convention for the Unification of Certain Rules for International Carriage by Air of 28 May 1999 (*Gesetz zu dem Übereinkommen vom 28 Mai 1999 zur Vereinheitlichung bestimmter Vorschriften über die Beförderung im internationalen Luftverkehr*). The Montreal Convention is in force in well over 100 states. See ICAO, 'Convention for the Unification of Certain Rules for International Carriage by Air of 1999 (Montreal Convention): Status Table', www.icao.int/secretariat/legal/List%20of%20Parties/Mtl99_EN.pdf.

[9] There is nothing to suggest that courts in the relevant jurisdictions would not decide in the same way in respect of the interpretation of the Montreal Convention.

[10] In Germany, comparing French and US authority, see *Decision of the Federal Court of Justice from 23 March 1976* (BGH, VI. Zivilsenat) VI ZR 150/74, NJW 1976, 1587, 1587–88.

[11] In *King v Bristow Helicopters Limited* 2001 SC 54, the Court of Session seems to have been heavily influenced by the academic contributions of a member of the German delegation to the negotiations of the Warsaw Convention, although the Court noted the lack of actual decisions from a German-speaking jurisdiction. Case law from, inter alia, the US was referred to in the decision. See HL MacQueen, 'Mixing It? Comparative Law in the Scottish Courts' (2003) 6 *European Review of Private Law* 735, 740.

[12] In the UK, comparing French and US authority, *Fothergill v Monarch Airlines Ltd* [1981] AC 251, 277.

The Hague Child Abduction Convention[13] is a further example of where there has been extensive, comparative discourse between the highest courts of the various contracting states to better interpret and uniformly apply the instrument,[14] inter alia, in respect of habitual residence,[15] rights of custody[16] and the concept of repudiatory retention,[17] and there are many other further examples from other contexts.[18]

Foreign law can also be used by a court purely for the purposes of comparative analysis, ie where a case has no material international element, to develop domestic law. In the British courts, foreign law is frequently drawn on in such circumstances when deciding difficult cases,[19] and particularly in the highest courts,[20] where more resources are available to support the necessary

[13] There are over 100 signatories, including the UK and Germany, of the Hague Convention of 25 October 1980 on the Civil Aspects of International Child Abduction (Hague Child Abduction Convention). See HCCH, 'Convention of 25 October 1980 on the Civil Aspects of International Child Abduction: Status Table', www.hcch.net/en/instruments/conventions/status-table/?cid=24. In the UK, its implementing legislation is the Child Abduction and Custody Act 1985 and, in Germany, the IntFamRVG.

[14] See the insightful judgment of the Supreme Court of Canada in *Office of the Children's Lawyer v Balev* [2018] SCC 16, which states, at [33], that 'domestic courts should give serious consideration to decisions by the courts of other contracting states on its meaning and application' and refers inter alia to Art 31(3)(b) of the Vienna Convention on the Law of Treaties of 1969 that mandates, in interpreting international treaties, that states take account of 'any subsequent practice in the application of the treaty which establishes the agreement of the parties regarding its interpretation' and also comments in the UK Supreme Court in a similar regard, *In re D (A Child) (Abduction: Rights of Custody)* [2007] 1 AC 619 (INCADAT Cite: HC/E/UKe 880), 632: 'In the absence of a supranational body to define and refine these autonomous terms, member states must strive for consistent practice – not in the content of their domestic laws but in the effect that they give to the particular features of one another's laws.'

[15] See, for example, *Monasky v Taglieri* 140 S Ct 719 (2020), which is discussed, in addition to several other important cases, in PR Beaumont and J Holliday, 'Habitual Residence in Child Abduction Cases: The Hybrid Approach is Now the Norm but How Much Weight Should Be Given to Parental Intention?' in M Pfeiffer and others (eds), *Liber Amicorum Monika Pauknerová* (Wolters Kluwer, 2021).

[16] See, for example, *In re K (A Child)* [2014] AC 1401, 1421ff; *Abbott v Abbott* 560 US 1 (2010) 16ff.

[17] See, for example, *In re C and another (Children)* [2018] 2 WLR 683, 757.

[18] See, in the context of the Convention on the Contract for the International Carriage of Goods by Road of 1956, *Decision of the Federal Court of Justice from 14 July 1983* (BGH, I. Zivilsenat) I ZR 128/81, NJW 1984, 565, 566. For analysis of this and other examples from Germany, see Drobnig (n 6), 615ff.

[19] Hector MacQueen argues that comparative law plays its greatest role in both Scotland and England when their respective courts are faced with making a fundamental choice in respect of the law. See MacQueen, 'Mixing It? Comparative Law in the Scottish Courts' (n 11), 743. There is particularly strong evidence that Scottish courts have long had recourse to foreign approaches. See, for example, the analysis of the Lord Justice-Clerk in the seminal Scottish case of *Knight v Wedderburn* [1778] Hailes 776, 778, which rejected the property rights of slave owners to slaves brought into Scotland, and *Thomson v James* (1855) 18 D 1, 9, where it was said by the Lord President: 'Very great research was exhibited in bringing before us authorities, ancient and modern, and the dicta of writers not only of our own country, but of Continental Europe and of America.' Prior to the 1707 Union and for a short period following it, it was common for Scottish jurists to study at continental universities such as Bologna, Heidelberg, Leiden, and Utrecht, which would inevitably have had an influence on their willingness to refer to foreign sources of law. Andrew D Gibb, 'International Private Law in Scotland in the Sixteenth and Seventeenth Centuries' (1927) 39 *Juridical Review* 369, 374; DJ Llewelyn Davies, 'The Influence of Huber's De Conflictu Legum on English Private International Law' (1937) 18 *British Yearbook of International Law* 49, 53.

[20] E Mak, 'Comparative Law before the Supreme Courts of the UK and the Netherlands' in M Andenas and D Fairgrieve (eds), *Courts and Comparative Law* (Oxford University Press, 2015).

research.[21] In *Cavendish Square Holding* (2015), when considering the penalty rule in English contract law,[22] the UK Supreme Court made detailed reference to the laws of a number of other legal systems,[23] and did so simply on the basis of materials lodged by one of the parties.[24] Although reference was made to several common law jurisdictions including, inter alia, Canada,[25] New Zealand,[26] and Australia,[27] it is notable that the judgments did not restrict their analysis only to common law jurisdictions,[28] with detailed reference being made to provisions of German law,[29] and by Lord Mance in particular.[30]

While such cases demonstrate the value that comparative law can bring to the adjudication of legal disputes, recourse to comparative law does carry some notable risks,[31] and it has not always been universal practice in the British courts even

[21] This applies particularly in respect of the UK Supreme Court, but also applies to a lesser extent to the Court of Appeal (England and Wales) and the Inner House of the Court of Session (Scotland). For a recent Scottish example, see *Compugraphics International Ltd v Nikolic* 2011 SC 744, 755, where reference is made to South African law.

[22] Other examples include tortious liability in relation to deprived beneficiaries in *White v Jones* [1995] 2 AC 207, where reference is made, at 255, to the German legal concept of *Vertrag mit Schutzwirkung für Dritte* (contract with protective effect in favour of third parties); the freezing of terrorist assets in *Reynolds v Times Newspapers Ltd* [2001] 2 AC 127, 198ff, where reference is made inter alia to US, Canadian, Indian, and Australian law; and anonymity orders in *Ahmed v Her Majesty's Treasury (Justice intervening) (Nos 1 and 2)* [2010] 2 AC 534, 666, where reference is made to Australian, New Zealand, and Canadian law.

[23] *Cavendish Square Holding BV v Makdessi* [2016] AC 1172.

[24] *Cavendish Square Holding BV v Makdessi* [2016] AC 1172, 1252. The court was provided with an analysis of the law, together with relevant academic commentary, of several countries in an appendix. It is notable that the strict rules of proof are not applied when a British court is referring to foreign law in the comparative context. The significance of this will become clear in due course.

[25] *Cavendish Square Holding BV v Makdessi* [2016] AC 1172, 1252–53.

[26] *Cavendish Square Holding BV v Makdessi* [2016] AC 1172, 1272.

[27] *Cavendish Square Holding BV v Makdessi* [2016] AC 1172, 1271–72, but see also 1252–53.

[28] The particular importance of drawing the jurisprudence of other common law countries to the UK Supreme Court's attention was made clear in *Jones v Kaney* [2011] 2 AC 398, where Lord Collins commented, at 424, that: 'It is highly desirable that at this appellate level, in cases where issues of legal policy are concerned, the court should be informed about the position in other common law countries. This court is often helped by being referred to authorities from other common law systems, including the United States.'

[29] See *Cavendish Square Holding BV v Makdessi* [2016] AC 1172, 1206, 1252, and 1280. It appears that German law has tended to feature more prominently in decisions of the UK Supreme Court than the laws of other European countries. See R Reed (Lord Reed), 'Comparative Law in the Supreme Court of the United Kingdom' (2018) 82 *Rabels Zeitschrift für Ausländisches und Internationales Privatrecht* 563, 565ff. In addition to *Cavendish Square Holding BV v Makdessi* [2016] AC 1172, Lord Reed gives other examples where German law has (had) a role to play in the court's jurisprudence, including the law of unjustified enrichment. The Scots law of unjustified enrichment has been greatly influenced by German law, having particularly influenced the writings of Professors Whitty and Evans-Jones. See HL MacQueen, 'The Sophistication of Unjustified Enrichment: A Response to Nils Jansen' (2016) 20 *Edinburgh Law Review* 312, 313. Professor Whitty's contribution to the Scots law of unjustified enrichment was noted and referred to by Lord Hope in the landmark case of *Morgan Guaranty Trust Company of New York v Lothian Regional Council* 1995 SC 151.

[30] *Cavendish Square Holding BV v Makdessi* [2016] AC 1172, 1252.

[31] A good summary of the advantages and disadvantages of comparative law in the court context is provided by Graziano. TK Graziano, 'Is it Legitimate and Beneficial for Judges to Compare?' in

in the context of interpreting international treaties and conventions.[32] Indeed, German courts appear to be significantly more reluctant than British courts to voluntarily engage with foreign sources of law. Thus, there is relatively limited evidence that German courts make comparative reference to other legal systems,[33] a situation viewed with regret by some.[34] A Federal Court of Justice (BGH) decision, where extensive reference was made to English and US law, was caveated accordingly:

> Foreign decisions, which, solely on the basis of differing legal foundations, can only have a limited meaning for domestic law. [Translation by author][35]

Nonetheless, comparisons with foreign law have played a role in German court decisions in certain areas, such as questions of classification,[36] and, as discussed above, where the interpretation of a multilateral instrument has been at issue.[37] The reason for the lack of comparative reference to foreign law in German court decisions perhaps has something to do with the less discursive nature of German court decisions,[38] and the overriding importance of the German Civil Code and

M Andenas and D Fairgrieve (eds), *Courts and Comparative Law* (Oxford University Press, 2015), 26ff. Graziano sensibly frames his discussion by asking two important questions: Is it legitimate to use comparative methodology and, if so, is it beneficial to do so? Perhaps the biggest risk is that the court inevitably risks focusing on those legal systems which support the approach it is seeking, to the possible exclusion of other legal systems, risking flawed judicial analysis, the obstruction of the real issues in dispute, and the possible unwarranted distortion of domestic legal principles. Graziano describes this (at 29) as the 'danger of cherry picking.' It is also clear that merely referencing legal practice in state A, B, and C does not per se assist the court if little other analysis is offered of the merits of a particular approach. See the apt comment of Lord Steyn in *McFarlane v Tayside Health Board* [2000] 2 AC 59, 81: 'the discipline of comparative law does not aim at a poll of the solutions adopted in different countries.' Thus, it is the reasoning, not the fact of the foreign practice, that is important. EA Young, 'Foreign Law and the Denominator Problem' (2005) 119 *Harvard Law Review* 148, 153.

[32] In refusing to have recourse to French and Dutch authority when interpreting the UN Convention on the Contract for the International Carriage of Goods by Road of 1956, Lord Salmon commented in *James Buchanan & Co Ltd v Babco Forwarding & Shipping (UK) Ltd* [1978] AC 141, 162: 'It would seem that our system of administering justice enjoys considerable confidence abroad and that we can safely leave our courts to apply their own methods of interpreting the Convention until such time, if ever, as better methods are devised abroad and universally accepted.'

[33] Drobnig (n 6), 621; H Kötz, 'Alte und neue Aufgaben der Rechtsvergleichung' (2002) 6 *Juristenzeitung* 257, 258. Kötz also observed that other civil law countries, for example Switzerland and Holland, are more likely than Germany to draw comparisons with foreign legal systems. US courts also appear to be more reluctant to refer to foreign law in their judgments, at least, in the domestic context. Levasseur (n 6), 58–59. Thus, the matter is not necessarily one of a distinction between the common and civil law traditions. See *Muller v Oregon* 208 US 412 (1908), 419, which refers to counsel's brief, and references a number of jurisdictions in the footnotes; and *McGowan v Maryland* 366 US 420 (1960), 482ff, which refers in particular to England, but also to a number of continental European legal systems.

[34] See, for example, Kötz (n 33), 258.

[35] *Decision of the Federal Court of Justice from 18 January 1983* (BGH, VI. Zivilsenat) VI ZR 114/81, BGHZ 86, 240, 250: 'Ausländische Entscheidungen, die aber schon wegen der verschiedenen Rechtsgrundlagen nur beschränkt für das inländische Recht Bedeutung haben können.'

[36] Drobnig (n 6), 613.

[37] ibid, 614.

[38] It is not being suggested that German judgments are less thorough than British judgments, and perhaps German courts simply find their intellectual inspiration elsewhere. For example, there appears

other statutory sources as sources of law,[39] although the renowned German jurist Hein Kötz also refers to a lack of training in foreign law and lack of sufficient court time as causes.[40] Moreover, subject to limited exceptions,[41] German court decisions, strictly speaking, do not have the same binding precedent value that lawyers with a common law background will be familiar with,[42] and so the potential for German appeal courts to develop domestic law is less when compared with their British counterparts. Nevertheless, important exceptions are provided by cases such as the famous[43] *Linoleumrollenfall* (1911),[44] which was a milestone in the development of the doctrines of *culpa in contrahendo* (fault in conclusion of the contract) and third party rights in German law.[45]

It should be clear from the foregoing that a domestic court can choose to refer to foreign law to improve the quality of its adjudication, but it does not have to and indeed there may be cogent reasons not to. On the other hand, in the context of private international law, the application of foreign law takes place through the conduit of a choice of law rule. This interaction between domestic and foreign

to be a comparatively stronger dialogue between German judges and German legal academia, which manifests itself in German judgments and no doubt leads to their enrichment. See, for an enthusiastic analysis from a former judge of the German Federal Court of Justice, which discusses this dialogue in the context of developments in German company law: W Goette, 'Dialog zwischen Rechtswissenschaft und Rechtsprechung in Deutschland am Beispiel des Gesellschaftsrechts' (2013) *Rabels Zeitschrift für Ausländisches und Internationales Privatrecht* 309. Several reasons for this are suggested at 311–13, for example, that German professors have often served as judges and that German judges often have connections to German academic institutions.

[39] H Köhler, *BGB Allgemeiner Teil*, 45th edn (CH Beck, 2021), § 1 para 6: 'Das Privatrecht beruht fast ausschließlich auf Gesetzen im formellen Sinn (BGB, HGB usw.)' ('The private law is based almost exclusively on laws in a formal sense (the German Civil Code, the German Commercial Code, etc.)') [Translation by author].

[40] Kötz (n 33), 258. Kötz is a particularly strong advocate of comparative law.

[41] For example, decisions of the German Constitutional Court (BVerfG) by virtue of § 31 of the BVerfGG.

[42] See Köhler (n 39), § 1 para 12, although it is made clear that higher instance decisions nonetheless have great importance in practice in Germany, eg on the basis that the court is likely to decide in similar terms in the future.

[43] J Cartwright and M Hesselink, 'Introduction' in J Cartwright and M Hesselink (eds), *Precontractual Liability in European Private Law* (Cambridge University Press, 2008), 12.

[44] *Decision of the Imperial Court of Justice from 7 December 1911* (RG) VI 240/11, RGZ 78, 239. In the case, the court held the proprietor of a shop responsible for the actions of his employees not by virtue of vicarious liability, which has restricted application in German law, but by virtue of his duties under contract law towards prospective customers injured by falling rolls of linoleum, despite no contract having actually been concluded. See, for an excellent historical analysis of the case, J Thiessen, 'Von der (Linoleum-)Rolle. Die heimliche Anerkennung der culpa in contrahendo im Streit der Reichsgerichtsräte' in HC Grigoleit, J Neuner and J Petersen (eds), *Privatrechtsdogmatik im 21. Jahrhundert: Festschrift für Claus-Wilhelm Canaris zum 80. Geburtstag* (De Gruyter, 2017).

[45] In the case, because of injuries sustained by the son of the prospective purchaser, the doctrine of *Vertrag mit Schutzwirkung zugunsten Dritter* (contract with protective effect in favour of third parties) was developed in German law. For a concise comparative analysis of the concept of third party rights, including coverage of both Scots and English law, see S Vogenauer, 'Vertrag zugunsten Dritter' in J Basedow, KJ Hopt and R Zimmermann (eds), *Handwörterbuch des Europäischen Privatrechts* (Mohr Siebeck, 2009). Note that the Scots common law doctrine of *jus quaesitum tertio* was recently replaced with statutory provision by the Contract (Third Party Rights) (Scotland) Act 2017.

law is conceptually different from the foregoing interaction in so far that the application of foreign law through the conduit of choice of law rules is in relevant circumstances – in theory at least – obligatory rather than voluntary, and a foreign rule of law is being applied rather than merely being referred to.

An example of a choice of law rule is that the law applicable to a non-contractual obligation arising out of a delict shall be the law of the country in which the damage occurs (*lex loci delicti*).[46] Thus, as recently happened, if a car accident takes place in Spain between a Scottish driver and a Spanish pedestrian,[47] the substantive applicable law, assuming that the case falls to be heard before a court applying the Rome II Regulation,[48] which includes all courts in the relevant jurisdictions, should be Spanish law.[49]

The first stage of the choice of law process is known as characterisation or classification.[50] Thus, a given set of facts, eg a car accident in Spain, must be sorted into a juridical category such as delict, unjustified enrichment, *culpa in contrahendo*, or contract to identify the applicable choice of law rule.[51] The German academic Jan Kropholler wrote:

> Put simply, at issue is the scope of application of the choice of law rules. [Translation by author][52]

Although this quote aptly describes the process, it understates the complexities inherent in the characterisation process, which, though also a feature of pure domestic law, can present acute difficulties in the private international law context.[53] The traditional approach of the British courts is to classify an issue based

[46] See Art 4(1) of Regulation (EC) No 864/2007 of the European Parliament and of the Council of 11 July 2007 on the law applicable to non-contractual obligations [2007] OJ L 199/40 (Rome II Regulation).

[47] These facts arose in *Gilmour v Linea Directa Aseguradora Sa Compania Se Seguros y Reaseguros* [2017] SC EDIN 81.

[48] This regulation, albeit in a slightly modified form, has been incorporated into UK domestic law by means of The Law Applicable to Contractual Obligations and Non-Contractual Obligations (Amendment etc.) (EU Exit) Regulations 2019. Thus, the position in this regard will not be altered by Brexit.

[49] In terms of the Rome II Regulation (n 46), Art 4(3), some flexibility is allowed where there is a manifestly closer connection with another law. This seems unlikely on the facts presented in the example.

[50] EB Crawford and JM Carruthers, *International Private Law: A Scots Perspective*, 4th edn (W Green, 2015), para 4-02; JJ Fawcett and P Torremans (eds), *Cheshire, North & Fawcett: Private International Law*, 15th edn (Oxford University Press, 2017), 41ff; PR Beaumont and PE McEleavy, *Anton's Private International Law*, 3rd edn (W Green, 2011), para 4.06ff; L Collins (Lord Collins of Mapesbury) and J Harris (eds), *Dicey, Morris & Collins on the Conflict of Laws*, 15th edn & 5th supp (Sweet & Maxwell, 2018), para 2-001ff. The concept is known in continental Europe as qualification, following an analysis published by Etienne Bartin in 1897. See EG Lorenzen, 'The Qualification, Classification, or Characterization Problem in the Conflict of Laws' (1941) 50 *Yale Law Journal* 743.

[51] See Crawford and Carruthers (n 50), para 4-02; Collins (Lord Collins of Mapesbury) and Harris (eds) (n 50), para 2-003.

[52] J Kropholler, *Internationales Privatrecht*, 6th edn (Mohr Siebeck, 2006), 114: 'Schlicht gesagt geht es um die Frage des sachlichen Anwendungsbereichs der Kollisionsnormen.'

[53] Crawford and Carruthers (n 50), para 4-02.

on the principles of classification that the *lex fori* generally applies to an issue,[54] with the reservation that judges must not rigidly confine themselves to principles familiar to them by having a parochial attitude.[55] Nonetheless, debate as to how the process should be undertaken is fierce, with the literature surrounding the subject having been described as 'immense'.[56] The practical significance of the debate has been questioned in Great Britain:

> The problem of characterisation has given rise to a voluminous literature, much of it highly theoretical. The consequence is that there are almost as many theories as writers and the theories are for the most part so abstract that, when applied to a given case, they can produce almost any result.[57]

The debate surrounding the German approach to classification (*Qualifikation*) is more nuanced, thorough, and convincing than in Great Britain.[58] The most persuasive German viewpoint, depicted in Jan Kropholler's seminal textbook on private international law, is the functional or teleological classification based on identifying the *purpose* of the relevant foreign provision.[59] This approach differs from the *lex fori* approach in so far that it allows legal concepts which are foreign to the *lex fori* to be properly classified.[60] The approach favoured by Kropholler has been summarised as the *aufgeklärte lex-fori-Theorie*,[61] and appears to have been similarly described in English as the enlightened *lex fori* approach.[62] Though never having been described in exactly these terms by the German courts, there

[54] See, in relation to England, *Macmillan Inc v Bishopsgate Investment Trust Plc (No 3)* [1996] 1 WLR 387, 407, and, in relation to Scotland, *Atlantic Telecom GmbH (Noter)* 2004 SLT 1031, 1044, which itself draws on *Macmillian Inc* (1996). See also Fawcett and Torremans (eds) (n 50), 43, and Crawford and Carruthers (n 50), para 4-02.

[55] Fawcett and Torremans (eds) (n 50), 44. Lord Brodie in *Atlantic Telecom GmbH (Noter)* 2004 SLT 1031, 1044, described this as a having 'a broad internationalist spirit'.

[56] Crawford and Carruthers (n 50), para 4-02.

[57] Collins (Lord Collins of Mapesbury) and Harris (eds) (n 50), para 2-008.

[58] For a concise summary of the problem of characterisation from a German standpoint, see A Junker, *Internationales Privatrecht*, 4th edn (CH Beck, 2021), § 7 para 16ff, in which it is argued that there are four possible approaches to characterisation: (1) the *lex fori* approach; (2) the *lex causae* approach; (3) the comparative approach; and (4) the functional approach. See also Kropholler (n 52), 113ff. A slightly outdated but fairly exhaustive list of the literature available on the subject of characterisation was provided in 2004 in G Kegel and K Schurig, *Internationales Privatrecht*, 9th edn (CH Beck, 2004), 325–27. It is notable that some of the most well-known contributions to the English language classification debate have been made by professors with backgrounds in German law.

[59] Kropholler (n 52), 126ff.

[60] ibid, 127.

[61] J von Hein, 'Einleitung zum Internationalen Privatrecht' in J von Hein (ed), *Münchener Kommentar zum Bürgerlichen Gesetzbuch: Band 12 (Internationales Privatrecht I, Europäisches Kollisionsrecht, Einführungsgesetz zum Bürgerlichen Gesetzbuche (Art 1-26)*, 8th edn (CH Beck, 2020), para 121, which is referred to in Junker, *Internationales Privatrecht* (n 58), § 7 para 19.

[62] C Forsyth, 'Characterisation revisited: an essay in the theory and practice of the English conflict of laws' (1998) 114 *LQR* 141, 152, citing O Kahn-Freund, *General Problems of Private International Law* (Kluwer Academic Publishers, 1976).

are significant decisions giving support to such a functional approach.[63] In a 1967 decision, the Federal Court of Justice held:

> Since the legal institution of separation from table and bed is unknown in German law, it is necessary to classify it in terms of German choice of law rules, to grasp the meaning and purpose of this legal institution, to assess its significance from the point of view of the foreign law and to compare it with institutions of the German legal system. On the basis of this foundation, it must be assigned to the German choice of law rule, which is based on the concepts and definitions of the German legal system. [Translation by author][64]

Whether there is any substantial difference in outcome between the prevailing traditional British approach, ie the *lex fori* approach combined with 'a broad internationalist spirit',[65] and the enlightened or *aufgeklärte lex fori* approach is questionable. Moreover, the traditional understanding of classification in the relevant jurisdictions has been unsettled by the introduction of European instruments with harmonised choice of law rules,[66] with their strong emphasis on an autonomous interpretation independent of domestic law.[67] For example, German law

[63] See also the *Decision of the Federal Court of Justice from 19 December 1958* (BGH, IV. Zivilsenat) IV ZR 87/58, BGHZ 29, 137, known as the *Handschuhehe* (or wedding by proxy) case, in which it was held at 139: 'Die dem deutschen Richter dabei obliegende Aufgabe ist es, die Vorschriften des ausländischen Rechts, insbesondere wenn sie eine dem deutschen Recht unbekannte Rechtsfigur enthält, nach ihrem Sinn und Zweck zu erfassen, ihre Bedeutung vom Standpunkt des ausländischen Rechts zu würdigen und sie mit Einrichtungen der deutschen Rechtsordnung zu vergleichen. Auf der so gewonnenen Grundlage ist sie den aus den Begriffen und Abgrenzungen der deutschen Rechtsordnung aufgebauten Merkmalen der deutschen Kollisionsnormen, im vorliegenden Fall dem Begriff der Formvorschrift oder dem der materiell-rechtlichen Norm zuzuordnen.' ('The task required of the German judge is to grasp the terms of the foreign law, especially if they contain a legal institution unknown to German law, according to their meaning and purpose, to assess their significance from the standpoint of the foreign law and to compare them with institutions of the German legal system. On the basis of this foundation, it is possible to classify the institution in accordance with the characteristics of the German choice of law rules, in this case, that of a concept of a requirement of form or that of a substantive legal provision, which are based on the concepts and definitions of the German legal system.') [Translation by author].

[64] *Decision of the Federal Court of Justice from 22 March 1967* (BGH, IV. Zivilsenat) IV ZR 148/65, NJW 1967, 2109, 2111, known as the *Trennung von Tisch und Bett* (literally separation from table and bed) case: 'Da das Rechtsinstitut der Trennung von Tisch und Bett dem deutschen Recht unbekannt ist, kommt es dafür, wie es den deutschen Kollisionsvorschriften einzuordnen ist, darauf an, diese Rechtseinrichtung nach ihrem Sinn und Zweck zu erfassen, ihre Bedeutung vom Standpunkt des ausländischen Rechts zu würdigen und sie mit Einrichtungen der deutschen Rechtsordnung zu vergleichen; auf der so gewonnenen Grundlage ist sie den aus den Begriffen und Abgrenzungen der deutschen Rechtsordnung aufgebauten Merkmalen der deutschen Kollisionsnorm zuzuweisen.' The functional approach appears to have been developed further by the Federal Court of Justice (BGH) during the mid-twentieth century on the basis of jurisprudence first emanating from the Imperial Court of Justice (RG). See H Weber, *Die Theorie der Qualifikation* (JCB Mohr (Paul Siebeck), 1986), 150, which considers a number of decisions of the Imperial Court of Justice starting from 1929.

[65] *Atlantic Telecom GmbH (Noter)* 2004 SLT 1031, 1044.

[66] Collins (Lord Collins of Mapesbury) and Harris (eds) (n 50), para 2-007: 'Although it would be possible to describe the process of determining whether and how the Regulations apply as being a form of characterisation … it is one to be undertaken wholly without reference to the common law of characterisation. It is for this reason better understood as an entirely distinct, self-contained, exercise.'

[67] The case law of the CJEU supports such an approach, see *Fonderie Officine Meccaniche Tacconi SpA v Heinrich Wagner Sinto Maschinenfabrik GmbH*, Case C-334/00, [2002] ECR I-7357, [19]. For

traditionally treats pre-contractual liability (*culpa in contrahendo*) as a contractual obligation,[68] whereas the applicable law rules in relation to pre-contractual liability are found in the Rome II Regulation, which provides choice of law rules for non-contractual obligations.[69] Although the importance of classification in the context of the relevant jurisdictions has diminished, there remain risks of the process being manipulated (ie manipulative classification)[70] to achieve a result favoured by the court. These risks have been concisely outlined by Symeonides with reference to US case law.[71] For example, in the initial stages of the US movement away from the traditional *lex loci delicti* rule,[72] the Californian Supreme Court was prepared to classify an obviously tortious non-contractual relationship in terms of family law to afford a claim to an injured family member.[73] As will be shown, the risk of manipulation arises at many stages of the choice of law process, including where foreign law is being applied by domestic courts.

Following classification and identification of the applicable choice of law rule, the next stage is to identify the applicable substantive law. In terms of the straightforward example of the Spanish car accident given above, the Scottish court correctly recognised that Spanish law was applicable on the basis that the accident was a delict, which had taken place in Spain. The specific choice of law rule, ie that the law of the place of the accident shall apply,[74] was therefore the means through which foreign law came to be applied in the case.

But taking a step back for a moment, faced with the prospect of applying Spanish law, the Scottish court would have had many questions to consider. How was the relevant substantive Spanish law to be identified and its content proved? Whose responsibility was it to prove the applicable Spanish law? What should happen if the parties failed to prove the content and effect of Spanish law? Indeed, who was responsible for introducing the matter of Spanish law at all? Were the parties obligated to draw the choice of law rule to the court's attention? Could the parties simply have ignored Spanish law and proceeded on the basis that Scots law

a thorough, albeit somewhat dated explanation of what is meant by autonomous interpretation, see M Gebauer, 'Uniform Law, General Principles and Autonomous Interpretation' (2000) 5 *Uniform Law Review* 683.

[68] H Bernstein, 'Kollisionsrechtliche Fragen der Culpa in Contrahendo' (1977) 41 *Rabels Zeitschrift für Ausländisches und Internationales Privatrecht* 281.

[69] The point is directly addressed in the Rome II Regulation (n 46), Recital (30). See JD Lüttringhaus, 'Das internationale Privatrecht der culpa in contrahendo nach den EG-Verordnungen "Rom I" und "Rom II"' (2008) *Recht der Internationalen Wirtschaft* 193. To understand the background, see P Mankowski, 'Die Qualifikation der culpa in contrahendo – Nagelprobe für den Vertragsbegriff des europäischen IZPR und IPR' (2003) *Praxis des Internationalen Privat- und Verfahrensrechts* 127.

[70] Crawford and Carruthers (n 50), para 4-05.

[71] SC Symeonides, *Choice of Law* (Oxford University Press, 2016), 65–67.

[72] AM Sherwood, '*Babcock v Jackson*: The Transition from the *Lex Loci Delicti* Rule to the Dominant Contacts Approach' (1964) 62 *Michigan Law Review* 1358. The *lex loci delicti* rule remains prevalent in Europe, see Rome II Regulation (n 46), Art 4(1) and Recitals (15), (16) and (18).

[73] Symeonides refers to the case of *Haumschild v Continental Casualty Co* 95 NW 2d 814 (Wis 1959) in Symeonides, *Choice of Law* (n 71), 65. See also commentary in Sherwood (n 72), 1364.

[74] Rome II Regulation (n 46), Art 4(1).

is the same as Spanish law? If they had taken this approach, would the sheriff have had any obligation or right to object? What if the parties had agreed the content of the relevant Spanish law prior to the proof (trial), even if such agreement incorrectly reflected the content of Spanish law? These questions lie at the very heart of the choice of law process. These questions and others are the focus of this work.

B. The Delimitation of Procedure and Substance in the Choice of Law Process

The domestic law of procedure traditionally governs matters such as the conduct and language[75] of the oral proceedings, the structure of the judgment, and the judge's role during the proceedings[76] (*forum regit processum*).[77] The *lex fori* rule is not regulated by statute in any of the relevant jurisdictions, but, for example, Italian law provides such a rule:

> Civil proceedings which are conducted in Italy are regulated by Italian procedural law. [Translation by author][78]

The domestic law of procedure can be likened to the rules of the game in so far as it provides the parties with a framework in which to conduct their litigation. On the other hand, substantive domestic law – for example, rules governing the formation of contracts – is law in the fullest sense. By way of example, P is injured by D in a road traffic accident in Edinburgh. Assuming D is at fault, P has a right in delict against D to be compensated to the extent of his injuries. Assuming that the financial value of the action is at least £100,000,[79] P will have the choice of raising an action at Edinburgh Sheriff Court or in the Court of Session,[80] each governed by the respective court's distinct procedure rules.[81] Regardless of whether P chooses to raise his

[75] See GVG § 184, which states, as a general principle, that German is the language of the German courts.

[76] See ZPO § 136 regarding the power of the presiding judge to manage the course of the proceedings (*Prozessleitung durch Vorsitzenden*). See W Grunsky and F Jacoby, *Zivilprozessrecht*, 16th edn (Franz Vahlen, 2018), para 140.

[77] H Schack, *Internationales Zivilverfahrensrecht*, 8th edn (CH Beck, 2021), para 45; A Junker, *Internationales Zivilprozessrecht*, 5th edn (CH Beck, 2020), § 24 I para 1.

[78] L. 31 maggio 1995, nº. 218 (1). Riforma del sistema italiano di diritto internazionale privato (1/circ). (Law of 31 May 1995 reforming the system of Italian private international law), Art 12: 'Il processo civile che si svolge in Italia è regolato dalla legge italiana.'

[79] Actions with a value of less than £100,000 must be raised in a sheriff court under the Court Reform (Scotland) Act 2014, s 39. If an action is worth more than £100,000 then it is a party's choice as to where they raise their action, although factors such as importance and complexity may mitigate towards the Court of Session.

[80] This assumes that D is domiciled in Edinburgh. If D is resident, for example, in Glasgow, then he may also be sued in Glasgow Sheriff Court, under the Civil Jurisdiction and Judgments Act 1982, sch 8, r 1.

[81] In the sheriff courts, most civil actions are governed by the Ordinary Cause Rules (OCR) and in the Court of Session all actions are governed by the Rules of the Court of Session (RCS). Scotland is unique amongst the relevant jurisdictions in having separate procedure rules for different tiers of court.

action at Edinburgh Sheriff Court or in the Court of Session, his outcome should not differ. This is because P's substantive underlying right against D, ie a right in delict under Scots law,[82] determining both liability and quantum, forms the basis of the action.

If D, now resident in Germany, were to have been on holiday in Edinburgh at the time of the accident, P would have a further choice. P would be entitled to raise his action in Scotland as the place where the harmful event occurred,[83] or in Germany as the place where D is domiciled.[84] If P chose to initiate proceedings in Germany, he would be required to follow German procedural law.[85] However, regardless of the differences in procedure, the German court would be required to consider the relevant Scots law as *lex loci delicti*,[86] the terms of which would extend to determine both liability and quantum.[87] Once both matters are determined, the German court would grant judgment (*Urteil*),[88] and any enforcement (*Zwangsvollstreckung*)[89] would then take place in terms of German law. The crucial point is that P should theoretically be awarded the same sum of money by the German court as he would be awarded by a Scottish court. Thus, his right should be vindicated in the same way in Germany as it would be in Scotland, even if the processes involved would differ.

While applying Scots law to determine both liability and quantum following an accident is a sensible outcome, regardless of which court hears the case, the question of quantification of damages has not always been considered a substantive

[82] See J Thomson, *Delictual Liability*, 5th edn (Bloomsbury Professional, 2014).

[83] See sch 8, r 2(c) of the Civil Jurisdiction and Judgments Act 1982. It should be noted that Scotland essentially chose to replace its own rules of jurisdiction with those found in the Brussels Convention, and there has been no suggestion of reverting to the old rules. Justice Directorate at the Scottish Government, 'Cross-border civil and commercial legal cases after Brexit: guidance for legal professionals', www.gov.scot/publications/cross-border-civil-commercial-legal-cases-brexit-guidance-legal-professionals/. See, for a detailed discussion of the implications of the end of the Brexit transition period for UK and European private international law: A Dickinson, 'Realignment of the Planets – Brexit and European Private International Law' (2021) *Praxis des Internationalen Privat- und Verfahrensrechts* 213, at 215, in which it is noted that the Scottish rules of jurisdiction are more restrictive than the English rules, which permit jurisdiction based on service on the defendant in England, although it should be noted that the exorbitant Scottish rules of jurisdiction now also apply to EU domiciled defenders, eg where moveable property is arrested in Scotland under sch 8, r 2(h)(i) of the 1982 Act.

[84] Regulation (EU) No 1215/2012 of the European Parliament and of the Council of 12 December 2012 on jurisdiction and the recognition and enforcement of judgment in civil and commercial matters (recast) [2012] OJ L 351/1 (Brussels I bis Regulation), Art 4(1). Note the specific meaning of 'domicile' under the Brussels I bis Regulation, which is not the same as the concept of domicile with which many British lawyers will be famliar. See Fawcett and Torremans (eds) (n 50), 213. The German language version of the Brussels I bis Regulation uses the word *Wohnsitz* (residence), which seems clearer as to the jurisdictional test in this context.

[85] A straightforward introduction to the German Code of Civil Procedure (ZPO) is provided in Grunsky and Jacoby (n 76). Two examples of German procedural rules, ie § 184 GVG and § 136 ZPO, were given above.

[86] Rome II Regulation (n 46), Art 4.

[87] ibid, Art 15.

[88] § 300 ZPO.

[89] § 704ff ZPO; H-J Musielak and W Voit, *Grundkurs ZPO*, 15th edn (CH Beck, 2020), § 8.

issue in Great Britain in the context of private international law. Quantum is therefore a good example of the impact that the classification of a matter as either procedural or substantive can have on a case, as well as the risk of manipulation in the choice of law process.

In *Boys* (1968), an English domiciled plaintiff had raised an action in England against an English domiciled defendant for injuries sustained in Malta.[90] Had the plaintiff raised his action in Malta, he would have been awarded just £53.[91] Maltese law would thus have awarded him nothing for his pain, suffering, or loss of amenity, as Maltese law did not recognise such heads of claim.[92] In terms of English law, the trial judge awarded him £2,303.[93]

Much of the discussion in the Court of Appeal turned on the applicable choice of law rule for the determination of the plaintiff's entitlement to damages in the context of the common law rule of double actionability,[94] with the judges significantly divided.[95] Lord Denning MR considered that English law should determine liability and quantum on the basis that it was the proper law of the tort, essentially because the parties involved were English.[96] Lord Justice Diplock was in favour of awarding the plaintiff only £53[97] on the basis that Maltese law was the *lex loci delicti*,[98] which should also govern which heads of damage were applicable.[99] Lord Upjohn considered that the question of which substantive law applied was fundamentally irrelevant, as:

> All questions of remedy, both as to its nature and kinds or heads of assessment of pecuniary damage, must be determined in an English action entirely by English principles.[100]

He then went on to argue that the *lex fori* rule in relation to matters of remedy:

> is clear and simple and gives rise to no difficulty in its application.[101]

[90] *Boys v Chaplin* [1968] 2 QB 1.

[91] *Boys v Chaplin* [1968] 2 QB 1, 20.

[92] *Boys v Chaplin* [1968] 2 QB 1, 19–20.

[93] *Boys v Chaplin* [1968] 2 QB 1, 20.

[94] The rule is concisely set out in Beaumont and McEleavy (n 50) para 14.305: 'to justify an action in tort in England in respect of a tort committed abroad it was necessary to prove that the conduct was actionable in tort both in the place of tort and in England as the lex fori (the double actionability rule).'

[95] Diplock LJ's comment in the Court of Appeal in *Boys v Chaplin* [1968] 2 QB 1, 45, was particularly poignant: 'I am sorry that we have been unable to agree on the relevant conflicts rule. Lex propria delicti, lex fori, lex loci delicti; quot judices tot sententiae.'

[96] *Boys v Chaplin* [1968] 2 QB 1, 24. Lord Denning MR's analysis demonstrated a particularly high degree of judicial creativity. *Boys v Chaplin* [1968] 2 QB 1, 20: 'I will show how the English authorities can be fitted in so as to achieve this result.' Later Lord Denning states: 'He gets justice here in that he gets fair compensation. Whereas the law of Malta gives him less than fair compensation.' *Boys v Chaplin* [1968] 2 QB 1, 25.

[97] *Boys v Chaplin* [1968] 2 QB 1, 45, although he noted at 44: 'My sympathies are naturally with the plaintiff. He suffered serious physical injuries for which I should like to award him compensation at the defendant's insurance company's expense.'

[98] *Boys v Chaplin* [1968] 2 QB 1, 44.

[99] *Boys v Chaplin* [1968] 2 QB 1, 41.

[100] *Boys v Chaplin* [1968] 2 QB 1, 32.

[101] *Boys v Chaplin* [1968] 2 QB 1, 33.

Lord Upjohn was clear as to what he perceived to be the difficulty in applying a foreign rule to some parts of the remedy and not to others, and raised doubts about the practical difficulties involved in applying foreign law in such cases.[102]

When the case came before the House of Lords in *Boys* (1971),[103] the court was mired in a similar level of controversy as in the Court of Appeal, with various strands of competing reasoning.[104] Those judges, especially Lord Denning MR in the Court of Appeal and Lord Hodson in the House of Lords,[105] who argued in favour of the proper law of tort[106] being English law argued with the most logical consistency in so far that their argumentation favoured adopting a choice of law with (in their view at least) a substantially closer connection to the factual matrix of the case.[107] Lord Wilberforce, whose opinion came to 'embody the correct approach'[108] in clarifying the double actionability rule,[109] and setting out a flexible exception to it,[110] gave recognition to the artificiality of splitting issues between substance and procedure.[111]

In the context of this work, *Boys* demonstrates three important points. First, the case demonstrates the crucial importance of the classification of an issue as either substantive or procedural, principally because the classification of a matter as procedural, as opposed to substantive, leads to the application of the *lex fori*. While the material difference between substance and procedure in the private international law context – with procedure being a matter for the *lex fori*, regardless of the

[102] *Boys v Chaplin* [1968] 2 QB 1, 33.

[103] *Chaplin v Boys* [1971] AC 356.

[104] The question as to whether it is possible to identify what was decided in *Chaplin v Boys* [1971] AC 356 is a matter subject to long-standing debate. See A Briggs, 'What did Boys v Chaplin decide?' (1983) 12 *Anglo-American Law Review* 237 and R Mortensen, 'Brexit and private international law in the Commonwealth' (2021) 17 *Journal of Private International Law* 18, 35–36. Lord Slynn noted in *Red Sea Insurance Co Ltd v Bouygues SA* [1995] 1 AC 190, 198, that their Lordships' reasons for deciding the case 'varied to such an extent that both academic writers and judges in other cases have expressed doubt as to whether there can be extracted from the speeches one binding ratio decidendi.'

[105] *Chaplin v Boys* [1971] AC 356, 380.

[106] The proper law of tort argument found its roots in the US case *Babcock v Jackson* 12 NY 2d 473 (1963). See Sherwood (n 72), 1368ff.

[107] Lord Guest favoured the traditional separation between procedure and substance, ie that quantification of damages is for the *lex fori*: *Chaplin v Boys* [1971] AC 356, 381. He recognised (at 382) that his reasoning differed from the majority in the Court of Appeal. Lord Donovan essentially agreed (at 383) in full with the Court of Appeal judgment of Lord Upjohn. Lord Pearson favoured the *lex fori* approach, which he considered as having 'advantages of certainty and ease of application. It enables the English courts to give judgment according to their own ideas of justice'. *Chaplin v Boys* [1971] AC 356, 406.

[108] Beaumont and McEleavy (n 50) para 14.306.

[109] See Lord Wilberforce's analysis in *Chaplin v Boys* [1971] AC 356, 389. Described in Beaumont and McEleavy (n 50), para 14.305, as the 'one clear element' of the decision.

[110] *Chaplin v Boys* [1971] AC 356, 391. See Beaumont and McEleavy (n 50) para 14.306 and Mortensen (n 104), 36, where it is argued that 'This approach eventually pre-dominated in England, with a more rational statement of the rule eventually being given by Lord Slynn in the Privy Council's decision in *Red Sea Insurance Company Ltd v Bouyges SA* … Lord Slynn effectively adopted Dicey and Morris' recast of Lord Wilberforce's approach in *Boys*'.

[111] *Chaplin v Boys* [1971] AC 356, 392.

substantive choice of law position – is almost uniformly accepted both by courts[112] and commentators in the relevant jurisdictions,[113] it is clear the real difficulty lies in classifying issues as substantive or procedural.[114] Indeed, making that distinction has been described as the 'fulcrum, or axis, of the choice of law process.'[115]

Second, *Boys* is a poignant example of British judges seeking to reduce the impact of foreign law to serve the perceived ends of justice, be it by classifying a matter as procedural, or by inventing a choice of law rule leading to the application of the *lex fori*.

Third, through the manipulation of choice of law rules, or the reduction of the scope of the foreign law applied through the conduit of them, it is possible to avoid dealing with the practicalities involved in proving foreign law. Lord Hodson explicitly alluded to this:

> Furthermore, difficulty and inconvenience is involved in many cases in ascertaining the details of the relevant foreign law.[116]

The issues discussed in *Boys* in relation to the classification of quantum as a procedural matter were ultimately resolved by Article 15 of the Rome II Regulation,[117] which states that both liability and quantum are matters for the *lex causae*. However, *Boys* is by no means the only example demonstrating the difficulties surrounding

[112] See, in Great Britain, *Cox v Ergo Versicherung AG* [2014] AC 1379, 1388, and *AS Latvijas Krajbanka v Antonov* [2016] EWHC 1679 (Comm), [5]. In Germany, *Decision of the Federal Court of Justice from 27 June 1984* (BGH, IVb. Zivilsenat) IVb ZR 2/83, NJW 1985, 552, 553, and *Decision of the Federal Court of Justice from 29 June 1987* (BGH, II. Zivilsenat) II ZR 6/87, NJW 1988, 647.

[113] The relevant points are well summarised in Fawcett and Torremans (eds) (n 50), 73, and Junker, *Internationales Zivilprozessrecht* (n 77), § 24 I para 1ff.

[114] Schack, who is sceptical as to the traditional approach, is certainly right in so far as the devil is in the detail, ie the exceptions and, in particular, the delimitation between the applicable substantive law and the supposedly applicable procedural law of the *lex fori*: Schack (n 77), para 45: 'steckt der Teufel im Detail, und zwar in den notwendigen Ausnahmen und vor allem in der Grenzziehung zwischen dem vom IPR berufenen materiellen Recht und dem angeblich der lex fori unterliegenden Prozessrecht.' While Dicey was clear in 1908 that the 'principle that procedure is governed by the lex fori is of general application and universally admitted', he noted that the difficulty 'lies in discriminating between matters which belong to procedure and matters which affect the substantive rights of the parties' and noted that 'English lawyers give the widest possible extension to the meaning of the term "procedure"'. AV Dicey, *A Digest of the Law of England with reference to the Conflict of Laws*, 2nd edn (Stevens and Sons; Sweet & Maxwell, 1908), 709.

[115] JM Carruthers, 'Substance and Procedure in the Conflict of Laws: A continuing debate in relation to damages' (2004) 53 *ICLQ* 691, 694: 'Whatever may be the justification for the principle, it is not so much the principle itself as its application which gives rise to difficulties', ie making the substance/procedure distinction.

[116] *Chaplin v Boys* [1971] AC 356, 380.

[117] The classification of the rules on quantification of damages as procedural continued as late as *Harding v Wealands* [2007] 2 AC 1, which was decided under the Private International Law (Miscellaneous Provisions) Act 1995 and not the common law. The old rule will apply to events giving rise to damage which pre-date the Rome I Regulation, as briefly discussed in *JXJ v Province of Great Britain of the Institute of Brothers of the Christian Schools* [2020] EWHC 1914 (QB), [8].

the classification of an issue as either procedural or substantive. A rule which stood for a particularly long time in England was to approach the classification of prescription or limitation as either substantive or procedural depending on how the *lex causae* classified the issue, ie has the right been substantively extinguished by the passage of time under the *lex causae* or is there merely a procedural bar to raising an action?[118] It is fair to say that the rule made a random and arbitrary distinction, an approach that was recognised by the English Law Commission in 1980 as being 'anomalous'.[119] The matter was remedied in England by the Foreign Limitation Periods Act 1984, which stated that a foreign limitation period would be recognised by the English courts regardless of whether the bar was procedural or substantive in terms of the *lex causae*, with the same issue having been addressed in Scotland by the Prescription and Limitation (Scotland) Act 1973.[120] This was also confirmed in Article 15 of the Rome II Regulation, which has generally been interpreted as giving the *lex causae* a very wide scope of application compared to the historic position.[121]

Questions involving the introduction and application of foreign law have also traditionally been classed as procedural;[122] however, whether and how foreign law is applied in a case can undoubtedly have a substantive impact on the parties' rights. In short, manipulation of this process can be viewed as a potential device for reducing or distorting the application of foreign law in a case,[123] which should be borne in mind in the context of this work.

[118] *Phillips v Eyre* (1870–71) LR 6 QB 1, 29. Explained succinctly in *Deutsche Bahn AG v Mastercard Inc* [2016] CAT 14, [39].

[119] The Law Commission, 'Classification of Limitation in Private International Law: Working Paper No 75' (1980), s3-eu-west-2.amazonaws.com/lawcom-prod-storage-11jsxou24uy7q/uploads/2016/08/No.075-Classification-of-Limitation-in-Private-International-Law.pdf, 16. See comments in *Deutsche Bahn AG v Mastercard Inc* [2016] CAT 14, [40].

[120] See The Law Commission (n 119), 28–29.

[121] It might have been thought that service of the proceedings, where this is specifically required by the applicable law to interrupt a limitation period, would be considered purely procedural and fall outwith the scope of the Rome II Regulation (n 46) under Art 1(3). However, in both *Pandya v Intersalonika General Insurance Co SA* [2020] EWHC 273 (QB), in respect of Greek law, and *Johnson v Berentzen* [2021] EWHC 1042 (QB), in respect of Scots law – both of which require service of the proceedings (summons) to interrupt the limitation period – the English court held that the *lex causae* should determine this matter, under the Rome II Regulation (n 46), Art 15(h), even though English law does not require this additional step to be completed to interrupt the limitation period.

[122] *Iranian Offshore Engineering and Construction Co v Dean Investment Holdings SA* [2019] 1 WLR 82, 90, citing Dicey's r 25(2) in Collins (Lord Collins of Mapesbury) and Harris (eds) (n 50).

[123] Although no longer relevant in respect of Great Britain, such outcomes have been criticised as undermining the coherence of EU private international law: see J Basedow, 'Kohärenz im Internationalen Privat- und Verfahrensrecht der Europäischen Union – Eine einleitende Orientierung' in J von Hein and G Rühl (eds), *Kohärenz im Internationalen Privat- und Verfahrensrecht der Europäischen Union* (Mohr Siebeck, 2016), 13–14.

C. Transformation of the Applicable Choice of Law Rules and the Impact of Brexit

Since the Treaty of Amsterdam entered into force in 1999,[124] the EU in its ambition to achieve ever closer union, together with its aim of maintaining and developing an area of freedom, security and justice,[125] has legislated for EU rules of private international law[126] to determine, inter alia, international jurisdiction in civil, commercial,[127] and family matters;[128] and to determine the applicable law in contractual,[129] and non-contractual matters.[130] These rules have been incorporated into EU Member States' law as regulations, which apply in EU Member State courts as binding, directly applicable rules of law.[131]

The UK, a Member State of the EU throughout this period,[132] enjoyed a special status with regards to EU legislation in the area of private international law,[133] which enabled it to opt-into instruments as it saw fit.[134] In a sense, the UK's opt-in allowed it to stand at the edge of the EU project to standardise the rules of private international law throughout the EU Member States.[135] Crucially, the UK chose

[124] See, regarding the Treaty of Amsterdam generally: PP Craig and G de Búrca, *EU Law: Text, Cases, and Materials*, 7th edn (Oxford University Press, 2020), 14ff. A Fiorini, 'The Codification of Private International Law in Europe – Could the Community Learn from the Experience of Mixed Jurisdictions?' (2008) 23 *Tulane European and Civil Law Forum* 89, 97: 'On 1 May 1999 the private international law landscape changed dramatically within Europe with the entry into force of the Treaty of Amsterdam.' Basedow (n 123), 5ff.

[125] Brussels I bis Regulation (n 84), Recital (3).

[126] For an understanding of the evolution of European private international law, see PE McEleavy, 'The Evolution of European Private International Law' (2008) 57 *ICLQ* 969, and J von Hein, 'EU Competence to Legislate in the Area of Private International Law and Law Reforms at the EU Level' in PR Beaumont and others (eds), *Cross-Border Litigation in Europe* (Hart Publishing, 2017). In German academic literature, the process has been referred to as 'Kollisionsrechtsvereinheitlichung.' See T Rauscher, *Internationales Privatrecht: Mit internationalem Verfahrensrecht*, 5th edn (CF Müller, 2017), para 91.

[127] Brussels I bis Regulation (n 84).

[128] Council Regulation (EC) No 2201/2003 of 27 November 2003 concerning jurisdiction and the recognition and enforcement of judgments in matrimonial matters and the matters of parental responsibility [2003] OJ L 338/1 (Brussels II bis Regulation).

[129] Regulation (EC) No 593/2008 of the European Parliament and of the Council of 17 June 2008 on the law applicable to contractual obligations [2008] OJ L 177/6 (Rome I Regulation).

[130] Rome II Regulation (n 46).

[131] TFEU (n 1), Art 288.

[132] The UK's membership of the EU ended on 31 January 2020.

[133] Under Protocol (No 21) to the TFEU on the Position of the United Kingdom and Ireland in respect of the area of Freedom, Security and Justice [2016] OJ C 202/295, Art 3(1) (Protocol (No 21)), the UK could notify the President of the Council in writing, within three months after a proposal or initiative had been presented to the Council, that it wished to take part. See Von Hein, 'EU Competence to Legislate in the Area of Private International Law and Law Reforms at the EU Level' (n 126), 20.

[134] Von Hein, 'EU Competence to Legislate in the Area of Private International Law and Law Reforms at the EU Level' (n 126), 33.

[135] M Sonnentag, *Die Konsequenzen des Brexits für das Internationale Privat- und Zivilverfahrensrecht* (Mohr Siebeck, 2017), 20–21.

to opt-into both the Rome I and Rome II Regulations,[136] although the UK did not opt-into the regulations on applicable law in divorce,[137] succession,[138] and matrimonial property,[139] or the 2007 Hague Protocol on Maintenance,[140] which the EU became a party to, all of which are in force in Germany.[141] Where the UK chose to voluntarily opt-in, the EU regulations applied with their full legal force,[142] and accordingly, as in all other EU Member States, were binding, directly applicable rules of law in the British courts.[143]

The rapid development of choice of law rules throughout the EU has given rise to the apt description that there has been a communitarisation,[144] or Europeanisation,[145] of private international law in EU Member States,[146] although the extent to which these developments have proceeded on a coherent basis has been questioned.[147] Nonetheless, since at least the inception of the 1980 Rome Convention on the law applicable to contractual obligations, but most prominently since 1999, it is clear that there have been fundamental changes to the choice of law rules in effect in the relevant jurisdictions. In Great Britain, for example, traditional common law doctrines, eg the proper law of contract,[148] have largely been replaced by provisions found in the EU regulations. In Germany, there is

[136] See, for a brief summary of which EU regulations the UK opted-into: Von Hein, 'EU Competence to Legislate in the Area of Private International Law and Law Reforms at the EU Level' (n 126), 33.

[137] Council Regulation (EU) No 1259/2010 of 20 December 2010 implementing enhanced cooperation in the area of the law applicable to divorce and legal separation [2010] OJ L 343/10 (Rome III Regulation).

[138] Regulation (EU) No 650/2012 of 4 July 2012 on jurisdiction, applicable law, recognition and enforcement of decisions and acceptance and enforcement of authentic instruments in matters of succession and on the creation of a European Certificate of Succession [2012] OJ L 201/107 (EU Succession Regulation).

[139] Council Regulation (EU) 2016/1103 of 24 June 2016 implementing enhanced cooperation in the area of jurisdiction, applicable law and the recognition and enforcement of decisions in matters of matrimonial property regimes [2016] OJ L 183/1 (EU Matrimonial Property Regulation).

[140] See the HCCH, 'Protocol of 23 November 2007 on the Law Applicable to Maintenance Obligations', www.hcch.net/en/instruments/conventions/full-text/?cid=133.

[141] See, as regards choice of law in divorce and matrimonial property law, Junker, *Internationales Privatrecht* (n 58), § 18, and, with regards choice of law in succession law, Junker, *Internationales Privatrecht* (n 58), § 20.

[142] The terms of the transition period meant that EU regulations continued to have direct effect until 31 December 2020. See, for the relevant provisions in UK domestic law, the European Union (Withdrawal Agreement) Act 2020, s 1.

[143] European Communities Act 1972, s 2.

[144] McEleavy (n 126), 981.

[145] Fiorini (n 124), 91.

[146] One wonders if Lord Denning MR's famous comment regarding the effect (at that time) of EC law in British law in *Shields v E Coomes (Holdings) Ltd* [1978] 1 WLR 1408, 1416, is apt to describe recent developments in European private international law: 'All this shows that the flowing tide of Community law is coming in fast. It has not stopped at high-water mark. It has broken the dykes and the banks. It has submerged the surrounding land. So much so that we have to learn to become amphibious if we wish to keep our heads above water.'

[147] Fiorini (n 124), 98.

[148] M McParland, *The Rome I Regulation on the Law Applicable to Contractual Obligations* (Oxford University Press, 2015), para 10.10.

now a much greater focus on habitual residence as a connecting factor rather than nationality.[149] However, the changes in Great Britain, in terms of the structure of choice of law rules, have been far more pronounced than in Germany, at least in so far as flexible, somewhat vague common law doctrines have been replaced by rigid rules and terminology.[150]

On 23 June 2016, the British people voted to leave the EU. Nine months later, on 29 March 2017, the then UK Prime Minister sent a letter[151] to the President of the European Council, under Article 50(2) of the TEU, indicating the UK's intention to withdraw from the EU.[152] This started the two-year period for withdrawal negotiations, under Article 50(3) of the TEU.[153] Following three extensions and two general elections, the UK finally left the EU on 31 January 2020 and entered an 11-month implementation[154] or transition[155] period, which ended on 31 December 2020.[156]

The full, long-term political, legal, and economic ramifications of the UK's decision to leave the EU remain to be seen. This work has essentially been written during the period since the 2016 Brexit referendum. Regardless of any potential merits of the UK's withdrawal from the EU, it is fair to say that the resultant legal uncertainty has cast a dark shadow over this work, as it has no doubt cast a shadow over many other academic works addressing UK (and EU) private international law. In the context of private international law, it is unclear how continued close cooperation between the UK and the EU can properly function going forward,[157] although Professor Paul Beaumont, for example, has strongly argued that the UK's future focus should be on those instruments developed by the Hague Conference

[149] For example, the EU Succession Regulation (n 138), Art 21. See Junker, *Internationales Privatrecht* (n 58), § 20 para 1. The change was described as a *Paradigmenwechsel* (paradigm shift) in the third edition of the same text. A Junker, *Internationales Privatrecht*, 3rd edn (CH Beck, 2019), § 20 para 1.

[150] See, for example, Rome I Regulation (n 129), Art 4(1)(b): 'a contract for the provision of services shall be governed by the law of the country where the service provider has his habitual residence.'

[151] The Prime Minister, 'Letter of the UK Prime Minister in terms of Article 50(2) of the Treaty of the European Union' (2017), assets.publishing.service.gov.uk/government/uploads/system/uploads/attachment_data/file/604079/Prime_Ministers_letter_to_European_Council_President_Donald_Tusk.pdf.

[152] This step required further legislation, ie the European Union (Notification of Withdrawal) Act 2017, by virtue of the decision of the UK Supreme Court in *R (Miller) v Secretary of State for Exiting the European Union* [2017] UKSC 5.

[153] Sonnentag (n 135), 1. For a detailed analysis of the Article 50 process, see PP Craig, 'The Process: Brexit and the Anatomy of Article 50' in F Fabbrini (ed), *The Law & Politics of Brexit* (Oxford University Press, 2017).

[154] This is the term used in UK domestic law. See the European Union (Withdrawal Agreement) Act 2020, s 1.

[155] This is the term used by the EU and in the Agreement on the withdrawal of the United Kingdom of Great Britain and Northern Ireland from the European Union and the European Atomic Energy Community [2019] OJ C 384 I/01 (Withdrawal Agreement).

[156] PR Beaumont, 'Some reflections on the way ahead for UK private international law after Brexit' (2021) *Journal of Private International Law* 1, 2.

[157] An analysis of the various options is provided in Sonnentag (n 135), 3ff.

on Private International Law (HCCH),[158] with which the EU has an existing, close, free-standing relationship,[159] and where the European Commission also sees the future UK–EU relationship in terms of private international law.[160]

Nonetheless, in so far as this work is concerned, two material points are clear. First, secondary legislation has been passed giving continuing effect to the Rome I and Rome II Regulations in UK domestic law, both of which will continue to operate largely as before.[161] Second, as the rules of civil procedure, eg the English Civil Procedure Rules (CPR) and associated case law, at least in so far as they govern the actual proceedings,[162] are only tangentially affected by EU law, there has been little impact of Brexit on them.

In terms of the future, it seems unlikely, in the absence of an obvious alternative, that the fixed rules provided by those EU regulations on applicable law, which do not require reciprocity (*Gegenseitigkeit*),[163] currently in force in the UK will be substantively reformed any time soon.[164] This accords with previous legislative

[158] See Beaumont, 'Some reflections on the way ahead for UK private international law after Brexit' (n 156), particularly 15–17, but note criticism, for example, of some of the UK's decisions regarding the refusal of accession to certain HCCH instruments from Commonwealth countries in Africa, the Caribbean, and Asia, as well as the lack of expertise of the UK's representatives at HCCH negotiations, and also PR Beaumont, 'Private international law concerning children in the UK after Brexit: comparing Hague Treaty law with EU Regulations' (2017) *CPIL Working Paper* No 2017/2, www.abdn.ac.uk/law/documents/CPIL%20Working%20Paper%20No%202017_2.pdf, 18–19.

[159] For example, the EU signed the Convention of 23 November 2007 on the International Recovery of Child Support and Other Forms of Family Maintenance on behalf of the EU Member States. See HCCH, 'European Union Declarations at the time of the approval of the Hague Convention of 23 November 2007 on the International Recovery of Child Support and other forms of Family Maintenance (the "Convention") in accordance with Article 63 thereof' (2007), www.hcch.net/en/instruments/conventions/status-table/notifications/?csid=1109&disp=resdn.

[160] In the context of the UK's application to accede to the Convention on jurisdiction and the recognition and enforcement of judgments in civil and commercial matters, 21 December 2007 [2007] OJ L 339 (Lugano Convention), the European Commission said 'The United Kingdom is a third country without a special link to the internal market. Therefore, there is no reason for the European Union to depart from its general approach in relation to the United Kingdom. Consequently, the Hague Conventions should provide the framework for future cooperation between the European Union and the United Kingdom in the field of civil judicial cooperation.' European Commission, 'Communication from the Commission to the European Parliament and the Council: Assessment on the application of the United Kingdom of Great Britain and Northern Ireland to accede to the 2007 Lugano Convention' (2021), ec.europa.eu/info/sites/default/files/1_en_act_en.pdf, 4.

[161] The Law Applicable to Contractual Obligations and Non-Contractual Obligations (Amendment etc.) (EU Exit) Regulations 2019. In addition, under the Withdrawal Agreement (n 155), Art 66(a), the Rome I Regulation (n 129) shall apply in respect of contracts concluded before the end of the transition period, and, under the Withdrawal Agreement (n 155), Art 66(b), the Rome II Regulation (n 46) shall apply in respect of events giving rise to damage, where such events occurred before the end of the transition period. This means that these regulations will continue to play a significant role in choice of law in British court proceedings well into the future.

[162] Certain areas of civil procedure will be directly affected by Brexit, eg service. See Regulation (EC) No 1393/2007 of the European Parliament and of the Council of 13 November 2007 on the service in the Member States of judicial and extrajudicial documents in civil or commercial matters (service of documents) (Service Regulation).

[163] See Sonnentag (n 135), 78–79.

[164] See also, for a sense of UK Government thinking on private international law after Brexit: HM Government, 'Providing a cross-border civil judicial cooperation framework: A future partnership paper', www.gov.uk/government/uploads/system/uploads/attachment_data/file/639271/Providing_a_cross-border_civil_judicial_cooperation_framework.pdf.

practice. The Private International Law (Miscellaneous Provisions) Act 1995 provides fixed rules for the determination of which law applies to govern a tort (or delict); for example, that the law of the place where the individual sustained his personal injury is to apply (*lex loci delicti*).[165] This, now largely superseded,[166] legislation, which was not based on provisions of EU law, is evidence that the UK is unlikely to revert to common law concepts such as the proper law of contract,[167] which was, in any case, superseded by the Contracts (Applicable Law) Act 1990 in its transposition into UK domestic law of the Rome Convention of 1980,[168] prior to the introduction of the Rome I Regulation in 2008. In short, the substantive analysis contained in this work, which focuses on the application of foreign law through the conduit of choice of law rules, does not appear to be materially affected by Brexit.

An interesting question, at least as far as matters concern Germany, which is not considered in detail in this work, is the extent to which these regulations, and their underlying legislative background,[169] place obligations on courts in EU Member States to give them mandatory effect and to apply them equivalently and effectively,[170] lest those Member States risk being held in breach of EU law. In summary, while other principles of EU law also potentially come into play,[171] the most relevant principle appears to be that of *effet utile*, which also has meaning in the context of public international law.[172] The CJEU has said:

> The national courts, whose task it is to apply the provisions of Community law in areas within their jurisdiction, must ensure that they take full effect.[173]

[165] Private International Law (Miscellaneous Provisions) Act 1995, s 11(2)(a).

[166] Most questions of applicable law in tort (or delict) are now addressed by the Rome II Regulation.

[167] See, for an explanation of the concept, Fawcett and Torremans (eds) (n 50), 682.

[168] Convention on the law applicable to contractual obligations, opened for signature in Rome on 19 June 1980 (Consolidated Version) (80/934/EEC) (Rome Convention).

[169] Most prominently, TFEU (n 1), Art 288(2): 'A regulation shall have general application. It shall be binding in its entirety and directly applicable in all Member States.'

[170] For a detailed analysis of the issues in the German language, see C Trautmann, *Europäisches Kollisionsrecht und ausländisches Recht im nationalen Zivilverfahren* (Mohr Siebeck, 2011), 265ff. This study has effectively come to be considered the leading study on the matter. See comments in MR Isidro, 'The Application of European Private International Law and the Ascertainment of Foreign law' in J von Hein, E-M Kieninger and G Rühl (eds), *How European is European Private International Law?* (Intersentia, 2019), 149ff. Another German language academic text covering similar ground, published three years later, builds on Trautmann's analysis: R Hübner, *Ausländisches Recht vor deutschen Gerichten* (Mohr Siebeck, 2014), 138ff. The point has also been alluded to by others: see G Rühl, 'Die Kosten der Rechtswahlfreiheit: Zur Anwendung ausländischen Rechts durch deutsche Gerichte' (2007) 71 *Rabels Zeitschrift für Ausländisches und Internationales Privatrecht* 559, 577. The point has been touched on in the British literature. See Fawcett and Torremans (eds) (n 50), 107; Crawford and Carruthers (n 50), para 8-32; TC Hartley, 'Pleading and Proof of Foreign Law: The Major European Systems Compared' (1996) 45 *ICLQ* 271, 290ff, albeit in relation to the Rome Convention, which is underpinned by different considerations as it is an international convention and not part of EU law.

[171] The principle of mutual trust is also potentially relevant, ie there may be an expectation that the instruments are being applied consistently. See M Weller, 'Mutual trust: in search of the future of European Union private international law' (2015) 11 *Journal of Private International Law* 64.

[172] A detailed summary of the principle is provided in M Potacs, 'Effet utile als Auslegungsgrundsatz' (2009) *Zeitschrift Europarecht* 465, 466ff. See also Hübner (n 170), 175ff, and Trautmann (n 170), 319ff.

[173] *Antonio Munoz y Cia SA and Superior Fruiticola SA v Frumar Ltd and Redbridge Produce Marketing Ltd*, Case C-253/00, [2002] ECR I-7289, [28].

At issue appears to be the extent to which potentially long-standing domestic rules of civil procedure allocating responsibilities to various actors, eg the parties and the judge, can continue to operate without modification, despite the fact that such domestic rules of civil procedure can lead to provisions of EU law potentially being left out of account by EU Member State courts. Perhaps one of the most significant contributions to the debate regarding the relationship between EU law and domestic rules of civil procedure was made by A-G Jacobs in his Opinion in *Van Schijndel and Van Veen* (1995). A-G Jacobs did not advocate a general requirement to reform domestic rules of civil procedure to ensure the mandatory application of EU law, ie to require Member State courts to introduce points of EU law *ex proprio motu*:

> To impose on all national courts a requirement to apply Community law of their own motion, although it might not be impossible to put into practice in any system, would cause a degree of disruption which might vary in different systems but would probably be significant in all of them. There would also be difficulty in deciding whether such treatment of Community law was required for the whole of Community law or only for certain parts of it, and if so which parts.[174]

However, that is not to say that A-G Jacobs advocated giving Member States a completely free hand, with the matter, in his view, being one essentially of fact and degree.[175] The CJEU appears to have adopted A-G Jacobs's argumentation in its judgment in the case,[176] and, moreover, has since held:

> The detailed procedural rules applicable are a matter for the domestic legal order of each Member State, under the principle of procedural autonomy of the Member States, provided that they are not less favourable than those governing similar domestic situations (principle of equivalence) and that they do not render impossible in practice or excessively difficult the exercise of rights conferred by the Community legal order (principle of effectiveness).[177]

Nonetheless, a recent decision of the Court of Justice of the European Union (CJEU) in *Amazon EU Sàrl* (2016), in so far as it concerned consumer protection, suggests that the CJEU may be prepared to be significantly more interventionist in contractual circumstances involving consumers.[178] Thus, some favour the

[174] *Van Schijndel and Van Veen v Stichting Pensioenfonds voor Fysiotherapeuten*, Joined Cases C-430/93 and C-431/93, [1995] ECR I-4705, Opinion of A-G Jacobs, [37].

[175] *Van Schijndel and Van Veen v Stichting Pensioenfonds voor Fysiotherapeuten*, Joined Cases C-430/93 and C-431/93, [1995] ECR I-4705, Opinion of A-G Jacobs, [30]: 'It is therefore only exceptionally that the Court will need to intervene to ensure that effect is given to Community law.'

[176] *Van Schijndel and Van Veen v Stichting Pensioenfonds voor Fysiotherapeuten*, Joined Cases C-430/93 and C-431/93, [1995] ECR I-4705, [21].

[177] *The Queen, on the application of Wells v Secretary of State for Transport, Local Government and the Regions*, Case C-201/02, [2004] ECR I-0723, [67].

[178] *Verein für Konsumenteninformation v Amazon EU Sàrl*, Case C-191/15, [2016] 2 WLR 19, [71]. In the case, which involved a choice of law clause in favour of Luxembourgish law, the CJEU stated that the failure of a business to draw a consumer's attention in its terms and conditions to the mandatory protection he derives from his own law is unfair.

mandatory application of choice of law rules in EU Member States in situations, at least, where there is a weaker party involved in the litigation.[179]

II. Prerequisites to Applying Foreign Law by Means of Choice of Law Rules

A. Necessity of a Foreign Element in the Factual Matrix of the Case

A basic requirement for fully engaging with private international law, and applying its attendant choice of law rules, is a foreign element in the factual matrix of the case, which is undoubtedly a *sine qua non* for the application of foreign law through the conduit of choice of law rules. In many EU private international law instruments there is explicit recognition of the requirement for a foreign element before the relevant regulation's scope of application is engaged. For example, Article 1(1) of the Rome I Regulation states:

> This Regulation shall apply, in situations involving a conflict of laws, to contractual obligations in civil and commercial matters.

Perhaps the term 'conflict of laws', in this context, is unsatisfactory, as this term of art leaves the fundamental question open: What exactly constitutes a conflict of laws? Does the term seek to identify the factual and legal situation involving a conflict of laws, or does the term make reference to the field of conflict of laws, which is an unsatisfactory term generally to describe the field of private international law.[180] Article 1(1) of the predecessor Rome Convention contained clearer language, with an emphasis on choice of law, which characterises the issue more precisely:

> The rules of this Convention shall apply to contractual obligations in any situation involving a choice between the laws of different countries.[181]

[179] Trautmann (n 170), 303ff. See also more cautiously PR Beaumont, 'When should EU private international law require that foreign law be applied?' in J von Hein, E-M Kieninger and G Rühl (eds), *How European is European Private International Law?* (Intersentia, 2019), 180.

[180] There are a number of academic discussions about the appropriateness of the term conflict of laws to describe the field, as opposed to private international law or international private law. See, for example, A Briggs, *The Conflict of Laws*, 2nd edn (Oxford University Press, 2008), 2. However, it should be noted that the German concept of *internationales Privatrecht* cannot be equated with the British concept of private international law (or international private law) for the reason that German law clearly distinguishes questions of international civil procedure (*internationales Zivilverfahrensrecht*) from questions of choice of law (*Kollisionsrecht*). See Kropholler (n 52), 1ff. The term international private law, encompassing both questions of international civil procedure and choice of law, is well-established in Scotland. See Crawford and Carruthers (n 50), para 1-03.

[181] Rome Convention (n 168), Art 1(1).

The 1980 Giuliano-Lagarde Report, in respect of the aforementioned article of the Rome Convention, clarified the ultimately chosen terminology to include situations involving:

> one or more elements foreign to the internal social system of a country (for example, the fact that one or all of the parties to the contract are foreign nationals or persons habitually resident abroad, the fact that the contract was made abroad the fact that one or more of the obligations of the parties are to be performed in a foreign country, etc.) thereby giving the legal systems of several countries claims to apply.[182]

While the French and Italian language versions of the Rome I Regulation both use the equivalent of the English term conflict of laws, ie '*comportant un conflit de lois*' and '*comportino un conflitto di leggi*', the German language version uses the phrase '*die eine Verbindung zum Recht verschiedener Staaten aufweisen*' (that show a connection to the law of different states).[183] This terminology is preferable as it is the clearest as to the essential requirement.

Nonetheless, in our globalised world, it is hard to find a factual matrix not involving at least some trivial foreign element.[184] The real gateway test for lawyers considering a factual matrix is establishing whether the foreign element is a *material one* such as to involve the possible application of a foreign law through the conduit of a relevant choice of law rule. Relevant foreign elements are defined in private international law in terms of connecting factors[185] (*Anknüpfungsmomente*),[186] which feature in choice of law rules throughout various systems of private international law. It might be that a party has a foreign domicile[187] or habitual residence.[188] It might be that the contract was defectively executed in terms of the

[182] M Giuliano and P Lagarde, 'Report on the Convention on the law applicable to contractual obligations' (1980), eur-lex.europa.eu/legal-content/EN/TXT/PDF/?uri=CELEX:31980Y1031(01)&from=EN, Art 1(1).

[183] There is a detailed discussion about how the respective terminology in English and French of the Rome Convention, Art 1(1), and the Rome I Regulation (n 129), Art 1(1) came to be chosen, in McParland (n 148), para 6.02ff.

[184] There is sensible debate in Germany as to whether the engagement of choice of law rules requires any foreign element in the factual matrix of the case at all or whether choice of law rules should nominally be applied in a purely domestic case. The majority opinion appears to favour the latter approach. See, for example, Junker, *Internationales Privatrecht* (n 58), § 1 para 13, which draws on Kegel and Schurig (n 58), 6–7. It is argued persuasively in Kegel and Schurig (n 58), 7, that the necessity to search for a foreign connection in order for a choice of law rule to be applicable unnecessarily adds an additional step to the process, ie either domestic law or a foreign law is applicable through the relevant choice of law rule, and, while the relevant choice of law rule is always applied, in certain domestic cases the application of domestic law will be simply be self-evident.

[185] Collins (Lord Collins of Mapesbury) and Harris (eds) (n 50), para 1-079ff. This process is succinctly described in Symeonides, *Choice of Law* (n 71), 64, as 'localisation', ie placing the connecting factor on the map.

[186] Kropholler (n 52), 136ff.

[187] For example, the English choice of law rule in relation to the inheritance of moveable property, *Pipon v Pipon* (1744) Amb 25; 27 ER 14. See also Fawcett and Torremans (eds) (n 50), 1339.

[188] For example, see the rules in relation to the applicable law in the absence of choice in a matrimonial property regime in the EU Matrimonial Property Regulation (n 139), Art 26. For an explanation of the complicated interplay between matrimonial property law and the law of property, which is

lex fori's rules of formal validity but was validly entered into abroad;[189] that the accident took place abroad;[190] or that the parties involved in the accident had a shared foreign domicile.[191]

B. Willingness to Apply Foreign Law

The fundamental proposition underlying the principle of territoriality is that the laws of state A do not permeate the boundaries of state B. Any decision of state B to give effect to the laws of state A is a voluntary one, even if the choice by state B as to whether to give effect to the laws of state A a priori affects the rights of a citizen of state A in state B. Thus, for there to be an application of the laws of state A within state B, there is required a willingness by state B to apply the laws of state A. Recognition of the principles underlying these propositions is long-standing. Early recognition of the principle of territoriality came from the Dutch academic lawyer Ulrich Huber,[192] who, in the late seventeenth century, prominently advocated the comity theory as justifying the application of foreign law,[193] notwithstanding the emergence of separate, sovereign nation states in Europe.[194] Huber's analysis particularly influenced English and Scottish lawyers.[195] It also

generally based on the *lex rei sitae*, see C Rupp, 'Die Verordnung zum europäischen internationalen Ehegüterrecht aus sachenrechtlicher Perspektive' (2016) *Zeitschrift für das Privatrecht der Europäischen Union* 295.

[189] For example, the rules in relation to the formal validity of contracts, Rome I Regulation (n 129), Art 11.

[190] For example, the *lex loci delicti* rule, Rome II Regulation (n 46), Art 4(1).

[191] For example, the rule developed in the US in *Babcock v Jackson* 12 NY 2d 473 (1963), and discussed in DF Cavers and others, '*Babcock v Jackson*, 12 NY 2d 473, 191 NE 2d 279, 240 NYS 2d 743 (1963)' (1963) 63 *Columbia Law Review* 1212 and Sherwood (n 72). There is a similar rule in the Rome II Regulation (n 46), Art 4(2), where the parties have a shared habitual residence.

[192] RD Carswell, 'The Doctrine of Vested Rights in Private International Law' (1959) 8 *ICLQ* 268, 271–72, which describes the territorial principle as having been 'expounded with impressive clarity and brevity by Ulrich Huber in 1689'; DJ Llewelyn Davies, 'The Influence of Huber's De Conflictu Legum on English Private International Law' (1937) 18 *British Yearbook of International Law* 49, 57; EG Lorenzen, 'Huber's De Conflictu Legum' (1919) Paper 4563 *Faculty Scholarship Series*, digitalcommons.law.yale.edu/fss_papers/4563, accessed 14 May 2020. Lorenzen argued, at 376, that Huber went further in proclaiming the principles underlying the theory of territoriality than any of his predecessors; A Mills, 'Rethinking Jurisdiction in International Law' (2014) 84 *The British Yearbook of International Law* 187, 202.

[193] Kropholler (n 52), 13; Carswell (n 192), 272; Lorenzen, 'Huber's De Conflictu Legum' (n 192), 378: 'Huber was the first writer who made it clear beyond a doubt, that the recognition in each state of so-called foreign created rights was a mere concession which such state made on grounds of convenience and utility, and not as the result of a binding obligation or duty.'

[194] JR Paul, 'The Isolation of Private International Law' (1988) 7 *Wisconsin International Law Journal* 149, 157; Beaumont and McEleavy (n 50), para 2.08. The first explicit mention of sovereignty as an issue has been attributed to the French lawyer and philosopher Jean Bodin's *De Republica*, which was published in 1576. See Carswell (n 192), 271.

[195] See Paul (n 194), 158, though there is no evidence of English lawyers studying in Holland during the eighteenth century in any significant numbers. The impact of Huber on Scottish lawyers is thought to have influenced Lord Mansfield, who, in turn, made Huber's ideas (better) known in England. See Llewelyn Davies (n 192), 53.

featured prominently in Joseph Story's nineteenth-century account of the conflict of laws,[196] which propounded ideas such as exclusivity, sovereignty, and territoriality. For example:

> A state may prohibit the operation of all foreign laws, and the rights growing out of them, within its own territories. It may prohibit some foreign laws, and it may admit the operation of others.[197]

The principle of territoriality has been described by Symeon C Symeonides – who attributes its prominence in the Anglo-American world to the writings of Joseph Beale – as having been the favourite, 'if not the prevailing', principle driving conflict of laws thinking in the Anglo-American world.[198] Indeed, it was a fundamental principle underlying the American Law Institute's[199] (albeit heavily criticised) Restatement (First) of Conflict of Laws,[200] and has long-standing roots in English case law:

> There can be no doubt, but that every action tried here must be tried by the law of England; but the law of England says, that in a variety of circumstances, with regard to contracts legally made abroad, the laws of the country where the cause of action arose shall govern.[201]

It is said in *Dicey, Morris and Collins*, the leading English textbook on private international law:

> Theoretically, it would be possible for English courts, while opening their doors to foreigners, to apply English domestic law in all cases.[202]

However, the principle of territoriality as a pressing concern in private international law has been heavily criticised.[203] Perhaps its greatest flaw is its rank simplicity. The inconvenience and injustice caused by a complete refusal to recognise the laws of other states would be so great that it scarcely warrants contemplation:

> But if [the English courts] did so, grave injustice would again be inflicted not only on foreigners but also on Englishmen. For instance, if two English people married in France in accordance with the formalities prescribed by French law, but not in accordance with the formalities prescribed by English law, the English court, if it applied English law to

[196] J Story, *Commentaries on the Conflict of Laws*, 3rd edn (Maxwell and Son, 1846), 28ff.
[197] ibid, 34.
[198] Symeonides, *Choice of Law* (n 71), 54.
[199] Symeonides has described the Restatement (First) of Conflict of Laws as having been 'inextricably tied with its drafter Professor Beale.' See SC Symeonides, 'The First Conflicts Restatement through the Eyes of Old: As Bad as Its Reputation' (2007) 32 *Southern Illinois University Law Journal* 39, 41ff.
[200] Symeonides, *Choice of Law* (n 71), 56: 'Gradually, the Restatement became the favorite punching bag of virtually every conflicts teacher and writer.'
[201] *Holman v Johnson* (1775) 1 Cowper 341, 343; 98 ER 1120. See also Carswell (n 192), 272.
[202] Collins (Lord Collins of Mapesbury) and Harris (eds) (n 50), para 1-006.
[203] See Symeonides, *Choice of Law* (n 71), 56–57; Carswell (n 192), 286. See also the closely linked theory of comity, which seeks to provide justification as to why foreign law should be applied. Referred to in Kropholler (n 52), 12–13, and concisely described in Beaumont and McEleavy (n 50), para 2.08ff.

> the validity of the marriage, would have to treat the parties as unmarried persons and their children as illegitimate.[204]

The renowned German lawyer Friedrich Carl von Savigny admitted the truth of the propositions inherent to the principle of territoriality in his eighth volume, but justifiably believed that they afford little real help in resolving the problems involved in private international law:

> To carry out the principle of the independent sovereignty of the state to the utmost possible extent with regard to aliens, would lead to their complete exclusion from legal rights.[205]

AV Dicey, who was a prominent advocate of the principle of vested rights as a justification for the application of foreign law,[206] argued that:

> The application of foreign law is not a matter of caprice or option; it does not arise from the desire of the sovereign of England, or of any other sovereign, to show courtesy to other states. It flows from the impossibility of otherwise determining whole classes of cases without gross inconvenience and injustice to litigants, whether natives or foreigners.[207]

Nonetheless, Dicey's justification was itself open to criticism. In his 1959 article, RD Carlswell, in arguing that the doctrine of vested rights had 'outlived its usefulness', and following consideration of some of the, then, existing theories, succinctly argued that:

> the best reason for not applying local law to the exclusion of rights created by foreign law seems to be that of justice, the ultimate basis of all legal principles.[208]

With few exceptions,[209] the considerations involved in private international law do not raise any significant questions of sovereignty; nor are the state's interests served by taking a restrictive attitude towards the application of foreign law in civil proceedings; not least because it is now firmly recognised that respect for party autonomy should permit citizens and businesses to choose both a forum and law

[204] Collins (Lord Collins of Mapesbury) and Harris (eds) (n 50), para 1-006. See, for a similar analysis, C Ludwig von Bar, *Theorie und Praxis des internationalen Privatrechts*, 2nd edn (Hahn'sche Buchhandlung, 1889), 4.

[205] FC von Savigny, *A Treatise on the Conflict of Laws*, William Guthrie trans (T&T Clark, 1869), 26. It is thought that acceptance of the principle that foreign law should be applied in appropriate circumstances can be traced to medieval Italy. See K Schurig, 'Das Fundament trägt noch' in H-P Mansel (ed), *Internationales Privatrecht im 20. Jahrhundert* (Mohr Siebeck, 2014), 6.

[206] Carswell (n 192), 271.

[207] Dicey, *A Digest of the Law of England with reference to the Conflict of Laws* (n 114), 10–11. The same line of analysis first appeared in his 1890 article: AV Dicey, 'On Private International Law as a Branch of the Law of England' (1890) 6 *LQR* 1, 10.

[208] Carswell (n 192), 277.

[209] State immunity is a well-known exception. See, in relation to the UK, Beaumont and McEleavy (n 50), para 6.01ff and, in relation to Germany, Junker, *Internationales Zivilprozessrecht* (n 77), § 4. One area in which territoriality does undoubtedly play a role in private international law is in relation to enforcement. See HL Buxbaum, 'Territory, Territoriality, and the Resolution of Jurisdictional Conflict' (2009) 57 *The American Journal of Comparative Law* 631, 673.

to settle their disputes in accordance with their wishes.[210] Dismissing notions that sovereignty has any real relevance in the overall context of modern international civil litigation, Lord Sumption recently said, in the context of the international service of documents:

> Litigation between residents of different states is a routine incident of modern commercial life. A jurisdiction similar to that exercised by the English court is now exercised by the courts of many other countries.[211]

Although the concept of sovereignty has no significant role to play in private international law (at least in the choice of law context), and states should take a permissive attitude towards the application of foreign law,[212] it is recognised that there do remain circumstances where the state should refuse to apply foreign law – circumstances generally approached in terms of the concept of public policy (*ordre public*).[213] Indeed, there may be very cogent reasons to refuse to apply the law of a foreign state, such as where it is discriminatory.[214]

C. Existence of a Norm Compelling the Application of Domestic Law

The definition of law, eg domestic law or public international law,[215] is an intractable problem of jurisprudence.[216] In Great Britain, without in any way trivialising

[210] Mills, 'Rethinking Jurisdiction in International Law' (n 192), 235.

[211] *Abela v Baadarani* [2013] 1 WLR 2043, 2062, although note that some states see the international service of documents as being a matter potentially encroaching on their sovereignty. See the Swiss Federal Office of Justice, 'International Judicial Assistance in Civil Matters' (2003), www.rhf.admin.ch/dam/data/rhf/zivilrecht/wegleitungen/wegleitung-zivilsachen-e.pdf, 2: 'According to the Swiss view – as well as that of numerous other states – the service of judicial or extra-judicial documents as well as the obtaining of evidence for court proceedings constitute the exercise of public powers … Accordingly, these procedures cannot simply be undertaken from beyond the frontiers of the state concerned without authorisation.'

[212] It has been said that the Scottish courts 'approach foreign law in a spirit of toleration.' Beaumont and McEleavy (n 50), para 5.18.

[213] German law provides a statutory basis for the doctrine of public policy in EGBGB, Art 6. There is 'abundant authority that an English court will decline to recognise or apply what would otherwise be the appropriate foreign rule of law when to do so would be against English public policy' (*Vervaeke v Smith* [1983] 1 AC 145, 164). The EU regulations on private international law also contain ordre public rules, eg Rome I Regulation (n 129), Art 21. The existence of rules mandating the application of domestic law should also be noted, eg Rome I Regulation (n 129), Art 9. It is said that the doctrine of public policy has assumed far less prominence in England than in France and Germany on the basis, inter alia, that English law does not apply foreign law in many areas of family law. See Collins (Lord Collins of Mapesbury) and Harris (eds) (n 50), para 5-004. For a very concise summary of the effect of ordre public in German law, see Junker, *Internationales Privatrecht* (n 58), § 5 para 39, and for a more detailed, albeit outdated, account see Kropholler (n 52), 244ff.

[214] A prominent example is given by the German citizenship decree of 1941, which deprived all Jews living outside of Germany of their German citizenship. For a case where the issue was considered, see *Oppenheimer v Cattermole (Inspector of Taxes)* [1976] AC 249, 277–78.

[215] Debate is particularly heated as to whether public international law can be described as law. Two major contributions to the debate were made by Austin and Hart. See M Payandeh, 'The Concept of

the quality of other works, HLA Hart's *The Concept of Law*[217] has without doubt made a particularly substantial, albeit controversial, contribution to the debate,[218] and is said to have built upon[219] arguments previously put forward, inter alia, by John Austin.[220] Hart suggested, through his rule of recognition theory,[221] a mechanism for identifying legal rules, as opposed to those rules lacking the characteristic of law. Regardless of its flaws, Hart's analysis perhaps helps to distinguish foreign from domestic law,[222] even if only as a starting point.

The potential difficulties in identifying domestic law are made particularly obvious when considering a nascent legal system. The nascent legal system may have little developed jurisprudence and thus may have an absence of established rules for many of the legal problems faced by its courts. Theoretically, its judges have a largely free hand to solve its legal problems, although consistently exercising an approach guided by a free hand would mire the system in legal uncertainty, as many cases would be solved on the basis of giving justice in each individual case (*Einzelfallgerechtigkeit*), rather than placing appropriate emphasis on the development of a coherent body of rules. However, where the nascent legal system's judges are schooled in the academic study of law, eg canon or Roman law, the most likely approach is that they will draw upon functioning rules from such existing

International Law in the Jurisprudence of HLA Hart' (2010) 21 *European Journal of International Law* 967, 969: 'Austin defines a sovereign as habitually obeyed by the bulk of a society and not habitually obeying to another human superior. On the basis of this general command theory Austin does not regard international law as law. According to him international law does not stem from the command of a sovereign but is set by general opinion and enforced by moral sanctions only.' Later in his article, at 970, Payandeh argues that 'Hart is regarded as the legal philosopher who most effectively refuted Austin's denial of international law's legal validity.' Although exactly how Hart himself sees international law is not entirely clear. See Payandeh (ibid), 974ff.

[216] Glanville Williams argued that 'it is a verbal dispute, and nothing else' in GL Williams, 'International Law and the Controversy Concerning the Word "Law"' (1945) 22 *British Yearbook of International Law* 146.

[217] HLA Hart, *The Concept of Law*, 3rd edn (Oxford University Press, 2012).

[218] Payandeh (n 215), 967–68. Hart's text has given rise to copious academic contributions, much of which is critical. A small sample of the literature is M Payne, 'Hart's Concept of a Legal System' (1976) 18 *William and Mary Law Review* 287; M Gilbert, 'Social Rules: Some Problems for Hart's account, and an alternative Proposal' (1999) 18 *Law and Philosophy* 141; R Sartorius, 'The Concept of Law' (1966) 52 *Archiv für Rechts- und Sozialphilosophie* 161; LL Fuller, 'Positivism and Fidelity to Law – A Reply to Professor Hart' (1957) 71 *Harvard Law Review* 630. SM Brown, 'Review: The Concept of Law by HLA Hart' (1963) 72 *The Philosophical Review* 250, 252: 'But if what I have said here is correct, the concept of law in Hart's treatment is confused. He describes the concept in one way when he is talking about his problem, whereas his solution describes it in a different and incompatible way.' J Bell, 'Sources of Law' (2018) 77 *CLJ* 40, 51: 'Overall, is it helpful to consider that this is a single legal rule?'.

[219] See, in particular, the article by Fuller (n 218), which is perhaps as well-known as Hart's text itself.

[220] J Austin, *The Province of Jurisprudence Determined and The Uses of the Study of Jurisprudence: with an Introduction by HLA Hart* (Hackett Publishing Company, 1998). Hart concisely summarises Austin's command doctrine at page x of his introduction to the text. In particular, Austin is said to have focused on the delimitation between morality and religion on one hand, and law on the other.

[221] See, especially, Hart (n 217), 100ff.

[222] Some of the thoughts explored in this context build upon the article by AM Godfrey, 'Ratio Decidendi and Foreign Law in the History of Scots Law' in S Dauchy, WH Bryson and MC Mirow (eds), *Ratio decidendi: Guiding Principles of Judicial Decisions* (Duncker & Humblot, 2010), 81.

legal systems, even if there is no compulsion on them to do so, in addition to any established sources of domestic law. In allowing its judges to take a relatively flexible approach to different sources of law, the nascent legal system may have little interest in strict delimitations as to what its sources of law are:

> Tracing how courts regarded 'foreign' law therefore presupposes some recognition of a category of law which was identified as 'foreign'.[223]

Mark Godfrey argues that there is evidence of a flexible approach in the early Scottish legal system,[224] which appears to have drawn on different legal sources, eg canon law and Roman law, to solve cases and develop domestic rules.[225] This receptiveness to different sources was influenced by the fact that Scottish lawyers often undertook at least part of their legal education at continental European universities.[226] However, by the eighteenth century, at the latest, Scottish judges were clearly familiar with concepts inherent to sovereignty and territoriality such as jurisdiction,[227] and a distinct Scottish domestic law requiring application,[228]

[223] ibid, 82.

[224] There also appears to have been considerable flexibility in the application of local laws, as opposed to the *ius commune*, in the various states of medieval continental Europe. Gebauer argues that neither the *ius commune* nor the local laws of the various medieval states can properly be described as law in terms of its modern conception. Rather, medieval lawyers were required to orientate themselves in what was essentially a multilayered system. See M Gebauer, *Grundfragen der Europäisierung des Privatrechts: Eine Untersuchung nationaler Ansätze unter Berücksichtigung des italienischen und des deutschen Rechts* (Universitätsverlag C Winter, 1998), 32–37. There is remarkable similarity between the development of the legal systems of medieval continental Europe and the Scottish legal system, a characteristic that separates the Scottish and English legal systems. See JW Cairns, 'Ius Civile in Scotland, ca. 1600' (2004) 2 *Roman Legal Tradition* 136, who notes, at 138, that Scotland, unlike England, had 'no law existing from time immemorial evidenced by authoritative statements in the reports of the courts.' Writing about the sixteenth-century Scottish legal system, Godfrey (n 222), with reference to Cairns, argues at 94: 'We are in the world of interaction between the categories of *ius commune* and *ius proprium* as understood by medieval jurists, and in which the *ius commune* had a powerful supplementary role alongside the strict interpretation of local laws.' See, for discussion of the various sources of late sixteenth-century Scots law and their respective authority, including the *ius commune* and canon law, Cairns, 'Ius Civile in Scotland, ca. 1600' (n 224), 150ff, which draws on Thomas Craig's *Jus feudale*, said by Cairns to have been written about 1600.

[225] Godfrey (n 222), 82. The extent of the impact of both sources on sixteenth- and seventeenth-century Scots law is discussed in detail in Cairns, 'Ius Civile in Scotland, ca. 1600' (n 224).

[226] AD Gibb, 'International Private Law in Scotland in the Sixteenth and Seventeenth Centuries' (1927) 39 *Juridical Review* 369, 374.

[227] *Scott v Carmichael* [1775] Hailes 663: 'No judge has power beyond his territory; but every judge has power over persons and things within his territory.'

[228] In relation to canon law, see *Maxwell v Gordon* [1775] Hailes 624, 626: 'The canon law is not the law of Scotland; but the law of Scotland contains much of the canon law'; and, in relation to Roman law, see *Campbell v Campbell* [1775] Hailes 641, 642: 'the relief given is founded on the *actio negotiorum gestorum* by the Roman law. Our law has gone further, and has given the same action, not against the debtor only, but also against the co-cautioners' or *Scott v Carmichael* [1775] Hailes 663, 664: 'Our notions of foreigners are taken from the Roman law; but I should be sorry to think that we should follow the Roman law in all its niceties.' See, more generally, *Hinton v Donaldson and Others* [1773] Hailes 535, 540: 'The sources of our common law are: *First*, Usages and established consuetude; *Second*, Feudal law; *Third*, Civil law, in so far as received by us; *Fourth*, every apparent principle of justice which has been received by the other civilized nations of Europe.'

although there was clearly some willingness following the 1707 Union to draw on English sources of law to develop Scots law.[229] If Hart's analysis was applied to this point in time, it would clearly have been possible to identify a rule of recognition relating to a distinct body of Scots law,[230] even if it is unhelpful to think in terms of a single rule of recognition.[231]

It has already been made clear that the exclusive application of domestic law to cases involving foreigners can result in injustice. One tactic that the early Scottish legal system could have employed to avoid injustice in cases involving foreigners is to have introduced or adopted a separate legal code for dealing with them. Such an approach appears to have been taken in England by means of the application of a Law Merchant (*Lex mercatoria*) to cases of international commerce,[232] and there is evidence of the Court of Session's sole recourse to the *ius commune* in some early cases where foreigners were involved.[233] Indeed, it is suggested by Dewar Gibb that there were some efforts in Scotland to develop a law of nature to address problems raised by the presence of foreigners,[234] although Dewar Gibb himself was dismissive of the value of this approach.[235] The difficulty with such an approach

[229] There was a marked tendency of the Scottish courts to adopt English law in certain areas following the 1707 Union, for example, in admiralty and insurance matters. See ADM Forte, 'Opinions by "Eminent English Counsel": Their Use in Insurance Cases before the Court of Session in the Late Eighteenth and Early Nineteenth Centuries' (1995) *Juridical Review* 345, which is discussed in Godfrey (n 222), 103–04, and mentioned in JW Cairns, 'Historical Introduction' in K Reid and R Zimmermann (eds), *A History of Private Law in Scotland: Introduction and Property* (Oxford University Press, 2000), 161.

[230] It became possible to speak in these terms as Scottish legal literature developed in the seventeenth century. See Cairns, 'Ius Civile in Scotland, ca. 1600' (n 224), 170. The matter is considered in more detail later.

[231] See the analysis of Professor John Bell (n 218), at 50ff, who refers inter alia to the Italian scholar Alessandro Pizzorusso.

[232] See C von Bar and P Mankowski, *Internationales Privatrecht: Band I – Allgemeine Lehren*, 2nd edn (CH Beck, 2003), § 2 para 7, in which strong parallels are drawn between the English and Roman approaches to cases involving a foreign element. As regards the Roman approach, which appears to have favoured the application of a *ius gentium* between different peoples, see Von Bar and Mankowski (n 232), § 2 para 5.

[233] *A Frenchman v An Englishman* [1550] Mor 7323, which is cited in Gibb (n 226), 380. The *ius commune* was an important source of Scots law at that time. See JW Cairns, 'Attitudes to Codification and the Scottish Science of Legislation, 1600–1830' (2007) 22 *Tulane European and Civil Law Forum* 1, 5. The particular feature of the 1550 case is that the Court of Session held, first, that it is competent in actions between strangers and, second, that it 'sould decern and judge thairanent conform to the commoun law, and not efter the municipal law of this realme.' Cairns argues, at 6, that at that time 'municipal law' did not include practicks, ie decided cases, but did include 'statutes (and presumably customs).'

[234] Gibb (n 226), 382. The term *ius gentium* may be a more apt description and, indeed, Gibb later refers to a 'standard furnished by some outside system, whether the Law of Rome or the Law of Nations.' It appears true that there was a developed, sustained interest in the *ius naturale* and *ius gentium*, alongside the *ius commune*, in the late seventeenth century. See Cairns, 'Attitudes to Codification and the Scottish Science of Legislation, 1600–1830' (n 233), 32–33. The extent to which this line of thought existed solely in academic thinking is questionable.

[235] Gibb (n 226), 382: 'The artificiality of such a proceeding is flagrant. An international code of law for legal intercourse with foreigners is as likely to succeed as an international language such as Esperanto for communicating with them.'

is that it creates parallel legal systems within one jurisdiction, stoking confusion, as well as running the risk that the legal rules applicable only to foreigners are not of particular benefit to them, ie the rules are no more closely connected to their circumstances than the *lex fori*.

The possible application of foreign law through the conduit of choice of law rules therefore provides the court with a mechanism to do justice in the circumstances of a case where there is a material foreign element by facilitating the application of the law that is best suited to the circumstances of the case. However, the first step is recognition by the court that the starting point is that it is bound to apply domestic law, even if there can be some doubt as to exactly what that is,[236] particularly in the context of a legal system with potentially contradictory precedents,[237] and notwithstanding the fact that foreign decisions may well provide justification for decisions in the comparative context.[238] Nonetheless, only where domestic substantive law can be identified, with its compulsive effect clear, does the role of private international law become relevant. If the court had a free hand, it would not need a domestic choice of law rule to facilitate the application of a foreign law; it would simply apply foreign law where it felt it was just to do so.[239] Thus, fundamental requirements for the application of foreign law through the conduit of domestic choice of law rules are: (1) a sufficiently developed body of domestic law; (2) the ability of the court to delineate domestic, as opposed to any other law; (3) a compulsion on the court to apply domestic law; (4) a domestic choice of law rule through which foreign law can be applied; and (5) circumstances justifying its application in respect of a foreign law.

[236] Bell correctly notes that there is no 'list' of sources of law in the UK. Bell (n 218), 41. Bell points out (at 47) that while most legal systems lack such specificity, the Italian civil code begins with several articles addressing sources of law. Bell correctly talks (at 49) of a 'basket of sources which apply in appropriate ways in different circumstances.'

[237] For discussion see, for example, T Prime and G Scanlan, 'Stare decisis and the Court of Appeal; judicial confusion and judicial reform?' (2004) 23 *CJQ* 212. The difficulties in identifying, for example, the English common law at any one point in time, with its numerous potentially contradictory precedents, seem obvious, a problem that becomes particularly acute when a foreign legal system is seeking to draw upon it. See H Pope, 'The English Common Law in the United States' (1910) 24 *Harvard Law Review* 6, 13. In the US, the authoritative value of the decisions of various State and federal courts is subject to controversy. Notably, one federal circuit does not bind the other, nor do decisions of federal courts necessarily bind state courts. JW Mead, 'Stare Decisis in the Inferior Courts of the United States' (2012) 12 *Nevada Law Journal* 787, 794ff.

[238] See the discussion by Leslie Green contained in 'Notes' in Hart (n 217), 294, especially with regards foreign and other sources: 'They are therefore more than merely historical or casual influences since such writings are recognized as "good reasons" for decisions.'

[239] It is interesting to note the debate surrounding the role of choice of law rules in international arbitration. This is an environment where one might think that the arbitral tribunal has a free hand, but matters are not as simple as that. See B Wortmann, 'Choice of Law by Arbitrators: The Applicable Conflict of Laws System' (1998) 14 *Arbitration International* 97.

D. A Choice of Law Rule

Choice of law rules provide the conduit through which foreign law can be applied in cases with a (material) foreign connection.[240] What unifies choice of law rules[241] is that in each case there must be a domestic rule leading either to the application of a substantive rule – be that a rule of the *lex fori* or the law of a foreign state – or, in certain circumstances, to the application of a further foreign choice of law rule (*renvoi*).[242] Where the domestic rule in question provides per se the solution to the case then it is not a choice of law rule but a substantive rule of law.[243] As has been stated by the German Federal Court of Justice:

> The relevant choice of law rule, determined on the basis of characterisation, of German private international law, regulates the extent and limit of the reference to the relevant foreign legal system. [Translation by author][244]

When faced with a factual matrix involving a (material) foreign element, the domestic court could be tasked, by means of a loosely worded choice of law rule,

[240] The role of choice of law rules in private international law is clear and well-summarised in many places. See, for example, K Otte, 'Betrachtungen zur Interessenlehre' in H-P Mansel (ed), *Internationales Privatrecht im 20. Jahrhundert* (Mohr Siebeck, 2014), 27 and Kropholler (n 52), 103ff. The traditional conception of (the body of) choice of law rules has been criticised as being one dimensional, especially when considered in the context of the private international law and fundamental freedoms of the European Union, eg the freedom to move between Member States and have one's same sex-marriage recognised. For a recent detailed and illuminating analysis of the subject, considering both the historical and modern context, which argues that it is necessary to approach choice of law in terms of three pillars: (1) choice of law rules; (2) sovereignty; and (3) vested rights, see F Berner, *Kollisionsrecht im Spannungsfeld von Kollisionsnormen, Hoheitsinteressen und wohlerworbenen Rechten* (Mohr Siebeck, 2017).

[241] Much academic discussion has been dedicated to the principles and interests underlying choice of law rules. A concise analysis, which both drew on and developed the discussion, was an article published in 2014 by Klaus Schurig. Schurig summarises and separates Savigny's analysis from modern private international law, while drawing on the substantial contributions of, inter alia, Franz Kahn and Gerhard Kegel. See Schurig, 'Das Fundament trägt noch' (n 205). See also K Schurig, *Kollisionsnorm und Sachrecht* (Duncker & Humblot, 1981), in particular 184ff.

[242] The problem of *renvoi* is not considered in this work but it is a well-recognised problem in private international law. It addresses the consequences of a reference to a foreign choice of law rule, which itself points to a different legal system. The impact of *renvoi* has been minimised in the European private international law instruments. See Article 20 of the Rome I Regulation (n 129). An excellent summary of the problem is provided in Junker, *Internationales Privatrecht* (n 58), § 8 para 2ff. For a discussion of how the problem entered 'the consciousness of the English judiciary', see Crawford and Carruthers (n 50), para 5-02ff.

[243] In German, such a rule is known as a *Sachnorm*, as opposed to a *Kollisionsnorm* (choice of law rule). See Schurig, *Kollisionsnorm und Sachrecht* (n 241), 58: 'Die Sachnorm dagegen entscheidet in der Sache selbst; sie beurteilt die widerstreitenden materiellen Interessen unmittelbar und abschließend.' ('The substantive rule of law, on the other hand, determines the matter itself; it assesses the conflicting material interests directly and conclusively.') [Translation by author].

[244] *Decision of the Federal Court of Justice from 21 September 1995* (BGH, VII. Zivilsenat) VII ZR 248/94, NJW 1996, 54, 55: 'Die aufgrund der Qualifikation ermittelte maßgebliche Kollisionsnorm des deutschen internationalen Privatrechts regelt den Umfang und die Grenzen der Verweisung auf die maßgebliche fremde Rechtsordnung.'

with choosing whichever law it felt was most appropriate in the circumstances. However, to provide greater legal certainty, it is much better to provide carefully drafted, well-defined choice of law rules allowing for the identification in advance of the substantive law that ought to apply to a set of facts.[245] Indeed, the absence of well-defined applicable law rules would be incompatible with the rules-based structures on which the relevant jurisdictions are based. Such a line of argumentation is advanced by the German scholar Kropholler, who argues:

> Legal certainty requires, above all, unambiguous, clear rules as well as foreseeable, predictable decisions. [Translation by author][246]

Choice of law rules can vary greatly in their scope and complexity. However, two principles which most often appear to underpin them in the relevant jurisdictions are, first, the principle of party autonomy,[247] and, second, the principle of the closest connection.[248] The EU regulations on private international law provide some very good examples as to how various important considerations can be woven into a workable instrument. Thus, under Article 3 of the Rome I Regulation, the contract shall be governed by the law chosen by the parties.[249] Where such a choice has not been made, Article 4 of the Rome I Regulation provides a number of rules, eg that:

> A contract for the sale of goods shall be governed by the law of the country where the seller has his habitual residence.[250]

[245] It cannot be denied that rigid choice of law rules can lead to harsh results in individual cases. The judgments of the various judges in *Boys v Chaplin* [1968] 2 QB 1 are instructive as to the issues involved.

[246] Kropholler (n 52), 30: 'Die Rechtssicherheit verlangt vor allem eindeutige, klare Regeln sowie voraussehbare, berechenbare Entscheidungen.'

[247] See, for the importance of party autonomy in private law generally from a German standpoint, Köhler (n 39), § 5 para 1 and, in a private international law context, Symeonides, *Choice of Law* (n 71), 363: 'Today, party autonomy enjoys the status of a self-evident proposition, a truism.' See A Mills, *Party Autonomy in Private International Law* (Cambridge University Press, 2018), 313: 'Party autonomy has become widely (but not universally) accepted in choice of law in contract, including under the common law, under EU regulation, in the US, and under international codifications on choice of law.' The role of party autonomy is particularly pronounced in international contract law. See Rühl (n 170), 562. The extent of the importance that parties actually place on choice of law clauses, which often form boilerplate clauses in contracts, has been questioned. See JF Coyle, 'The Canons of Construction for Choice-of-Law Clauses' (2017) 92 *Washington Law Review* 631, 641.

[248] An emphasis on the closest connection (*engste Verbindung*) has particularly strong roots in German law. See Kropholler (n 52), 25ff. Prior to the adoption of the Rome Convention, British law favoured the proper law approach. *Bonythen v Commonwealth of Australia* [1951] AC 201, 219: 'the substance of the obligation must be determined by the proper law of the contract, ie the system of law by reference to which the contract was made or that with which the transaction has its closest and most real connexion.' See McParland (n 148), para 10.10ff.

[249] See also Rome I Regulation (n 129), Recital (11): 'The parties' freedom to choose the applicable law should be one of the cornerstones of the system of conflict-of-law rules in matters of contractual obligations.'

[250] Rome I Regulation (n 129), Art 4(1)(a). Recital (19) implies that these presumptions have been defined on the basis of ascertaining the centre of gravity in the respective contractual relationship. A history of how Rome I Regulation, Art 4, came to be drafted can be found in McParland (n 148), para 10.04ff.

However, the application of these rules remains subject to the discretion of the court in the form of the general exception provided in Article 4(3) of the Rome I Regulation. Thus, where there is a manifestly more closely connected law than the one indicated by the relevant rule, the court retains discretion to apply that law.

E. A Mechanism to Facilitate the Investigation and Determination of Foreign Law

Once the court has undertaken the often difficult and complicated process of choosing which law it should apply to govern the dispute by means of the relevant choice of law rule, the court has the task of investigating and determining the applicable foreign law.

There are numerous ways in which a court could establish the relevant foreign law on an issue. The court could read legislation, cases, and academic materials produced in relation to the relevant legal system. The court could invite the parties to make submissions based solely on such material. The court could delegate responsibility for investigating the content of the applicable foreign law to an external party, such as an institution specialising in comparative law.[251] The court could invite (or allow the parties to invite) expert witnesses to report on and testify about the content of the applicable foreign law.

The purpose of the mechanism facilitating the investigation is to afford the judge the knowledge required to be able to draw conclusions on the relevant foreign law so that he can successfully apply it to the circumstances of the case. However, the difficulties involved in investigating and determining the content of foreign law can be substantial. As has astutely been said:

> Experience shows that often it is less difficult to choose the appropriate law than to discover its content.[252]

In certain cases, it will be impossible to establish the foreign law on a particular matter, for example, because the applicable foreign law offers no clear rule.[253] Possible consequences that could follow from a failure to prove, or attempt to prove, the applicable foreign law are that the judge could dismiss the case[254] or apply the *lex fori*,[255] both outcomes leading to a result that is not in conformity with the relevant choice of law rule and is potentially unjust.

[251] An example of such an institution is the Max Planck Institute for Comparative and International Private Law based in Hamburg. For further information on the possibility of obtaining an expert opinion from the institute, see Max Planck Institute for Comparative and International Private Law, 'Legal Advice', www.mpipriv.de/1074018/rechtsauskuenfte-und-gutachten.

[252] M Furmston, 'Proof of Foreign Law' (1959) 22 *Modern Law Review* 317.

[253] See, for example, *Decision of the Federal Court of Justice from 24 November 1960* (BGH, II. Zivilsenat) II ZR 9/60, NJW 1961, 410.

[254] *Global Multimedia International Limited v ARA Media Services* [2006] EWHC 3612 (Ch), [38], though, as will be discussed in due course, the authoritative value of this case has been doubted.

[255] *Sharp v Ministry of Defence* [2007] EWHC 224 (QB), [11].

What is clear is that the mechanism for the investigation and determination of the relevant foreign law is fundamental to the choice of law process. Thus, regardless of the technical legal quality of the relevant choice of law rule, this will be of no benefit if the applicable law cannot be successfully determined. Failure to provide an effective mechanism to allow investigation and determination of the content of the applicable foreign law means that the choice of law rule becomes, at best, merely academic or, at worse, a nuisance and hindrance to the effective delivery of justice.

The law does not exist in a vacuum and private international law is no exception. Litigation is often expensive, long-running, and can have a 'ruinous' impact on parties, especially private individuals.[256] Where a matter of private international law is involved in a case, the cost and time required often increases significantly, especially where it is necessary to rely on expert evidence to prove the content of foreign law.[257] As will be explored in more detail, if applied to their full extent, certain choice of law rules place onerous obligations on courts.[258] Moreover, the growing phenomenon, in England especially,[259] of unrepresented parties places arduous burdens on courts and the judiciary, which, though not subject

[256] See the well-known comments of Sir James Munby in respect of ancillary relief proceedings in which he went as far as to refer to *Jarndyce v Jarndyce*, a fictional case from Charles Dickens' *Bleak House*: *KSO v MJO* [2008] EWHC 3031 (Fam), [76]–[81].

[257] A prominent English example of the difficulties that can be involved in proving foreign law is provided by *Macmillan Inc v Bishopsgate Investment Trust Plc (No 3)* [1995] 1 WLR 978, 1013: 'Opinions on foreign law were obtained from 12 witnesses, almost all of whom were cross-examined at length. Documents in the case filled more than 120 lever arch files. The experts' reports on foreign law with accompanying authorities filled 24 files. The parties' opening and closing submissions with accompanying authorities filled a further 40 files.' A prominent German example of the difficulties involved in proving foreign law is provided by the *Decision of the Federal Court of Justice from 21 January 1991* (BGH, II. Zivilsenat) II ZR 49/90, NJW-RR 1991, 1211, in which, according to Jürgen Samtleben, eight expert witness reports were obtained during the course of the case, with no satisfactory outcome. J Samtleben, 'Der unfähige Gutachter und die ausländische Rechtspraxis' (1992) *Neue Juristische Wochenschrift* 3057, 3062: 'Die Sache ist inzwischen vor dem OLG Bremen verglichen worden. Den Parteien war es offenbar wichtiger, endlich an den Versteigerungserlös zu kommen, als die vom II. Senat geforderte Einholung eines neunten Gutachtens zum venezolanischen Recht abzuwarten.' ('The case has meanwhile been settled before the Bremen Court of Appeal. It was clearly more important to the parties to finally get access to the proceeds of the auction than to wait for the ninth expert opinion on Venezuelan law, which had been requested by the second senate.') [Translation by author].

[258] An example is provided by the consumer provisions in the Rome I Regulation (n 129), Art 6, which theoretically require an onerous exercise in comparative law.

[259] See Wong S and R Cain, 'The impact of cuts in legal aid funding of private family law cases' (2019) 41 *Journal of Social Welfare and Family Law* 3, though the writers' reference to the UK should not be thought to include Scotland, the legal aid provision of which was not affected by the Legal Aid, Sentencing and Punishment of Offenders Act 2012; L Trinder and others, 'Litigants in person in private family law cases' (Ministry of Justice, 2014), assets.publishing.service.gov.uk/government/uploads/system/uploads/attachment_data/file/380479/litigants-in-person-in-private-family-law-cases.pdf, and K Williams, 'Litigants in person: a literature review' (Ministry of Justice, 2011), assets.publishing.service.gov.uk/government/uploads/system/uploads/attachment_data/file/217374/litigants-in-person-literature-review.pdf. The issues surrounding unrepresented parties in Scotland have been the subject of less research (and the problem seems less critical than in England in view of the fact that Scottish legal aid provision remains comparatively generous) but a recently published

to independent research specifically, has potential to cause significant difficulties where foreign law is at issue.[260]

The problems in Great Britain in investigating and determining foreign law are not confined to cases where parties are unrepresented.[261] In a recent case which came before the English Court of Appeal[262] a marriage had been dissolved by order of the Slovenian court,[263] and the wife had subsequently raised financial remedy proceedings in England under Part III of the Matrimonial and Family Proceedings Act 1984.[264] The Slovenian judgment appears to have included various orders, the force of which was subject to dispute. The ex-husband pleaded at first instance that a 'decision' as regards maintenance had been made in Slovenia because his ex-wife had withdrawn her claim for maintenance prior to the court giving judgment.[265] The husband's defence was rejected at first instance.[266] He appealed.[267] At issue was whether the judgment of the Slovenian authority could be classed as a 'decision' in terms of the EU Maintenance Regulation:[268]

> Unusually for proceedings which involve the construction of the terms of foreign court orders, neither party has presented any expert evidence as to the law of Slovenia and, on this particular point, the English court is left to try to understand the effect of the words in various court documents for itself.[269]

In *Villiers* (2016), an English High Court judge was faced, inter alia, with the question as to whether maintenance proceedings were ongoing in Scotland, ie, was the

PhD thesis sheds light on the issue, see H Turner, 'The party litigant in the Scottish civil courts' (2018) *University of Glasgow*, https://theses.gla.ac.uk/30665/. In many proceedings in Germany, parties' representation by a lawyer is mandatory, known as *Anwaltszwang*. See R Zuck, 'Postulationsfähigkeit und Anwaltszwang: Die Rolle des Anwalts in einer sich wandelnden Welt' (1993) *Juristenzeitung* 500, 504ff. Moreover, as will be discussed in more detail, German judges have significantly more control over cases and are also more numerous, which significantly reduces the difficulties involved in dealing with unrepresented parties.

[260] An example involving two unrepresented parties is provided by *Padero-Mernagh v Mernagh* [2020] EWFC 27, which involved a question of status. At [18], the judge commented: 'Regrettably I did not have expert evidence on Philippine Family Law which might have confirmed both the substantive law but perhaps more importantly the practice and application of that law to marriages in the Philippines.' It is said, at [5], that 'at some stage extracts from the Philippine civil code and the Philippine family code were filed with the court', on which the judge had to rely to make his conclusions. The case is considered in more detail in due course in Chapter three at section II.A.(ii)(b), fn 180.

[261] This work does not necessarily agree with Professor Fentiman's view that 'courts in contested cases seldom want for evidence of foreign law.' See R Fentiman, 'Foreign Law in National Courts: A Common Law Perspective' in M Andenas and D Fairgrieve (eds), *Courts and Comparative Law* (Oxford University Press, 2015), 79.

[262] *R v R* [2015] EWCA Civ 1138.

[263] *R v R* [2015] EWCA Civ 1138, [3].

[264] *R v R* [2015] EWCA Civ 1138, [4].

[265] *R v R* [2015] EWCA Civ 1138, [33].

[266] *R v R* [2015] EWCA Civ 1138, [27].

[267] *R v R* [2015] EWCA Civ 1138, [29].

[268] *R v R* [2015] EWCA Civ 1138, [29]. See the Council Regulation (EC) No 4/2009 of 18 December 2008 on jurisdiction, applicable law, recognition and enforcement of decisions and cooperation in matters relating to maintenance obligations [2009] OJ L 7/1 (EU Maintenance Regulation), Art 2(1).

[269] *R v R* [2015] EWCA Civ 1138, [46].

Scottish court seised of the issue of maintenance?[270] The wife was represented but the husband was not. The wife initially relied on a letter from her Scottish solicitor as expert evidence,[271] although, as observed by the court, such a witness could not be said to be sufficiently independent.[272] The unrepresented husband relied on an article placed on the website of a Scottish firm of solicitors.[273] For various reasons, the judge was not prepared to allow the husband a further opportunity to obtain expert evidence,[274] having previously given him ample opportunity;[275] nor was the judge, for reasons that will be explored in due course, permitted to carry out independent research. Ultimately, the judge felt sufficiently informed to determine the matter without further evidence.[276] There are many other recent cases where the issues involved in the investigation and determination of foreign law have caused difficulties for British judges.[277]

The practical difficulties involved in dealing with foreign law are not confined to Great Britain. There is also evidence in Germany of significant difficulties for courts required to investigate and determine foreign law. A recent study conducted by the University of Konstanz is thought-provoking.[278] The focus of the study was

[270] *Re V* [2016] EWHC 668 (Fam), [30]. The UK Government made the decision to apply the EU Maintenance Regulation (n 268) to internal UK cases (eg involving only Scotland and England) in terms of the Civil Jurisdiction and Judgments (Maintenance) Regulations 2011. This approach was critically discussed by Lord Wilson in *Villiers v Villiers* [2020] UKSC 30, [119]–[120], and no longer applies post-Brexit. For discussion of the current position, and, in particular, the odd failure, post-Brexit, to include maintenance creditor jurisdiction in sch 4 of the Civil Jurisdiction and Judgments Act 1982 (intra-UK rules), despite its inclusion in sch 8 of the 1982 Act (Scotland only), see Beaumont, 'Some reflections on the way ahead for UK private international law after Brexit' (n 156), 11f.

[271] *Re V* [2016] EWHC 668 (Fam), [66].

[272] *Re V* [2016] EWHC 668 (Fam), [71].

[273] *Re V* [2016] EWHC 668 (Fam), [66].

[274] *Re V* [2016] EWHC 668 (Fam), [84].

[275] *Re V* [2016] EWHC 668 (Fam), [78]. The unrepresented husband claimed that he did not have funds to instruct an expert opinion.

[276] *Re V* [2016] EWHC 668 (Fam), [87]. The jurisdiction issues involved in the case were appealed to the UK Supreme Court, but neither its decision (*Villiers v Villiers* [2020] UKSC 30) nor the decision of the Court of Appeal (*Villiers v Villiers* [2018] EWCA Civ 1120) questioned the first instance judge's conclusion as regards Scots law.

[277] Interim applications involving foreign law appear to have caused difficulties recently in the English courts in so far that parties have, on a number of occasions, adduced too much evidence without the court's permission. See *Deutsche Bank AG v Comune di Savona* [2018] EWCA Civ 1740, [15]: 'I must confess to considerable unease about the proliferation of expert evidence of foreign law on jurisdiction applications which are supposed not to be excessively complicated and to be capable of determination in hours rather than days.' See also *BNP Paribas SA v Trattamento Rifiuti Metropolitani SPA* [2018] EWHC 1670 (Comm), [50], and the comments of Mr Justice Andrew Baker in *BB Energy (Gulf) DMCC v Al Amoudi* [2018] EWHC 2595 (Comm), [48]–[50]. These were echoed in *Gulf International Bank BSC v Aldwood* [2019] EWHC 1666 (QB), [8], where the court described 'the highly unsatisfactory state of affairs' in relation to expert evidence in a jurisdiction dispute as being 'strikingly similar' to that in *BB Energy (Gulf) DMCC* (2018). An example of the general difficulties involved in dealing with expert evidence on foreign law is provided by *Exportadora de Sal SA de CV v Corretaje Maritimo Sud-Americano Inc* [2018] EWHC 224 (Comm), [29], which is discussed in detail in Chapter three at section II.B.(vii). A recent Scottish example of some of the difficulties involved in leading evidence on foreign law is provided by *Ted Jacob Engineering Group Inc v Morrison and Thompson* [2018] CSOH 51.

[278] M Stürner and F Krauß, *Ausländisches Recht in deutschen Zivilverfahren: Eine rechtstatsächliche Untersuchung* (Nomos, 2018).

online questionnaires and interviews with members of the judiciary in Baden-Württemberg,[279] one of Germany's largest federal States. The survey exposes failings in the knowledge and support of the judiciary when it comes to the investigation of the content of foreign law,[280] with difficulties cited, inter alia, in relation to language,[281] understanding of the structure of foreign laws,[282] and obtaining access to foreign case law.[283] The study conveys the impression that German first instance judges are 'just getting on with it', seldom choosing to instruct an expert other than as a last resort.[284] But it is questionable how effectively one can independently research the content of a foreign legal system from a computer in anything other than the most straightforward of cases, especially considering that professional electronic legal databases (eg Westlaw) require paid subscriptions. Although the survey area was limited to Baden-Württemberg, there is no reason to think that such difficulties are not widespread.[285]

[279] ibid, para 76.
[280] See, in particular, ibid, paras 288–305, 400–427.
[281] ibid, para 215.
[282] ibid, para 233.
[283] ibid, para 213.
[284] ibid, para 291. There is further reference in the German literature to this being viewed as the option of last resort. See Rühl (n 170), 570. On the other hand, it is suggested elsewhere that the instruction of an expert is the usual manner of proceeding in the German courts. G Wagner, 'Fakultatives Kollisionsrecht und prozessuale Parteiautonomie' (1999) *Zeitschrift für Europäisches Privatrecht* 6, 7. Similarly, Junker suggests that, in practice, an expert opinion is usually ordered by the trial court. Junker, *Internationales Privatrecht* (n 58), § 11 para 8.
[285] More generally, it has been suggested in the German academic literature that, especially in lower instance courts, the relevance of foreign law is often either not considered or intentionally ignored. See R Geimer, *Internationales Zivilprozessrecht*, 8th edn (Otto Schmidt, 2020), para 2628, and Von Bar and Mankowski (n 232), § 5 para 66.

2

Historical

I. Great Britain

To provide some context, it is briefly necessary to consider the historical development of private international law as a field of law in both Scotland and England. For significant periods prior to the Union of Scotland and England in 1707, the two countries endured a troubled relationship:

> The two countries were kept asunder by the most bitter hatred and enmity, stronger possibly on the side of Scotland because of the wanton aggressiveness of English kings from Edward Plantagenet onwards. And so, though strong in earlier times, English influence during our period was at a discount.[1]

Thus, prior to the 1707 Union, the development of the English and Scottish legal systems essentially took place separately,[2] with Scotland developing stronger connections with continental Europe.[3] These connections appear to have influenced the early development of Scottish private international law,[4] driven inter alia by the practice of Scottish lawyers studying in continental Europe, including in France and Holland.[5] Some evidence of their continental education can be seen,

[1] AD Gibb, 'International Private Law in Scotland in the Sixteenth and Seventeenth Centuries' (1927) 39 *Juridical Review* 369, 370; see also A Donaldson, 'Some Conflict Rules of Scots Law' (1953) 39 *Transactions Year* 145, 146.

[2] This meant that, by the seventeenth century, Scotland and England had two 'quite different legal systems.' JW Cairns, 'Attitudes to Codification and the Scottish Science of Legislation, 1600–1830' (2007) 22 *Tulane European and Civil Law Forum* 1, 8. However, there is evidence that English law (or Anglo-Norman law, as it was in the late twelfth century), did impact on the development of the early Scottish legal system, ie prior to the early modern period. See AM Godfrey, 'Ratio Decidendi and Foreign Law in the History of Scots Law' in S Dauchy, WH Bryson and MC Mirow (eds), *Ratio decidendi: Guiding Principles of Judicial Decisions* (Duncker & Humblot, 2010), 100–101. Thereafter, from the fourteenth century, Scots law developed independently of English law. Significant English influence then followed the 1707 Union. Godfrey, ibid, 102ff.

[3] Gibb (n 1), 373; Donaldson (n 1), 146.

[4] Scottish cases considered in this chapter include some originating from the early seventeenth century. The history of private international law in Scotland is considered in detail in PR Beaumont and PE McEleavy, *Anton's Private International Law*, 3rd edn (W Green, 2011), para 1.26ff, and EB Crawford and JM Carruthers, *International Private Law: A Scots Perspective*, 4th edn (W Green, 2015), para 2-03.

[5] Gibb (n 1), 374; AE Anton, 'The Introduction into English Practice of Continental Theories on the Conflict of Laws' (1956) 5 *ICLQ* 534, 536. Anton argues that 'in the sixteenth and seventeenth centuries the universities of the Netherlands were especially favoured.' Prior to this, it was the universities of

for example, in early-eighteenth-century references in Scottish cases to the teachings of Ulrich Huber.[6]

Nonetheless, one should not exaggerate the state of development of Scottish private international law at the turn of the eighteenth century, which can only fairly be described as having been rudimentary.[7] What appears to have most separated Scotland and England at this point in time, in terms of the field of private international law, was the bare awareness in Scotland of the issues involved in the field, and the Scottish courts' willingness to apply foreign law in cases heard before them.[8] Kames argued that an important cause of this was that jurisdiction for cases involving foreigners had been reserved to the Scottish Court of Session by a law of the Scottish Parliament from 1487, together with the fact that the Scottish court operated outwith the constraints of the English common law:

> Lucky it is for Scotland, that chance, perhaps more than good policy, hath appropriated foreign matters to the court of session, where they can be decided on rational principles, without being absurdly fettered as in England by common law.[9]

Perhaps the state of development of private international law in England at the beginning of the eighteenth century was best summarised by Professor Frederic Harrison in 1919, then Professor of the English Inns of Court:

> What during all this time had been the position of England with regard to this science? It had been absolutely null … (D)own to the middle of the eighteenth century in England I cannot find a single opinion or decision which seemed to show the consciousness on the part of English lawyers that there was any branch of law such as that we are

France. See Cairns, 'Attitudes to Codification and the Scottish Science of Legislation, 1600–1830' (n 2), 5. It appears that the practice of Scottish advocates studying at universities in Holland continued as late as the middle of the eighteenth century, with Scottish advocates, until 1750, admitted solely on the basis of examinations in Latin on Roman law, see Cairns (n 2), 30.

[6] See, for example, *Cockburn* [1709] Mor 2877, 2878; *Watson v M'Kenzie* [1711] Mor 3455, 3456; *Craig v Craig* [1712] Mor 15494, at 15495 and 15497; *Steedman v Coupar* [1743] Mor 7337, 7339. Anton suggests in Anton (n 5), 536, that Huber was first cited in Scotland in 1713 but it appears to have been a little earlier than this. It has been argued that the first English case in which Huber was discussed was *Robinson v Bland* (1760) 1 W Bl 234; 96 ER 129. See DJ Llewelyn Davies, 'The Influence of Huber's De Conflictu Legum on English Private International Law' (1937) 18 *British Yearbook of International Law* 49, 54.

[7] See, for some principles which developed, Donaldson (n 1), 147; Gibb argued that Scottish private international law could not be expected to be found, 'in the sixteenth and seventeenth centuries, otherwise than in a very rudimentary condition.' Gibb (n 1), 369. In terms of Scots law generally, Cairns argues that at the beginning of the seventeenth century, Scots law 'was in an uncertain, confused and disorganised state, while by 1700, modern Scots law had definitely taken shape.' JW Cairns, 'Institutional Writings in Scotland Reconsidered' (1984) 4 *Journal of Legal History* 76, 89.

[8] Anton (n 5), 535.

[9] H Home (Lord Kames), *Principles of Equity*, 4th edn (Bell & Bradfute, and W Creecii, 1800), 541. See also Anton (n 5), 535. It is argued in PR Beaumont and P Bremner, 'Inter-regional conflicts within the United Kingdom relating to Private International Law of Succession – The development of the applicable law rule' (2010) 54 *Revista Valenciana d'Estudis Autonòmics* 238, 245–46 that the Scottish mixed legal system's ability to draw on a wider range of sources than existing precedents, including Scottish institutional writers and foreign jurists, 'means that it may have been more likely to produce a more rigorous and thoroughly-reasoned rule.'

> now considering … Our insular position, our complete detachment from the civil law, and our complete indifference to any systematic treatment of legal theory apart from cases of practice, explain the fact that down to the beginning of the nineteenth century Private International Law was absolutely unknown in this country.[10]

Alexander Sack referred to the historical lack of English intra-national conflicts, with its uniform common law,[11] and the peculiarities of English rules of jurisdiction,[12] acting in combination with its jury system,[13] when he concluded in 1937, in one of the most important contributions to the historical study of English private international law written to date,[14] that:

> The English law on the conflict of laws actually originated only in the middle of the eighteenth century, when other countries of Europe had a developed system of rules governing conflicts of laws.[15]

The conclusion that can be drawn from the academic literature is that there was virtually no discernible field of private international law in England by the turn of the eighteenth century. However, by the turn of the nineteenth century, the field of private international law in England had evidently begun to develop. It was said by Lord Ellenborough in *Potter* (1804):

> We always import together with their persons the existing relations of foreigners as between themselves, according to the laws of their respective countries.[16]

Although Lord Ellenborough CJ's statement, especially in his use of the word 'always', appears to have been rather optimistic in view of the infancy of the field in England at that time, it suggests that there was, by the early nineteenth century, a willingness amongst the English judiciary to apply foreign law in the English

[10] F Harrison, *On Jurisprudence and the Conflict of Laws* (Clarendon Press, 1919), 117–118.

[11] AN Sack, 'Conflicts of Laws in the History of the English Law' in New York University (ed), *Law: A Century of Progress (1835–1935)* (New York University Press, 1937), 344.

[12] ibid, 344. Early English rules of jurisdiction meant that actions could only be raised if some elements of the case took place in England. During the sixteenth century, jurisdictional rules developed such that it was possible to create a fiction so that the English courts would have jurisdiction in all cases, providing that the cause of the action was transitory. See W Holdsworth, 'The Rules of Venue, and the Beginnings of the Commercial Jurisdiction of the Common Law Courts' (1914) 14 *Columbia Law Review* 551, 553–54. Whether an action was local or transitory depended on whether all the facts took place in one place (ie the action was local, requiring only a jury from the locality), or whether the facts took place in a number of places (ie the action was transitory, requiring a jury from each of those places). The distinction was addressed succinctly by the then Lord Chancellor, Lord Herschell, in *British South Africa Co v Companhia de Mocambique* [1893] AC 602, 617–18.

[13] Sack (n 11), 346: 'Thus the rule became established that a jury could not inquire into any matter that did not take place within the given locality.'

[14] For example, Sack's 1937 article forms the basis of the historical introduction to the 2017 fifteenth edition of *Cheshire, North and Fawcett on Private International Law*. See JJ Fawcett and P Torremans (eds), *Cheshire, North & Fawcett: Private International Law*, 15th edn (Oxford University Press, 2017), 17ff, which refers to the article as the 'only separate work in English of an historical nature.'

[15] Sack (n 11), 398.

[16] *Potter v Brown* (1804) 5 East 124, 131; 102 ER 1016.

courts, and this crucial development appears to have taken place during the course of the eighteenth century.

But why did the field of private international law start to develop in England during the eighteenth century? One argument that has been floated is the influence of existing principles of Scottish private international law in England following the 1707 Union. Thus, it was suggested in the late nineteenth century by John Westlake in the second edition of his book on private international law that the continental approach may have found its way into England through Scotland. Writing in 1880[17] he said:

> I do not know enough of the history of Scotch law to assert it, but probably the union with Scotland, coupled with the fact that it had been usual for Scotch advocates to complete their legal education in Holland, may have had some effect in the same direction.[18]

Westlake is not the only source of the argument that existing Scottish practice may have played an important role in the development of private international law in England. The fifteenth edition of one of the leading English textbooks on private international law, *Dicey, Morris and Collins on The Conflict of Laws* argues:

> Although the conflict of laws has been intensively studied by continental jurists since the 13th century, it is of comparatively recent origin in England. A few rules of the English conflict of laws can be traced back the late 17th century. But the subject first came into prominence in English courts towards the end of the 18th century, mainly because of conflicts between the laws of England and Scotland.[19]

It is very likely that the influence of existing Scottish private international law, as well as the necessity for the House of Lords to engage with problems of Scots law and questions of internal private international law, as between the separate legal systems of the UK, accelerated the development of the field in England. For example,[20] the Scottish appeal to the House of Lords in *Gray* (1709) considered the formal validity of a bond executed and assigned in England,[21] and referred both to the pre-Union English case of *Foubert* (1703)[22] and the Scottish case of *Salton* (1673).[23]

[17] Despite Westlake having drawn on Scottish cases in his first 1858 edition – for example, at 40, as matters relate to domicile – there does not appear to be any mention of this theory in this first edition of his book. See J Westlake, *A Treatise on Private International Law or the Conflict of Laws* (W Maxwell, 1858).

[18] J Westlake, *A Treatise on Private International Law*, 2nd edn (William Maxwell & Son, 1880), 8.

[19] L Collins (Lord Collins of Mapesbury) and J Harris (eds), *Dicey, Morris & Collins on the Conflict of Laws*, 15th edn & 5th supp (Sweet & Maxwell, 2018), para 1-018.

[20] Other examples include *Paterson v Ogilvie and Murray* (1724) Robertson 499; *Brand v Cumming* (1725) Robertson 511; *Fullerton v Kinloch* (1740) 1 Paton 265.

[21] *Gray v Duke of Hamilton* (1709) Robertson 1.

[22] *Foubert v Turst* (1703) 1 Brown 129; 1 ER 464. The importance of this case is discussed further below.

[23] *Salton v Salton* [1673] Mor 4431, although the older case of *Harper v Jaffrey* [1630] Mor 4431 is clearer on the point, at least in so far as the court's terse reasoning is concerned.

Nonetheless, the argument that private international law was introduced into England through existing Scottish practice must be approached with a degree of caution. Perhaps the greatest difficulty with the argument is that while there was evidently a willingness to apply foreign law in Scotland and to engage with the associated issues, there was, as has been stated, a lack of any coherent Scottish system of private international law by the turn of the eighteenth century that could have been adopted in England.

Another argument that has been advanced is that Lord Mansfield, a born Scot,[24] heavily involved in litigating Scottish cases early in his career,[25] was, by means of his acquired knowledge of Scots law,[26] a significant driving force behind the development of English private international law.[27] Again, while Lord Mansfield, in his capacity as an English judge, was responsible for some very important decisions,[28] and was thus extremely influential in the development of the field of private international law in England,[29] it does appear that some initial advances were already being made in England by the early eighteenth century, ie well before Lord Mansfield came into practice either as a barrister or as a judge.[30]

In short, it is difficult to say with any certainty why there was a rapid development of private international law in England during the eighteenth century. It is unlikely that there was any one cause. By way of speculation, an important cause, but one that is difficult to fully substantiate from the available sources, was likely the rapidly increasing trade and movement of people between England, Scotland, Ireland, the continent, and further afield, which made it increasingly untenable to ignore foreign law in English cases. Indeed, it should come as no surprise that the potential injustice of refusing to recognise, for example, the terms of a foreign marriage settlement would have been clear to the early-eighteenth-century English judge.[31] Further impetus was no doubt given during the course of the eighteenth

[24] E Heward, *Lord Mansfield* (Barry Rose (Publishers) Ltd, 1979), 1.

[25] ibid, 16ff.

[26] Lord Mansfield, despite his Scottish heritage and upbringing, was an English barrister educated in Oxford.

[27] Llewelyn Davies (n 6), 53, an analysis which is critically discussed in Anton (n 5).

[28] See comments, in respect of Lord Mansfield's contribution to English law generally, from Lord Hodge, current Deputy President of the UK Supreme Court: 'His judgments on contract, commercial law, insurance, and unjust enrichment continue to be cited in our courts.' P Hodge (Lord Hodge), 'The Scope of Judicial Law-Making in the Common Law Tradition' (2020) 84 *Rabels Zeitschrift für Ausländisches und Internationales Privatrecht* 211, 216.

[29] *Mostyn v Fabrigas* (1774) 1 Cowper 161; 98 ER 1021 is, perhaps, the best example but see also *Robinson v Bland* (1760) 1 W Bl 234; 96 ER 129 and *Holman v Johnson* (1775) 1 Cowper 341; 98 ER 1120.

[30] An early English case addressing choice of law in respect of foreign marriages, decided before Lord Mansfield came onto the bench in 1756, was *Scrimshire v Scrimshire* (1752) 2 Hagg (Consist) 395; 161 ER 782, which engaged inter alia with writers of the Dutch school such as Voet. Cases such as *Scrimshire* (1752) are further authority that it is difficult to pin down the development of English private international law to one cause.

[31] See *Foubert v Turst* (1703) 1 Brown 129; 1 ER 464, which case is considered below. Some of the theoretical issues involved were considered in Chapter one, Section II. E.

century by the 1707 Union and the influence of Lord Mansfield, both of which accelerated the development of English private international law. But even then, it was probably not until the mid-nineteenth century, following the publication of the first editions of both Story's[32] and Westlake's[33] textbooks, that the field of private international law really started taking shape in England and the wider common law world,[34] driven in no small part by the developing US legal system.[35]

A. Scotland

(i) Sources

The most comprehensive source of early Scottish case law is the *Decisions of the Court of Session in the Form of a Dictionary*, known as *Morison's Dictionary*,[36] which was first published between 1801 and 1804,[37] with later additions to remedy a number of significant omissions.[38] The editor, William Maxwell Morison, after whom *Morison's Dictionary* is named, stated in the short introduction to the first volume of the compilation that he should perform an 'acceptable service' to the:

> Law, and to his country – by publishing a COMPLETE AND UNIFORM EDITION, of the whole cases, which have been reported; as well those which have been printed, as those which remain in manuscript.[39]

The editor also stated in the introduction that most existing printed decisions, including the collections of Lords Durie, Stair, Dirleton, and Fountainhall, were

[32] J Story, *Commentaries on the Conflict of Laws* (Hilliard, Gray, and Company, 1834).

[33] Westlake, *A Treatise on Private International Law or the Conflict of Laws* (n 17).

[34] See Llewelyn Davies (n 6), 49, who argued 'When Story's Commentaries on the Conflict of Laws appeared in 1834 no serious attempt had been made to construct a system of Conflict of Laws on the basis of the existing English and American decisions.' As noted by Llewelyn Davies, Story, in the preface to his first edition, described the materials on the subject as 'loose and scattered' and 'absolutely repulsive, to the mere Student of the Common Law.' Story (n 32), Preface. Lorenzen argued that with the publication of Story's *Commentaries on the Conflict of Laws* 'a new era began in the treatment of the subject.' EG Lorenzen, 'Story's Commentaries on the Conflict of Laws: One Hundred Years after' (1934) 48 *Harvard Law Review* 15.

[35] For example, *Church v Hubbart* 6 US 187, 2 Cranch 187 (1804) is an important early US case in the context of this work.

[36] Cases referred to from *Morison's Dictionary* (n 39) are referred to by *Party A v Party B* [YEAR] Mor [PAGE NUMBER], as in eg nn 6 and 23 above.

[37] K Reid and R Zimmermann (eds), *A History of Private Law in Scotland: Introduction and Property* (Oxford University Press, 2000), lvi; JS Leadbetter, 'The Printed Law Reports: 1540–1935' in The Stair Society (ed), *An Introductory Survey of the Sources and Literature of Scots Law* (Robert Maclehose & Co Ltd, 1936), 52.

[38] Reid and Zimmermann (eds) (n 37), lvi.

[39] William Maxwell Morison, *The Decisions of the Court of Session from its first institution to the present time, digested under proper heads, in the form of a Dictionary*, vol 1 (Bell & Bradfute, 1801), Advertisement VI.

'very scarce and high priced',[40] and also that the volumes of the Faculty Collection[41] were 'nearly out of print'[42] and contained many 'errors' and 'deficiencies'.[43]

Morison's Dictionary is indeed a substantial and impressive compilation of decisions of the early Scottish Court of Session, with the earliest decision dating from 1540, and the latest from 1808.[44] The decisions contained within *Morison's Dictionary* are categorised by subject, for example, *Adultery*,[45] *Annualrent*,[46] and *Apprentice*.[47] The most relevant chapters for the purpose of this work are *Foreign* (volume 6) and *Proof*[48] (volume 15).

However, the cases contained within *Morison's Dictionary* suffer from some fundamental flaws as sources of legal authority. Aside from the inevitable risks of inaccuracy associated with any compilation of law reports,[49] especially early law reports, the main difficulty with the decisions contained within *Morison's Dictionary* is that they lack the depth of analysis that a modern judgment would be expected to have.[50] Indeed, some of the earliest potentially relevant decisions contain, at most, a few sentences of judicial reasoning.[51] The value of these early

[40] ibid, Advertisement V.

[41] See, for explanation of the Faculty Collection, Reid and Zimmermann (eds) (n 37), lvi.

[42] WM Morison (n 39), Advertisement V.

[43] ibid, Advertisement VI.

[44] *Morison's Dictionary* (n 39) as currently bound contains 19 full volumes with the last subject 'WRONGOUS IMPRISONMENT' ending at page 17074 (which does not account for the numerous appendixes to the categories), together with several supplementary books. It is understood to have originally comprised 38 volumes. A full explanation is given in Leadbetter (n 37), 52.

[45] WM Morison (n 39), 327, which starts with a decision from 1573.

[46] ibid, 473, which starts with a decision from 1705.

[47] ibid, 583, which starts with a decision from 1686.

[48] Proof is the term used by Scottish lawyers today in relation to the substantive evidential hearing stage of a civil court action.

[49] This point is developed later in more detail in relation to England, which, unsurprisingly considering its size relative to Scotland, has a greater range of available law reports.

[50] One important reason for this, though not the only one, is that it was not until the nineteenth century that an established system of precedent (stare decisis) began fully taking hold in Scotland. Prior to this, recourse was had to statute and custom, failing which, the *ius commune*, although it must be stressed that the authoritative value of the different sources of Scots law was a matter of controversy. See discussion in Cairns, 'Attitudes to Codification and the Scottish Science of Legislation, 1600–1830' (n 2), 21–24. It is said (at 24) that Scottish writers were 'very cautious about ascribing a direct and clear law-making role to the judges.' However, there is evidence, said Cairns (at 56), that by the end of the eighteenth century thinking was turning in favour of a system of precedent, as opposed to legislation, being seen as the best mode of law-making in Scotland. This was, in part, Cairns maintained (at 68) because the 'Westminster Parliament neglected Scots law: lawyers were compelled to seek for development through the working of the Court of Session.' See also Hodge (Lord Hodge) (n 28), 215: 'Until the early nineteenth century, judges relied on the authoritative institutional writers, such as Stair and Erskine, and the published notebooks, or 'Practicks' of some judges rather than judicial precedent, although some leading cases were seen as settling certain points of law.' Lord Hodge described Scottish law reporting prior to the nineteenth century as 'a summary of the pleadings and the result.' Hodge (Lord Hodge) 'The Scope of Judicial Law-Making in the Common Law Tradition' (n 28), 215.

[51] The decision of *Scot v Toish* [1676] Mor 4502 contains little to no judicial reasoning: 'An assignation, being made in Holland, according to the custom there, by way of instrument, under the hand of a notary, a tabellion having retained the warrant in his hands, signed by the parties, was sustained, in respect of the custom and consueiudo loci.' See also *Falconer v Heirs of Beatie* [1627] Mor 4501, where

decisions can therefore be questioned on the basis that they lack any discernible *ratio decidendi*.[52] The merits of trying to catalogue them were described by the respected Scottish private international law scholar Sandy Anton as 'pointless'.[53] It should also not be overlooked that the procedural background of practice in the Court of Session at that time was very different.[54]

Nonetheless, *Morison's Dictionary* does provide a useful source of information for historical legal research. In particular, there is useful information contained in some of the reports as to the method with which the court carried out its investigation into the content of foreign law.

Moreover, the potential contemporary legal importance of these terse decisions must not be underestimated.[55] In *Glasgow Corporation* (1959)[56] and *Morgan Guaranty Trust Company of New York* (1994),[57] both of which concerned the law of unjustified enrichment, the Inner House of the Court of Session considered whether a *condictio indebiti* could be sustained through an error of fact or,

the court was prepared to give recognition to an assignation made in Germany not in Scottish form and lacking witnesses, which has slightly more expansive reasoning and explanation of the circumstances, although the operative part of the judgment is terse: 'the LORDS would sustain the assignation, albeit made betwixt two Scotsmen, and albeit pursued in Scotland, and disconform to the Scots law.' The cases appear to be early examples of the *in favorem* approach in respect of formal validity. See, for explanation, Crawford and Carruthers (n 4), para 15-33 and J Kropholler, *Internationales Privatrecht*, 6th edn (Mohr Siebeck, 2006), 310.

[52] See also Beaumont and Bremner (n 9), 248. For an illuminating discussion of what is meant by *ratio decidendi*, see: AL Goodhart, 'Determining the Ratio Decidendi of a Case' (1930) 40 *Yale Law Journal* 161.

[53] Anton (n 5), 535.

[54] See NR Whitty, 'Civil Procedure (Reissue) (2007): Introduction (paras 1–45)', *The Laws of Scotland: Stair Memorial Encyclopaedia* (LexisNexis) para 4: 'the system of civil procedure was based on the romano-canonical procedure of the *ius commune* from at least the foundation of the Court of Session in 1532 to the early nineteenth century when the reforms of 1808 to 1830 consciously changed its character to a variant of the common law system of procedure.' Whitty notes, at para 5, the predominance of writing; remoteness of judges from parties, witnesses and real evidence; undue formalism of rules of evidence; and inefficient procedure characterised by repetitious and inconclusive stages in procedure as well as by unstructured and unfocused written pleadings and frequent appeals from interlocutory orders. He then notes, at para 6: 'As an inevitable consequence of the foregoing features, litigation in late eighteenth century Scotland could drag on interminably just as in continental procedure, actions lasting several decades were not unusual.'

[55] However, notable scepticism in relying on dated authorities was expressed by Lord Reed in a dissenting judgment in *Willers v Joyce* [2016] UKSC 43, where he noted, at [182], that his 'own conclusion in the present case would have been the same even if a judgment had been discovered which unequivocally demonstrated that a right of action had been held to lie 300 years ago', and that 'the court must not lose sight of the fact that it is deciding law for the 21st century.' While he recognised the merit in 'looking back to the achievements of our predecessors', he noted that it would often be more pertinent to look to 'contemporaries in other jurisdictions'. For support, he cites Frederic William Maitland's observation 'that every age should be the mistress of its own law', found in 'The Making of the German Civil Code' in HAL Fisher (ed), *The Collected Papers of Frederic William Maitland* vol 3 (Cambridge University Press, 1911), at 487, and argues that the great judges of the past, such as Holt and Mansfield, would be the first to recognise that. Lord Reed in *Willers v Joyce* also noted, at [183], the difficulty in properly understanding and applying old judgments made in 'an unfamiliar procedural context, and an equally unfamiliar remedy-centred approach to legal thinking.'

[56] *Glasgow Corporation v Lord Advocate* 1959 SC 203.

[57] *Morgan Guaranty Trust Company of New York v Lothian Regional Council* 1995 SC 151.

alternatively, through an *errore iuris* (error of law). A central point of consideration for both courts was the case of *Stirling* (1733) which, albeit consisting of a mere ten words, supported the proposition that an *errore iuris* does indeed give rise to a right *condictio indebiti*:

> *Condictio indebiti* sustained to one who had paid *errore juris*.[58]

The decision is remarkably short, even when compared to other meagre decisions contained in *Morison's Dictionary*, with most other decisions generally containing at least some background facts or submissions. In *Glasgow Corporation* (1959), Lord Wheatley was dismissive of the case's importance and concluded that the decision was 'a mere statement unsupported and unvouched for by any argument.'[59] However, in the landmark decision of *Morgan Guaranty Trust Company of New York* (1994), Lord President Hope concluded that:

> The decision itself is clear and it was regarded both in subsequent decisions and by the institutional writers and other commentators as having settled the point.[60]

While it appears that *Morison's Dictionary* successfully collated many early Scottish law reports, with many of the reports from earlier compilations appearing in *Morison's Dictionary* in similar or identical terms,[61] certain cases are reported differently throughout the various law reports, especially those cases reported in the useful collection by Lord Hailes.[62] For example, in a decision about *legitim* in *Sinclair* (1768), the parties' pleadings are contained in *Morison's Dictionary* in detail, but the decision of the court is reported merely as: 'THE LORDS adhered.'[63] However, in the report of the same case contained in Lord Hailes' reports there is, it appears, verbatim citation of what the judges actually said when considering the case.[64] This adds significant depth to the exceptionally terse judgment contained in *Morison's Dictionary*, and the decisions contained in Lord Hailes' reports are a rare opportunity to read the judges' discussions amongst themselves about those cases calling before the court.

[58] *Stirling v Earl of Lauderdale* [1733] Mor 2930.

[59] *Glasgow Corporation v Lord Advocate* 1959 SC 203, 221–22.

[60] *Morgan Guaranty Trust Company of New York v Lothian Regional Council* 1995 SC 151, 163.

[61] See, for example, the decision of *Stranger of Middleburg* (1626), which is reported in *Stranger of Middleburg v Executors of Smith* [1626] Mor 12420 and in Alexander Gibson of Durie, *The Decisions of the Lords of Council and Session in Most cases of Importance, Debated, and brought before them: From July 1621 to July 1642* (Printed by the Heir of Andrew Anderson 1690), 242–43. Please note that the decisions relative to this case in *Durie* are separated by an unrelated decision.

[62] SD Dalrymple (Lord Hailes), *Decisions of the Lords of Council and Session: From 1766 to 1791* (vol 1, William Tait 1826). Cases referred to from Lord Hailes' collection of cases are referred to by *Party A v Party B* [YEAR] Hailes [PAGE NUMBER], as in eg nn 64, 95 and 97 below.

[63] *Sinclair v Sinclair* [1768] Mor 8188.

[64] *Sinclair v Sinclair* [1768] Hailes 247, per Lord Monboddo: 'I would give some operation to the general discharge; but a right of future succession must be discharged in express words. This sort of renunciation was quite improbated by the Roman law: It has been admitted, indeed, in modern practice, as appears in Antonius Faber's *Decisiones Sabaudicae*; but the renunciation must be upon oath.'

In terms of early Scottish legal literature, the texts of the Scottish institutional writers are undoubtedly significant,[65] although there is debate as to which texts have the status of institutional texts[66] and, even, the extent to which institutional texts have special status.[67] Although the significance of the Scottish institutional texts is waning in terms of their contemporary authoritative legal value,[68] these texts are extremely important when it comes to historical analysis of the development of Scots law.

There is reference to the approach that should be taken to foreign law[69] as early as the late seventeenth century in the seminal text of Stair,[70] which is widely regarded as being the most influential institutional text in Scots law,[71] although the quality of Stair's analysis in so far as it concerns matters of private international law has been criticised.[72] In addition, highly regarded institutional texts which have relevance to this work are Bankton, Erskine, and (although perhaps not an institutional text in the traditional sense)[73] Kames. Lord Kames is noted[74] for having been the first Scottish writer to have published, in the mid-eighteenth century, a serious account of private international law.[75] These (institutional) texts are important because they demonstrate contemporaneous understanding of the meaning of the early Scottish cases and, as will be demonstrated during the course of this chapter, provide good evidence as to how the approach to the application of foreign law in the Scottish courts came to develop.

[65] TB Smith, 'English Influences on the Law of Scotland' (1954) 3 *The American Journal of Comparative Law* 522, 522. Cairns argues that Scots lawyers accord much more importance to Stair's work than, for example, English lawyers do to Blackstone's *Commentaries on the Laws of England*. Cairns, 'Institutional Writings in Scotland Reconsidered' (n 7), 76.

[66] AC Black, 'The Institutional Writers: 1600–1826' in The Stair Society (ed), *An Introductory Survey of the Sources and Literature of Scots Law* (Robert Maclehose & Co Ltd, 1936). Lord Hodge refers to Stair, Erskine, and Bell as being the 'principal institutional writers'. Hodge (Lord Hodge) (n 28), 216.

[67] Cairns, 'Institutional Writings in Scotland Reconsidered' (n 7), 99: 'there is no rational or historical basis for this modern canon of institutional writers.'

[68] Although note the extensive reference to institutional texts in *Morgan Guaranty Trust Company of New York v Lothian Regional Council* 1995 SC 151, for example, at 158 of Lord President Hope's decision.

[69] The discussion regarding the development of the Scottish legal system at 39ff should be borne in mind. While, by the turn of the eighteenth century, it would certainly have been possible to talk of foreign, as opposed to, Scots law, it would have been increasingly difficult to do so as one went further back in time. Cairns seems to pinpoint the modern development of distinct Scots law to the late seventeenth century and the publication of Stair's institutional text. JW Cairns, 'Ius Civile in Scotland, ca. 1600' (2004) 2 *Roman Legal Tradition* 136, 170. In terms of the sixteenth century, Godfrey (n 2) argues, 'we have still obviously not reached the position in which it is accurate to speak of "Scots law"'.

[70] JD Viscount of Stair, *The Institutions of the Law of Scotland* (Printed by the Heir of Andrew Anderson, 1693), I, 1, 11.

[71] Black (n 66), 63: 'Every body of men has its own special idol, and of Scots lawyers it is safe to say that Stair's position is impregnable.'

[72] Gibb (n 1), 379: 'Yet in his Institutes of the Law of Scotland he not only displays no clear idea of International Private Law but no idea whatsoever of the need for such a system.'

[73] Cairns, 'Institutional Writings in Scotland Reconsidered' (n 7), 101.

[74] Beaumont and McEleavy (n 4), para 1.31.

[75] Lord Kames' analysis with regards private international law is mostly contained in H Home (Lord Kames) *Principles of Equity* (n 9), 536ff, in which the title of his chapter eight is: 'Jurisdiction of the court of session with respect to foreign matters.'

Finally, there is an excellent examination of the various instruments of the pre-Union Scottish Parliament relevant to private international law in Andrew Dewar Gibb's article 'International Private Law in Scotland in the Sixteenth and Seventeenth Centuries',[76] notably the Act of 1487, which provided exclusive jurisdiction to the Court of Session in actions involving 'strangers'.[77] However, drawing on Gibb's analysis, early Scottish legislation appears to have been very rudimentary in so far as it concerned private international law and, other than the Act of 1487, no significant reference is made to it.

(ii) The Application of Foreign Law in Early Scottish Case Law

As will be shown, questions involving foreign law in the early Scottish courts most often concerned matters such as formal validity, eg was the contract validly entered into in terms of the *lex loci contractus*?, and the recognition of judgments, including judgments dealing with questions of status.[78]

Scottish private international lawyers have,[79] for obvious reasons, tended to focus on the sections of *Morison's Dictionary* entitled *Foreign*[80] and *Forum Competens*,[81] which are contained in volume 6 of *Morison's Dictionary*, to the exclusion of the albeit small number of cases concerned with private international law contained in *Proof*,[82] found in volume 15 of *Morison's Dictionary*; *Arbitration*,[83] found in volume 1; and *Literary Property*,[84] found in volume 10. It is not suggested that these sections account for all of the cases contained in *Morison's Dictionary* with a private international law dimension, and there are likely to be other relevant cases in other sections. The absence of any reference by Dewar Gibb to cases contained in *Proof* may explain why he commented in his article that 'there is very little that can be said on [the] subject [of procedure]', in so far as early Scottish

[76] See Gibb (n 1), 371, for example, where various discriminating laws against the English are analysed.

[77] The full text of the Scottish Act of 1487, c 105, appears in JD Viscount of Stair, *The Institutions of the Law of Scotland*, A new edition, with notes and illustrations, by John S More (Bell & Bradfute, 1832), 547: 'That all civil actions, questions, and pleas, moved between whatsomever parties, be determined and decided before their Judge-Ordinar, sua that na action shall be deduced, called nor determined before our Sovereign Lord's Council, except allenarly actions pertaining in special to our Sovereign Lord, actions and complaints made be kirk-men, widows, orphans, and pupils, actions of strangers of other realms, and complaints made upon officers for fault of execution of their office, or where the officers are parties themselves.'

[78] A very good summary is contained in a speech given in 1953 by Alex Donaldson, then lecturer in Private International Law at the University of Glasgow, see Donaldson (n 1), 147ff. Some examples are also discussed in Anton (n 5), 535.

[79] Anton (n 5), 535; Gibb (n 1).

[80] The first decision in *Foreign* being *Fortoun v Shewan* [1610] Mor 4429.

[81] The first decision in *Forum Competens* being *Anderson v Hodgson and Ormiston* [1747] Mor 4779.

[82] The first decision in *Proof* being *Blackstock v Wilson* [1542] Mor 12263.

[83] The first decision in *Arbitration* being *Melvill v Strang* [1539] Mor 623.

[84] The first decision in *Literary Property* being *Midwinter v Hamilton* [1748] Mor 8295.

private international law is concerned.[85] Thus, this work seeks to draw out some cases from these more neglected sections of *Morison's Dictionary*.

(a) Concept of Foreign Law as Fact

The first explicit reference in the Scottish institutional authorities to foreign law being a question of fact appears to originate from the late seventeenth century.[86] Thus, Stair wrote in 1693:

> But the Law of *England* and other Forraign Nations, being matter of Fact to us, the fame was found probable by the Declaration of the Judges there. Jan. 18. 1676. *Cunningham* contra *Brown*.[87]

A similar reference to the case of *Cuninghame* (1676)[88] is to be found in other institutional texts, with the decision cited by both Bankton[89] and Erskine,[90] when stating the general proposition that foreign law should be approached as a matter of fact. Although the institutional texts seem to have been united in the way that foreign law should be approached, it is not clear from the *Cuninghame* (1676) decision where the concept of categorising foreign law as fact derives from. The fact approach is certainly not explicitly mentioned in the decision, the operative part of the decision being:

> The Lords found the allegeance relevant, and for the proving thereof, granted commission to the Judges of the Common Pleas, to declare what was their law in the case.[91]

[85] Gibb (n 1), 399.

[86] When considering the method of ascertaining foreign law there does appear to be a suggestion in Balfour's *Practicks*, SJ Balfour (Lord Pettindreich), *Practicks: Or, a System of the more ancient Law of Scotland* (A Kincaid and A Donaldson, 1754), 292, that matters of foreign law should be referred to judges of other countries for proof by way of commission, implying that foreign law was approached as fact, although there is no reference to foreign law being a question of fact in Balfour's text. Although Balfour's *Practicks* were not published until 1754, they are said to have been compiled in the 1570s. See DT Fergus and G Maher, 'Sources of Law (General and Historical) (Volume 22) (Original Date of Publication: 30 November 1986)', *The Laws of Scotland: Stair Memorial Encyclopaedia* (LexisNexis), para 540. It has been long argued that the Practicks were not, in fact, written by Balfour but this work expresses no view on the matter. See ÆJG Mackay, 'Who Wrote "Balfour's Practicks"?' (1898) 13(49) *The Scottish Antiquary, or, Northern Notes and Queries* 1.

[87] Viscount of Stair, *The Institutions of the Law of Scotland* (n 70), I, 1, 11.

[88] The decision appears in *Morison's Dictionary* in *Cuninghame v Brown* [1676] Mor 12323 with a slightly differently spelled name to that found in Stair but it is certainly the same case.

[89] AM Bankton, *An Institute of the Laws of Scotland in Civil Rights* (A Kincaid and A Donaldson, 1751), 32: 'for the law of foreign countries is matter of fact to us: the competent proof in such case is a declaration from the judges there, concerning the law of their country, and the validity of the deed in question, upon recommendatory letters from the court where the action is sued.'

[90] J Erskine, *An Institute of the Law of Scotland*, New edition by James Badenach Nicolson (Bell & Bradfute, 1871), 718: 'As the law of one country is in most cases matter of fact to the judges of every other country, the proper way of proving it, in points which carry the least degree of doubtfulness, is by a written opinion of the foreign judges, which is readily granted *ex comitate*, upon a recommendation from the court before whom the question which gave rise to the doubt has been brought.'

[91] *Cuninghame v Brown* [1676] Mor 12323.

Significance can potentially be found in the fact that Stair, who was Lord President of the Court of Session at the time of the case,[92] would likely have heard the case or, at least, would have been familiar with the approach of the court to matters of foreign law at the time.

By the middle of the eighteenth century, the principle that foreign law was to be considered a matter of fact was well-established in Scottish jurisprudence. In *Randal* (1768), there is reference, in what was pleaded by the parties, to the principle that the laws of every country are a matter of fact, capable of proof when disputed,[93] together with reference to *Cuninghame* (1676).[94] As Lord Hailes' report of the case insightfully reveals from the judges' discussions, the Lord President went as far as saying:

> I have been early taught that foreign law is fact, and, like all other facts, the knowledge of it may be attained.[95]

In *Hinton* (1773), which considered whether Scotland recognised a subsisting common law right to prevent copyright infringement,[96] Lord Hailes himself commented:

> I am of the opinion that, in England, an author may have a common-law right in his works after publication. So the English lawyers have said: so it has been determined in the Court of King's Bench. English law, as to us, is foreign law. Foreign law is a matter of fact; and of the fact, I ask no better evidence, for I can have no better evidence than the opinion of lawyers and judges in that foreign country.[97]

(b) Mechanisms of Proof

(aa) Proof by Written Opinion of Foreign Judges

Both Erskine[98] and Bankton[99] argued that the proper means of proving foreign law, at least in cases with the least degree of doubt,[100] was to obtain a written opinion from foreign judges.[101] Erskine suggested that such an opinion would be readily granted *ex comitate*.[102] Thus, in *Cuninghame* (1676), the case was referred

[92] Black (n 66), 64.
[93] *Randal and Elliot v Captain Innes' Executors* [1768] Mor 4520, 4521.
[94] *Randal and Elliot v Captain Innes' Executors* [1768] Mor 4520.
[95] *Randal v Alexander and George Innes* [1768] Hailes 225, 227.
[96] In addition to any rights granted under the Copyright Act 1710.
[97] *Hinton v Donaldson and Others* [1773] Hailes 535, 536.
[98] Erskine (n 90), 718.
[99] Bankton, *An Institute of the Laws of Scotland in Civil Rights* (n 89), 32.
[100] Erskine (n 90), 718.
[101] There is also earlier, albeit more ambiguous, reference to this method of proof in Balfour (Lord Pettindreich) (n 86), 292, in so far that reference may be made to 'ordinar Jugeis' of the relevant foreign 'realme'.
[102] Erskine (n 90), 718.

to 'Judges of the Common Pleas'[103] in England for consideration as to whether the defender could be held liable to a 'double bond' in English form involving multiple parties.[104]

The practice of Scottish courts referring cases to foreign judges, or at least seeking their view, appears to have begun earlier than *Cuninghame* (1676), suggesting that it was, albeit to a limited extent, established practice.[105] In *Paterson* (1620), the court, having allowed averments to proceed to an evidential hearing (probation) founded on the Irish custom of subscribing writs for illiterate parties, refused to accept evidence (testimonial) from three Irish Justices of the Peace as to Irish custom on the matter, on the basis that their evidence was not sufficient to prove the point.[106] The Scottish court adjourned the case to allow the defender to obtain evidence from 'a sitting judge in Ireland having power to decide on the validity or invalidity of the writs.'[107]

According to the first report in *Morison's Dictionary*, dated 6 December 1626, of the *Stranger of Middleburg* (1626), the pursuer offered to prove that a bond made by a deceased in Flanders was valid, as it was the custom in Flanders that bonds were effective against the subscriber, despite the lack of witnesses.[108] The court admitted the bond to probation, but insisted that evidence as to the custom in Flanders be provided by testimony of judges of that country.[109] The case is reported in similar terms in Durie, which is an older set of case reports.[110] In *Salton* (1673), the court (Présidial) in Rheims was granted a commission to report on a custom that a bond without witnesses, which the defender averred to be null, was valid according to local law.[111] In response to the report returned by the foreign court, the court sustained the bond.[112] As stated previously, *Salton* (1673) was referred to by the House of Lords in *Gray* (1709).[113]

However, while the practice of Scottish courts referring matters to foreign courts appears to have been relatively common in the seventeenth century at least,[114]

[103] The Judges of the Common Pleas appear to have had jurisdiction, together with the Court of King's Bench and the Court of Exchequer, over most important legal matters that would have arisen in early English law. Their judgments contributed to the development of the English common law. D Klerman, 'Nonpromotion and Judicial Independence' (1999) 72 *Southern California Law Review* 455, 456; HW Jones, 'Our Uncommon Common Law' (1975) 42 *Tennessee Law Review* 443, 450–52.

[104] *Cuninghame v Brown* [1676] Mor 12323.

[105] See Balfour (Lord Pettindreich) (n 86), 292, and the case of *Merchandis of Avinzeon v airis of Fastcastell* (1532) contained therein.

[106] *Paterson v Hall* [1620] Mor 12419.

[107] *Paterson v Hall* [1620] Mor 12419. The note refers to 'a supreme Judge there, having power to decide in such cases.'

[108] *Stranger of Middleburg v Executors of Smith* [1626] Mor 12420.

[109] *Stranger of Middleburg v Executors of Smith* [1626] Mor 12420.

[110] Alexander Gibson of Durie (n 61), 242.

[111] *Salton v Salton* [1673] Mor 4431, 4432.

[112] *Salton v Salton* [1673] Mor 4431.

[113] *Gray v Duke of Hamilton* (1709) Robertson 1, 3. Note that the case is spelled '*Saltoun*' in the *Gray* (1709) report.

[114] It has been noted elsewhere, albeit in a slightly different context, that it is particularly difficult drawing conclusions from sixteenth-century Scottish case law, although seventeenth-century Scottish

the practice appears to have died out by the turn of the eighteenth century,[115] at least until the later introduction of relevant legislation by the UK Parliament in the mid-nineteenth century.[116] There is no evidence available from the authorities as to why the practice died out as it did. However, there are likely to have been formidable obstacles. It is not clear how these references to foreign courts operated in practice. Although there is evidence in *Salton* (1673) that the case was successfully passed by the Scottish court to the foreign court for consideration, it is unlikely that such references could have worked in every case. Indeed, the case report explicitly refers to the fact that the report was returned by the foreign court.[117] It might be that other foreign courts rejected or simply did not respond to attempts by Scottish courts to refer cases to them for an opinion, which led to an end of the practice. The barriers to the system working effectively in every case were obviously substantial. Even the conveyance of the relevant documents would have taken weeks, using unreliable methods of transport, without any clear opportunity for the foreign court to ask follow-up questions, not to mention the language difficulties involved. During that time, many European countries had hostile relationships with each other or were even at war.[118] Responding to a Scottish court would surely have created additional work for the foreign court. It is not clear how such work would have been remunerated. In *Salton* (1673), it might have been that historically strong Franco-Scottish relations[119] meant that the court in Rheims was particularly obliging in that case. It can only be speculated that other Scottish cases sat waiting for a response from foreign courts, potentially for many months.

(bb) Proof by Witness Evidence

There are conflicting accounts in the authorities as to whether witness evidence was sufficient to satisfy the Scottish court as to the content of a foreign law. The suggestion in some important early authorities is that it was not. As stated above, both Erskine[120] and Bankton[121] were clear that the proper method of proving foreign law was remit to foreign judges.

Nonetheless, there is evidence of foreign law being proven by witnesses in the earliest reported Scottish cases. In the case of *Dingwall* (1619), which is reported

case law tends to be much more fruitful. See Beaumont and McEleavy (n 4), para 1.27. However, there is no evidence that a different approach was taken in any earlier cases. The reference in Balfour (Lord Pettindreich) (n 86), 292, though ambiguous, is supportive of this proposition.

[115] In *Fyffe v Fyffe* (1840) 2 D 1001, 1003, the Scottish court held that it had no power to send a case for consideration to the English court. However, there is mention of the practice in submissions made by the pursuer to the court in *Earl of Selkirk v Gray* [1708] Mor 4453, 4454: 'the law of England, which being matter of fact to us, must be proven by a declaration of their judges.'

[116] The legislation which was introduced by the UK Parliament in the mid-nineteenth century, and its associated cases, are considered in Chapter three. These later developments did not have anything to do with the early Scottish practice considered here.

[117] *Salton v Salton* [1673] Mor 4431, 4432.

[118] D Pennington, *Europe in the Seventeenth Century*, 2nd edn (Routledge, 1989).

[119] Fergus and Maher (n 86), para 603.

[120] Erskine (n 90), 718.

[121] Bankton, *An Institute of the Laws of Scotland in Civil Rights* (n 89), 32.

in *Morison's Dictionary*, both in *Foreign*[122] and in *Proof*,[123] the court granted a commission allowing witnesses, inter alia, to be heard on the matter of English law. The case concerned an alleged vicious intromission[124] by the defender in her late husband's goods. The defender averred that intromission was necessary, involving only 'household-gear', which could not be 'cast furth', and that any intromission should be judged by the law of England, where the goods were meddled with.[125] The defender averred that English law limited the pursuer's remedy to mere restitution. The court appears to have allowed the defender's averments to proceed to an evidential hearing (probation),[126] which, if successful, would presumably have restricted the pursuer's remedy to the value of the specific goods, rather than placing a general liability for the deceased's debts on the defender.[127]

By the late eighteenth century, with the practice of referring cases to foreign courts having died out, the Scottish court appears to have become more favourable towards the use of expert witness opinions from foreign lawyers.[128] In the case of *Johnstone* (1775), which considered whether an arbitral award was subject to review by the Dutch court, the case was made up:

> for the opinion of Dutch counsel, as to what was the law of Holland with regard to the privilege of challenging decrees-arbitral, and this opinion (which mentioned such decrees not to be challengeable) being laid before the court.[129]

Another relatively early case where an expert opinion appears to have been sought is *Wightman* (1802), where the Scottish court was persuaded on the basis of English counsel's opinion as to the content of English law regarding a testamentary instrument executed in India.[130] A note to *Wightman* (1802) states that another case, *Austin* (1802), was also decided on the basis of opinions from English counsel.[131]

[122] *Dingwal v Vandosme* [1619] Mor 4449. Note the slightly different spelling.

[123] *Dingwall v Vandosme* [1619] Mor 12419. The report consists only of the words 'Foreign laws and customs found relevant to be proved by witnesses.' The report in *Foreign* is accordingly more substantial.

[124] The concept of vicious (or vitious) intromission appears to have left a confirmed Scottish executor liable for all the deceased's debts should there have been any interference with the deceased's moveable property. See AM Bankton, *An Institute of the Laws of Scotland in Civil Rights* (A Kincaid and A Donaldson, 1752), 420: 'Executors confirmed have the only active title, with safety, to administer and dispose of the effects of persons deceased; but, if any wrongfully intermeddle therewith, he is liable, upon the passive title of vitious intromission, to make payment of the deceased's debts. This is justly introduced, to deter people from meddling with such moveables unwarrantably, which are easily embezzled. It is a singularity in our law, that vitious intromitters, or intermeddlers with moveables of a person deceased, are subjected universally to his debts.'

[125] *Dingwal v Vandosme* [1619] Mor 4449.

[126] *Dingwal v Vandosme* [1619] Mor 4449.

[127] The principle that an intromission with goods in England, or in a foreign place, does not give rise to liability for the deceased's debts in Scotland appears to have been confirmed in *Archbishop of Glasgow v Bruntsfield* [1683] Mor 4449.

[128] The extent to which these opinions may have been considered binding is discussed in Chapter three.

[129] *Johnson v Crawford and Mason* [1776] Mor in Arbitration, Appendix, Part I, No 4, 5. Also reported at *Johnstone v Executors of James Crawford* [1775] Hailes 729. It is clear from the reports that the opinion of Dutch counsel was successfully obtained and relied upon by the court.

[130] *Wightman v Delisle's Trustees* [1802] Mor 4479.

[131] *Austin v Austin* [1802] Mor 4480.

A further, essentially contemporaneous, trend that can be observed in the cases originating from around the turn of the nineteenth century was the practice of the Court of Session to seek opinions from English counsel to deal with areas of Scots law that were yet to be developed, in particular, in commercial cases such as those dealing with insurance and admiralty law.[132] However, this was essentially an example of the Scottish court applying substantive English law to disputes for which there was no suitable Scottish rule. In other words, such an application of English law did not take place in terms of choice of law rules.

There were several early cases where there was a dispute as to whether it was acceptable to lead witness evidence in the Scottish court in relation to foreign bonds, where such practice was permissible under the procedural law of the *lex loci actus*.[133] However, such cases really concerned the question of whether Scottish procedural law or foreign law ought to govern the introduction of evidence into Scottish proceedings. By *Scot* (1664),[134] the Scottish court appears to have recognised that Scots law ought to regulate procedural matters on the basis that it:

> Would furnish an ordinary delay in such cases, to the disadvantage of merchants, and hindering of trade, by always offering to prove payment in England, by witnesses, which could require long time.

A further case report by Newbyth, also contained in *Morison's Dictionary*, regarding the same case states that the court found the averments:

> Probable only, by writ, or oath of party, and not by witnesses; and declared they would judge so in all time coming, especially the bond being made after the Scots manner.[135]

The same approach appears to have been taken in *Chatto* (1702).[136] Thus, these cases appear to have been an early assertion of the now universally accepted principle[137] that the *lex fori* regulates matters of procedure.

(cc) Ascertainment of Foreign Law with No Clear Indication of the Source

Despite there being fairly cogent evidence as to how foreign law was ascertained in most of the cases considered above, there are a number of cases appearing in the

[132] See, for example, *Wilson and Company v Elliot and others* [1776] Hailes 679 and *Wood and Company v Hamilton* [1788] Hailes 1052.

[133] See *Galbraith v Cunningham* [1626] Mor 4430, in which such evidence was allowed and admitted to probation, which is reported later more clearly on the point in *Galbraith v Cunningham* [1626] Mor 4446. Also allowed in both *Laird of Balbirnie v Laird of Arkhill and Relltrees* [1633] Mor 4446 and *Hyde v Williamson* [1634] Mor 4447.

[134] *Scot v Henderson and Wilson* [1664] Mor 4450. This case appears to have had a stronger connection with both Scotland and England, the form of bond in question having been used ordinarily between merchants of both countries.

[135] *Scot v Henderson and Wilson* [1664] Mor 4450, 4451.

[136] *Chatto v Ord* [1702] Mor 4456.

[137] Fawcett and Torremans (eds) (n 14), 73, although, for a more critical view, see H Schack, *Internationales Zivilverfahrensrecht*, 8th edn (CH Beck, 2021), para 45ff.

early reports in which there is some discussion of foreign law but no substantial evidence of the basis on which the court drew its conclusions.[138] For example, in *Davidsons* (1682), in relation to a notarially sealed assignation in Dutch form, the court required the principal assignation or proof of Dutch custom that a writ subscribed by the secretary of the town was valid.[139] Accordingly, a report seems to have been ordered by the court in the case, the outcome of which was presented to the court just over six months later.[140] Although the case report refers to 'Newton's report', there is little conclusive evidence of who that might have been and how he determined Dutch law on the matter.[141]

Equally, there are cases where the Scottish court did not seek evidence of foreign law, essentially choosing to draw its own conclusions from the documents available. Thus, in several cases concerning the effect of English bankruptcies, there was discussion as to the effect of the English Lord Chancellor's certificate. While the question as to whether to give recognition in Scotland to an English bankruptcy would have been a matter of Scots law, the question as to the certificate's effect in terms of the discharge of any English debts, or any conditions relating to the discharge, would have been a matter of English law, a fact that was alluded to in *Rochead* (1724).[142] However, despite significant discussion as to the effect of the certificate in the cases, no Scottish court appears to have heard evidence on English law on the matter, although this cannot be completely ruled out.[143] In *Lamington* (1627), proof of Bordeaux custom was forgone entirely, as:

> it was known to the Lords that it was the custom of that part to make the bond after that form.[144]

[138] For example, *Galbraith v Cunningham* [1626] Mor 4430, where the custom of Ireland was found proven but there is no clear evidence as to how this was done. There is mention of witnesses in the report from 16 November 1626, but that seems to have been as regards proof of payment and whether proof by witnesses should be allowed in the case. Again, in *Harper v Jaffrey* [1630] Mor 4431, the court found the custom of Normandy relevant and proven, but there is no evidence in the case report as to how this was done.

[139] *Davidsons v Town of Edinburgh* [1682] Mor 4444.

[140] The report by Fountainhall, which follows the shorter Folio Dictionary report, contained in *Morison's Dictionary* clearly sets out the various hearings. The case first called (ie was heard) on 22 June 1681, at which point the court set out the requirement for the principal assignation or evidence as to Dutch custom. The case then called again on 11 February 1682, at which point the court found Dutch custom proven on the basis of 'Newton's Report.' The case report's author appears to have been sceptical of the value of the delay: 'This has been so oft tried now, that the custom scarce needs any more probation; many testimonials from the Magistrates of these towns attesting it, and Grotius in his *introdutio ad jus Batavum*, and other lawyers, affirming it.'

[141] Newton is, however, mentioned in another case from the era: *Bromley v Fraser* [1682] Mor 4378, 4381. It is likely that Newton was an advocate.

[142] *Rochead v Scot* [1724] Mor 4566, 4567. Compare *Galbreath v Galbreath* [1762] Mor 4574; *Watson v Renton* [1792] Mor 4582; *Coalston v Stewart* [1770] Mor 4579 and *Marshall v Yeaman and Spence* [1746] Mor 4568.

[143] Although there is ambiguous reference to a 'report' in *Christie v Stration* [1746] Mor 4569, 4571.

[144] *Lamington v Kincaid* [1627] Mor 4443.

B. England

(i) Sources

There appears to have been little substantive academic discussion of private international law in England until John Westlake published the first edition of his text *Private International Law* in 1858.[145] Early sources of English private international law, to the extent that such a field can be said to have existed by the turn of the nineteenth century, are to be found almost entirely in case law.[146]

In common with Scotland, law reporting in England prior to the nineteenth century was flawed, being often brief and of questionable accuracy, with many cases, as today, being left unreported.[147] The case report of *Ranelaugh* (1700) is to be found in Vernon's case reports, the second edition of which was published in 1806. The case report appears as follows:

> The court upon the account allowed the defendant but 61. *per Cent, per Ann*, for a debt contracted in Ireland, because the bond for securing of it was executed here in *England*.[148]

This suggests that the English court refused to apply the Irish rate of interest, despite the *lex loci contractus* being Irish law. However, when one looks at a different set of case reports there is a suggestion that the court took a very different approach to the issue:

> If a Debt be contracted in *Ireland*, and a Bond given for securing it in *England*, it shall carry *English* Interest, Mich. 1700, L *Ranelaugh* and Sir *John Champant* 2 Vern. 395, but *Quære* of this Report; for it appears, that Sir *John Champant* was Deputy-Receiver to L *Ranelaugh*, who was Vice-Treasurer of *Ireland*; and that he had accepted and paid several Bills drawn on him by my Lord from *England*, amounting to a great deal more than the Fees and Profits of his Place; and that my Lord sent him over a Bond for the Overplus payable there; and it was held, that this Bond, on a Suit here, should carry *Irish* Interest.[149]

[145] Joseph Story's seminal work *Commentaries on the Conflict of Laws*, first published in 1834, is nonetheless credited with being the first substantive discussion of private international law in the English-speaking world, a substantial portion of which engaged with issues originating from Scotland and England: Story (n 32). Lorenzen (n 34), 19: 'Very little had been done on the subject of the conflict of laws in England and America prior to Story.'

[146] Lorenzen argued that there were upwards of 500 decisions from Anglo-American courts on private international law by the time Joseph Story came to write his seminal work, although the same author argued that 'Problems of the conflict of laws did not come before the English courts before the middle of the eighteenth century', which is not quite correct. See Lorenzen (n 34), 18. As will be shown, there *are* earlier relevant decisions.

[147] Although law reporting in England was of a higher standard than in Scotland. Its history in England is analysed in depth in VV Veeder, 'The English Reports (I): 1292–1865' (1901) 15 *Harvard Law Review* 1; VV Veeder, 'The English Reports (II): 1292–1865' (1901) 15 *Harvard Law Review* 109.

[148] *Ranelaugh v Champante* (1700) 2 Vern 395; 23 ER 855.

[149] *Ranelaugh v Champant* (1700) 1 Eq Ca Abr 289; 21 ER 1052.

The clear weaknesses of early English case law can make it difficult to draw definitive conclusions on matters of English law prior to or at the turn of the eighteenth century. Despite this, there is a tendency when considering historical points of English law to state propositions that may not be justifiable based on the evidence available. It has been argued in relation to the case of *Earl of Dungannon v Hackett* (1702):[150]

> Interest thus takes a special place in English conflict of laws: *Dungannon* v *Hackett* was the first decision in which an English court ever applied foreign (Irish) law. It is the springboard with which England broke away from the pre-choice of law, one dimensional, domestic law approach. [Translation by author][151]

The submission that *Dungannon* (1702) was the first case in which foreign law was applied in England is questionable, even based on the case report itself.[152] Thus, *Dungannon* (1702) appears to state that other precedents were cited to the court for the purposes of deciding the case, for example, the undated case of *Lane*, in which Turkish interest was allowed on a contract made in Turkey, though both parties had long been in England.[153] In other words, as the case of *Lane* is said to have been cited as a precedent in *Dungannon* (1702), it follows that *Lane* must have been heard by the English court before it. The reality is that it may be impossible to say with certainty when foreign law was first applied by the English court.

Moreover, the argument that *Dungannon* (1702) was the springboard for the development of choice of law rules in England generally is questionable, absent there being a demonstrable chain of cases drawing on *Dungannon* (1702), which there is not. For example, the case only appears to be mentioned once in Joseph Story's 1834 first edition text[154] and once in Westlake's 1858 first edition text,[155] although the case is referred to in at least one important case of the time.[156] In short, cases originating from pre-nineteenth century England should be approached with the greatest degree of caution. It is in this light that the following analysis is conducted.

[150] The case is mentioned at *Earl of Dungannon v Hackett* (1702) 1 Eq Ca Abr 289; 21 ER 1051.

[151] O Brand, *Das Internationale Zinsrecht Englands* (JCB Mohr (Paul Siebeck), 2002), 116: 'Der Zins nimmt damit einen besonderen Rang im englischen Kollisionsrecht ein: *Dungannon v Hackett* war die erste Entscheidung, in der ein englisches Gericht überhaupt ausländisches (irisches) Recht zur Anwendung brachte … Es ist das Sprungbrett, mit dem sich England aus der vorkollisionsrechtlichen Eindimensionalität heimischen Rechts löste.'

[152] Note that in Brand (ibid, at 116), it is implied that '*Dungannon v Hackett*, *Lane v Nichols*, *Harvey v East India Company* und *Bodily v Bellamy*' were decided by or close to the end of the eighteenth century. However, the cases all appear to have been decided earlier than this. For example, the case of *Dungannon* (1702) is dated the Trinity term of 1702, ie the start of the eighteenth century. This may be a typographical error.

[153] *Lane v Nichols* 21 ER 1051.

[154] Story (n 32), 257.

[155] Westlake, *A Treatise on Private International Law or the Conflict of Laws* (n 17), 192.

[156] *Robinson v Bland* (1760) 1 W Bl 234; 96 ER 129, 130, although *Dungannon* (1702) can hardly be viewed as forming the crux of the court's reasoning in the case, being only referred to in the plaintiff's submissions. It is notable that the Scottish court appears to have been aware of developments in England in relation to the application of foreign interest to English judgments. See *Savage v Craig*

(ii) Conceptual Treatment

One of the earliest references in English case law to the concept that foreign law was not a matter of judicial notice was the case of *Fremoult* (1718),[157] which drew on the earlier case of *Foubert* (1703).[158]

Foubert (1703) concerned a French marriage contract, which the deceased wife's relatives sought to rely on. The case was first heard by the Court of Chancery but with a differently spelled name: *Feaubert* (1702).[159] The defendant argued that the plaintiff could not take advantage of Parisian law, which was only local law, to which the plaintiff responded:

> Marriage Contracts are to be supported in all Countries, without Regard to the Place where made; and that this Contract did extend to the whole Fortune of the Wife, and not only to the Particulars mentioned; and the saying the rest should go according to the Custom of Paris, is as much as if the Custom had been recited at large, and that the Fortune should go so.[160]

The Court of Chancery appears to have refused to recognise the marriage contract, but no substantive reasoning is given in the case report. However, it was subsequently held by the House of Lords that the marriage contract should be given effect to,[161] and it can be inferred from the case report that evidence was led as to the effect of the marriage contract in France. Nonetheless, the appellant appears to have played down the idea that the House of Lords was being asked to apply foreign law in the case:

> The right of the appellants arose from the express agreement of the parties, that there should be a community of all goods or estates, moveable and immoveable; and that the additional words, *pursuant to the custom of* Paris, were but explanatory of what was meant by the word *community* … but by no means an attempt to introduce *foreign* laws or customs as binding here, any otherwise than by experts and positive agreement.[162]

Thus, the plaintiff appears to have sought to frame matters in terms of contractual interpretation rather than as an application of Parisian law, while, importantly, acknowledging the possibility of proving foreign law in a case using experts.

[1710] Mor 4530. In *Scrimshire v Scrimshire* (1752) 2 Hagg (Consist) 395, the English court discussed choice of law in respect of foreign marriages, but there is no mention of *Dungannon* (1702). At 412 of *Scrimshire* (1752), it was held, with extensive reference to, inter alia, writers of the Dutch school such as Voet: 'They may change the forum, but they must be tried by the laws of the country which they left. This doctrine of trying contracts, especially those of marriage, according to the laws of the country where they were made, is conformable to what is laid down in our books, and what is practised in all civilized countries, and what is agreeable to the law of nations, which is the law of every particular country, and taken notice of as such.'

[157] *Fremoult v Dedire* (1718) 1 P Wms 429; 24 ER 458.
[158] *Foubert v Turst* (1703) 1 Brown 129; 1 ER 464.
[159] *Feaubert v Turst* (1702) Prec Ch 207; 24 ER 101, 102.
[160] *Feaubert v Turst* (1702) Prec Ch 207; 24 ER 101, 102.
[161] *Foubert v Turst* (1703) 1 Brown 129, 132; 1 ER 464.
[162] *Foubert v Turst* (1703) 1 Brown 129, 131; 1 ER 464.

While *Foubert* (1703) does appear to have given the most restrictive application to Parisian law possible, the case is significant in the development of private international law in England for two reasons. First, the case was appealed to the House of Lords, which in turn appears to have countenanced, in principle, the possibility for the recognition and application of foreign law in an English court. Second, *Foubert* (1703) impacted on two subsequent cases, namely *Fremoult* (1718) and *Mostyn* (1774).

In *Fremoult* (1718), the marriage contract being relied on had been made in Holland. It was argued:

> That these marriage articles were made in *Holland*, and that by the law of *Holland*, such articles take place of any other debts, wherefore they should be here construed according to the law of *Holland*, where they appeared to have been made, which was said to have been held in the case of *Feaubert* and *Turst*.[163]

An important issue in the case was the fact that the plaintiff had failed to aver the content of the relevant foreign law:

> To which it was answered, and so ruled, that it ought to have been proved in this case what is the law of Holland, as in the case of *Feaubert and Turst* it was proved what was the law of France, without which proofs our courts cannot take notice of foreign laws.[164]

Thus, *Fremoult* (1718) provided clear authority that the English court would not take notice of foreign law in the absence of averments and proof adduced by the party seeking to rely on it. Subsequently, in *Mostyn* (1774), Lord Mansfield held:

> The way of knowing foreign laws is, by admitting them to be *proved* as *facts*, and the court must assist the jury in ascertaining what the law is. For instance, if there is a *French* settlement the construction of which depends upon the custom of *Paris*, witnesses must be received to explain what the custom is; as evidence is received of customs in respect of trade. There is a case of the kind I have just stated.[165]

Lord Mansfield's reference in *Mostyn* (1774) to the custom of Paris was undoubtedly an implied reference to *Foubert* (1703) and, indeed, *Foubert* (1703) is referenced with an asterisk in the *Mostyn* (1774) case report.[166] *Mostyn* (1774) is a particularly important case in so far that it appears to have crystallised the development of the fact approach in English law. It also played a significant role in the development of the fact approach in the US, being cited, together with *Fremoult* (1718), in the foundational US Supreme Court case of *Church* (1804).[167]

[163] *Fremoult v Dedire* (1718) 1 P Wms 429, 431; 24 ER 458.
[164] *Fremoult v Dedire* (1718) 1 P Wms 429; 24 ER 458.
[165] *Mostyn v Fabrigas* (1774) 1 Cowper 161, 174; 98 ER 1021.
[166] *Mostyn v Fabrigas* (1774) 1 Cowper 161, 174; 98 ER 1021.
[167] *Church v Hubbart* 6 US (2 Cranch) 187 (1804); The case of *Talbot v Seeman* 5 US (1 Cranch) 1 (1801) first mentioned the fact approach and was heard a little earlier than *Church v Hubbart* 6 US (2 Cranch) 187 (1804) but appears to have been a little less influential. *Church* (1804) is cited in RB Schlesinger, 'Die Behandlung des Fremdrechts im Amerikanischen Zivilprozess' (1962) 27 *Rabels Zeitschrift für Ausländisches und Internationales Privatrecht* 54, 57; MJ Ahn, '44.1 Luftballons: The

However, it should not be thought that *Mostyn* (1774) itself created the fact approach in English law.[168] It rather appears that the fact approach developed in English law through the combination of *Foubert* (1703), *Fremoult* (1718), and *Mostyn* (1774). First, *Foubert* (1703) afforded the House of Lords an opportunity to give support to the principle that an English court can take heed of foreign law when reaching its decisions. Second, *Fremoult* (1718) established the principles that a failure to plead and adduce evidence of foreign law means that a party cannot later rely on it when stating their case; nor can the court judicially note it. Finally, in *Mostyn* (1774), Lord Mansfield stated the principle that foreign law should be regarded as a matter of fact requiring proof in English law.

(iii) Influence of Scottish Practice

Assuming that Lord Mansfield was responsible for crystallising the fact approach in English law through his decision in *Mostyn* (1774), the question is whether existing Scottish practice played a role in his reasoning, especially in the circumstances that (as proven in the previous section) the fact approach had developed in Scotland prior to the turn of the eighteenth century. There are several factors suggesting the existence of a link.

First, Lord Mansfield, an English barrister with a Scottish heritage, essentially built his career on the presentation of Scottish appeals to the House of Lords.[169] He was accordingly familiar with Scottish case law and institutional writings. Second, the Scottish institutional writers were consistent in their treatment of foreign law as fact, and the principle that foreign law should be treated as fact had been established in their writings by the mid-eighteenth century. Third, the principle that foreign law should be considered a matter of fact does not appear to have been clearly enunciated in England prior to *Mostyn* (1774). Thus, Lord Mansfield may have been influenced by existing Scottish authority when he decided this pivotal case.

On the other hand, the basic approach to be taken to foreign law in England had probably been settled by the House of Lords as early as *Foubert* (1703), something recognised by the references to *Foubert* (1703) in *Fremoult* (1718). In addition, foreign law was being applied by English courts during the early eighteenth century

Communication Breakdown of Foreign Law in the Federal Courts' (2014) 89 *New York University Law Review* 1343, 1351. Both cases were, however, recently referred to by the US Supreme Court in *Animal Science Products Inc v Hebei Welcome Pharmaceutical Co Ltd* (2018) 585 US ___ (Slip Opinion), 7, as setting out the fact approach.

[168] It is respectfully suggested that T Rogoz, *Ausländisches Recht im deutschen und englischen Zivilprozess* (Mohr Siebeck, 2008), 68, placed too much weight on *Mostyn v Fabrigas* (1774) 1 Cowper 161; 98 ER 1021.

[169] Heward (n 24), 16ff. William Murray (later Lord Mansfield) appears in numerous Scottish appeals to the House of Lords from 1733, including *Fullerton v Kinloch* (1740) 1 Paton 265; *Wauchope and Agnes v Wauchope* (1737) 1 Paton 200; *Bayne and Morrison v Earl of Sutherland* (1750) 1 Paton 454; *Midwinter v Kincaid* (1751) 1 Paton 488; and *Gordon v HM Advocate* (1754) 1 Paton 558.

in cases other than *Foubert* (1703), for example, in cases involving the application of foreign interest,[170] meaning that English judges were required to apply their minds to the application of foreign law before *Mostyn* (1774) was decided.[171] These points, together with a lack of any explicit reference by Lord Mansfield in *Mostyn* (1774) to Scottish authority, mean that Scottish influence in the development of the fact approach in England, while likely, can ultimately only ever be a matter of speculation.[172]

(iv) Mechanisms of Proof

The process involved in proving the content of foreign law in the English courts throughout the eighteenth and early nineteenth centuries appears to have followed few rules. It was, however, recognised as a matter of some controversy in the courts and the academic community. Thus, Westlake argued in 1858 that:

> The nature of the evidence which must be given of the foreign law has been the subject of much doubt, nor is it certain that the same views are now entertained on it in England and the United States.[173]

In the earliest English cases, as in Scotland, it is often unclear how foreign law was proven. For example, in *Foubert* (1703), there is inconclusive reference to the use of experts, and, on the basis of the report, one is left guessing as to how the court established Parisian law in the case.[174] Whilst there is a suggestion in *Fremoult* (1718) that the content of the relevant Parisian law was proven in some way in *Foubert* (1703), there is no evidence of how this was done in the *Fremoult* (1718) case report either.[175] In *Fremoult* (1718) itself, it was the failure of the plaintiff to even attempt to prove the law of Holland that appears to have formed the basis of the court's refusal to apply foreign law.[176]

There is no evidence that early English courts referred matters to foreign courts for consideration, such as appears to have been done by Scottish courts during the seventeenth century. The two methods which appear to have been used in the

[170] *Ranelaugh v Champant* (1700) 1 Eq Ca Abr 289; 21 ER 1052 and *Dungannon v Hackett* (1702) 1 Eq Ca Abr 289; 21 ER 1051. See the discussion in Brand (n 151), 115ff, although, as discussed previously, issue is taken with the view stated as to the importance of foreign interest in, and the sequence of, the development of English private international law.

[171] It is also certainly possible that existing Scottish practice had found its way into other (unreported) English cases in the period preceding *Mostyn v Fabrigas* (1774) 1 Cowper 161; 98 ER 1021, with the decision in *Mostyn* (1774) simply confirming existing (imported) English practice.

[172] One proposition put forward is that Lord Mansfield's expertise in dealing with evidence of trade customs gave him a basis with which to approach foreign law. See Rogoz (n 168), 63. Another proposition is that, at the relevant point in the English legal system's development, having applied judicial notice only to English law, there was no other way to approach foreign law other than by treating it as fact. See R Fentiman, *Foreign Law in English Courts: Pleading, Proof and Choice of Law* (Oxford University Press, 1998), 5.

[173] Westlake, *A Treatise on Private International Law or the Conflict of Laws* (n 17), 394.

[174] *Foubert v Turst* (1703) 1 Brown 129; 1 ER 464.

[175] *Fremoult v Dedire* (1718) 1 P Wms 429; 24 ER 458.

[176] *Fremoult v Dedire* (1718) 1 P Wms 429, 431.

English courts to prove the content of foreign law were proof by way of authenticated documentary evidence and proof by means of evidence from witnesses. In most cases, the two were used together. Thus, in *Dalrymple* (1811), when considering the validity of a Scottish marriage in England, the English court referred to a range of sources to determine the content of Scottish marriage law:

> The authorities to which I shall have occasion to refer are of three classes; first, the opinions of learned professors given in the present or similar cases; secondly, the opinions of eminent writers as delivered in books of great legal credit and weight; and, thirdly, the certified adjudication of the tribunals of Scotland upon these subjects.[177]

The court stated that, as a matter of principle, it was not prepared to conclude whether any one of those sources should be considered more authoritative than the other considering that:

> It will be the undoubted duty of the Court which has to weigh them, stare decisis.[178]

In *Lacon* (1822), the judge appears to have required, and accepted, a printed copy of the written law of France, *Code Civil*,[179] as well as the evidence of a French diplomatic official,[180] to prove the content of that law.[181] However, parties waived 'all objection as to the admissibility of the evidence of the marriage law in France',[182] with the court noting that the 'general rule certainly was, that the written law of a foreign country must be provided by an examined copy'.[183]

There is authority which suggests that oral evidence alone was not sufficient evidence of written foreign law in English courts of the time. Thus, in *Boehtlinch* (1799), in response to the plaintiff's request to call evidence from a witness conversant in Russian law to prove the content of that law without any written evidence, it was asked:

> Can the laws of a foreign country be proved by a person who may be casually picked up in the street? Can a court of justice receive such evidence of such a matter? I shall expect it to be made out to me, not by such loose evidence, but by proof from the country, whose laws you propose to give in evidence, properly authenticated.[184]

The same approach appears to have been taken by the English court in *Millar* (1815), in which it was held:

> That will not do. Foreign laws not written are to be proved by the parol examination of witnesses of competent skill. But where they are in writing, a copy properly authenticated must be produced.[185]

[177] *Dalrymple v Dalrymple* (1811) 2 Hagg (Consist) 54, 81; 161 ER 665.
[178] *Dalrymple v Dalrymple* (1811) 2 Hagg (Consist) 54; 161 ER 665.
[179] *Lacon v Higgins alias Isaac* (1822) Dowl & Ry NP 38; 171 ER 910, 912.
[180] *Lacon v Higgins alias Isaac* (1822) Dowl & Ry NP 38; 171 ER 910, 913.
[181] *Lacon v Higgins alias Isaac* (1822) Dowl & Ry NP 38; 171 ER 910, 912.
[182] *Lacon v Higgins alias Isaac* (1822) Dowl & Ry NP 38; 171 ER 910, 913.
[183] *Lacon v Higgins alias Isaac* (1822) Dowl & Ry NP 38; 171 ER 910, 912.
[184] *Boehtlinck v Schneider* (1799) 3 Espinasse 58, 59.
[185] *Millar v Heinrick* (1815) 4 Campbell 155, 155–56.

In *Middleton* (1802), the court recognised the existing English authority 'that it ought to have had an authentic exemplification of the laws and ordinances of those countries', but noted the practical difficulties in obtaining such evidence, and the fact that the relevant parts of the foreign law had been referred to and copied into the foreign lawyers' opinion.[186] Thus, the plaintiff's eight (!) gentlemen witnesses 'well acquainted with the laws of those countries' were considered to provide sufficient evidence to satisfy the court that the marriage was null and void.[187] In terms of the recognition of foreign judgments, it appears that an authenticated judgment was not always accepted as sufficient by the English court, which sometimes expected further evidence as to the relevant country's substantive law.[188]

Notable scepticism towards documentary evidence alone appears to have developed in the English courts by the mid-nineteenth century.[189] In *Baron de Bode's Case* (1845), it was held:

> The question for us is, not what the language of the written law is, but what the law is altogether, as shewn by exposition, interpretation and adjudication. How many errors might result if a foreign Court attempted to collect the law from the language of some of our statutes … I am merely shewing that our Courts require, not the actual written words of a foreign law, but the law itself; for which purpose a professional witness is required to expound it.[190]

[186] *Middleton v Janverin, falsely calling herself Middleton* (1802) 2 Hagg (Consist) 437, 442; 161 ER 797.

[187] *Middleton v Janverin, falsely calling herself Middleton* (1802) 2 Hagg (Consist) 437, 443; 161 ER 797.

[188] *Ganer v Lady Lanesborough* (1790) Peake 25, 25–26.

[189] Some concerns agitating English judges of the time were spelled out by Lord Langdale in *Earl Nelson v Lord Bridport* (1845) 8 Beavan 527, 535; 50 ER 207: 'Even if we suppose it to be proved, that the law has not been legislatively repealed or varied, and has not fallen into disuse, and that the words have been accurately translated, still the words require due construction, and the construction depends on the meaning of words to be considered with reference to otherwords not contained in the mere text of the law, and also with reference to the subject-matter, which is not insulated from all others. The construction may have been, probably has been, the subject of judicial decision: instead of one decision, there may have been a long succession of decisions, varying, more or less, from each other, and ultimately ending in that which alone ought to be applied in the particular case.'

[190] *Baron de Bode's Case* (1845) 8 QB 208; 115 ER 854, 875. See also *Earl Nelson v Lord Bridport* (1846) 8 Beavan 547, 560; 50 ER 207 (Lord Langdale), which draws attention to the risk of authorities cited having been subsequently 'repealed or altered.' The reasoning of *Baron de Bode's Case* (1845) 8 QB 208; 115 ER 854 was referred to by the House of Lords in the famous case *The Sussex Peerage* (1844) 11 Cl & Fin 85, 116; 8 ER 1034, with Lord Langdale also sitting as a judge in the case. In response to a suggestion from Lord Campbell that 'the most authoritative form of getting at foreign law, is to have the book which lays down the law', Lord Brougham replied (at 114–15) that 'it is perfectly clear that the proper mode of proving a foreign law is not by showing to the House the book of the law; for the House has not the organs to know and to deal with the text of that law, and therefore requires the assistance of a lawyer who knows how to interpret it.' These competing viewpoints were noted and discussed by the US Supreme Court in *Ennis v Smith* 55 US (14 How) 400 (1852), 426–30, which itself considered, at 429, that the French *Code Civil* 'certified to the court as it is, is sufficiently authenticated to make it evidence in this suit, and that it would be so in any other case in which it may be offered.' Thus, the US Supreme Court did not consider it necessary to have expert evidence to apply the French Civil Code, stating the general principle, at 429: 'In our view it is this, that a foreign written law may be received, when it is found in a statute book, with proof that the book has been officially published by the government which made the law.'

Westlake, referring to *Baron de Bode's Case* (1845), also appears to have been sceptical about documentary evidence on its own on the basis that foreign law is liable to change:

> And I may add that the point to be proved is always what the foreign law was at a certain moment of time, so that if the written law be of an earlier date, it may have been altered during the interval.[191]

English case law from the mid-nineteenth century onwards is considered in the next chapter. However, by the mid-nineteenth century, the English approach towards the proof of foreign law reflected, on one hand, the main weakness of the common law system in so far that the case law was fluid and inconsistent, while on the other, the fact that English judges were weighing up the strength of the evidence in the individual cases before them. Nonetheless, a distinct preference had developed in favour of requiring expert evidence in all cases, regardless of whether the applicable foreign law was in statutory form or not.

II. Germany

To understand the following discussion, it should be noted that prior to 1871, Germany was not a unified nation-state. Accordingly, different legal systems existed throughout the territorial States that later came to comprise Germany. The British historian Martin Kitchen described Germany at the turn of the nineteenth century as:

> A ramshackle empire, made up of hundreds of petty principalities, free cities, and ecclesiastical and aristocratic estates.[192]

It follows that there was no uniform German Code of Civil Procedure (ZPO)[193] as there is today, and different rules of civil procedure were to be found throughout the pre-unification States.[194] Moreover, there was no uniform German Civil Code (BGB).[195] Rather, the various pre-unification cities and States mostly still had multi-layered legal systems comprising both local (or particular) laws and a form of the *ius commune*,[196] although by the turn of the nineteenth century steps

[191] Westlake, *A Treatise on Private International Law or the Conflict of Laws* (n 17), 394.

[192] M Kitchen, *A History of Modern Germany: 1800 to the Present*, 2nd edn (Wiley-Blackwell, 2012), 1.

[193] The uniform German Code of Civil Procedure (then referred to as the CPO) entered into force on 1 October 1879. See L Gaupp (ed) and F Stein, *Die Civilprozeßordnung für das Deutsche Reich*, 4th edn (JCB Mohr (Paul Siebeck), 1901), 3ff. Further discussion of its drafting history follows in due course.

[194] A Heffter, *System des römischen und deutschen Civil-Proceßrechts* (Adolph Marcus, 1843), 24ff.

[195] The uniform German Civil Code (BGB) entered into force on 1 January 1900. See, for a concise account of its drafting history, FJ Säcker, 'Einleitung (Einl. BGB)' in C Schubert (ed), *Münchener Kommentar zum Bürgerlichen Gesetzbuch: Band 1 (Allgemeiner Teil §§ 1–240, AllgPersönlR, ProstG, AGG)*, 9th edn (CH Beck, 2021), para 11ff.

[196] There were circumstances where either or none could apply, ie a just solution would have to be found. A lawyer would have had to orientate themselves within this flexible, multilayered system.

had been taken in some pre-unification States towards codifying elements of their private law.[197]

The following analysis focuses on the major pre-unification German States, eg Prussia, and is substantively based on three sources: (1) legislation, which comprises the codes and draft codes of civil procedure of the pre-unification German States; (2) academic literature; and (3) case law emanating from appellate courts. The sources, which are dealt with in turn, are explained as they are addressed.

A. Legislative[198]

One of the most significant pre-unification States comprising what later became Germany was Prussia.[199] A relatively comprehensive code of civil procedure, the *Allgemeine Gerichtsordnung für die Preußischen Staaten* (Prussian Code of

See M Gebauer, *Grundfragen der Europäisierung des Privatrechts: Eine Untersuchung nationaler Ansätze unter Berücksichtigung des italienischen und des deutschen Rechts* (Universitätsverlag C Winter, 1998), 32–37. It is thought that the influence of Roman law was comparatively greater in the pre-unification German states, than, for example, in France. This was, in part, due to the lack of a centralised legal focal point (eg a capital city such as Paris or London) as well as the strong, independent territorial States of medieval Germany. See K Zweigert and H Kötz, *Einführung in die Rechtsvergleichung: auf dem Gebiete des Privatrechts*, 3rd edn (JCB Mohr (Paul Siebeck), 1996), 131–33. Interestingly, the approach taken in the pre-unification German States appears to find resonance in sixteenth- and seventeenth-century Scotland. See the early seventeenth-century manuscript of a Scottish lawyer for an English audience, which was printed and discussed in JD Mackie and WC Dickinson, 'Relation of the Manner of Judicatores of Scotland' (1922) 19 *The Scottish Historical Review* 245, especially, 268: 'There is noe common lawe in Scotland, but the Judge eyther proceedeth accordinge to warrant of the municypall lawe, which is the statutes of Parliament, and that faylinge they have recourse and doe decide accordinge to the ymperiall civill law.' The reference to the imperial civil law, rather than the *ius commune*, is thought to have been to avoid confusion with the English conception of the common law. See Cairns, 'Ius Civile in Scotland, ca. 1600' (n 69), 148. For a summary of the complex and controversial interplay in Scotland between the *ius commune* and *ius proprium*, see Cairns, ibid, 168. It should be noted that reference to the *ius commune* in Scots law was wider than simply as subsidiary law. See, Cairns, 'Attitudes to Codification and the Scottish Science of Legislation, 1600–1830' (n 2), 8. The matter is also touched on at 6ff.

[197] For example, see the *Allgemeines Landrecht für die Preußichen Staaten* of 1794, which applied in the pre-unification State of Prussia. Zweigert and Kötz (n 196), 134–36; G Wesenberg and G Wesener, *Neuere deutsche Privatrechtsgeschichte: im Rahmen der europäischen Rechtsentwicklung*, 3rd edn (Moritz Schauenburg, 1976), 145–46; SF Fortunato, 'Vom römisch-gemeinen Recht zum Bürgerlichen Gesetzbuch' (2009) *Zeitschrift für das Juristische Studium* 327. For a comprehensive list of which form of private law was applied to the different cities and states prior to the entering into force of the uniform German Civil Code (BGB), see Säcker (n 195), paras 13–14.

[198] The focus of this analysis is on the period covering the late eighteenth century to the late nineteenth century. Civil procedure in pre-unification Germany prior to this was constituted by many local procedural codes based, in part, on Roman law. It was during the period of this analysis that substantial reform took place. See H-J Musielak, *Die Grundlagen der Beweislast im Zivilprozeß* (Walter de Gruyter GmbH & Co KG, 1975), 265–66. There is no evidence that the legislative position prior to the late eighteenth century influenced the unified German Code of Civil Procedure (ZPO), as it relates to the content of this work.

[199] Kitchen (n 192), 1.

Civil Procedure), was introduced throughout Prussia in 1795.[200] The Prussian Code of Civil Procedure was a substantial work divided into 52 sections and spanned well over a thousand pages. It covered a wide range of procedural matters, including those of evidence, appeals, and costs.[201] It was stated at § 53 of the tenth section:[202]

> If, on the other hand, there is a dispute regarding a matter which must be judged according to foreign laws, which the judge is not required to know; and matters depend on what this law actually prescribes for the present case: so, as with other facts, evidence must be taken. [Translation by author][203]

This rule of the Prussian Code of Civil Procedure thus clearly stated matters of foreign law to be a question of fact. In treating foreign law as a question of fact requiring evidence, § 55 of the tenth section addressed matters of custom in a similar way:

> When the parties are not in agreement, it should be, as other disputed facts, proven through the taking of evidence. [Translation by author][204]

It is notable that § 55 of the tenth section provided the possibility for parties to agree the content of the relevant rule of custom, an approach that would not be considered acceptable today as modern German procedural law does not allow the court to be bound by party agreement as to the content of rules of custom (or foreign law).[205]

Bavaria first published its *Codex Iuris Bavarici Iudiciarii* in 1753, which was subsequently introduced throughout the State.[206] While the *Codex Iuris Bavarici Iudiciarii* did not use the term *ausländisches Recht* (foreign law), § 3 of the ninth chapter stated:

> One should prove only the history (or narrative), but not the law itself, *particular statuta*, and customs excluded, which, when they are not publicly known, must also be proven. [Translation by author][207]

[200] The *Allgemeine Gerichtsordnung für die Preußischen Staaten* replaced the *Corpus Juris Fridericianum*, which had been introduced in 1781. See MCFW Grävell, *Praktischer Kommentar zur allgemeinen Gerichts-Ordnung für die preußischen Staaten* (Keyser'sche Buchhandlung, 1825), 13ff.

[201] This is clear from its well-presented table of contents.

[202] The tenth section (*Zehnter Titel*) is headed: 'Von der Instruktion der Sache zum Definitiverkenntnisse' ('From the beginning of the action to the conclusion of the evidential stage') [Translation by author].

[203] § 53 of the tenth section of the Prussian Code of Civil Procedure: 'Wenn hingegen über ein Geschäft gestritten wird, welches nach fremden Landesgesetzen, die der Richter zu kennen nicht schuldig ist, beurtheilt werden muß; und es darauf ankommt, was diese Gesetze für den vorliegenden Fall eigentlich verordnen: so muß darüber, so wie über eine andere Thatsache, Beweis aufgenommen werden.'

[204] § 55 of the tenth section of the Prussian Code of Civil Procedure: 'wenn die Parteien darüber nicht einig sind, gleich andern bestrittenen Thatsachen, durch Beweisesaufnehmung ins Licht gesetzt werden.'

[205] Schack (n 137), para 756.

[206] JA Seuffert, *Handbuch des deutschen Civilprozesses auf der Grundlage und nach der Ordnung der bayerischen Gesetzgebung*, 2nd edn (JJ Palm & Ernst Enke, 1853), 1ff.

[207] § 3 of the ninth chapter of the *Codex Iuris Bavarici Iudiciarii*: 'Soll man nur die Geschichte, nicht aber das Recht selbst beweisen, Particular-Statuta, und Gewohnheiten ausgenommen, welche, wann sie nicht offentlich Kundbar seien, ebenfalls dargetan werden müssen.'

This suggests that foreign law under the *Codex Iuris Bavarici Iudiciarii* was subject to the rules of evidence governing facts, assuming the law of any foreign state was encapsulated by (or treated in the same way as) particular law.[208] There is some evidence in a commentary from 1755 that particular and customary law should indeed be considered a matter of fact rather than law,[209] together with the question:

> How and in what way are particular laws in foreign places to be proved? [Translation by author][210]

The 1839 draft Commercial Code for the Kingdom of Württemberg (*Entwurf eines Handelsgesetzbuches für das Königreich Württemberg*) appears to have left the potential application of foreign law in the hands of the parties, though it did not address the question of evidence. Article 997 of the draft code stated:

> In those cases where the law allows the judge to apply foreign law, this may only happen at the request of a party. [Translation by author][211]

As the nineteenth century progressed, the approach to be taken when applying foreign law began featuring more consistently in the procedural laws of the pre-unification German States. § 216 of the 1850 Hannover Code of Civil Procedure (*Allgemeine bürgerliche Prozessordnung für das Königreich Hannover*)[212] stated:

> The burden of proof must be allocated in such a way that the individual particulars of those facts, foreign laws, statutes, customs and also laws, in so far as the latter are permitted in terms of § 185, are specifically given. [Translation by author][213]

The approach in the pre-unification German states in respect of foreign law appears to have taken a modern turn during the later nineteenth century, ie giving the court control of the issue rather than the parties. Thus, § 321 of the

[208] It is notable that the approach traditionally taken to the customary law of the cities and States in pre-unification Germany has similarities to the modern treatment of foreign law under § 293 of the German Code of Civil Procedure, at least in terms of how § 293 is worded, as well as to the English fact approach. Customary law required to be proven, even if it was applicable in the locality of the court. Otherwise, the *ius commume* (or a form of it) would be applied to the facts of the case. See Wesenberg and Wesener (n 197), 80, and Gebauer (n 196), 38–39.

[209] Unknown Authors, *Anmerkungen über den Codicem Juris Bavarici Judiciarii* (Johann Jacob Vötter, 1755), 318.

[210] ibid, 318: 'Wie und auf was Weis aber Particular-Statuta an fremden Orten bewiesen werden müssen?'

[211] Article 997 of the 1839 draft commercial code for the Kingdom of Württemberg in Unknown Authors, *Entwurf eines Handelsgesetzbuches für das Königreich Württemberg* (JB Meßler'schen Buchhandlung, 1839), 299–300: 'In denjenigen Fällen, wo das Gesetz dem Richter erlaubt das ausländische Recht in Anwendung zu bringen, hat dies nur auf Anrufen der Partei zu geschehen.'

[212] The Hannover Code of Civil Procedure of 1850 appears to have been particularly renowned and influential at the time. See C Wolf and S Klein, 'Die Wiege der ZPO' in T Freudenberg (ed), *70. Deutscher Juristentag in Hannover: 16. bis 19. September 2014* (Redaktionsbeilage zu NJW, CH Beck, 2014).

[213] § 216 of the 1850 Hannover Code of Civil Procedure: 'Der Beweissatz ist so zu bestimmen, daß die einzelnen eines Beweises bedürfenden Thatsachen, fremden Gesetze, Statuten und Gewohnheiten oder auch Rechte, insofern lezteres nach § 185 zulässig ist, genau anegeben werden.'

revised 1869 Bavarian Code of Civil Procedure (*Prozessordnung in bürgerlichen Rechtsstreitigkeiten*) dealt with matters of foreign law by allowing the judge to use his own knowledge, failing which, giving him the power to order that evidence be provided:

> The court can require evidence to be produced with regards foreign laws and statutes, when these are not reliably known to it. [Translation by author][214]

Work towards a code of civil procedure for a unified Germany essentially appears to have begun as early as 1867, in the form of work carried out with view to creation of a Code of Civil Procedure for the North German Confederation (*Prozeßordnung in bürgerlichen Rechtsstreitigkeiten für den Norddeutschen Bund*). A commission is said to have worked on the draft over a period of about two years and to have met 288 times.[215] The initial draft, published in 1870, provided a rule for the application of foreign law at § 439:

> The law of another state requires evidence only insofar as it is unknown to the court. In determining this law, the court is not limited to the evidence provided by the parties, it is authorised to use other sources and to order what is necessary *ex proprio motu*. [Translation by author][216]

Following unification of Germany in 1871, the law of civil procedure became a matter regulated by federal law.[217] Work then officially started in May 1871 on a uniform code of civil procedure.[218] The draft code of civil procedure was based substantially on the draft 1870 Code of Civil Procedure for the North German Confederation. A draft was laid before the Reichstag in 1874.[219]

At § 255, the 1874 draft German Code of Civil Procedure (the Civilprozessordnung (CPO)) contained substantially the same wording as what came to be numbered § 265 of the CPO when enacted in 1877. As has been previously stated, § 265 of the 1877 CPO was in the same terms as is § 293 of the current

[214] § 321 of the revised 1869 Bavarian Code of Civil Procedure: 'Ueber ausländische Gesetze und Statuten kann das Gericht Beweis verlangen, wenn sie ihm nicht zuverlässig bekannt sind.'

[215] This information appears on the first page after the title page of Unknown Authors, *Entwurf einer Prozeßordnung in bürgerlichen Rechtsstreitigkeiten für den Norddeutschen Bund* (Königlichen Geheimen Ober-Hofbuchdruckerei, 1870). A different account of how many times and when the commission met is provided in Gaupp (ed) and Stein (n 193), 7, where it is said that the commission met 390 times over a slightly longer period of time.

[216] This is effectively what is currently set out in relation to foreign law in § 293 of the German Code of Civil Procedure, although there is no mention of custom in § 439 of the draft code: 'Das in einem anderen Staate geltende Recht bedarf des Beweises nur insofern, als es dem Gerichte unbekannt ist. Bei Ermittelung dieses Rechts ist das Gericht auf die von den Parteiein beigebrachten Nachweise nicht beschränkt, es ist befugt, auch andere Erkenntnißquellen zu benutzen und zum Zwecke einer solchen Benutzung geeignetenfalls das Erforderliche von Amtswegen anzuordnen.'

[217] C Hahn, *Die gesammten Materialien zur Civilprozessordnung und dem Einführungsgesetz zu derselben vom 30 Januar 1877* (RV Decker, 1880), Begründung des Entwurfs, § 1.

[218] ibid, Vorwort.

[219] Gaupp (ed) and Stein (n 193), 9.

German Code of Civil Procedure (Zivilprozessordnung (ZPO)), the terms of which were outlined in the introduction to this work. The current wording of § 293 can therefore be traced directly back to the 1874 draft German Code of Civil Procedure.

In the explanatory memorandum to the draft German Code of Civil Procedure,[220] there is little evidence of controversy, but also little useful information as to how the, then, § 255 ought to be interpreted. Many questions, such as the possibility for appeal on points of foreign law, and the mechanisms for proof of its content, were neither discussed by the parliamentary committee nor addressed in the vague terms of the paragraph itself. There is reference in the explanatory memorandum to a number of codes of civil procedure, including the draft 1870 Code of Civil Procedure for the North German Confederation and the 1869 revised Bavarian Code of Civil Procedure.[221] It is stated that the draft § 255, which was later adopted, reflected new (or recent) doctrine and practice.[222]

By the time the justice committee of the Reichstag looked at the paragraph, it had been renumbered as § 265.[223] It then appears to have been adopted by the justice committee without any discussion.[224]

The conclusion that can be drawn from the legislative sources is that during the nineteenth century there was a shift away from (a form of) the fact approach to the modern German approach towards foreign law in the pre-unification German States. The shift was then confirmed by the terms of the then § 265 of the German Code of Civil Procedure (CPO), as introduced in 1877.

B. Judicial

The main source referred to in this section is *Seuffert's Archiv*.[225] This substantial compilation comprises decisions from the appellate courts of the pre-unification German States, usually those of the various *Oberappellationsgerichte* (OAG). However, as with the early case reports emanating from England and Scotland, the case reports contained in *Seufert's Archiv* suffer from numerous flaws. The main difficulty is that *Seufert's Archiv* often comprises summaries of case reports from other sources. For example, at page 103 of volume four of *Strippelmann's Neue Sammlung*,[226] a different compilation published in 1846, there is a note stating the

[220] Hahn (n 217), Begründung des Entwurfs.
[221] ibid, Begründung des Entwurfs, 212.
[222] ibid, Begründung des Entwurfs, 212.
[223] ibid, Protokolle der Justiz-Kommission des Deutschen Reichstags, 97.
[224] ibid, Protokolle der Justiz-Kommission des Deutschen Reichstags, 97.
[225] The compilation's full title is *Seuffert's Archiv für Entscheidungen der obersten Gerichte in den deutschen Staaten* (Seuffert's archive of decisions of the highest courts in the German States). It comprises numerous volumes, with the first appearing to have been published in 1847 by JG Cotta'sche Buchhandlung.
[226] The compilation's full title is *Strippelmann's Neue Sammlung bemerkenswerter Entscheidungen des Ober-Appellations-Gerichtes zu Kassel* (Strippelmann's new compilation of notable decisions of the Kassel Court of Appeal).

general principle that foreign laws must be proven by means of evidence. The note then goes on to state, inter alia, the principle that, where the relevant applicable foreign law is in similar terms to domestic law, the court may refer to domestic law when applying foreign law. The decision then appears in substantially the same terms as case 218 in volume two of *Seufert's Archiv*, which was published in 1849. However, the report in *Strippelmann's Neue Sammlung* was not a proper case report, but rather was a brief summary of a case of an unknown date. The lack of a date in both the report in *Seufert's Archiv* and the summary in *Strippelmann's Neue Sammlung* suggests that the author of the report contained in *Seufert's Archiv* simply transcribed the summary from *Strippelmann's Neue Sammlung* when writing the report. It is highly questionable whether there was enough specific information in the *Strippelmann's Neue Sammlung* summary to be able to write a later case report.

It is also regrettable that there was no (serious) attempt to categorise the decisions contained in *Seufert's Archiv*, as was done in Scotland by the authors of *Morison's Dictionary*, even if the categorisation of the cases in *Morison's Dictionary* was far from perfect. The cases appear in *Seufert's Archiv* in no chronological or other discernible order. This means that researching the cases in *Seufert's Archiv* is more time consuming than interrogating those found in its Scottish equivalent, as the cases are spread randomly throughout the various volumes. In addition, as with *Morison's Dictionary*,[227] *Seufert's Archiv* appears to have been re-bound using different volume numbers at least once during the nineteenth century. This is confusing as it is possible to refer to either the case number in the original volume, the page number in the original volume, or the page number in the re-bound volume. In the following, the case number, together with the original volume number, is referred to.

It appears that early pre-unification German courts generally treated foreign law as a matter of fact, although the approaches taken varied somewhat, and, as with the legislation, there was a movement towards the modern German approach during the nineteenth century. Thus, in a decision from Dresden Court of Appeal (OAG) from 16 November 1843, it was held:

> The judge only needs to know the law of his country; he may ignore the foreign law and demand evidence from the party which derives its right from the foreign law. [Translation by author][228]

A similar approach was taken in an 1849 decision from the same court, although the later decision appears to have made it clear that the judge is entitled to look independently at foreign law if he wishes to:

[227] Leadbetter (n 37), 52.

[228] Decision of OAG Dresden from 16 November 1843, Case 79, in *Seuffert's Archiv für Entscheidungen der obsersten Gerichte in den deutschen Staaten* (vol 12): 'Der Richter braucht zwar an sich nur das Recht seines Landes zu kennen, das ausländische Recht darf er ignorieren und von der Partei, welche ihr Recht aus demselben ableitet, den Beweis desselben verlangen.'

> The rule *jura novit curia* should not be extended to the extent that the judge has the obligation, if he does not know a foreign law, unbidden and *ex officio*, to study it to decide an individual case, but he must be free to do so. [Translation by author][229]

In a case from December 1855, the same court appeared to reject any notion that foreign law was anything other than a question of fact:

> The recourse of a defendant in a case to foreign law and his assertion that it contains favourable, completely different provisions, to those contained in the law applicable in the Kingdom of Saxony, constitutes upmost prevarication as an *exceptio facti*. For legislation of an external state, in this questionable form, deviating from domestic law, is a matter of fact. Facts, however, must, if they are to be eligible for consideration, be expressly cited, and as a rule require special evidence. [Translation by author][230]

Of the pre-unification courts, it appears that it was not only the Dresden Court of Appeal that took a fact-based approach to foreign law during the mid-nineteenth century. For example, in decisions of the Darmstadt Court of Appeal from 20 December 1853,[231] and the Berlin Court of Appeal from 5 December 1870, similar approaches appear to have been taken, at least in so far as the decisions confirmed that a court does not have an *ex officio* duty (*von Amts wegen*) to investigate the terms of foreign law which is of a different character to domestic law.[232]

However, the approach taken by the courts of the pre-unification German States was not consistent, with evidence of a more modern approach being taken in the years following the publication of Friedrich Carl von Savigny's seminal analysis in 1840, which is considered below. For example, in an 1864 decision of the Oldenburg Court of Appeal it was held:

> The evidence in this case of foreign law is not to be judged, in terms of procedural, evidential requirements, as evidence of fact, but because the matter concerns the existence of a rule of law, the judge must use all means at his disposal to determine it.

[229] Decision of OAG Dresden from 1849, Case 322, in *Seuffert's Archiv für Entscheidungen der obsersten Gerichte in den deutschen Staaten* (vol 2): 'Die Regel: *jura novit curia* ist allerdings nicht dahin auszudehnen, daß der Richter die Verpflichtung habe, wenn er ein fremdes Recht nicht kennt, unaufgefordert und *ex officio* daselbe behufs der Entscheidung des vorkommenden einzelnen Falles zu studieren. Wohl, aber muß es ihm frei stehen …'

[230] Decision of OAG Dresden from December 1855, Case 208, in *Seuffert's Archiv für Entscheidungen der obsersten Gerichte in den deutschen Staaten* (vol 11): 'Die Berufung eines Beklagten auf ausländisches Recht und seine Behauptung, daß dieses für den concreten Fall zu seinen Gunsten ganz andere Bestimmungen enthalte, als das im Königreich Sachsen geltende Recht, stellt sich als zerstörliche Ausflucht als exceptio facti dar. Denn daß die Gesetzgebung eines auswärtigen Staates in der fraglichen Bestehung besondere, vom inländischen Recht abweichende Bestimmungen getroffen, ist eine Thatsache. Thatsachen aber müssen, wenn sie Anspruch auf Berücksichtigung erlangen sollen, ausdrücklich angeführt werden, und bedürfen in der Regel des besonderen Beweises.'

[231] Decision of OAG Darmstadt from 20 December 1853, Case 248, in *Seuffert's Archiv für Entscheidungen der obsersten Gerichte in den deutschen Staaten* (vol 9). But note a decision on the same page of *Seuffert's Archiv* of the OAG Lübeck from 30 January 1850, which rejected an implied (*stillschweigende*) choice of law in favour of the *lex fori*.

[232] Decision of OAG Berlin from 5 December 1870, Case 215, in *Seuffert's Archiv für Entscheidungen der obsersten Gerichte in den deutschen Staaten* (vol 26).

That is how the role of the judge is to be understood today when it comes to evidencing a particular custom, as has been known by our courts since the statements of Puchta … and … Savigny. [Translation by author][233]

The Oldenburg Court of Appeal, drawing on Puchta's and Savigny's analyses, thus explicitly rejected the treatment of foreign law as fact, and endorsed a similar treatment of custom and foreign law.

C. Academic

The starting point for the following analysis comes from the second edition of Carl Ludwig von Bar's text, published in 1889, in which it was stated:

According to the old, strict view, foreign law is merely fact to the judge and is treated procedurally as such; therefore, without express reference by the parties, the judge does not appear to be entitled to apply a foreign rule of law. [Translation by author][234]

Thus, according to von Bar, the traditional academic view had been, in terms of procedure, that foreign law should be treated as fact. As has been shown, this accords with both the prevailing legislative and judicial approaches in the major pre-unification German States. Von Bar referred to two academic sources in stating what he considered to be the traditional view. First, he referred to a text on public international law by Heinrich Oppenheim, who argued in his first edition text:

This also includes foreign laws, which form the basis of a legal relationship; for domestic laws would also have to be proved if the judge did not know them in terms of his responsibilities and had to apply them *ex officio*. [Translation by author][235]

[233] Decision of OAG Oldenburg from 1864, Case 101, in *Seuffert's Archiv für Entscheidungen der obersten Gerichte in den deutschen Staaten* (vol 18): 'Der hier fragliche Beweis eines im Auslande geltenden Rechts ist hinsichtlich der processualischen Verpflichtungen des Beweisführers nicht wie ein Beweis über Thatsachen zu beurteilen, sondern weil es um die Existenz einer Rechtsregel sich handelt, muß der Richter mit den ihm zu Gebote stehenden Hilfsmitteln von Amtswegen mit thätig werden. Daß die Stellung des heutigen Richters in dieser Weiße aufzufassen sei, wenn es um den Beweis eines particularen Gewohnheitsrecht sich handelt, ist bekanntlich von unseren Gerichten seit den Ausführungen von Puchta … und … Savigny.' The court refers generally to the fourth chapter of Book three of GF Puchta, *Das Gewohnheitsrecht* vol 2 (Palm'sche Buchhandlung, 1837), although the discussion from 170ff seems most relevant, and FC von Savigny, *System des heutigen Römischen Rechts* (Veit und Comp, 1840), 186ff.

[234] C Ludwig von Bar, *Theorie und Praxis des internationalen Privatrechts*, 2nd edn (Hahn'sche Buchhandlung, 1889), 132–33: 'Nach der älteren strengen Ansicht ist das auswärtige Recht für den Richter lediglich Thatsache und als solche processual zu behandeln; daher der Richter ohne ausdrücklichen Hinweis der Parteien nicht befugt erscheint, eine ausländische Rechtsnorm anzuwenden.'

[235] HB Oppenheim, *System des Völkerrechts* (Literarische Anstalt (J Rütten), 1845), 381: 'Ebenso die ausländischen Gesetze, welche die Basis eines Rechtsverhältnisses bilden; denn auch die inländischen müßten erwiesen werden, wenn sie der Richter nicht von Amtswegen kennen und *ex officio* anwenden müßte.' The second edition of Oppenheim's text is more detailed on the point and makes comparative reference to English law stating, with regards to the English courts, that they also take no 'judicial notice of the laws of a foreign country'. See HB Oppenheim, *System des Völkerrechts*, 2nd edn (A Kröner, 1867), 316–17.

Second, von Bar referred to an 1858 article by W Langenbeck, who argued that where no reference is made by the parties to the existence of a foreign rule, the judge should apply his own law.[236] Langenbeck also referred to another rule familiar to British lawyers, which allows the possibility for the content of foreign law to be admitted by a party, regardless of its veracity.[237] The possibility of admission (*Geständnis*) of a foreign rule by parties is a clear facet of the fact approach, with such a possibility being rejected by German academics today.[238]

However, von Bar did not consider that academics were uniform in their approach. He referred to one of the first German academic journal articles substantively analysing the treatment of foreign law, which was authored by Mittermaier in 1835.[239] Mittermaier acknowledged that the traditional view had been to treat law essentially as fact.[240] Mittermaier referred to the writings of Adolf D Weber and Franz Gesterding.[241] Weber had argued in 1805:

> The judge is not required to know the laws of a foreign state. However, where they do apply in a case which a judge has to decide, the judge is entitled to place the obligation on the parties to provide evidence or verification of the foreign law. [Translation by author][242]

Similarly, Gesterding had argued in 1832 that the existence and content of foreign law should be treated as fact and, in so arguing, drew on Weber.[243]

Mittermaier, in his 1835 article, referred to two further academic sources. One reference was to Story,[244] who was clear in 1834 as to the treatment of foreign law in US law:

> The established doctrine now is, that no court takes judicial notice of the laws of a foreign country, but they must be proved as facts.[245]

[236] W Langenbeck, 'Beiträge zur Lehre von dem Beweise fremder Rechte vor inländischen Gerichten' (1858) 41 *Archiv für die civilistische Praxis* 129, 132–33.

[237] ibid, 133.

[238] Schack (n 137), para 756; H Prütting, '§ 293' in W Krüger and T Rauscher (eds), *Münchener Kommentar zur Zivilprozessordnung: Band 1 (§§ 1–354)*, 6th edn (CH Beck, 2020), para 14.

[239] Mittermaier, 'Ueber den Beweis ausländischer Gesetze in Rechtsstreitigkeiten' (1835) 18 *Archiv für die civilistische Praxis* 67.

[240] ibid, 68.

[241] ibid, 68.

[242] AD Weber, *Ueber die Verbindlichkeit zur Beweisführung im Civilprozeß* (Rengerische Buchhandlung, 1805), 21: 'Ist der Richter nicht schuldig, die Gesetze eines auswärtigen Staats zu kennen. Kommen diese gleichwohl bei Rechtssachen, die er zu entscheiden hat, in Anwendung, so ist er allerdings berechtig, den Parteien die Beibringung deserselben oder die Bewahrheitung der auswärtigen Rechtsnorm aufzugeben.' The same approach is taken by Weber in his 1832 second edition text of the same name. See AD Weber, *Ueber die Verbindlichkeit zur Beweisführung im Civilprozeß*, 2nd edn (Rengerische Buchhandlung, 1832), 16.

[243] F Gesterding, *Ausbeute von Nachforschungen über verschiedene Rechtsmaterien* (Koch, 1832), 28.

[244] Mittermaier (n 239), 68.

[245] Story (n 32), 527.

Mittermaier's other reference was to an article published in 1833 by the Austrian academic Franz Xaver Haimerl,[246] which Mittermaier considered to be the only German-language article which had engaged with the question as to how foreign law should be approached by courts:

> Only one German writer has, to our knowledge, provided a very commendable contribution to the field's academic debate … [Translation by author][247]

Haimerl's article was written from the Austrian point of view and thus made extensive reference to the 1781 Austrian Code of Civil Procedure. Haimerl was clear that foreign law should essentially be treated as a matter of fact:

> Accordingly, foreign laws require, in a domestic court, just as much proof as any other fact. [Translation by author][248]

Later in his article, Haimerl confirmed the option for parties to admit the content of foreign law, which he considered to be a possibility available to all facts, of which foreign law should be no exception.[249]

While von Bar in his 1889 text sought to distinguish Mittermaier's approach from, for example, Langenbeck,[250] it appears that Mittermaier, while recognising the difficulty in treating facts and foreign law as equivalents,[251] essentially agreed with the fact approach to foreign law, or at least, its practical outcome:

> Which law applies in the foreign place? And the courts in such cases place the evidential burden on the person who invokes the foreign law. This procedure is also absolutely correct … [Translation by author][252]

The 1840 analysis of the pre-eminent German jurist Friedrich Carl von Savigny in volume one of his seminal *System des heutigen Römischen Rechts* focused primarily on custom.[253] Savigny referred to the fact that the judge is required to undertake legal studies and thus should be expected to act differently when confronted with custom, as opposed to material that he has studied.[254] Savigny referred to the

[246] FX Haimerl, 'Ueber den Beweis ausländischer Gesetze; als Beitrag zur Erklärung des § 104 der allgemeinen Gerichtsordnung' (1833) Bd. 2 *Zeitschrift für österreichische Rechtsgelehrsamkeit und politische Gesetzkunde* 281.

[247] Mittermaier (n 239), 68: 'nur ein deutscher Schriftsteller hat unseres Wissens sehr dankenswerte Beiträge zur Erörterung der Lehre geliefert …'

[248] Haimerl (n 246), 283: 'Hiernach bedürfen also fremde Gesetze vor einem inländischen Gerichte eben so eines Beweises, wie ein jedes andere Factum.' However, Haimerl is clear, at 285, that foreign law requires special evidence. Thus, normal witnesses, who would normally speak to their sensory perceptions, are not sufficient evidence, as legal, academic knowledge is necessary to give evidence on foreign law.

[249] ibid, 286.

[250] Ludwig von Bar (n 234), 132–33.

[251] Mittermaier (n 239), 68–69.

[252] ibid, 68: 'welches Gesetz an dem fremden Orte gilt? und die Gerichte legen in diesen Fällen demjenigen, welcher sich auf das fremde Gesetz beruft, den Beweis desselben auf. Dies Verfahren ist auch völlig richtig …'

[253] Von Savigny (n 233), 186ff. Von Bar, at 133 of his second edition text, refers to page 191 of Savingny's text, although the relevant analysis appears to start on page 186.

[254] ibid, 189–90.

doctrine of *iura novit curia*,[255] later making clear that the judge is expected to know and apply statute law, and fails in his duties where he does not correctly refer to it.[256] On the other hand, Savigny argued that custom should be drawn by the parties to the judge's attention, with the relevant party being required to take responsibility (and suffer any negatives) where they fail to do so.[257] While recognising practical similarities between fact and custom, Savigny was clear that there are differences.[258] He pointed out that facts may never be supplemented by the judge, whereas rules of custom can and should be taken account of where the judge has knowledge of them.[259] Equally, custom is not subject to the strict rules of evidence applicable to questions of fact.[260] In making these arguments, Savigny developed a nuanced analysis in relation to custom that can be construed as a third way between law and fact. Importantly, Savigny likened foreign law to custom.[261] As with custom, Savigny argued that no knowledge of foreign law can be imputed to the judge, with detail having to be given and proven by the parties. While Savigny suggested that parties should suffer the consequences of failing to draw a foreign rule to the judge's attention[262] – a facet of the fact approach – it appears that Savigny was advocating the modern German approach when he argued, first, for similar approaches in respect of foreign law and custom, and, secondly, different approaches towards those two and fact. In terms of the potential influences which Savigny had when writing his analysis, he referred a number of times to the 1837 text on custom by Georg Friedrich Puchta,[263] who himself had substantively referred to Mittermaier's 1835 article.[264] This means that Mittermaier's analysis, which is not itself referred to in Savigny's text, appears to have materially impacted on Savigny's approach.[265]

As shown, there is evidence from the cases that German courts were taking account of Savigny's writings by the mid-nineteenth century. While it can only be a matter of speculation, it also seems highly probable that Savigny's 1840 analysis influenced the codes of civil procedure developed in Germany from the mid-nineteenth century. Nonetheless, Savigny was more nuanced than might be thought. Thus, Savigny did not leave foreign law or custom purely in the hands of the court, but rather required the parties to draw both to the attention of the court in cases where the court did not have existing knowledge.

[255] ibid, 187. Savingny describes it as *jus novit curia*.
[256] ibid, 190.
[257] ibid, 190.
[258] ibid, 190.
[259] ibid, 190.
[260] ibid, 190.
[261] ibid, 190–91.
[262] ibid, 190–91.
[263] ibid, 181, 188, 190, 191, 192, 195, which refer to Puchta (n 233).
[264] Puchta (n 233), 172.
[265] Mittermaier drew parallels between the treatment of custom and foreign law. See Mittermaier (n 239), 68.

It appears that by the late nineteenth century, academic debate in Germany had orientated itself in essentially modern terms,[266] eg the parties may aid the judge in his investigation, but their assistance is not a necessary part of the process of applying foreign law in a German court, and the judge may draw on any materials he considers necessary.[267] The specifics of the modern German approach are analysed in more detail in the following chapter.

D. Mechanisms of Proof

Drawing on legislative, judicial, and academic sources, there is limited evidence to allow conclusions to be drawn as to the mechanisms by which foreign law was proven in early German cases. There was reference made to an expert opinion regarding the law of Massachusetts in a decision of the Obertribunal Berlin from 10 July 1860.[268] There is also early authority that foreign consular officials would be permitted to provide expert evidence as to their countries' respective law in a case report of the Kassel Court of Appeal (OAG) from an unknown date.[269] Seuffert, writing in 1856, recommended official correspondence as a means of investigating the content of the *lex causae*.[270]

§ 53 of the Prussian Code of Civil Procedure was previously outlined. An 1826 commentary, by Maximilian Grävell, in addition to making clear that foreign law, where it was disputed by the parties, was a matter of evidence to be dealt with like every other fact,[271] went into significant detail as to how foreign law ought to be proven in the Prussian courts. For example, Grävell argued that a distinction required to be drawn between written and unwritten law.[272] In terms of written law, Grävell argued that the most reliable source of information were those copies authenticated by authorities of the relevant country, but he also drew a distinction

[266] The shift appears to have taken place during the nineteenth century. In 1868, Wilhelm Endemann was clear that while the German judge has a duty to apply foreign law, it is nonetheless a matter which can be treated as evidential. W Endemann, *Das Deutsche Civilprozeßrecht* (Bangel & Schmitt, 1868), 106, and W Endemann, *Das Deutsche Civilprozeßrecht* (Bangel & Schmitt, 1868), 675. Otto Stobbe, writing in 1871, in likening the treatment of custom to that of foreign law, also rejected the old approach that custom (and so foreign law) should be treated as a matter of fact. He attributed the reason for the shift in thinking to Puchta's analysis. Stobbe was clear that the judge must apply foreign law but that he is entitled to order the parties to seek evidence as to the content of the applicable foreign law. See O Stobbe, *Handbuch des Deutschen Privatrechts* (Wilhelm Hertz, 1871), 139–40 and 179.

[267] Ludwig von Bar (n 234), 136–37; L Gaupp, *Die Civilprozeßordnung für das Deutsche Reich*, 2nd edn (Akademische Verlagsbuchhandlung von JCB Mohr (Paul Siebeck), 1890), 538.

[268] Decision of the Obertribunal Berlin from 10 July 1860, Case 164, in *Seuffert's Archiv für Entscheidungen der obsersten Gerichte in den deutschen Staaten* (vol 14).

[269] F Strippelmann, *Neue Sammlung bemerkenswerter Entscheidungen des Ober-Appellations-Gerichtes zu Kassel*, Bd. 4 (1846), 103.

[270] JA Seuffert, *Handbuch des deutschen Civilprozesses auf der Grundlage und nach der Ordnung der bayerischen Gesetzgebung*, 2nd edn (J J Palm und Ernst Enke, 1856), 23.

[271] MCFW Grävell, *Praktischer Kommentar zur allgemeinen Gerichts-Ordnung für die preußischen Staaten* (Keysersche Buchhandlung, 1826), 178.

[272] ibid, 180.

between general statute law and, presumably, local regulations.[273] He placed the obligation on the party averring foreign law to produce the relevant evidence.[274] In terms of unwritten foreign law, Grävell considered that witnesses or judicial precedents were the most simple and certain way of proving it, on the basis that every court in a country ought to know its own law.[275] Grävell considered acceptable expert opinions from men with the requisite professional status to know the laws of their country, whose testimony would be assessed as any other expert witness.[276] In its totality, Grävell's approach shows a great deal of similarity with the approach taken in England at the time. Indeed, Grävell referred specifically to the proof of English law.[277] In doing so, he referred to a Prussian regulation dated 8 December 1819 stating that proof of English law should take place by way of legalised opinions from two well-known English learned jurists (*Rechtsgelehrter*).[278] It should be open to the opposing party to bring a contradictory opinion.[279] The opinions should concern themselves only with the terms of English law and would be subject to the ultimate conclusions of the court.[280] Such an approach would have found particularly great resonance in the English courts of the time (and today).

III. Conclusions

In Scotland, the fact approach is of some antiquity, having developed in the seventeenth century through a combination of case law and the contributions of the Scottish institutional writers, especially that of Stair. There is evidence that existing Scottish practice influenced the later development of the fact approach in England during the eighteenth century, first, in so far that the fact approach was already established in Scotland by the end of the seventeenth century and, second, due to Lord Mansfield's contribution as an English judge. As a result of his work presenting Scottish appeals before the House of Lords during the mid-eighteenth century, Lord Mansfield would inevitably have been familiar with the writings of the Scottish institutional writers when he decided the pivotal case of *Mostyn* (1774).[281] If Scottish practice did influence English practice, then perhaps the fact approach is, in part, a Scottish export to the common law world. In terms of how foreign law was proven in the Scottish courts during the seventeenth century, the preference

[273] ibid, 180.
[274] ibid, 180.
[275] ibid, 181.
[276] ibid, 181.
[277] ibid, 186.
[278] ibid, 186.
[279] ibid, 186.
[280] ibid, 186.
[281] *Mostyn v Fabrigas* (1774) 1 Cowper 161; 98 ER 1021.

appears to have been remits to foreign judges to give a ruling on their law, despite the huge practical difficulties that such a remit would have entailed. This approach then developed in favour of remits to foreign lawyers for them to give expert opinions on the relevant points of foreign law. The English courts did not refer cases to foreign courts prior to the mid-nineteenth century.[282] There appears to have been an early trend requiring authenticated copies of written foreign law, although such evidence was usually accompanied by witness evidence. By the mid-nineteenth century, the preference in the English courts was very much in favour of expert witness evidence, with written law never being considered sufficient on its own. This was motivated by concerns that the English courts were ill-equipped to understand foreign law without expert assistance, as well the risk that written foreign law may have changed or been subject to (further) judicial decision.

Late-eighteenth- and early-nineteenth-century German legislative, judicial, and academic sources demonstrate a strong tendency towards treating foreign law as fact. However, both German courts and commentators appear to have taken inconsistent approaches to foreign law during the early-to-mid-nineteenth century. Savigny's 1840 first volume appears to have been decisive in moving German jurisprudence away from the fact approach, a trend which culminated in § 265 (later § 293) of the German Code of Civil Procedure. Nonetheless, the approach taken in § 265 is not strictly reflected in what Savigny wrote, which was more nuanced. The evidence available on how foreign law was proven in pre-unification Germany is comparatively limited. The most relevant evidence is that from Prussia, which provided in legislation that evidence of English law should be given by two well-known English jurists (*Rechtsgelehrter*).

[282] Legislation was introduced by the UK Parliament in the mid-nineteenth century to permit references by British courts to foreign courts on points of foreign law. This is addressed in Chapter three.

3

Present

I. Introduction

The main purpose of this chapter is to compare the current approaches taken to the application of foreign law through the conduit of choice of law rules in the relevant jurisdictions. The analysis is based on two fundamental considerations, with their associated component parts. The first fundamental consideration is whether the relevant choice of law rule is introduced and applied in the court proceedings. The question of which law should apply is not considered in the analysis.[1] The second fundamental consideration, where it is decided by the court that a foreign law *does* apply, is that of the three-stage process of investigating, determining, and applying the relevant foreign law to the facts of the case.

The investigative stage is the inquiry into the content of the *lex causae*. This might involve the collection of relevant materials, eg textbooks and court decisions, the instruction of an expert, or the direction of a question to a foreign authority. The determinative stage is the point at which the foreign law regarding the matter at hand is decided, ie the decision-maker determines, with reference to the evidence available, what the applicable foreign law is. The person investigating the content of the foreign law can, and often will, be different from the person determining the foreign rule of law. As will be shown, in the British courts, the parties have responsibility for conducting the investigation into the relevant foreign law, necessarily with the assistance of an expert. However, they have no right to determine its content. This right lies exclusively with the court:

> Foreign law must be proved as a matter of fact. This often means that parties will adduce experts in the foreign law to explain the relevant rules and principles. The task of ascertaining foreign law remains that of the court.[2]

On the other hand, in Germany, it is the court which is tasked with both the investigation and determination of the content of the *lex causae*, although the investigation is sometimes contracted out to an expert by the court.

[1] This analysis does not engage with the complexities involved in determining the applicable law under choice of law rules and assumes that any reference to a foreign law is to the substantive law of a state, ie without the application of *renvoi*. See, for example, Article 20 of Regulation (EC) No 593/2008 of the European Parliament and of the Council of 17 June 2008 on the law applicable to contractual obligations [2008] OJ L 177/6 (Rome I Regulation) for a provision that implements such an approach in EU private international law.

[2] *DNO Oman Ltd v Clouston* 2019 SLT 395, 407.

The distinction between the investigative and determinative stages becomes clearer when comparing the treatment of foreign law as a question of fact or as one of law. Even if foreign law is considered a matter of law, there must almost inevitably be an investigation into the content of the *lex causae*, as no judge can know the laws of every foreign legal system.[3] However, at the determinative stage, the content of the *lex causae* is no longer a matter of evidence but of law. On the other hand, if foreign law is strictly considered a matter of fact, both the investigative and determinative stages are evidential, with the determination of the content of the *lex causae* purely being an assessment by the judge of which party's evidence is most persuasive; ie little or no emphasis is placed on establishing the correct position under the foreign law.

The application stage is the process of applying the relevant rule of foreign law to the facts of the case. While there is a close connection, the determination and application stages are logically distinct.[4] For example, the application stage involves consideration of other matters such as whether a rule of public policy of the forum is breached by the application of the foreign rule to the facts of the case.[5]

Throughout the various stages, many ancillary questions arise, eg what should happen if the applicable foreign law cannot be established to the court's satisfaction, where should the costs fall for investigating the content of the *lex causae*, and what aspects should be appealable? Where, following investigation, it has been decided by the domestic court that the foreign rule cannot be determined, the question as to whether the application of the *lex fori*, or even an alternative foreign law, is appropriate then becomes relevant.

In terms of the various strands of analysis, there are several actors involved in the process with differing responsibilities. In all the relevant jurisdictions, the principal actors are the court and the parties (together with their legal representatives). In terms of responsibility, first, for introducing the issue of foreign law and, second, for investigating foreign law, the court and the parties each potentially have a role to play. As experts, including the various possible permeations thereof,[6] play a role only with regard to the investigation of foreign law, their involvement is relevant for consideration at the investigative stage only. This is because questions involving the introduction and application of choice of law rules, a part of domestic law, should never be a matter of expert evidence, regardless of how obscure or

[3] G Kegel and K Schurig, *Internationales Privatrecht*, 9th edn (CH Beck, 2004), 501: 'Natürlich kann man vom Richter nichts Übermenschliches fordern' ('Of course one cannot demand something superhuman from the judge') [Translation by author].

[4] An example of the distinction can be found in the case of *JXJ v Province of Great Britain of the Institute of Brothers of the Christian Schools* [2020] EWHC 1914 (QB), in which, following thorough analysis of a joint expert report on the Scots law of limitation, in terms of the investigative stage, Mr Justice Chamberlain first sets out, at [101], his 'Conclusions on Scots limitation law', and then moves on, at [102], to the 'Application of Scots limitation law to the facts of this case'.

[5] J Kropholler, *Internationales Privatrecht*, 6th edn (Mohr Siebeck, 2006), 245.

[6] For example, in Germany, the Max Planck Institute for Comparative and International Private Law based in Hamburg provides courts and agencies with reports and information on foreign law. See H Prütting, '§ 293' in W Krüger and T Rauscher (eds), *Münchener Kommentar zur Zivilprozessordnung: Band 1 (§§ 1–354)*, 6th edn (CH Beck, 2020), para 30.

complicated.[7] This is even though parts of domestic law, eg tax law, can be more complicated than relatively simple provisions of foreign law, relative to which an expert opinion may be instructed.[8]

The following analysis first addresses the role of the two principal actors in civil proceedings: (section II) the court and (section III) the parties, both in respect of their roles in the introduction and application of choice of law rules, and in the investigation and determination of foreign law. The analysis then considers (in section IV) the role of experts in investigating the content of the *lex causae*, including the costs associated with instructing experts. This work is concerned only with the particular costs involved in the application of foreign law. Thus, while there can be high legal costs involved for the parties in paying their legal representatives to consider complicated choice of law rules, such legal costs will almost inevitably arise in any complicated area of the law, e.g. tax or competition law. The consequences of failure to prove the content of the *lex causae* are then considered (section V). All the foregoing essentially falls within the purview of first instance proceedings. This leaves opportunity (in section VI) for consideration of outstanding questions regarding appeals.

II. The Court

This section is about the role of the court in the (A) introduction and application of choice of law rules, and (B) the investigation and determination of the content of foreign law. Before moving on to deal with substantive matters, a few points are made about the procedural background in which courts operate in the relevant jurisdictions.

The respective approaches, including the role of the judge, to civil litigation in the British and German courts have traditionally been thought to differ substantially. Perhaps Zweigert and Kötz best captured the continental European view of the English judge as a passive actor, a form of umpire, when they wrote:

> The romantic image of a judge in a scarlet robe and horsehair wig in front of one's eyes, who, sitting in a splendid panelled courtroom, and, with just as much wisdom as authority, scoops the law out of thick collections of law reports. [Translation by author][9]

[7] The point is clear in German law: *Decision of the Federal Court of Justice from 14 March 1966* (BGH, VII. Zivilsenat) VII ZR 171/63, NJW 1966, 1364; H Schack, *Internationales Zivilverfahrensrecht*, 8th edn (CH Beck, 2021), para 751. There is limited academic material available in English but see a US journal article considering the problem in the context of the US Federal Rules of Civil Procedure: TE Baker, 'The Impropriety of Expert Witness Testimony on the Law' (1992) 40 *University of Kansas Law Review* 325. The writer can anecdotally confirm that expert opinions on questions of domestic law are regularly referred to in Scottish cases, although the propriety of this is unclear. However, such reports are not ordered by the court but by the parties.

[8] Schack, *Internationales Zivilverfahrensrecht* (n 7), para 763; Prütting, '§ 293' (n 6), para 29.

[9] K Zweigert and H Kötz, *Einführung in die Rechtsvergleichung: auf dem Gebiete des Privatrechts*, 3rd edn (J C B Mohr (Paul Siebeck), 1996), 202: 'Das romantische Bild eines Richters in scharlachroter Robe und bezopfter Perücke vor Augen, der in prachtvoll getäfeltem Saale zu Gericht sitzt und mit ebensoviel Weisheit wie Autorität aus dickleibigen Entscheidungssammlungen das Recht schöpft.'

While there may have been an element of truth in this view in the past, the role of the English judge has changed considerably in recent years,[10] prompted in no small part by the significant changes introduced by the replacement of the old County Court Rules and Supreme Court Rules with the new Civil Procedure Rules in 1998, which now apply generally throughout the ordinary civil courts of England. The introduction of the Civil Procedure Rules followed an extensive investigation by Lord Woolf, who was assigned the task by the Lord Chancellor in March 1994,[11] and who produced a detailed report entitled Access to Justice.[12] Lord Woolf considered that civil litigation in England was plagued by a number of serious problems. He argued that litigating in England was too expensive,[13] slow, unequal, uncertain, fragmented, and adversarial.[14] He saw an increased role of the court as critical to ensuring that civil litigation proceeded efficiently:

> Ultimate responsibility for the control of litigation must move from the litigants and their legal advisers to the court.[15]

Since the introduction of the Civil Procedure Rules, English civil proceedings now require active case management. The role of the English court today includes encouraging co-operation; identifying issues at an early stage; helping parties to settle cases; and fixing timetables.[16] To enable the courts and the parties[17] to conduct litigation efficiently, the Civil Procedure Rules set out objectives and principles underpinning civil litigation in the English courts. The overriding objective is that the court should be enabled to 'deal with cases justly and at proportionate cost.'[18] This overriding objective is defined to include principles such as ensuring an equal footing between the parties; saving expense; proportionality; and the enforcement of rules, practice directions, and orders.[19] Factors referred to in defining the requirement to deal with cases expeditiously and fairly include consideration of the amount of money in dispute; the importance of the dispute; its complexity; and the financial position of each party.[20] These factors, and the considerations underlying them, appear to be highly relevant when considering the possible cost and time implications of proving foreign law in a case. Indeed, it has been argued that the changes introduced by the Civil Procedure Rules have

[10] That the quotation was not a true reflection of matters even in 1996 is acknowledged by Zweigert and Kötz.
[11] A Zuckerman, 'Lord Woolf's Access to Justice: Plus ça change …' (1996) 59 *Modern Law Review* 773.
[12] H Woolf (Lord Woolf), 'Access to Justice – Final Report' (1996), webarchive.nationalarchives.gov.uk/20060213223540/http://www.dca.gov.uk/civil/final/contents.htm.
[13] Unpredictable, excessive, and disproportionate costs in English litigation was a particularly acute concern leading to the Woolf Report. See Zuckerman, 'Lord Woolf's Access to Justice' (n 11), 773.
[14] Woolf (Lord Woolf) (n 12), Section I – Overview, para 2.
[15] ibid, Section II, Chapter 1, para 1.
[16] CPR 1.4.
[17] The obligations on the parties under the CPR are referred to at CPR 1.3.
[18] CPR 1.1(1).
[19] CPR 1.1(2).
[20] CPR 1.1(2)(c).

made such fundamental inroads into the adversarial system, as it was once known in England, that it is possible to talk in terms of its 'evisceration'.[21]

The Scottish rules of civil procedure have not yet been reformed in a similar manner to that undertaken in England. As it stands, there remain different rules for the sheriff courts[22] and the Court of Session,[23] and the processes and terminology involved have been criticised as inconsistent and unnecessarily complicated.[24] Indeed, many of the problems highlighted in Lord Woolf's Access to Justice Report appear to find resonance in Scotland. The Lord President, the highest judge in Scotland, perhaps captured the essence of the problem in a recent report on Scottish civil procedure when he commented that while an advocate from the nineteenth century would no doubt find modern day Edinburgh to be a bewildering place:

> If they were to make their way to Parliament House, however, they would, once recovered from the shock of seeing women at the bar and on the bench, find our courts to be comfortingly familiar. They might even feel up to the task of taking some instructions.[25]

However, reform of Scottish civil procedure is coming and, indeed, has begun taking place. A significant and relevant change introduced by the Courts Reform (Scotland) Act 2014 was the introduction of Scottish simple procedure, which provides a special forum to adjudicate all civil cases up to a value of £5,000.[26] Simple procedure has specially drafted rules designed to be understandable to individuals representing themselves in court proceedings.[27] However, perhaps the

[21] JA Jolowicz, 'Adversarial and Inquisitorial Models of Civil Procedure' (2003) 52 *ICLQ* 281, 286.

[22] See the Act of Sederunt (Sheriff Court Ordinary Cause Rules) 1993.

[23] See the Rules of the Court of Session 1994.

[24] See Scottish Civil Justice Council, 'The New Civil Procedure Rules: First Report' (2017), www.scottishciviljusticecouncil.gov.uk/docs/librariesprovider4/consultations/scjc-consultations/the-new-civil-procedure-rules-first-report-and-annex.pdf?sfvrsn=2. It should be noted that debate regarding the reform of Scottish civil procedure is 'longstanding', with two themes said to have 'constantly recurred namely, first, the question of how far abbreviated written pleadings should be introduced; and, second, the issue of whether or how far there should be a change from party-management to judicial management of cases.' NR Whitty, 'Civil Procedure (Reissue) (Original date of publication 1 January 2007): Introduction (paras 1–45)', *The Laws of Scotland: Stair Memorial Encyclopaedia* (LexisNexis, 2007), para 16. There have been numerous reports in addition to the 2017 report, notably Lord Cullen's report titled the 'Review of the Business of the Outer House of the Court of Session' published in 1995 (the Cullen Report) and Lord Gill's 'Report of the Scottish Civil Courts Review' published in 2009 (the Gill Review), which led to the Courts Reform (Scotland) Act 2014.

[25] Scottish Civil Justice Council (n 24), 1. An analysis of Scottish civil procedure published in 1932 essentially remains valid today. See, for example, its account of Scottish procedural terminology in RW Millar, 'Civil Pleading in Scotland (I)' (1932) 30 *Michigan Law Review* 545, 553–54.

[26] Almost all Scottish civil actions not exceeding a value of £5,000, including actions for payment and actions *ad factum praestandum*, must be brought by way of simple procedure, by virtue of s 72 of the Courts Reform (Scotland) Act 2014. In relation to simple procedure, Lord Carloway, the then Chair of the Scottish Civil Justice Council, stated: 'The simple procedure has been designed with the party litigant in mind, using accessible language and incorporating user-friendly guidance into the rules.' See Scottish Courts and Tribunals Service, 'New Simple Procedure' (2016), www.scotcourts.gov.uk/about-the-scottish-court-service/scs-news/2016/11/29/new-simple-procedure.

[27] See the Act of Sederunt (Simple Procedure) 2016, sch 1.

greatest difficulty with simple procedure is the disparity in complexity between procedure and substance, ie between the rules of the court and the substantive law that must be applied in the case. Thus, while the procedural rules no doubt represent a significant simplification over their predecessor rules,[28] the substantive law that applies to the facts of the case remains essentially as complicated as it ever was.[29] Where a contractual dispute involves a question of foreign law there is an added level of complexity, with the choice of law rules found in the Rome I Regulation (as incorporated into UK domestic law) continuing to determine which law applies.[30] Thus, in a consumer contract dispute with a value of £500, where the contract contains a choice of law clause in favour of a foreign law, the choice of law clause, even in a consumer context, remains a valid one,[31] be that the law of Luxembourg in an Amazon purchase,[32] or the law of Germany in a purchase of tea,[33] albeit subject to the mandatory provisions of the law of the consumer's habitual residence.

As previously discussed,[34] the German Code of Civil Procedure (ZPO) derives from 1877 and governs most civil litigation in the German courts. Since its inception, the Code of Civil Procedure has been repeatedly reformed,[35] including substantially at the turn of this century,[36] although the most relevant paragraph, § 293, remains in the same terms as it was in 1877.[37] In general, the German civil courts do not necessarily operate in the manner which the common law lawyer might assume, since the parties also play a central role in German civil proceedings. The *Beibringungsgrundsatz*,[38] for example, places the responsibility on the parties to plead the facts of the case, the content of which generally binds the German court.[39] Moreover, the *Dispositionsgrundsatz* gives the parties significant control over the proceedings including the power to settle and end the proceedings.[40]

[28] For example, the Scottish simple procedure rules talk of a pause rather than a sist, a discussion rather than a hearing, and an application rather than a motion.

[29] Though improvements to UK domestic consumer law have been made by the Consumer Rights Act 2015. See P Giliker, 'The Consumer Rights Act 2015 – a bastion of European consumer rights?' (2017) 37 *Legal Studies* 78.

[30] The Law Applicable to Contractual Obligations and Non-Contractual Obligations (Amendment etc.) (EU Exit) Regulations 2019.

[31] See Article 6(2) of the Rome I Regulation (n 1). The particular complexities of this provision in the Rome I Regulation (n 1) are considered in more detail in Chapter four.

[32] 'Conditions of Use & Sale for Amazon UK', www.amazon.co.uk/gp/help/customer/display.html/ref=footer_cou?ie=UTF8&nodeId=201909000.

[33] 'Terms and Conditions of Teekampagne', shop.teekampagne.de/en/Shop/Info/termsandconditions.

[34] The history of § 293 and, briefly, the German Code of Civil Procedure (ZPO) was addressed in Chapter two, section II.A.

[35] There have been around 200 revisions to the German Code of Civil Procedure since 1950, some of which were substantial. See H Roth, 'Entwicklung und Reformen der ZPO' (2018) *Juristische Rundschau* 159, 160.

[36] R Greger, 'Die ZPO-Reform – 1000 Tage danach' (2004) 59(17) *Juristenzeitung* 805.

[37] See Chapter two, section II.A, text to fns 219–220.

[38] Also known as the *Verhandlungsmaxime*. See Prütting, '§ 293' (n 6), para 48.

[39] P Pohlmann, *Zivilprozessrecht*, 4th edn (CH Beck, 2018), para 66ff.

[40] ibid, para 52ff.

Nonetheless, there is little doubt that the German court has a more significant role to play in civil proceedings,[41] both in terms of case management and during the proceedings, when compared with the more adversarial English and Scottish courts.[42] For example, under § 139 of the Code of Civil Procedure, there is a requirement on the German judge to give the parties suggestions or warnings regarding factual matters pleaded and their legal implications.[43] A German court's failure to give such suggestions or warnings is a procedural irregularity, and can, in certain circumstances, breach a party's constitutional right to a fair hearing.[44] In England, it has been confirmed by the Court of Appeal that there is no such duty on English judges, even where parties are unrepresented,[45] and this is the case even in the context of tribunals that have the aim of ensuring a user-friendly environment for unrepresented parties.[46] Nonetheless, there is little doubt that many English (and Scottish) judges will legitimately choose to interfere in proceedings, where the interests of justice require it,[47] although case law dictates that they must be careful not to overstep the mark, which is impossible to define in exact terms.

[41] ibid, para 113ff.

[42] There are, of course, important differences between common law (including Scotland) and civil law procedure, including the former's emphasis on a concentrated trial. See Whitty (n 24), para 11.

[43] It is difficult to define exactly what is required of the German court, but any interventions must be clear, noted in the court file, and should certainly be more explicit than mere hints. The obligations placed on the German court were expanded by the legislator in 2001. See L Rosenberg, KH Schwab and P Gottwald, *Zivilprozessrecht*, 18th edn (CH Beck, 2018), § 77 para 17ff.

[44] ibid, § 77 para 18.

[45] *Lemas v Williams* [2009] EWCA Civ 360, [58]: 'There are, however, limits to what a judge can and should do in order to assist such a litigant. It is for the litigant himself to decide what case to make and how to make it, and what evidence to adduce and how to adduce it. It is not for the judge to give directions or advice on such matters. It is not his function to step into the arena on the litigant's side and to help him to make his case.' The English court may, however, warn a party as to the consequences of a particular course of action. In respect of a party's decision not to give evidence, the court held, also at [58]: 'When he indicated that he did not want to give evidence, the judge properly pointed out to him the consequences if he did not. I have no doubt that the judge made the position clear.'

[46] See *Muschett v HM Prison Service* [2010] EWCA Civ 25, [31], in which the court drew on *Lemas v Williams* [2009] EWCA Civ 360: 'Those observations were made in the context of a challenge to a decision of a circuit judge but I consider that essentially similar considerations apply to employment judges. It is not their role to engage in the sort of inquisitorial function that Mr Hopkin suggests or, therefore, to engage in an investigation as to whether further evidence might be available to one of the parties which, if adduced, might enable him to make a better case. Their function is to hear the case the parties choose to put before them, make findings as to the facts and to decide the case in accordance with the law.'

[47] There is a suggestion in *Lemas v Williams* [2009] EWCA Civ 360, [58], that failure by the judge to warn an unrepresented party as to the consequences of not giving evidence might have constituted a 'procedural error or other irregularity in the conduct of the trial', although there was no such error in the case, as the judge did so warn. However, in *Joseph v Brighton & Sussex University Hospitals NHS Trust* 2015 WL 3750910, [38], the court was clear that there is no general duty on the judge to assist: 'But it is one thing to say that this would have been permissible, another altogether to say that the Employment Tribunal was required by law to take that course. It is plain on the authorities that it was not.' The writer's experience of both appearing in and observing practice in the Scottish courts is that judges differ widely in their willingness to interfere in proceedings.

In addition to the ordinary civil courts operating throughout the relevant jurisdictions, there exist many additional courts and tribunals.[48] It is impossible to examine all the various rules governing these courts and tribunals here. In general, these *fora* exist outwith the sphere of normal civil proceedings, and their attendant rules often differ somewhat from the ordinary rules of civil procedure. Nonetheless, such courts and tribunals remain bound by rules of private international law,[49] and the following analysis applies to a significant extent to them.

A. The Introduction and Application of Choice of Law Rules

(i) General Position

(a) Germany

It is beyond dispute in German case law[50] and literature[51] that the principle of *iura novit curia*,[52] ie that the judge has imputed knowledge of the law, extends to choice of law rules, be it those choice of law rules contained in pure domestic law[53] or in EU law.[54] The court must, in principle, not only *ex proprio motu* introduce and apply any applicable domestic choice of law rule,[55] but must also *ex proprio motu* apply any applicable foreign law, including instigating and conducting any necessary investigation of the applicable foreign law to effectively do so.[56] It is said that

[48] For example, British law makes provision for the operation of employment tribunals under the Employment Rights Act 1996. German law makes provision for the operation of *Arbeitsgerichte* (employment courts) under the ArbGG.

[49] See, for example, the scope of application of the Regulation (EU) No 1215/2012 of the European Parliament and of the Council of 12 December 2012 on jurisdiction and the recognition and enforcement of judgments in civil and commercial matters (recast) [2012] OJ L 351/1 (Brussels I bis Regulation, Art 1(1)).

[50] *Decision of the Federal Court of Justice from 7 April 1993* (BGH, XII. Zivilsenat) XII ZR 266/91, NJW 1993, 2305, 2306. The court explicitly rejects the proposition that one of the parties must rely on foreign law in order that choice of law rules be engaged. See G Wagner, 'Fakultatives Kollisionsrecht und prozessuale Parteiautonomie' (1999) *Zeitschrift für Europäisches Privatrecht* 6, 9.

[51] A Junker, *Internationales Privatrecht*, 4th edn (CH Beck, 2021), § 11 para 2; Schack, *Internationales Zivilverfahrensrecht* (n 7), para 751; R Geimer, *Internationales Zivilprozessrecht*, 8th edn (Otto Schmidt, 2020), para 2571.

[52] See Schack, *Internationales Zivilverfahrensrecht* (n 7), para 751; Prütting, '§ 293' (n 6), para 2.

[53] Prütting, '§ 293' (n 6), para 8.

[54] Many elements of EU law, eg regulations, by virtue of the Consolidated version of the Treaty on the Functioning of the European Union of 26 October 2012 [2012] OJ C 326/47 (TFEU), Art 288, have direct effect in German law. See also Prütting, '§ 293' (n 6), para 9.

[55] *Decision of the Federal Court of Justice from 15 July 2008* (BGH, VI. Zivilsenat) VI ZR 105/07, BGHZ 177, 237, 239; Schack, *Internationales Zivilverfahrensrecht* (n 7), para 752.

[56] *Decision of the Federal Court of Justice from 25 January 2005* (BGH, XI. Zivilsenat) XI ZR 78/04, NJW-RR 2005, 1071, 1072; *Decision of the Federal Court of Justice from 18 March 2020* (BGH, IV. Zivilsenat) IV ZR 62/19, NJW-RR 2020, 802, 804; Schack, *Internationales Zivilverfahrensrecht* (n 7), para 756.

the court should neither rely on the parties to raise a relevant choice of law rule,[57] nor should it construe the parties' ignorance thereof as an implied choice in favour of the *lex fori*.[58]

Nonetheless, there are situations, even in the general context, where choice of law rules can potentially be left out of account by the German courts.

First, it is obvious that the court may simply not see the choice of law issue raised by a foreign element in the case. The possibility for mistake in the application of domestic law clearly exists in every legal system, although the potential for mistake to provide grounds for a successful appeal differs. In Germany, as is considered in more detail in due course, a mistake in the application of choice of law rules (including a failure to consider them) undoubtedly provides grounds for appeal.[59]

Second, where the *Beibringungsgrundsatz* applies,[60] ie the vast bulk of civil matters,[61] the German court does not take cognisance of facts which have not been introduced by the parties.[62] Thus, if a material fact, which would raise a choice of law issue, is not introduced by the parties, the court may not *ex proprio motu* introduce it, even if the fact is known to the court and such a fact would lead to the application of foreign law in a case.[63] The converse of the *Beibringungsgrundsatz* is the *Untersuchungsgrundsatz*,[64] by which principle the court is required to actively investigate the factual matrix of the dispute, and which principle applies in certain civil actions, including family actions.[65] Thus, in every case to which this principle applies, regardless of what the parties seek to lead by way of evidence, the facts ought to be established by the court, and any relevant choice of law rule should accordingly always be applied.

Third, the possibility has, it seems, been recognised, usually in the contractual context, for the parties to tacitly (*stillschweigend*) consent to the application of the

[57] Geimer (n 51), para 2572.

[58] Schack, *Internationales Zivilverfahrensrecht* (n 7), para 752. See below for discussion regarding the possibility of tacit (*stillschweigend*) consent, which Schack strongly opposes in principle.

[59] *Decision of the Federal Court of Justice from 15 July 2008* (BGH, VI. Zivilsenat) VI ZR 105/07, BGHZ 177, 237, 239; *Decision of the Federal Court of Justice from 30 April 2013* (BGH, VII. Zivilsenat) VII ZB 22/12, NZI 2013, 763, 765.

[60] Also known as the *Verhandlungsgrundsatz*. See W Grunsky and F Jacoby, *Zivilprozessrecht*, 16th edn (Franz Vahlen, 2018), para 96ff; Kegel and Schurig (n 3), 499.

[61] Rosenberg, Schwab and Gottwald (n 43), § 77 para 8.

[62] Pohlmann (n 39), para 66ff.

[63] Schack, *Internationales Zivilverfahrensrecht* (n 7), para 754. The situation differs in Austria, where the court is always under a duty to investigate all facts that could lead to the application of a choice of law rule. See Wagner (n 50), 11, drawing on the relevant provision of Austrian law. 'Austrian Federal Law on Private International Law of 15 June 1978, as at 12 May 2020 (Bundesgesetz vom 15 Juni 1978 über das internationale Privatrecht, Fassung vom 12.05.2020)', www.ris.bka.gv.at/GeltendeFassung.wxe?Abfrage=Bundesnormen&Gesetzesnummer=10002426, § 2.

[64] Also known as the *Amtsermittlungsgrundsatz*. See, C Gomille, 'Beweiserhebung – Unterschiede zwischen ZPO- und FamFG Verfahren' (2014) *Neue Zeitschrift für Familienrecht* 100, 101.

[65] Pohlmann (n 39), para 67; Rosenberg, Schwab and Gottwald (n 43), § 77 para 45ff; Kegel and Schurig (n 3), 499–500; Schack, *Internationales Zivilverfahrensrecht* (n 7), para 754.

lex fori through a failure to make any reference to foreign law throughout the duration of the proceedings.[66] It has been held that:

> Such a – tacit – choice of law can, according to established case law of the Federal Court of Justice, be assumed if the parties proceed on the basis of the application of a certain law during the case, in particular by citing its provisions [Translation by author].[67]

Although this seems pragmatic and reasonable, it is questionable to what extent a failure to refer to foreign law can truly be construed as consent, as it may be that the parties were unaware that foreign law was even applicable in their case.[68] Hübner has therefore argued that, in such circumstances, the parties ought to receive a suggestion or warning under § 139 of the Code of Civil Procedure.[69] Nonetheless, that the possibility of tacit consent has been recognised by the Federal Court of Justice suggests that German procedural law is not as dogmatically opposed to leaving the introduction of choice of law rules in the parties' hands as might initially be thought, although the matter is undoubtedly a grey area and the German court's right to intervene is beyond dispute.

(b) Great Britain

Although the British court undoubtedly takes judicial notice of domestic choice of law rules,[70] the traditional and general position in Great Britain is that choice

[66] *Decision of the Federal Court of Justice from 17 December 1957* (BGH, VIII. Zivilsenat) VIII ZR 315/56, JurionRS 1957, 13380; *Decision of the Federal Court of Justice from 17 March 1981* (BGH, VI. Zivilsenat) VI ZR 286/78, NJW 1981, 1606; *Decision of the Federal Court of Justice from 30 September 1987* (BGH, IVa. Zivilsenat) IVa ZR 22/86, NJW-RR 1988, 159; *Decision of the Federal Court of Justice from 12 December 1990* (BGH, VIII. Zivilsenat) VIII ZR 332/89, NJW 1991, 1292; *Decision of the Federal Court of Justice from 22 February 1994* (BGH, VI. Zivilsenat) VI ZR 309/93, NJW 1994, 1408, which was in the delictual context; *Decision of the Hamm Court of Appeal from 9 June 1995* (OLG Hamm) 11 U 191/94, NJW-RR 1996, 179. For discussion see Wagner (n 50), 6 and R Hübner, *Ausländisches Recht vor deutschen Gerichten* (Mohr Siebeck, 2014), 192–93.

[67] *Decision of the Federal Court of Justice from 12 December 1990* (BGH, VIII. Zivilsenat) VIII ZR 332/89, NJW 1991, 1292, 1293: 'Eine solche – stillschweigende – Rechtswahl kann nach ständiger Rechtsprechung des BGH dann angenommen werden, wenn die Parteien während des Rechtsstreits von der Anwendung einer bestimmten Rechtsordnung, vor allem durch Anführen ihrer Vorschriften, ausgehen.' It was noted that English law would have been applicable in terms of the Introductory Act to the Civil Code (EGBGB), Art 28, which pre-dated the Rome I Regulation (n 1), and provided the rules governing the applicable law of contracts in the absence of choice in terms of the rules provided in the Convention on the law applicable to contractual obligations opened for signature in Rome on 19 June 1980 (Consolidated Version) (80/934/EEC) (Rome Convention).

[68] Wagner (n 50), 44; Hübner (n 66), 192–93. See, for a particularly critical analysis of a tacit choice of law in favour of the *lex fori*, H Schack, 'Keine stillschweigende Rechtswahl im Prozeß!' (1986) *Praxis des Internationalen Privat- und Verfahrensrechts* 272, which view is echoed in Schack, *Internationales Zivilverfahrensrecht* (n 7) para 753.

[69] Hübner (n 66) 193.

[70] R Fentiman, *Foreign Law in English Courts: Pleading, Proof and Choice of Law* (Oxford University Press, 1998), 64: 'Being a question of law there is no doubt that an English court has judicial notice of English rules for choice of law, just as it has notice of every other aspect of English law.' See also K Hood, 'Drawing Inspiration? Reconsidering the Procedural Treatment of Foreign Law' (2006) 2 *Journal of Private International Law* 181, 183.

of law rules will not be applied by the court unless one of the parties pleads the content of the applicable rule of foreign law, and the court may not introduce a choice of law rule *ex proprio motu*. In respect of England, Fentiman summarised the position as follows:

> There is certainly no doubt that the introduction of foreign law is generally voluntary. More precisely, English law normally allows litigants to select the *lex fori* as the applicable law. This choice may apparently be effected without express agreement by a simple omission to plead any other law.[71]

In *Sharp* (2007), an accident had taken place on the Autobahn 11 in the direction of Berlin involving British military personal travelling in a convoy.[72] The claimant had been injured by girders protruding from the vehicle travelling in front of him as a result of the convoy requiring to stop suddenly.[73] In terms of the relevant choice of law rule,[74] German law was applicable as *lex loci delicti*, however, neither party pleaded its content. Under the applicable law, the judge noted:

> It would have depended on whether, in the particular circumstances of the case, the general rule in section 11(1) of the Private International Law (Miscellaneous Provisions) Act 1995 that the applicable law is the law of the country in which the events constituting the tort occurred had been disapplied by section 12. However, the parties agreed that English law should be the governing law, and in these circumstances no evidence as to what the relevant German law is has been assembled.[75]

Sharp (2007) was, of course, a case in which the English court engaged with the issue as to whether a choice of law rule applied, and the parties had agreed that the *lex fori* should apply. However, there are numerous reported cases, both from the English and Scottish courts, where the choice of law issue has been ignored.[76] There is no material difference in the approach taken in Scotland. In *Pryde* (1971), it was observed that:

> the pursuer in such an action must make adequate averment of the foreign law applicable to the situation, and as to his rights by that foreign law … But in the written

[71] Fentiman, *Foreign Law in English Courts* (n 70), 70.

[72] *Sharp v Ministry of Defence* [2007] EWHC 224 (QB).

[73] *Sharp v Ministry of Defence* [2007] EWHC 224 (QB), [7].

[74] Private International Law (Miscellaneous Provisions) Act 1995, s 11(1).

[75] *Sharp v Ministry of Defence* [2007] EWHC 224 (QB), [11].

[76] Examples are given in Fentiman, *Foreign Law in English Courts* (n 70), 159–61. There is no necessity to rehearse them here. A poignant example is provided by *Aluminium Industrie Vaassen BV v Romalpa Aluminium Ltd* [1976] 1 WLR 676, which involved a contract governed by Dutch law, with numerous other connections with the Netherlands. Dutch law was not pleaded and, at appeal, a judge merely commented, at 684, that 'it would have been interesting to have known what the position was under Dutch law, as indeed it would have been interesting to know how a Dutch lawyer would have construed some of those express terms.' However, it is important to note that there is a difference between the foreign law dimension being completely ignored and the implications of the presumption of similarity. Thus, in the Scottish cases of *Emerald Stainless Steel Ltd v South Side Distribution Ltd* 1982 SC 61 and *Deutz Engines Ltd v Terex Ltd* 1984 SLT 273, Lord Ross acknowledged the implications of the presumption at 64 and 274 respectively, but the foreign law dimension was not completely ignored in these cases.

> pleadings in the present case no question of foreign law is raised on either side, and in that situation I am of opinion that the Scottish court is entitled to decide the case according to the law of Scotland, or, at any rate, to proceed upon the view that the lex loci delicti is the same as the law of Scotland.[77]

Notwithstanding the fact that the traditional approach appeared to be well-settled, some recent doubts were expressed as to the proper approach that should be taken to choice of law rules deriving from the European choice of law instruments,[78] which rules are prima facie framed in mandatory terms, for example, that the law applicable to a delict shall be the law of the country in which the damage occurred.[79]

A clear example of argumentation in this direction is found in *Global Multimedia International Ltd* (2006).[80] In the case, pleadings failing to draw on the applicable foreign law led to the rejection of the defendant's counterclaim under Part 20 of the English Civil Procedure Rules.[81] The then Chancellor (Sir Andrew Morritt) of the English High Court, criticised the:

> Complete absence of any reference to Sharia or Saudi law.[82]

[77] *Pryde v Proctor and Gamble Limited* 1971 SLT (Notes) 18.

[78] It has been suggested that 'Although the court will apply the appropriate choice of law rule (even if the parties fail to plead it) in the absence of proof of foreign law, operation of the choice of law rule of the forum effectively will be frustrated.' EB Crawford and JM Carruthers, *International Private Law: A Scots Perspective*, 4th edn (W Green, 2015), para 8-28. Although there is certainly strength in the argument that it would be pointless to nominally apply choice of law rules without insisting on proof of the relevant applicable foreign law's content, it appears that choice of law rules in such cases are simply not applied at all. See, in relation to German law, Hübner (n 66), 189: 'Die amtswegige Berücksichtigung der Kollisionsnormen macht aber nur dann Sinn, wenn auch das durch sie berufene Recht entsprechend von Amts wegen in das Verfahren eingeführt wird' ('It only makes sense to take choice of law rules into account *ex proprio motu* if the law designated by them is also introduced into the proceedings *ex proprio motu*') [Translation by author].

[79] For example, under Article 4(1) of Regulation (EC) No 864/2007 of the European Parliament and of the Council of 11 July 2007 on the law applicable to non-contractual obligations [2007] OJ L 199/40 (Rome II Regulation), 'Unless otherwise provided for in this Regulation, the law applicable to a non-contractual obligation arising out of a tort/delict shall be the law of the country in which the damage occurs irrespective of the country in which the event giving rise to the damage occurred and irrespective of the country or countries in which the indirect consequences of that event occur.'

[80] *Global Multimedia International Limited v ARA Media Services* [2006] EWHC 3612 (Ch).

[81] CPR 20.4(2). It should be noted that the fact that the decision was made in the context of a Part 20 application gave the court an opportunity to scrutinise the claim in a way that is not normally available. CPR, Part 7, titled 'How to start Proceedings – The Claim Form', lays down very few requirements when raising civil proceedings in England. In essence, in addition to the court fee, a claim form, together with the particulars of claim, must be filed at court. The English court does have the power to strike out a claim under CPR 3.4(2)(a) if the statement of case discloses no reasonable grounds for bringing the claim, but this is a very low bar. In Scotland, the sheriff's powers to dismiss a claim were clearly set out in *Cabot Financial UK Limited v McGregor* [2018] SAC (Civ) 12, [34], as being essentially limited to questions of competency and jurisdiction. The point is considered in more detail as regards undefended actions. See section II.A.(ii)(a).

[82] *Global Multimedia International Limited v ARA Media Services* [2006] EWHC 3612 (Ch), [37].

The defendant relied on the traditional approach by failing to plead the content of the applicable foreign law;[83] however, the judge rejected the legitimacy of this approach in the case stating:

> Given the allegations in relation to the parties to and formation of the employment contracts the law there referred to must be the law of Saudi Arabia, yet there is no attempt to say what it is or, in the sense of legal source, where it is to be found. In my view such pleading is deficient. It is not a mere pleading point but one of justice.[84]

The judge took the view that the purpose of the pleading rule is so that a party can provide detail of the relevant foreign legal system, with such detail providing fair notice to opponents and preventing unnecessary cost.[85] However, the judge argued that such detail is not necessary for foreign law to be applicable in a case:

> But if the facts alleged demonstrate that, for example, the proper law of a contract is not the law of England then as the law of England includes the principles of private international law those principles may demonstrate that some other system of law is applicable to the claim and if the relevant principles of that system of law are not sufficiently proved the claim may fail for that reason.[86]

Indeed, the judge went as far as saying that a failure to plead the content of the applicable law would be inconsistent with the overriding objective.[87]

There was also suggestion that the choice of law rules found in the Private International Law (Miscellaneous Provisions) Act 1995 ought to be considered mandatory, in the first instance decision in *Belhaj* (2013), where it was held by Mr Justice Simon that:

> it is not consonant with the overriding objective of the CPR, in a case where the 1995 Act applies, for a party either to decline to plead the relevant provisions of the applicable law or to rely on a presumption that a foreign law is the same as English law. Such an approach is evasive.[88]

This analysis was echoed in the Court of Appeal in *Belhaj* (2015), which noted:

> We are not surprised that the judge was unimpressed by the claimants' arguments on this (pleading) point, which he characterised as evasive, unrealistic and contrary to the overriding objective. We would add that we do not accept that section 14(3)(b) of the 1995 Act (which provides a saving for 'any rules of evidence, pleading or practice')

[83] *Global Multimedia International Limited v ARA Media Services* [2006] EWHC 3612 (Ch), [37]. The court was referred to L Collins (ed), *Dicey and Morris on the Conflict of Laws*, 13th edn (Sweet & Maxwell, 1999), para 9.003: 'The general rule is that if a party wishes to rely on foreign law he must plead it in the same way as any other fact. Unless this is done the court will decide a case containing foreign elements as though it were a purely domestic English case.'

[84] *Global Multimedia International Limited v ARA Media Services* [2006] EWHC 3612 (Ch), [39].

[85] *Global Multimedia International Limited v ARA Media Services* [2006] EWHC 3612 (Ch), [39].

[86] *Global Multimedia International Limited v ARA Media Services* [2006] EWHC 3612 (Ch), [38].

[87] *Global Multimedia International Limited v ARA Media Services* [2006] EWHC 3612 (Ch), [38]. See CPR, Part 1.

[88] *Belhaj v Straw* [2013] EWHC 4111 (QB), [140].

affects the position as Mr Hermer argues. The issue of the applicable law is one of substantive law, not procedure.[89]

However, the extent to which the treatment of choice of law rules as mandatory can be aligned with the adversarial approach taken in English (and Scottish) civil procedure is questionable, even in the face of the reforms introduced in the English Civil Procedure Rules.[90] Particularly robust criticism of the mandatory approach alluded to in both *Global Multimedia International Ltd* (2006) and *Belhaj* (2013) was made by Mr Justice Baker in *Iranian Offshore Engineering and Construction Co* (2019),[91] who rejected the authoritative value of the cases in the context, suggesting that they were a source of confusion,[92] and rejected any notion whatsoever that a party should be required by the court to aver foreign law, where it is applicable to a case,[93] but does not form part of the pleadings.[94]

These conflicting authorities arguably left the law in a somewhat unsettled state, with the risk of further decisions finding that the English court may be under a general obligation to apply choice of law rules *ex proprio motu*.[95] Any such doubts were, however, authoritatively dispelled in the UK Supreme Court decision in *FS Cairo (Nile Plaza) LLC* (2021), by Lord Leggett, who, in the wake of further discussion of the various relevant principles in the Court of Appeal,[96] clearly set out the implications of what he described as the 'default rule':[97]

[T]he English court is not obliged to apply the choice of law rules contained in the Rome I and Rome II Regulations if neither party chooses to assert in its statement of

[89] *Belhaj v Straw* [2015] 2 WLR 1105, 1166.

[90] See section II, nn 10–21.

[91] *Iranian Offshore Engineering and Construction Co v Dean Investment Holdings SA* [2019] 1 WLR 82.

[92] *Iranian Offshore Engineering and Construction Co v Dean Investment Holdings SA* [2019] 1 WLR 82, 88.

[93] *Iranian Offshore Engineering and Construction Co v Dean Investment Holdings SA* [2019] 1 WLR 82, 85: 'A little care therefore must be taken when reading Dicey, rule 25(1), lest it be thought to suggest that whenever a claim is governed by foreign law, it is necessary for the claimant to plead and prove the material content of that law (or indeed, as a logically prior matter, to plead a case as to governing law at all). I am quite clear that is not the law.'

[94] *Iranian Offshore Engineering and Construction Co v Dean Investment Holdings SA* [2019] 1 WLR 82, 92. *Iranian Offshore Engineering and Construction Co* (2019) has been discussed in positive terms in a number of cases, including *GDE LLC and Goffe v Anglia Autoflow Limited* [2020] EWHC 105 (Comm), [34]; *Gulf International Bank BSC v Aldwood* [2019] EWHC 1666 (QB), [149]; *Qatar Airways Group QCSC v Middle East News FZ LLC* [2020] EWHC 2975 (QB), [190], in which the reasoning of Mr Justice Baker is described as 'clear and convincing'; and *FS Cairo (Nile Plaza) LLC v Brownlie* [2020] EWCA Civ 996, per Lord Justice Underhill at [197].

[95] There are no similar Scottish cases, and the traditional approach has never been seriously doubted in Scotland.

[96] *FS Cairo (Nile Plaza) LLC v Brownlie* [2020] EWCA Civ 996. At [190], Lord Justice Underhill specifically distanced himself from the reasoning advocated in *Global Multimedia International Limited v ARA Media Services* [2006] EWHC 3612 (Ch), and, at [197], drew on Mr Justice Baker's reasoning in *Iranian Offshore Engineering and Construction Co v Dean Investment Holdings SA* [2019] 1 WLR 82, regarding his analysis as 'to essentially the same effect as mine.'.

[97] It should be noted that much of Lord Leggett's analysis addressed the implications of the presumption of similarity, which is addressed later when considering the implications of a failure to prove the content of the relevant foreign law. See section V.B.(i).

> case that foreign law is applicable. That is so even if the case is one to which a foreign system of law would clearly have to be applied if either party chose to rely on that fact.[98]

In terms of justification, Lord Leggett referred to the fundamental rule of English civil procedure:

> that (with limited exceptions) the court is not obliged to decide a case in accordance with a rule of law on which neither party chooses to rely.[99]

Lord Leggett also suggested that the failure to plead a foreign rule of law may be considered to constitute tacit agreement that English law should be applied to the case, and noted that there is no rule of public policy preventing such an approach.[100] He also found support in the relevant regulations themselves, first, in so far that the regulations were not intended to 'apply to evidence and procedure', and, second, the extent to which the regulations allow parties to choose the law that should be applied to their dispute after the relevant event has occurred.[101]

The British approach has been aptly identified by German academics as essentially rendering choice of law rules voluntary (*fakultatives Kollisionsrecht*),[102] an approach that is almost uniformly criticised by them,[103] as well as by the Federal Court of Justice (BGH),[104] although perhaps the greatest practical difference in approach lies in the fact that the British court may not introduce a choice of law rule *ex proprio motu*, whereas the German court is manifestly entitled to do so if the circumstances warrant it. In terms of justification for the voluntary approach, Fentiman has argued:

> As well as lacking the doctrine *iura novit curia*, English law lacks those general principles which might also justify such mandatory introduction in other systems.[105]

The German lawyer FA Mann, in a 1977 article on civil procedure, noted the absence in England of the doctrine of *iura novit curia*,[106] which requires the German court

[98] *FS Cairo (Nile Plaza) LLC v Lady Brownlie* [2021] UKSC 45, [114].
[99] *FS Cairo (Nile Plaza) LLC v Lady Brownlie* [2021] UKSC 45, [114].
[100] *FS Cairo (Nile Plaza) LLC v Lady Brownlie* [2021] UKSC 45, [114]. As discussed above, there is some authority for this approach in Germany.
[101] See the Rome I Regulation (n 1), Art 3(2) and Rome II Regulation (n 79), Art 14(1)(a). This argument is a little less convincing as it means having recourse to the regulations themselves, and in certain contexts, it is not possible to fully align the voluntary choice of law approach with the terms of the regulations. For example, in the context of employment contracts. See Rome I Regulation (n 1), Art 8.
[102] The term voluntary choice of law is not well-known in Great Britain. See Wagner (n 50), 9.
[103] Schack, *Internationales Zivilverfahrensrecht* (n 7), para 752; C von Bar and P Mankowski, *Internationales Privatrecht: Band I – Allgemeine Lehren*, 2nd edn (CH Beck, 2003), § 5 para 66ff; Kropholler (n 5), 45–46. As previously stated, two prominent advocates of voluntary choice of law (*fakultatives Kollisionsrecht*) in Germany are Flessner (see A Flessner, 'Fakultatives Kollisionsrecht' (1970) *Rabels Zeitschrift für Ausländisches und Internationales Privatrecht* 547), and Sturm (see F Sturm, 'Fakultatives Kollisionsrecht: Notwendigkeit und Grenzen' in H Bernstein, U Drobnig and H Kötz (eds), *Festschrift für Konrad Zweigert zum 70 Geburtstag* (JCB Mohr (Paul Siebeck), 1981)).
[104] See *Decision of the Federal Court of Justice from 7 April 1993* (BGH, XII. Zivilsenat) XII ZR 266/91, NJW 1993, 2305, 2306. The court specifically refers to the academic debate surrounding voluntary choice of law (*fakultatives Kollisionsrecht*).
[105] Fentiman, *Foreign Law in English Courts* (n 70), 271.
[106] FA Mann, 'Fusion of the Legal Professions?' (1977) 93 *LQR* 367, 369. However, the point appears to be a controversial one. For example, Adrian Briggs argued that *iura novit curia* does apply in respect

to actively apply the law to the facts it is presented with, and drew attention, inter alia, to the role of the English barrister and dearth of judicial capacity in England in comparison to Germany. However, Mann's argumentation attracted criticism from A-G Jacobs in a well-reasoned 1995 Opinion, who took the view, in respect of the differences in practice between the civil and common law systems, that:

> Such contrasts between different categories of legal system often prove on closer examination to be exaggerated … An English court, for its part, is in no way precluded from raising a point which the parties have not relied upon.[107]

Indeed, the reasoning put forward by A-G Jacobs seems particularly relevant when a British court is confronted with unrepresented parties, whose involvement may require the court to engage with the law applicable to a case in a way that would not usually be required when dealing with represented parties.[108] While it is true that advocates in British courts decide which legal arguments to put to the court, in terms of the adversarial system, this does not absolve British judges of their responsibility for knowing and applying the law. Domestic law is not voluntary in the British courts, which presumably ought to include domestic choice of law rules. Thus, although the general position in respect of choice of law rules is beyond dispute, there arguably remains something odd[109] in the position that the British judge may not, in principle, refer to nominally binding choice of law rules unless they are referred to by parties.[110]

of English law: 'The principle that *curia novit jus*, that the court knows the law, begins and ends with English domestic law.' A Briggs, *Conflict of Laws*, 4th edn (Oxford University Press, 2019), 10. Crawford and Carruthers imply that *iura novit curia* applies in the British courts in respect of domestic law when they exclude its scope of application from foreign law. Crawford and Carruthers (n 78), para 8-31. When discussing whether *iura novit curia* should be applied to foreign law in the US courts, Sprankling and Lanyi appear to proceed on the basis that the principle does apply in respect of US courts applying domestic law; otherwise their other argumentation would make little sense. See JG Sprankling and GR Lanyi, 'Pleading and Proof of Foreign Law in American Courts' (1983) 19 *Stanford Journal of International Law* 3, 8ff. The writers also proceed, at 9, on the basis that *iura novit curia* is applied by German courts in respect of the *content* of foreign law. However, that viewpoint is controversial. See 36ff.

[107] *Van Schijndel and Van Veen v Stichting Pensioenfonds voor Fysiotherapeuten* Joined Cases C-430/93 and C-431/93, [1995] ECR I-4705, Opinion of A-G Jacobs, [34].

[108] *Muschett v HM Prison Service* [2010] EWCA Civ 25, [31]: 'Of course an employment judge, like any other judge, must satisfy himself as to the law that he must apply to the instant case; and if he assesses that he has received insufficient help on it from those in front of him, he may well be required to do his own homework.' The court then goes on to make clear that the judge is not required 'to step into the factual and evidential arena.'

[109] Hood suggests that the approach is 'open to an objection of illogicality.' Hood, 'Drawing Inspiration?' (n 70).

[110] It is notable that the position in US federal procedural law appears to be different in so far that, when not pleaded by either party, the US federal court is entitled to apply foreign law if it wishes, and even this has been criticised as not going far enough. The distinguished US judge Roger Miner commented in a 1995 article: 'It is strange indeed for a court to consciously apply the wrong law, based on the position taken by the parties, while acknowledging a discretionary authority to apply the right law. Such an approach with regard to questions of domestic law would be highly unusual.' Judge Miner favoured the mandatory application of choice of law rules. 'My own view of the matter is that a court has the affirmative obligation to seek out the applicable foreign law whether the parties have established that law or not.' See RJ Miner, 'The Reception of Foreign Law in the US Federal Courts' (1995) 43 *The American Journal of Comparative Law* 581, 583.

(ii) Special Circumstances

The foregoing analysis sought to consider the general approach taken to the introduction and application of choice of law rules in the relevant jurisdictions. It was shown that the German court is, in principle, required to introduce and apply choice of law rules *ex proprio motu*, whereas the British court is not required to do so and indeed should refrain from doing so. Nonetheless, as previously stated, the possibility of a British court raising, in limited circumstances, a matter *ex proprio motu*, even in the context of the adversarial system, is well-recognised and was indeed acknowledged in England by Mr Justice Baker in *Iranian Offshore Engineering and Construction Co* (2019):

> In our adversarial system, it is primarily for the parties, through their pleadings, to decide for themselves and define for the court (and each other) what is or is not to be relevant for the resolution of their dispute. My analysis recognises and allows for the possibility of the court of its own motion insisting that an issue not raised by the parties be considered.[111]

The focus of the following analysis is to seek to identify any exceptions to the general approach taken in each of the relevant jurisdictions. It should be noted that there have been some suggestions in British case law and academic authorities that a different approach should be taken towards choice of law rules in further circumstances not addressed in detail here, but it is not clear what the conceptual basis is for a different approach to be taken in the circumstances addressed.[112] As noted by Lord Leggett in *FS Cairo (Nile Plaza) LLC* (2021),[113] confusion has often derived from a tendency in the authorities to conflate the question as to whether a choice of law rule ought to be applied by the court in a specific situation with the

[111] *Iranian Offshore Engineering and Construction Co v Dean Investment Holdings SA* [2019] 1 WLR 82, [21]. Lord Leggett also left some limited scope for exceptions in *FS Cairo (Nile Plaza) LLC v Lady Brownlie* [2021] UKSC 45, [113], when he noted that 'in an adversarial system such as that in England and Wales, if a party does not rely on a particular rule of law even though it would be entitled to do so, it is not generally for the court to apply the rule of its own motion.'

[112] For example, there is no analysis in the following as to whether the English courts' current approach towards the incorporation of foreign law (or foreign legal terminology) into documents represents an encroachment of voluntary choice of law in English law. At issue is really a question of contractual incorporation, ie it may be necessary to have recourse to foreign law to properly understand the relevant document, the content of which will, of course, require to be investigated and determined. See L Collins (Lord Collins of Mapesbury) and J Harris (eds), *Dicey, Morris & Collins on the Conflict of Laws*, 15th edn & 5th supp (Sweet & Maxwell, 2018), para 32-056: 'There is a clear distinction in theory between reference to a foreign law as a choice of that law to govern the contract (or part of a contract), on the one hand, and incorporation of some provisions of a foreign law as a term or terms of the contract, on the other hand, although sometimes it is difficult to draw the distinction in practice … the effect is not to make French law the governing law of the contract but rather to incorporate the French articles as contractual terms into an English contract. This is a convenient "shorthand" alternative to setting out the French articles verbatim.' See also, on this point, C Trautmann, *Europäisches Kollisionsrecht und ausländisches Recht im nationalen Zivilverfahren* (Mohr Siebeck, 2011), 72–73, which talks of a *materiell-rechtliche Verweisung*.

[113] See *FS Cairo (Nile Plaza) LLC v Lady Brownlie* [2021] UKSC 45, [111]–[112].

approach that should be taken if foreign law is not proven to the requisite evidential standard,[114] a matter that is addressed in detail later in this work.

(a) Undefended Litigation

Particular considerations potentially arise where litigation is undefended. This is where the defendant fails to adequately respond to the action brought against him, for example, by failing to return the acknowledgement of service, as required in England,[115] or a notice of intention to defend, as required in Scotland,[116] or failing to appear or be represented in court by a lawyer, as required in most courts in Germany.[117] In such circumstances, the claimant is usually entitled to a (form of) default judgment.[118] At issue is whether, in the absence of the defendant, choice of law rules can potentially be applied by the court *ex proprio motu*.

The following analysis considers actions raised in ordinary civil litigation, eg actions of debt. Actions concerning questions of status raise different considerations and accordingly are considered in a subsequent section. It should be noted that the circumstances in which litigation is undefended are practically and conceptually different from those circumstances in which the defendant has no proper defence to an action, but nonetheless seeks to defend it. For example, in England, summary judgment may be granted where the defendant has no real prospect of successfully defending the claim, and there is no other compelling reason as to why judgment should not be granted.[119]

Scots law frames the judge's role in an undefended action as a question *pars judicis*, which a leading textbook on Scottish procedure defines as follows:

> Pars judicis essentially means what a judge has a duty to do. Under the inherent jurisdiction of the court to preserve the due administration of justice the sheriff is empowered

[114] An exception in respect of 'claims for infringement of foreign intellectual property rights' appears to have first originated in *Alfred Dunhill Limited v Sunoptic SA* [1979] FSR 337. The matter is briefly discussed in *FS Cairo (Nile Plaza) LLC v Brownlie* [2020] EWCA Civ 996 at [128] and [199]. However, this is a matter that is properly considered in respect of the presumption of similarity. It is worth noting that no clear line of reasoning seems to run through the authorities in support of this exception, and as observed by Lord Justice Underhill in *FS Cairo (Nile Plaza) LLC* (2020), at [199], the matter was addressed in *Alfred Dunhill Limited* (1979) in a few sentences with no serious analysis undertaken or authorities cited to the court.

[115] CPR 12.1.

[116] OCR r 7.2.

[117] ZPO § 331; See commentary in H Prütting, '§ 331' in W Krüger and T Rauscher (eds), *Münchener Kommentar zur Zivilprozessordnung: Band 1 (§§ 1–354)*, 6th edn (CH Beck, 2020).

[118] As it is known in England, under CPR 12.1. In Scotland, it is known generally as 'decree in absence', under OCR Chapter 7, and, in Germany, *Versäumnisurteil*, under ZPO § 330ff.

[119] CPR, Part 24. There is limited authority to suggest that the English court is more reluctant to grant summary judgment if a foreign law is applicable to the facts of the case. See *National Shipping Corp v Arab* [1971] 2 Lloyd's Rep 363, which is referred to in Fentiman, *Foreign Law in English Courts* (n 70), 206, as authority that the court may decline to employ the presumption of similarity in summary proceedings. However, it is important to be clear that considerations of fairness appear to have played the greater role in these cases, rather than any view that the presumption was not applicable. The English court has more recently rejected the argument that summary judgment should not be granted in such circumstances. *Podgorica v Bishopscourt (BB&Co) Ltd* [2002] EWCA Civ 1468, [16]: 'There is

> to take notice of certain matters whether or not they have been urged upon him by any of the parties to the action. It is thought that such matters include any aspect of the litigation which may cause prejudice to a specific public interest, such as the public interest in the regular conduct of litigation, or to the interests of third parties not called in the action, or which may require the court to exceed its proper powers; but that they do not include objections based on rules conceived only for the benefit of a party to the action.[120]

Pars judicis thus represents a limited encroachment on the adversarial system in order that the judge can represent the public interest in civil proceedings. However, its scope should not be overstated. In an undefended action, it is clear that the Scottish judge has no responsibility to consider the substantive merits of a claim, regardless of whether the action is raised under simple procedure or otherwise, a point recently considered by a Scottish appeal court.[121] Specifically, the Scottish judge is not permitted *ex proprio motu* to dismiss an undefended action on the basis of the relevancy of averments made by the pursuer,[122] or require further detail or clarification,[123] which almost certainly includes any averments relating to the content of foreign law. This means that in most undefended Scottish actions no possibility exists for the Scottish judge to consider *ex proprio motu* whether a choice of law rule is applicable in the circumstances of the case, or whether any averments made by the pursuer in relation to the content of foreign law are correct. A pursuer can therefore ignore the issue of foreign law or base their claim on an understanding of foreign law that is entirely incorrect, which will go unchallenged if the action is undefended.

There appear, however, to be some theoretical exceptions to this general principle. Two matters[124] which are recognised as requiring consideration by

no reason why a claimant on a summary judgment application should not be in the same position as a claimant at a trial. A claimant is entitled to plead his case on the basis that foreign law is the same as English law and swear that he has the right to judgment and, if the defendant wants to say there is a different result by the proper law, it is for the defendant to put that evidence in.' This approach, if applied rigidly, could result in harsh outcomes and, where the matter is contested, summary judgment should not be granted based on the fact approach. In such circumstances, the 'proper course is to allow the matter to go to trial where more complete evidence may be supplied.' Fentiman, *Foreign Law in English Courts* (n 70), 206. There is some support for this proposition from the English Court of Appeal in *Shaker v Al-Bedrawi* [2003] Ch 350, 372, in so far as considerations of fairness may mean that the so-called 'default rule' may not be applied where the result would be unfair. In *Al Misnad v Azzaman Limited* [2003] EWHC 1783 (QB), [37], a defamation case, the judge stated that he 'would be reluctant to dispose summarily of the Claimant's claims in relation to the publications on the foreign jurisdictions on the basis of the presumption [of similarity].'

[120] AM Cubie (ed), *Macphail's Sheriff Court Practice*, 4th edn (W Green, 2022), para 2.12.

[121] *Cabot Financial UK Limited v McGregor* [2018] SAC (Civ) 12, [35].

[122] Cubie (ed) (n 120), para 7.16; *Cabot Financial UK Limited v McGregor* [2018] SAC (Civ) 12, [35].

[123] *Cabot Financial UK Limited v McGregor* [2018] SAC (Civ) 12, [72].

[124] There are others, eg whether there has been effective service, which can be an issue of significant controversy. See, by way of example, *Abela v Baadarani* [2013] 1 WLR 2043. Service can raise questions of foreign law if the relevant court rules require effective service under a foreign country's law. See, for example, RCS 16.2(6), which requires, in certain circumstances, that the party executing service lodge in process a certificate by a person qualified in the law of the country, or a duly accredited

the Scottish judge *pars judicis* in undefended actions are those of jurisdiction[125] and prescription.[126] In terms of jurisdiction, the Scottish court should not grant decree in absence unless a valid ground of jurisdiction appears on the face of the writ.[127] It is clear that a question of jurisdiction can involve a point of foreign law, for example, in a contract case, under the relevant rule in schedule 8 to the Civil Jurisdiction and Judgments Act 1982, which can require the application of substantive foreign law to determine the place of performance of the obligation giving rise to the alleged basis of jurisdiction.[128] Would the Scottish court ever seek to apply choice of law rules *ex proprio motu* to establish whether it has jurisdiction in an undefended action? As matters stand, this seems highly unlikely.[129] The test laid out in the Ordinary Cause Rules, which apply to most proceedings in the sheriff courts, is not an onerous one; the rules require only that there exists a prima facie ground of jurisdiction, although the rules of the Court of Session arguably set a more onerous test by requiring that the court be satisfied that it has jurisdiction.[130] Moreover, even where a defended action involves a question of jurisdiction involving foreign law, the Scottish court has made clear that it will apply the *lex fori* in the absence of evidence of the content of foreign law. In *McGowan* (2002), the Court of Session held in respect of a dispute regarding its jurisdiction that:

> The contract provides that 'this Document shall be governed by the laws of England'. Given such a provision, Scottish private international law regards English law as the law governing the effect of the jurisdiction condition. The Scottish courts cannot take judicial notice of foreign law; and they cannot therefore apply any foreign system of law (including English law) unless it has been established as a fact. In the absence of any proof of foreign law, the Scottish courts proceed on the basis that foreign law coincides with Scots law. In the present case, there is no suggestion in the pleadings that the

representative of the country in which service was executed, stating that the method of service used is permitted by the law of that country. In such a case, it would be ludicrous to apply the presumption that foreign law is the same as Scots law.

125 This is made clear in OCR 7.2(2)(a).

126 In Scots law, the passing of the relevant prescription period, usually five years, has the effect of extinguishing an obligation, eg Prescription and Limitation (Scotland) Act 1973, s 6.

127 OCR 7.2(2)(a). See Cubie (ed) (n 120), para 7.13.

128 In matters relating to contract, sch 8, r 2(b) of the Civil Jurisdiction and Judgments Act 1982, allows a defender to be sued in Scotland if performance of the obligation in question has taken place there. The place of performance of the obligation in question, eg the obligation to make payment, is determined by the law applicable to the legal relationship in question: *Tessili v Dunlop*, Case 12/76, [1976] ECR 1473 and *De Bloos v Bouyer*, Case 14/76, [1976] ECR 1497. See, for consideration of both cases in a Scottish case, *Eddie v Alpa Srl* 2000 SLT 1062, 1063–64.

129 It is notable that the Scottish court has a duty under sch 8, r 9 of the Civil Jurisdiction and Judgments Act 1982 to consider its jurisdiction *ex proprio motu* in an undefended action: 'Where in any case a court has no jurisdiction which is compatible with this Schedule, and the defender does not enter an appearance, the court shall declare of its own motion that it has no jurisdiction.' However, the suggestion that a court must, as a rule, consider its jurisdiction *ex proprio motu* – then in the context of Article 27 of the original Brussels I Regulation – was doubted by Lord Clarke in *The Alexandros T* [2013] UKSC 70, [118], although the court recognised the uncertainty and the potential need for a reference to the CJEU to decide the issue.

130 RCS 19.1(4)(b).

> relevant English law differs in any way from Scots law, and no attempt has been made before us to establish English law as a fact. In these circumstances, this court can only proceed on the basis that the relevant English law is the same as Scots law.[131]

Averments setting out the alleged basis of jurisdiction are unlikely to be queried in a Scottish undefended action unless they are patently without basis.[132] Even if the Scottish court were to query grounds for jurisdiction, requiring consideration of foreign law in an undefended contract action, the Scottish court would likely determine the place of performance of the obligation in question exclusively in terms of Scots law.[133]

In terms of the potential roles of *pars judicis* and foreign law in respect of prescription in Scottish undefended actions, where a foreign law is applicable to the substance of an action, the relevant prescription period is determined by the *lex causae*.[134] Again, while the Scottish court ought to consider *ex proprio motu* whether an obligation has been extinguished by prescription in an undefended action,[135] it appears likely that, in the absence of proof of the applicable foreign law, it is Scots law that will determine the relevant prescription period, even if a foreign law is applicable in the case. This arguably undermines the purpose behind the adoption of rules in Scots law providing for prescription (and extinction of obligations),[136] rather than limitation,[137] to the extent that foreign prescription periods are relevant.

English law frames the court's responsibilities, first and foremost, in terms of its case management powers under the Civil Procedure Rules,[138] and, second, but

[131] *McGowan v Summit at Lloyds* 2002 SC 638, 644.

[132] Undefended litigation is dealt with administratively in the Scottish courts. Thus, in the sheriff court, the pursuer (claimant) is entitled to minute (ie, apply) for decree once the relevant notice period has expired and no notice of intention to defend has been lodged. The sheriff will not review the papers where an action is undefended, unless a matter is brought to his attention by the sheriff clerk. The procedure for minuting for decree is detailed in Cubie (ed) (n 120), para 7.05ff.

[133] In Scots law, the place of performance of the payment obligation is at the creditor's residence or place of business. See *Bank of Scotland v Seitz* 1990 SLT 584 and, for comment, PR Beaumont and PE McEleavy, *Anton's Private International Law*, 3rd edn (W Green, 2011), para 8.227. However, this varies according to legal system and can be at the debtor's residence or place of business. Where a foreign law is applicable in the case, it might be that the ground of jurisdiction on which the action has been raised by the creditor may not be available in terms of the substantially applicable law.

[134] See, for those matters covered by its material scope, the Rome I Regulation, Art 12(1)(d), and for the default position in Scots law, the Prescription and Limitation (Scotland) Act 1973, s 23A(1).

[135] *Cabot Financial UK Limited v McGregor* [2018] SAC (Civ) 12, [72].

[136] The wording of the Prescription and Limitation (Scotland) Act 1973 is clear in so far as obligations are extinguished by the passage of the relevant prescription period; ie prescription does not act merely as a procedural bar.

[137] The nature of prescription and what distinguishes it from limitation is clearly explained in D Johnston, *Prescription and Limitation of Actions*, 2nd edn (W Green, 2012), para 1.01ff. With regard to the definition of limitation, it is said by the author: 'Limitation, about which neither Stair nor Erskine has anything to say, does not involve the loss of any substantive right but is the procedural barring of an action after the lapse of a period during which the law insists that it must, if at all, be brought.'

[138] Many of the English court's powers are listed at CPR, Part 3. For example, the court may exclude an issue from consideration, in terms of CPR 3.1(2)(k), or dismiss or give judgment on a preliminary issue, in terms of CPR 3.1(2)(l).

more elusively, in terms of the concept known throughout the common law world as 'inherent authority'[139] or 'inherent power'.[140] The issue of limitation is not relevant in the context of this work because in England, unlike Scotland, the expiry of a limitation period is a procedural bar to raising a further action, with no substantive rights being extinguished.[141] Even in the course of contested proceedings, as is also the position in Germany,[142] the English court will only take note of an elapsed limitation period if it is drawn to the court's attention by a party,[143] making it essentially impossible that the English court will apply a foreign limitation period *ex proprio motu*.

In terms of the potential for the English court to raise an issue of foreign law *ex proprio motu* in respect of its jurisdiction, the issue could arise at two stages: first, where a party is seeking permission to serve out of the jurisdiction;[144] and second, where a party is seeking, by means of application, default judgment in respect of a foreign domiciled defendant, for which permission to serve out of the jurisdiction is not required.[145] It is more likely than in Scotland that the English court would seek evidence of its jurisdiction in these circumstances, as the necessary application will always be considered by a judge. It seems highly probable, however, that the English judge would accept the application of English law in relation to grounds of jurisdiction raising a substantive issue of foreign law.

In principle, the German court may grant default judgment (*Versäumnisurteil*) in circumstances where the defendant fails to appear or to be represented by a lawyer with rights of audience, at the oral hearing.[146] However, the requirements in relation to default judgments are greater in the German courts than in the British courts. First, the writ in German proceedings must be coherent and relevant (*schlüssig*),[147] and, unlike in Scotland,[148] consideration of this is undertaken by the German court *ex proprio motu*.[149] While the failure to appear is

[139] DJ Meador, 'Inherent Judicial Authority in the Conduct of Civil Litigation' (1995) 73 *Texas Law Review* 1805.

[140] JD Pinsler, 'The Inherent Powers of the Court' (1997) *Singapore Journal of Legal Studies* 1.

[141] A McGee, *Limitation Periods*, 8th edn (Sweet & Maxwell, 2018), para 1.010.

[142] H Grothe, 'BGB § 194 Gegenstand der Verjährung' in C Schubert (ed), *Münchener Kommentar zum Bürgerlichen Gesetzbuch: Band 1 (Allgemeiner Teil §§ 1–240, AllgPersönlR, ProstG, AGG)*, 9th edn (CH Beck, 2021), para 5.

[143] This is made clear in CPR, Practice Direction 16, para 13.1.

[144] CPR 6.36. The specifics are complicated and beyond the scope of this work. It suffices to say that permission is required in relation to many defendants located furth (outside) of the English jurisdiction.

[145] CPR 12.10(b), which requires that an application be made under CPR, Part 23, for default judgment, where the defendant is located furth (outside) of the jurisdiction, but permission was not required to start the action, eg in respect of defendants located in Scotland.

[146] ZPO § 331.

[147] There is no direct translation of the German legal concept of *schlüssig*. However, a comparison can be drawn with the Scottish concept of relevancy. As was said by Lord Normand in *Jamieson v Jamieson* [1952] AC 525, 534: 'The true proposition is that an action will not be dismissed as irrelevant unless it must necessarily fail even if all the pursuer's averments are proved.' See also Cubie (ed) (n 120), para 9.34.

[148] This is clear from Lord Normand's remarks in *Jamieson v Jamieson* [1952] AC 525, 534, in so far as the onus is on the defender, not the court, to demonstrate that the action is irrelevant.

[149] H-J Musielak and W Voit, *Grundkurs ZPO*, 15th edn (CH Beck, 2020), para 335.

usually considered to be an admission by the defendant of all the averments in the writ,[150] this principle does not apply to the content of foreign law.[151] Accordingly, where the pleadings contain facts indicating the applicability of a choice of law rule, the German court must apply such a choice of law rule *ex proprio motu*. Any averments made in the claimant's pleadings drawing on foreign law are not considered to be admitted, and the mere offer by the claimant to prove foreign law is insufficient.[152] Thus, in so far as matters of foreign law are concerned, the approach taken by the German court in undefended litigation is essentially the same as that taken by it in defended litigation. Schack justifiably argues that the very character of foreign law, in terms of German procedural law, is clearly demonstrated by the approach taken by the German courts to it in undefended litigation.[153]

(b) Questions of Status

Questions of status can arise where a preliminary question (*Vorfrage*)[154] is raised in proceedings, eg whether the parties are validly married, or where a party is seeking recognition of a foreign marriage.[155] The law of marriage can raise difficult questions in choice of law, even amongst the different legal systems of the UK. Until 2006, it was possible for parties in Scotland to be married by cohabitation with the requisite habit and repute.[156] Although marriage by cohabitation with habit and repute was constituted by the inferred intention of the parties to marry, it is normal for third parties to require evidence by means of a declarator of marriage; ie the declarator is a probative but not a necessary step for the parties to be married under the doctrine.[157] It is a trite principle of private international law that formal validity is measured by the place of the marriage, *locus regit actum*,[158] with this principle having been committed to statute in Scotland.[159] Where the *lex causae* recognises marriage by cohabitation and repute, a union so constituted will be recognised in England under the *locus regit actum* principle,[160]

[150] ZPO § 331(1).

[151] Schack, *Internationales Zivilverfahrensrecht* (n 7), para 756; K Bacher, '§ 293' in V Vorwerk and C Wolf (eds), *BeckOK ZPO*, 43rd edn (CH Beck, 2022), para 22; Geimer (n 51), para 2595.

[152] Prütting, '§ 293' (n 6), para 55.

[153] Schack, *Internationales Zivilverfahrensrecht* (n 7), para 756.

[154] Junker (n 51), § 10 para 1ff.

[155] For example, in England and Wales, the Family Law Act 1986, s 55.

[156] Family Law (Scotland) Act 2006, s 3.

[157] Scottish Law Commission, 'Report on Family Law: No 135' (1992), www.scotlawcom.gov.uk/files/5912/8015/2668/Report%20on%20family%20law%20Report%20135.pdf, para 7.2.

[158] *Berthiaume v Dastous* [1930] AC 79, 83: 'If there is one question better settled than any other in international law, it is that as regards marriage – putting aside the question of capacity – *locus regit actum*. If a marriage is good by the laws of the country where it is effected, it is good all the world over, no matter whether the proceeding or ceremony which constituted marriage according to the law of the place would or would not constitute marriage in the country of the domicile of one or other of the spouses.' See also JJ Fawcett and P Torremans (eds), *Cheshire, North & Fawcett: Private International Law*, 15th edn (Oxford University Press, 2017), 893.

[159] Family Law (Scotland) Act 2006, s 38(1).

[160] Collins (Lord Collins of Mapesbury) and Harris (eds) (n 112), para 17-011, which cites inter alia *Rooker v Rooker and Newton* (1863) 3 Swabey & Tristram 526.

a proposition recently confirmed by the English High Court.[161] In Germany, the *locus regit actum* principle is accepted under Article 11(1) of the Introductory Act to the Civil Code (EGBGB).[162] Where the marriage took place abroad, foreign law may then have to be proven in respect of it.[163]

In Great Britain, the potential importance of status in the context of the application of foreign law has been alluded to by academics,[164] for example, in Hartley's 1996 article[165] and, more extensively, in Fentiman's 1998 text, although perhaps not with the viewpoint which one might expect.[166] In terms of whether there is a public policy interest involved in questions of status, Fentiman was of the view that:

> To the extent that English law requires mandatory pleading in status cases, it does not do so because of any desire to protect rights in personal status in the interests of public policy.[167]

Thus, Fentiman, following detailed consideration of the topic, concluded that there is no general obligation in status cases requiring that foreign law be pleaded:

> At best, the law is uncertain, such uncertainty itself implying that there is no general rule requiring the proof of foreign law in cases involving personal status.[168]

However, there is clear authority from the Scottish and English courts emphasising that status is of fundamental importance in any society.[169] In *Abbassi* (2006), where the recognition of a *talaq* divorce pronounced in Pakistan was at issue, the English court was mindful that it would be a:

> matter of grave consequence to the wife were the court in this jurisdiction too lightly to uphold the husband's application, which would demonstrate that the wife had, for a period of some years after the dissolution of the marriage, been co-habiting with the husband under the same roof and holding herself out to be his wife.[170]

[161] *R v M* [2011] EWHC 2132 (Fam), [19].

[162] Junker (n 51), § 18 para 15ff. Article 13 of the EGBGB, which refers to the formalities necessary for marriage, is identified by Junker as *lex specialis*, as the private international law rules found in it apply only to marriages entered into in Germany. Otherwise, the general provisions found in Article 11 of the EGBGB apply.

[163] An example is provided by the English case of *Padero-Mernagh v Mernagh* [2020] EWFC 27.

[164] See also Briggs (n 106), 9.

[165] TC Hartley, 'Pleading and Proof of Foreign Law: The Major European Systems Compared' (1996) 45 *ICLQ* 271, 286–87.

[166] See comments made in Fentiman, *Foreign Law in English Courts* (n 70), 120–21, in so far that the author suggests that lawyers experienced in domestic family law are likely to see the issues involved in status differently from private international lawyers.

[167] ibid, 118.

[168] ibid, 122.

[169] See, for a Scottish example, *Ferguson v Binnie or Ferguson* 1936 SC 808, 809, where the Inner House of the Court of Session, following the death of a judge, was not prepared to let a draft judgment be treated as an opinion: 'If the action had not been a consistorial action it would have been competent for the Court, with the consent of parties … But the action is one of divorce. It involves a question of status. It concerns the position of a co-defender who did not lodge defences in the action and therefore is not a party in the action, but who obviously has a material interest in the result of the action.'

[170] *Abbassi v Abbassi* [2006] EWCA Civ 355, [10]. See also *M v P* [2019] EWFC 14, [115]: 'After all, divorce goes to status and the public at large has an interest in knowing whether or not someone's marriage has been dissolved and what that person's status is.'

Questions of status (and its potential modification by a court judgment) are thus too important to be left entirely in the hands of the parties, especially as changes of status can affect third party rights. It was held in *Niboyet* (1878) that:

> As has been frequently pointed out, a decree of dissolution of marriage cannot be the judicial declaration of a mere consequence agreed between the parties for the breach of a contract, as in ordinary cases of breach of contract, or a mere compensation or individual remedy for the breach of a private duty as in an action for damages, but can only be a judicial sentence of the law of the country in and for which the Court is acting, by which such Court assumes to alter not only the relation between the parties but the status of both.[171]

Despite recognition that the state does have an interest in questions of status, and the fact that the authorities show that the court may seek to be more interventionist generally in cases involving status, there are, nonetheless, cases that demonstrate that the voluntary choice of law approach is applicable in the British courts to cases involving status to its full extent.[172] It appears that these potentially competing propositions do not represent the full story, however, at least as far as England is concerned. The public interest has been, and can be, represented in English court proceedings through the fairly elusive[173] office of the Queen's Proctor,[174] which has not infrequently intervened in matrimonial matters.[175] Thus, the Queen's Proctor provides a mechanism to facilitate the state's interests in proceedings involving

[171] *Niboyet v Niboyet* (1878) 4 PD 1, 11.

[172] This was the approach explicitly taken by the Scottish court in *Prawdzic-Lazarska v Prawdzic-Lazarski* 1954 SC 98, 102. In *Szechter v Szechter* [1971] P 286, 295–96, the English court commented: 'If I also look (as I propose to do) at what English law says on the matter, it is because the annulment of a marriage is a very serious step, and because the expert witness on Polish law had to go into hospital for an operation, so that he had to give his evidence by affidavit and was not available for oral examination. If a party adduces no evidence, or insufficient evidence, of the proper foreign law, court perforce looks to English law'. However, as Fentiman recognises, in Fentiman, *Foreign Law in English Courts* (n 70), 117, the judge concluded in *Szechter* (1971), at 298, that Polish and English law were essentially to the same effect, a point that makes the case inconclusive. Consideration of English law was thus in addition to the (limited) evidence led on Polish law, the conclusions with regard to which no issue was taken by counsel for the Queen's Proctor. In *Buckland v Buckland* [1967] 2 WLR 1506, in an undefended action for a declaration of nullity, the English court nullified a Maltese marriage but did not make any mention of Maltese law.

[173] There are no contemporary official references to the role of the Queen's Proctor outwith legislation: See the Matrimonial Causes Act 1973, s 8. In response to a published request under the Freedom of Information Act 2000, on 4 July 2011, the Ministry of Justice wrote that the position of Queen's Proctor is held by the Treasury Solicitor. See UK Government, 'Bona Vacantia: About Us', www.gov.uk/government/organisations/bona-vacantia/about. However, there is no mention on the Treasury Solicitor's website as to its role as the Queen's Proctor. The response from the Ministry of Justice to the Freedom of Information Request can be found at What Do They Know, 'Queen's Proctor', www.whatdotheyknow.com/request/queens_proctor.

[174] The office of the Queen's Proctor appears to be one of some antiquity. See *Sheldon v Sheldon* (1865) 4 Swabey & Tristram 75 and *Clutterbuck v Clutterbuck and Reynolds (Queen's Proctor showing cause)* (1961) 105 Sol Jo 1012.

[175] The Queen's Proctor appears to have assumed a role in matrimonial matters shortly following the introduction of the Matrimonial Causes Act 1857 to examine the circumstances underlying divorce petitions and to avoid, inter alia, the risk of parties colluding to satisfy the then very strict requirements for divorce. For a detailed and interesting account of the role of the Queen's Proctor, see S Cretney, *Family Law in the Twentieth Century: A History* (Oxford University Press, 2005), 178ff.

status in England. Although the Queen's Proctor mostly appears to have intervened in cases where there has been fraud in obtaining divorce decrees,[176] the Queen's Proctor has also intervened in the private international law context. In *H* (2006), the Queen's Proctor intervened where the validity of a Japanese divorce was at issue, taking the lead role in instructing the main experts in the case, namely Japanese and Californian lawyers.[177] Equally, in *Abbassi* (2006), it appears that the Queen's Proctor was also involved in the case, and instructed an expert to provide an opinion on the validity of a divorce granted in Pakistan.[178] *In Duhur-Johnson* (2005), the court involved the Queen's Proctor in respect of the possible recognition of a Nigerian divorce, but no expert report was instructed as the divorce was refused on other grounds.[179] This is not to suggest that the Queen's Proctor will intervene in every case where the parties' status is at issue in a case,[180] but the existence of this possibility in English law cannot be doubted. There appears to exist no similar mechanism in Scotland,[181] and the voluntary choice of law approach likely applies to questions of status in Scots law without impediment.[182]

[176] *Ali Ebrahim v Ali Ebrahim (Queen's Proctor Intervening)* [1983] 1 WLR 1336; *Grasso v Naik v Bhatoo and twenty other petitions* [2017] EWHC 2789 (Fam); *Rapisarda v Colladon* [2014] EWFC 35, which involved 180 divorce petitions of persons mostly resident in Italy falsely claiming habitual residence in England.

[177] *H v H (Queen's Proctor Intervening) (Validity of Japanese Divorce)* [2006] EWHC 2989 (Fam), [11].

[178] *Abbassi v Abbassi* [2006] EWCA Civ 355, [2]. There is no specific reference to the term 'Queen's Proctor' in the case, although the Attorney General is referred to as having intervened in the case.

[179] *Duhur-Johnson v Duhur-Johnson (Attorney-General Intervening)* [2005] 2 FLR 1042. The Queen's Proctor was represented by standing counsel. The court noted that it was not able to make any decisions on the validity of the Nigerian divorce without expert evidence but decided to refuse recognition of the divorce under s 51(3)(a)(i) of the Family Law Act 1986, ie that reasonable steps were not taken to inform the respondent of the Nigerian divorce action. The court made clear, at 1057, that it would have required expert evidence on the effect of the divorce under the relevant Nigerian law had it not felt in a position to refuse recognition under s 51(3)(a)(i) of the 1986 Act.

[180] See *K v A* [2014] EWHC 3850 (Fam), [24]. Despite the efforts of the petitioner's counsel, the court was placed in some difficulty by the refusal of the Queen's Proctor to intervene in the case. See comments at [25] and [77] of the judgment. Even where the Queen's Proctor intervenes, there is no guarantee that it will seek to investigate and lead evidence on the content of foreign law. See *Padero-Mernagh v Mernagh* [2020] EWFC 27, [9], where the Queen's Proctor declined to do so despite the judge providing for the Queen's Proctor to apply for further directions in relation to expert evidence on the law of the Philippines as 'the prospect of the parties instructing a single joint expert on Philippine law was not viable given they were both acting in person and of limited means.' It is clear that the judge felt bound to consider the relevant provisions of Philippine family law, despite the lack of expert evidence and the failure of the Queen's Proctor to properly assist. Thus, at [49], he determined that 'The Philippine Family Code appears to require only five essential or formal requisites of marriage' and 'according to Philippine law she was lawfully married and she believed herself to be lawfully married.' At no point in *Padero-Mernagh v Mernagh* [2020] EWFC 27 does the judge doubt the need for proper evidence as to the content of Philippine law to resolve the question as to whether the parties were lawfully married.

[181] It is not impossible that the Scottish court could appoint a lawyer *amicus curiae* to represent the public interest in a status case with unrepresented parties: 'The role and function of the *amicus* is to assist the court by presenting a neutral appraisal of the issues which require to be decided and by raising considerations that might not otherwise come to the court's attention particularly in circumstances where the appellants are not legally represented.' *Hamilton v Glasgow Community and Safety Services* [2016] SAC (Civ) 3, [2].

[182] It should be noted that, in Scotland, decrees (other than a simplified divorce) affecting status may not be granted without evidence being led, even where an action is undefended, including evidence

In Germany, as has been explained, choice of law rules are mandatory and are applied by the court *ex proprio motu*. This applies to all actions, including actions involving questions of status. Nonetheless, as stated previously, in most civil actions there remains the possibility that a party will neglect to plead a fact having a bearing on a choice of law issue. This could lead to foreign law not being applied by the German court where foreign law is applicable under a choice of law rule. However, where a case involves a question of status, there is an enhanced role for the German court, which has a duty to investigate facts in terms of the *Untersuchungsgrundsatz* (duty to investigate). The court is not bound by party averments, with the factual matrix requiring to be established objectively by the court to the greatest possible extent.[183] It is also very unlikely that the German court would allow the parties to tacitly consent to the application of the *lex fori* in a case involving a question of status.

(c) Provisional Measures

Provisional measures[184] include interim injunctions[185] and freezing orders.[186] Each relevant jurisdiction has its own test to determine whether a provisional measure should be granted.[187] In short, provisional measures seek to preserve the existing position, pending a substantive decision by the court with jurisdiction.[188] However, provisional measures can have a significant impact on the progression of the litigation, potentially being largely determinative, both as an indication of what the trial judge is likely to decide,[189] and, due to their oppressive effect pending resolution of the substantive dispute.[190] It has been argued in Germany that the court should accordingly pay due respect to the consequences that a failure to take account of the substantive applicable law may have on the subsequent progression of the litigation.[191]

independent of the parties, under the Civil Evidence (Scotland) Act 1988, s 8(1) and (2), and it is *pars judicis* to refuse to grant an order if not persuaded by the evidence. See M Ross, J Chalmers and I Callander, *Walker and Walker: The Law of Evidence in Scotland*, 5th edn (Bloomsbury Professional, 2020), para 27.2.1 and para 27.5.2. This may give a Scottish court an opportunity to, at least, raise a choice of law issue.

[183] H Borth and M Grandel, *Familiengerichtliches Verfahren*, Hans-Joachim Musielak (ed), 6th edn, (Franz Vahlen, 2018), § 127 1.

[184] This is the term used in the Brussels I bis Regulation (n 49), for example, at Art 35 of that Regulation. In Germany, provisional measures are known as *einstweilige Rechtsschutz*, whereas interim remedies is the term used in England and interim diligence is the term used in Scotland.

[185] G Phillipson, 'Max Mosley goes to Strasbourg: Article 8, Claimant Notification and Interim Injunctions' (2009) 1 *Journal of Media Law* 73, 76.

[186] *Candy v Holyoake* [2017] EWCA Civ 92, [34].

[187] In England, the leading case is *American Cyanamid v Ethicon Ltd* [1975] AC 396, which set out the fundamental test. *American Cyanaid* (1975) is said not to apply in Scotland. See *NWL Ltd v Woods* [1979] 1 WLR 1294, 1309. For a summary of the position in Scotland, see Cubie (ed) (n 120), para 21.57, and, in Germany, Pohlmann (n 39), para 12.

[188] Cubie (ed) (n 120), para 11.01–11.03; J O'Hare and K Browne, *O'Hare & Browne: Civil Litigation*, 20th edn (Sweet & Maxwell, 2021), para 27-001; Pohlmann (n 39), para 11.

[189] O'Hare and Browne (n 188), para 27-001.

[190] Phillipson (n 185), 75.

[191] Schack, *Internationales Zivilverfahrensrecht* (n 7), para 757.

The determination as to whether a provisional measure should be granted by the German court is made using an accelerated procedure (*Eilverfahren*).[192] In such circumstances, the German court applies choice of law rules, ie it does not simply apply the *lex fori*, but a full investigation of the content of the *lex causae* need not be undertaken at the interim stage.[193] Rather, it is necessary for the applicant to provide a credible basis for their submissions, with reference to those sources on the applicable foreign law that are readily available.[194] A failure to provide such a basis means that the application for provisional measures should be refused.[195]

While strictly an evidential matter, the Scottish case of *Wilmington Trust Co* (2010) is authority that a British court may be reluctant to grant an interim application made at an early stage of proceedings, where such an application seeks to derive unfair advantage from the implications of the fact approach.[196] In this case, Lord Hodge rejected the pursuer's motion before calling,[197] which relied on the presumption of similarity,[198] as there was evidence that the defender was actively seeking to identify the terms of the (potentially) applicable foreign law:

> While it was incumbent on the defenders to obtain the needed legal advice with alacrity, I did not consider their behaviour to be unreasonable and, in any event, did not think that it entitled the court to deny them the right to obtain advice on the law of New York as well as that on the law of Connecticut, which they had obtained and produced. It is important to observe that the motion was heard before calling.[199]

Nonetheless, there remains little evidence that a British court will *ex proprio motu* insist on the application of a choice of law rule in an interim application, where no party is seeking to rely on foreign law,[200] and Lord Leggett made clear in *FS Cairo (Nile Plaza) LLC* (2021) that it is more likely that the court will accept the application of the presumption of similarity at an early stage of proceedings.[201] In *Wilmington Trust Co* (2010), it appears to have been primarily considerations of fairness that motivated the judge to refuse the motion at such an early stage of proceedings as, in the opinion of the judge, the defender had had insufficient time to investigate the position.[202]

[192] Pohlmann (n 39), para 11ff.
[193] Schack, *Internationales Zivilverfahrensrecht* (n 7), para 757; Geimer (n 51), para 2575. The matter is not without controversy. A detailed discussion of the competing viewpoints can be found in Prütting, '§ 293' (n 6), para 56, where the writer cautions against placing too great an evidential burden on the applicant, as well as against simple recourse to the *lex fori*.
[194] Schack, *Internationales Zivilverfahrensrecht* (n 7), para 757.
[195] ibid, para 757.
[196] *Wilmington Trust Co v Rolls Royce Plc* [2010] CSOH 157.
[197] A motion (application) before calling is made at a very early stage of Scottish Court of Session proceedings. Lord Hodge is currently Deputy President of the UK Supreme Court.
[198] *Wilmington Trust Co v Rolls Royce Plc* [2010] CSOH 157, [15].
[199] *Wilmington Trust Co v Rolls Royce Plc* [2010] CSOH 157, [20].
[200] It is not clear whether Lord Hodge meant to impinge upon the fact approach when he said in *Wilmington Trust Co v Rolls Royce Plc* [2010] CSOH 157, [19], 'If Scots law were to be applied as the *lex situs*, I would still require to know the extent to which the law of New York allowed the lessee to create a lien and the meaning it gave to the relevant terms of the lease. I needed to know the lessee's rights in order to apply the principle of *nemo dat quod non habet*.'
[201] *FS Cairo (Nile Plaza) LLC v Lady Brownlie* [2021] UKSC 45, [147].
[202] *Wilmington Trust Co v Rolls Royce Plc* [2010] CSOH 157, [20].

It is unclear whether a British court may insist on more protection for the defender in an ex parte application, ie could considerations of fairness prompt the court to raise the choice of law dimension *ex proprio motu* if an application is made at the earliest stage of the litigation? While certainly conceivable, this does seem unlikely in most cases and the same considerations as regards undefended litigation would seem to apply. An important question which arises in this context is whether a party has a duty in an ex parte application to raise the choice of law dimension, if relevant, when considering that there is a duty of disclosure on parties in ex parte applications,[203] a duty that has been described as a serious and onerous one.[204] This is properly a question that is dealt with in the section of this work addressing the parties' role in the introduction of choice of law rules.[205]

In interim applications before the British courts, any evidence, including that relating to the content of foreign law, should usually be provided only by way of written documents and statements, rather than oral evidence.[206] There is strong suggestion that a lesser amount of evidence on the content of foreign law is required from the parties at the interim stage as no substantive decisions may be taken,[207] which is the approach taken with regards to interim applications generally.[208]

(d) Foreign Illegality

The possibility that the factual matrix of a case may give rise to illegality under foreign law gives rise to potential difficulty for the British courts.[209] The general principle is well-known:

> The court will not lend its assistance for the purpose of enforcing an illegal contract, once the illegality has come to light and the court is satisfied of the illegality.[210]

[203] D Bean, I Parry and A Burns, *Injunctions*, 13th edn (Sweet & Maxwell, 2018), 5–12.

[204] *OJSC TNK-BP Holding v Beppler & Jacobson Ltd* [2012] EWHC 3286 (Ch), [320]. See also the Scottish case of *Fife v Orr* (1895) 23 R 8, where it is noted, at 10, that statements made in pursuit of interdict are made at a party's 'own peril', and, at 11, that no distinction is drawn between 'positive false statements' and 'suppression or non-disclosure of facts'.

[205] See section III below.

[206] See, generally, in respect of English law O'Hare and Browne (n 188), para 13-003. It is recognised that this analysis strays into matters dealt with in the next section of this chapter, but it is convenient to address the issue here.

[207] *Alfred Dunhill Ltd v Sunoptic SA* [1979] FSR 337, 368–69; *Shaker v Al-Bedrawi* [2003] Ch 350, 372; *PT Pan Indonesia Bank Ltd TBK v Marconi Communications International Ltd* [2005] EWCA Civ 422, [70], which places the burden on the party 'who asserts that the application of foreign law would provide a different result' but the evidence produced must only be 'sufficient to satisfy the court that an arguable defence or other relevant issue has been established for the purposes of a decision at that stage of the proceedings.'

[208] *American Cyanamid v Ethicon Ltd* [1975] AC 396, 404ff. There are differences between English and Scots law regarding the test for granting an interim remedy, with more emphasis in Scotland on the relative strength of the parties' cases. See Cubie (ed) (n 120), para 21.57, citing *NWL Ltd v Woods* [1979] 1 WLR 1294, 1310.

[209] There is no evidence of any difficulty in this area so far as concerns the German courts, which investigate and apply choice of law rules *ex proprio motu*.

[210] *Snell v Unity Finance Co Ltd* [1964] 2 QB 203, 219.

Difficulties involving foreign law can arise, first, where the contract is illegal under the *lex causae*, but neither party has pleaded the content of that law, or, second, but significantly less relevant for the purposes of this work, where the law of a third state is involved and an act is illegal under that law.[211] The relevant question is, despite neither party having pleaded the relevant rule of foreign law, can the British court apply choice of law rules *ex proprio motu* to determine whether an act is illegal under the *lex causae*?

Taking account of the existing case law, it is suggested that in circumstances where there is evidence of illegality, either under domestic law[212] or foreign law, the British court is entitled to make orders *ex proprio motu*;[213] for example, potentially dismissing a claim or ordering a party, under its case management powers, to obtain an expert opinion as to the content of the relevant foreign law. However, the matter seems somewhat academic.[214] First, the British court would be unlikely to know of the foreign illegality without any evidence being led on the point. Second, in such a situation, it is very unlikely that one of the parties would not benefit from pleading the illegality, and one of them would thus seek to do so. For example, in one of the few relevant cases, *Foster* (1929), the defendant pleaded that the agreement was illegal and void on the basis that it provided for the shipping and delivery of whisky into the United States, in violation of the prohibition laws of the country at that time.[215]

(e) Criminal Proceedings

This work is about the application of foreign law in civil proceedings. It does not attempt to substantially engage with the role that foreign law can play in criminal proceedings. However, for completeness, it is observed that there are situations in criminal proceedings where the private law position can have an impact as to whether the essential elements of a crime are satisfied. One example[216] is the criminal offence of theft (*Diebstahl*), the elements of which are similar throughout the relevant jurisdictions,[217] with all requiring that to constitute the crime, the misappropriated moveable property must belong to another (*Fremdheit der Sache*). There are other relevant offences such as the offence of bigamy,[218] which requires

[211] A good example is provided by *Regazzoni v KC Sethia (1944) Ltd* [1958] AC 301.

[212] This point is made clearly in *Snell v Unity Finance Co Ltd* [1964] 2 QB 203, 220: 'the court is bound to take a point of illegality of this kind of its own motion.'

[213] For example, a case management order under CPR, Part 3.

[214] See Fentiman, *Foreign Law in English Courts* (n 70), 113.

[215] *Foster v Driscoll* [1929] 1 KB 470, 478.

[216] For a very detailed discussion of the issues involved in respect of German law, see A-M Brutscher, *Zivilrechtsakzessorietät des Strafrechts bei Sachverhalten mit Auslandsbezug – am Beispiel des § 242 StGB* (Mohr Siebeck, 2014).

[217] Theft Act 1968, s 1(1); § 242 of the German Criminal Code (StGB); *Carmichael v Black* 1992 SLT 897. See, in relation to Scotland, J Chalmers and F Leverick, *The Criminal Law of Scotland*, 4th edn (W Green, 2016), para 21.01ff.

[218] Bigamy is a criminal offence in England under the Offences Against the Person Act 1861, s 57. Bigamy has long been recognised in England as an offence with a potential private international law

the existence of a subsisting marriage,[219] and the offence of handling stolen goods, which draws on the definition of theft.[220] Moreover, there is a distinction, not always observed, between applying the criminal law of another country,[221] and applying the private law of another country to determine a matter relevant to the constitution of a criminal offence under domestic law, eg who currently owns the previously stolen property? It is the latter with which this work is concerned.

By way of example, all relevant jurisdictions have recourse to the *lex situs* to determine real rights in property, which includes changes of ownership.[222] In other words, changes of ownership are determined by the *situs* of the property at the time of the alleged change of ownership. Circumstances may arise where there has been a change of ownership abroad, even in bad faith,[223] in respect of stolen property – even if the property was stolen in, removed from, and subsequently returned to the jurisdiction of the court. This change of ownership could have an impact as to whether an offence has been committed in the jurisdiction of the court, eg the offence of handling stolen property.

Considering that even German civil courts reject the voluntary choice of law approach,[224] it seems inconceivable that a German criminal court would take a different approach. Although the matter does not appear to have been considered

dimension. In 1752, in *Scrimshire v Scrimshire* (1752) 2 Hagg (Consist) 395, 402, it was held: 'It has been determined at common law that, if a man marries two wives, the first in France and another here, he may be tried and indicted here for that as felony.' Bigamy was recently made a statutory offence under Scots law, although the term bigamy is not used, under the Marriage (Scotland) Act 1977, s 24(A1). The offence is known in Germany as *Doppelehe*, under StGB, § 172.

[219] See, in relation to England, a detailed analysis of the offence of bigamy in M Lucraft, *Archbold: Criminal Pleading, Evidence and Practice*, 2021 edn (Sweet & Maxwell, 2020), para 31-5ff.

[220] ibid, para 21-221ff. The offence of handling is known as reset in Scotland and, in Germany, *Unterschlagung*, in terms of § 246 of the StGB. See, in relation to Scotland, Chalmers and Leverick (n 217), para 27.01ff, and, in relation to Germany, O Hohmann, '§ 246' in GM Sander (ed), *Münchener Kommentar zum StGB: Band 4 (§§ 185–262)*, 4th edn (CH Beck, 2021).

[221] An example is provided by the Theft Act 1968, s 24(1), which encapsulates stealing regardless of 'whether the stealing occurred in England or Wales or elsewhere, and whether it occurred before or after the commencement of this Act, provided that the stealing … amounted to an offence where and at the time when the goods were stolen; and references to stolen goods shall be construed accordingly.' In *R v Ofori; R v Tackie* (1994) 99 Cr App R 223, the English criminal appeal court quashed convictions for theft, where there had been a failure to prove illegality under Belgian and German criminal law respectively. A more recent example is provided by *R v Okolie*, CA (Crim Div), 15 May 2000, 2000 WL 699434. With reference to the relevant terms of the Theft Act 1968, s 24(1), the court made clear, at [11], that in criminal cases 'Foreign law must be proved strictly. It should be proved, as the case Ofori makes clear, by calling a properly qualified expert in that law, who will give evidence himself unless his testimony is agreed or no issue is taken. Just as in criminal cases foreign law cannot be the subject of judicial notice, and it is not possible to rely on any rebuttable presumption that it is the same as our law, so it cannot be derived from the basis of inference that is here put before us.' Thus, the fact approach does not apply in such cases.

[222] The authorities draw on each other in respect of England and Scotland. See *Cammell v Sewell* (1858) 3 H & N 617; 157 ER 615, 638: 'If personal property is disposed of in a manner binding according to the law of the country where it is, that disposition is binding everywhere.'; *Todd v Armour* (1882) 9 R 901; *Winkworth v Christie Manson & Woods Ltd* [1980] Ch 496, 506, which describes the Scottish Court of Session decision in *Todd* (1882) as 'particularly helpful'. In respect of Germany, see Art 43 EGBGB and Junker (n 51), § 17 para 34.

[223] Possession in bad faith can benefit from prescription under Italian law. See G Alpa and Zeno-Zencovich Vincenzo, *Italian Private Law* (Routledge-Cavendish, 2007), 153.

[224] See section II.A.(i)(a).

by a court either in Scotland or in England – despite the established position in civil proceedings – it seems likely that the requirements of criminal law, ie proof beyond reasonable doubt with the burden of proof resting with the state,[225] would indeed require the prosecutor to prove that no change of ownership had taken place abroad, under the applicable choice of law rule. Thus, it would not be acceptable for a prosecutor in a British criminal court to rely on a presumption that the terms of the *lex causae* are the same as the *lex fori*. A failure to take account of the relevant provisions of foreign law at the trial stage would likely entitle the defendant to an acquittal.[226] However, more detailed consideration of criminal procedure would exceed the scope of this work.

B. The Investigation and Determination of the Content of Foreign Law

This section considers the role of the court in the investigation and determination of the content of the applicable foreign law. It proceeds on the basis that the court has determined that a choice of law rule requires the application of foreign law. It assumes that the court is seeking to apply the relevant choice of law rule, ie there is no question as to whether the court can ignore it. The focus of this analysis is to identify what the court can do, must do, and must not do in respect of the investigation and determination of the content of the *lex causae*. The role of the parties and the experts in the investigation and determination of the content of foreign law will be considered in due course.

(i) Objective of the Court when Applying Foreign Law

Both the British and German courts have the stated aim of applying foreign law as the foreign court would do, which is a point that can scarcely be considered controversial. It has been said by the English court:

> In the case of disputed questions of foreign law, the task for the trial judge is to determine what the highest relevant court in the foreign legal system would decide if the point had come before it.[227]

[225] S Powles, L Waine and R May, *May on Criminal Evidence*, 6th edn (Sweet & Maxwell, 2015), para 4-03.

[226] *R v Bentley (Deceased)* [2001] 1 Cr App R 21, 326: 'The jury must be clearly and unambiguously instructed that the burden of proving the guilt of the accused lies and lies only on the Crown, that (subject to exceptions not here relevant) there is no burden on the accused to prove anything and that if, on reviewing all the evidence, the jury are unsure of or are left in any reasonable doubt as to the guilt of the accused that doubt must be resolved in favour of the accused. Such an instruction has for very many years been regarded as a cardinal requirement of a properly conducted trial.'

[227] *Dexia Crediop SPA v Comune di Prato* [2017] EWCA Civ 428, [34]. Similarly, the Scottish court recently held in *Ted Jacob Engineering Group Inc v Morrison* 2019 SC 487, 493: 'The task of the Scottish court is to determine how a foreign court would be likely to decide the issues of law that are relevant to the particular facts of the case before it.'

There is little material difference in approach by the German courts:

> Foreign law is to be applied by German courts as courts in foreign countries would interpret and apply it.[228] [Translation by author]

Moreover, it has been held that:

> Rather, what is required is that the law be investigated as a whole, as it has evolved in case law and jurisprudence, and how it is applied practice.[229] [Translation by author]

Nonetheless, the difficulties that domestic judges face when approaching the applicable foreign law are formidable. First, only a foreign judge can apply their law in the manner that they would do, usually with years of experience in the given legal system. Even when seeking to apply a foreign law, an English judge may place less emphasis than a foreign judge on academic commentaries than on case law,[230] which reflects the general approach in domestic English law. Second, the domestic judge faces obvious practical difficulties understanding foreign legal materials, eg lack of understanding of the full context, even if assisted by an expert. Third, foreign legal materials may, of course, be in a foreign language, which the judge does not know and, even if translated, may be formulated in a way that is difficult to follow, or the translation itself may be disputed.[231] Fourth, domestic judges face difficulties identifying even their own domestic law, which may be unclear or the subject of debate, and such difficulties clearly also exist in respect of foreign legal systems. In some cases, there will be no clear answer, or even no answer at all, to the question that the domestic court is seeking to answer under the applicable foreign law. In such a case:

> The judge may be faced with the frightening task of settling a question as yet unsettled by the *lex causae*.[232]

Thus, the stated objective of the exercise, ie to apply foreign law as the foreign judge would, while no doubt a laudable aim, belies the complexities involved.

[228] *Decision of the Federal Court of Justice from 7 June 2016* (BGH, Kartellsenat) KZR 6/15, BGHZ 210, 292, 320: 'Ausländisches Recht ist von deutschen Gerichten so anzuwenden, wie es die Gerichte des ausländischen Staates auslegen und anwenden.' See also Schack, *Internationales Zivilverfahrensrecht* (n 7), para 758; Junker (n 51), § 11 para 20; and Geimer (n 51), para 2604.

[229] *Decision of the Federal Court of Justice from 21 January 1991* (BGH, II. Zivilsenat) II ZR 49/90, NJW-RR 1991, 1211, 1212: 'er ist vielmehr gehalten, das Recht als Ganzes zu ermitteln, wie es sich in Rechtsprechung und Rechtslehre entwickelt hat und in der Praxis Anwendung findet.' See also *Decision of the Federal Court of Justice from 17 May 2018* (BGH, IX. Zivilsenat) IX ZB 26/17, IWRZ 2019, 80, 81.

[230] That is not to suggest that English courts will not take account of academic commentaries when investigating foreign law. See, for example, *Glencore International AG v Metro Trading International Inc* [2001] CLC 1732, 1751: 'Where the witnesses were in disagreement I have reached my decision only after giving careful consideration to their different opinions in the context of any relevant legislation and commentaries, preferring the views which seemed to me to be most consistent with a carefully constructed system of the kind which one can discern in the civil code as a whole.'

[231] *Bianco v Bennett* [2015] EWHC 626 (QB), [23]: 'Even where agreed translations of foreign materials are provided – which is not the case here – an English lawyer is liable to lack an understanding of the right approach to construing the foreign statutes or other materials relied on. And there may be much room for debate between those expert in the foreign law about the true interpretation of that law.'

[232] M Furmston, 'Proof of Foreign Law' (1959) 22 *Modern Law Review* 317, 317.

(ii) Knowledge Imputed to the Court

The term *iura novit curia* is used in Germany to describe the knowledge of the law imputed to the judge. The German judge's imputed knowledge is said to extend to all domestic laws,[233] ie all laws which apply in the Federal Republic of Germany, including those laws applying only to individual States (*Landesrecht*) or locally (*Partikularrecht*).[234] EU law, although not domestic German law, is viewed as being of equal status,[235] as are any rules of public international law which have been incorporated into domestic German law.[236]

The extent to which the principle of *iura novit curia* applies to foreign law appears to be controversial in Germany. For example, Junker is clear that *iura novit curia* does not apply to foreign law.[237] However, Mankowski, while recognising differences between foreign and domestic law, is of the view that *iura novit curia does* apply to foreign law.[238] What is clear is that no German judge can possibly know, nor can he be expected to know, all of the laws of the world.[239] Generally speaking, where the German judge is required to apply foreign law, he must acquire both knowledge and understanding of its content by means of evidence.[240] There needs to be a dividing line between foreign law – which usually requires evidence of its content, both to facilitate knowledge and understanding – and domestic law – which is not a matter of evidence, even where specific points may require research and consideration. The justification for such a dividing line has been conceptually recognised in Germany at least since Savigny's 1840 first volume of *System des heutigen Römischen Rechts*, not least because judges are required to pass academic exams in domestic German law before being appointed.[241]

In Great Britain, imputed knowledge of domestic law is covered by judicial notice, which is a nebulous concept,[242] especially in so far as it encompasses both

[233] Prütting, '§ 293' (n 6), para 8.

[234] For an example of a case involving *Partikularrecht*, see *Decision of the Federal Court of Justice from 25 October 1984* (BGH, III. Zivilsenat) III ZR 131/83, BGHZ 92, 326. Both *Landesrecht* and *Partikularrecht* play little role in German private law, which is essentially uniform throughout Germany. See FJ Säcker, 'Einleitung (Einl. BGB)' in C Schubert (ed), *Münchener Kommentar zum Bürgerlichen Gesetzbuch: Band 1 (Allgemeiner Teil §§ 1–240, AllgPersönlR, ProstG, AGG)*, 9th edn (CH Beck, 2021), para 1, and also the discussion in the Introduction to this work, as well as Chapter two at section II.

[235] Prütting, '§ 293' (n 6), para 9.

[236] ibid, para 10; Geimer (n 51), para 2600.

[237] Junker (n 51), § 11 para 3: 'Für das fremde Recht gilt der Grundsatz *iura novit curia* nicht.' A similar viewpoint appears to be held in Geimer (n 51), para 2597.

[238] P Mankowski, 'Privatgutachten über ausländisches Recht – Erstattungsfähigkeit der Kosten' (2001) *Monatsschrift für Deutsches Recht* 194. Sometimes it is not entirely clear whether a writer is arguing that the doctrine of *iura novit curia* extends to foreign law or whether the proper application of choice of law rules, which are beyond doubt subject to *iura novit curia*, requires that the applicable foreign law be investigated and applied. See, for example, G Rühl, 'Die Kosten der Rechtswahlfreiheit: Zur Anwendung ausländischen Rechts durch deutsche Gerichte' (2007) 71 *Rabels Zeitschrift für Ausländisches und Internationales Privatrecht* 559, 568.

[239] Kegel and Schurig (n 3), 501: 'Natürlich kann man vom Richter nichts Übermenschliches fordern.'

[240] Junker (n 51), § 11 para 3.

[241] FC von Savigny, *System des heutigen Römischen Rechts*, Bd 1 (Veit und Comp, 1840), 189–91.

[242] It is described in Fentiman, *Foreign Law in English Courts* (n 70), 314, as elusive.

imputed knowledge of fact[243] and law, with each striking at very different issues. Thus, as far as judicial notice is applied to domestic law,[244] evidence should not be adduced in relation to it, although the rules as to what is defined as domestic law are complicated.[245] Domestic law includes more obscure areas of law such as ecclesiastical law, in England at least,[246] of which most judges will have very limited, if any, knowledge. The retained law of the EU, including the treaties and decisions of the European courts, is subject to judicial notice,[247] as are cases emanating from the European Court of Human Rights.[248] Where law is not classified as domestic, it is classified as foreign, requiring proof, and no knowledge of its content may be imputed to the judge.[249] Although English and Scottish courts do not generally take judicial notice of the other country's respective laws,[250] this is, again, subject

[243] Judicial notice covers those notorious facts that fall within general knowledge or common sense, eg that the earth is round or that there are seven days in the week. See H Malek, J Auburn and R Bagshaw (eds), *Phipson on Evidence*, 20th edn (Sweet & Maxwell, 2021), para 3-17, which gives examples such as the standards of weights and measures, and that there are time differences east and west of Greenwich. It has been suggested that the internet has changed the scope of judicial notice as it relates to fact: 'In 1999 there was not available on the internet, as it had not then been invented, the sort of information that is readily available at the click of a mouse in 2020. Whilst it is plainly desirable that the court should have evidence, in proper form, it seems to me there must be some practical dilution of Lord Hoffmann's stern words.' *S v H* [2020] EWFC B16, [63] HHJ Booth. Perhaps the suggestion that the internet had not been invented in 1999 should not be taken too literally. § 291 of the German Code of Civil Procedure serves a similar function, a translation of which is: 'Facts that are common knowledge with the court need not be substantiated by evidence.' [Translation by C von Schöning, 'Translation of the German Code of Civil Procedure', www.gesetze-im-internet.de/englisch_zpo/englisch_zpo.html].

[244] See, in relation to legislation, the Interpretation Act 1978, s 3. In England, it has long been recognised that case law is judicially noticed. This included the law of equity in common law courts prior to the passing of the Judicature Acts in the late nineteenth century. *Sims v Marryat* (1851) 17 QB 281, 292, per Lord Campbell. See also, in relation to Scotland, G Maher, 'Judicial notice and statute law' (2001) 117 *LQR* 71.

[245] See, in relation to England, Malek, Auburn and Bagshaw (eds) (n 243), para 3-07. However, this text does leave one with some doubt in relation to the unwritten law of Ireland. It is said that 'Judicial notice will be taken of the existence and contents of all public statutes, and of all Acts of Parliament of a public nature, as well as of every branch of unwritten law obtaining in England or Ireland.' We are then referred to the Senior Courts Act 1981, s 19. However, this provision, which deals with the jurisdiction of the English High Court, does not seem to address this matter. It is submitted that Irish law is foreign law in the English courts, and has been so since, at least, 1949. See GD Nokes, 'Irish Law in English Courts' (1960) 9 *ICLQ* 564, especially 579, where it was correctly stated in 1960: 'The divergencies between English and Irish law are not inconsiderable today; an English lawyer who undertook to advise on some aspects of Irish law would be rash indeed; and the disparities are not likely to decrease in the future.' The point is not directly addressed in chapter 9 of Collins (Lord Collins of Mapesbury) and Harris (eds) (n 112), but the implication is clear that Irish law (or any element of it) is not covered by judicial notice. No judicial notice is taken of Irish law in Scotland, which, as foreign law, 'must, if it is to be founded on, be proved as a fact.' See *Faulkner v Hill* 1942 JC 20, 32.

[246] *Mackonochie v Lord Penzance and Martin* (1880–81) LR 6 App Cas 424, 446. It was once the case that two experts (doctors) were called to argue points of ecclesiastical law, 'but they came as advocates to argue the law, not as witnesses to state it.' See *Sims v Marryat* (1851) 17 QB 281, 292.

[247] The European Union (Withdrawal) Act 2018, sch 5, makes provision for judicial notice to be applied to retained EU law after 31 December 2020.

[248] Human Rights Act 1998, s 2(2).

[249] Malek, Auburn and Bagshaw (eds) (n 243), para 3-07; Beaumont and McEleavy, *Anton's Private International Law* (n 133), para 27.172.

[250] Despite ambiguous language in the Interpretation Act 1978, this includes legislation (or parts thereof) of the UK Parliament not applying in the respective jurisdiction of the court. See Maher (n 244), 75, who relies on *M'Elroy v M'Allister* 1949 SC 110.

to some limited, obscure exceptions, eg the cross-border enforcement of maintenance orders.[251] The UK Supreme Court, regardless of the background of the judges deciding the case, takes judicial notice of the laws of all the constituent parts of the UK.[252]

As recognised by Lord Blackburn in the House of Lords in *Mackonochie* (1881), a crucial difference between the recognition of law as domestic, as opposed to foreign, is that judicial notice allows argument founded on legal principles and authorities, rather than requiring expert witnesses to prove it.[253] There are limited exceptions to the rule that a British court may not take judicial notice of foreign law, aside from any exceptions in intra-UK cases.

A notable exception is Article 14 of the Hague Child Abduction Convention,[254] which allows courts to judicially notice the content of foreign law as regards the alleged wrongful removal or retention within the meaning of Article 3 of the Convention,[255] unusually, bringing elements of foreign law in child abduction proceedings within the terms of judicial notice.

There is authority suggesting that an English court may take judicial notice of notorious foreign laws, in the same way that it may judicially note notorious facts.[256] It was thus held in *Saxby* (1909) that the English court is entitled to judicially notice that roulette in Monte Carlo is not an unlawful game.[257] However, the

[251] See the Maintenance Orders Act 1950, s 22(2), which provides that a court in one part of the UK may, for that purpose, take notice of the law in force in any other part of the UK. Two other exceptions, which are of little relevance to this work, appear to be that the Scottish courts will judicially note the English law of charity under some tax statutes and, separately, will take note of English law in certain court-martial appeals. See ID Macphail (Lord Macphail), 'Research Paper on the Law of Evidence of Scotland' (1979) *Scottish Law Commission*, www.scotlawcom.gov.uk/files/1913/1463/2308/Macphail_ch_20-25.pdf, para 2.04ff.

[252] See *Elliot v Joicey* [1935] AC 209, 236, and *Bank of East Asia Ltd v Scottish Enterprise* 1997 SLT 1213, 1214. This applies even if a case on appeal from the English courts concerns a matter of Scots law, which would be a question of foreign law until the case reaches the UK Supreme Court.

[253] *Mackonochie v Lord Penzance and Martin* (1880–81) LR 6 App Cas 424, 446.

[254] This provision, of course, also applies in Germany, but its practical significance is far less than in Great Britain for reasons that should be obvious from this work.

[255] PR Beaumont and PE McEleavy, *The Hague Convention on International Child Abduction* (Oxford University Press, 1999), 63–64. In practical terms, an application under the Hague Convention of 25 October 1980 on the Civil Aspects of International Child Abduction (Hague Child Abduction Convention) is almost always accompanied with a certificate or affidavit under Art 8(f) of the Convention. The matter is considered in more detail when Article 15 of the Convention is addressed.

[256] In respect of notorious facts and the concept of judicial notice, see Malek, Auburn and Bagshaw (eds) (n 243), para 3-02.

[257] *Saxby v Fulton* [1909] 2 KB 208, 211: 'I was asked to assume, in the absence of evidence, that the law in Monte Carlo is the same as in England as regards gaming, but I decline to make this assumption; it is notorious that at Monte Carlo roulette is not an unlawful game.' While one may reasonably assume that gambling is not illegal in Monaco, it is perhaps little known that it is illegal for Monégasque citizens themselves to gamble in Monaco under the Monégasque law pertaining to gambling of 12 June 1987. This perhaps shows how dangerous making any assumptions regarding the content of foreign law can be. See LégiMonaco, 'Loi n. 1.103 du 12/06/1987 relative aux jeux de hasard (Act no. 1.103 of 12 June 1987 pertaining to gambling)', www.legimonaco.mc/305/legismclois.nsf/db3b0488a44ebcf9c12574c7002a8e84/9481c4afb3115dc4c125773f003bba6e!OpenDocument, Art 11: 'Les Monégasques, les fonctionnaires et agents de l'État, de la Commune et des établissements publics ne peuvent, dans les maisons de jeux, participer à ceux-ci.'

case does not seem to have been followed in subsequent cases, not least for the reason that what constitutes sufficient notoriety is a vague concept, and it appears that the parties were, in fact, in agreement as to the legality of gaming in Monte Carlo.[258] More recently, Lord Leggatt suggested in the UK Supreme Court decision of *FS Cairo (Nile Plaza)* (2021) that it can be judicially noted that the doctrine of *non cumul* is a basic principle of civil law,[259] which could represent a step towards significantly widening the scope of judicial notice as it applies to foreign law.[260]

(iii) Investigative Duties Incumbent on the Court

Before considering the various options available to courts in the relevant jurisdictions to facilitate the investigation of the content of foreign law, it is important to be clear as to what the domestic judge must do and must not do in terms of any investigation into the content of foreign law.

In terms of what the German judge is required to do, there can be little doubt that while the text of § 293 of the Code of Civil Procedure itself provides few answers,[261] substantial relevant case law has been forthcoming. Thus, case law has determined that the German judge has a duty to investigate the content of the applicable foreign law.[262] While German appeal courts have recognised that it is difficult to define the necessary extent and intensity of the required investigation in exact terms,[263] the German court is certainly tasked with the investigation of the applicable foreign law.[264] Although § 293 of the Code of Civil Procedure allows the court to call on the aid of the parties, it is not restricted to the evidence they have provided and can turn to other sources.[265] It is accordingly a matter for the German judge's discretion, subject to review by an appeal court,[266] as to how he seeks to

[258] *R v Ofori; R v Tackie* (1994) 99 Cr App R 223, 227.

[259] *FS Cairo (Nile Plaza) LLC v Lady Brownlie* [2021] UKSC 45, [159].

[260] It is respectfully submitted that many judges are unlikely to be familiar with the concept of *non cumul*, and in any case the principle, as it applies in France, appears to be under legislative review. Any future assumptions as to its terms could well be erroneous. See J Knetsch and Z Jacquemin, 'France' in E Karner and BC Steininger (eds), *European Tort Law 2020* (De Gruyter, 2021), 179.

[261] E Huzel, 'Zur Zulässigkeit eines "Auflagenbeschlusses" im Rahmen des § 293 ZPO' (1990) *Praxis des Internationalen Privat- und Verfahrensrechts* 77, 77; G Otto, 'Der verunglückte § 293 ZPO und die Ermittlung ausländischen Rechts durch "Beweiserhebung"' (1995) *Praxis des Internationalen Privat- und Verfahrensrechts* 299, 300. The translated text of § 293 is provided in the Introduction to this work.

[262] For example, see *Decision of the Federal Court of Justice from 30 April 1992* (BGH, IX. Zivilsenat) IX ZR 233/90, BGHZ 118, 151, 162. The role of the German judge in this context has been described as active, as opposed to the passive role played by the judge in this context in Great Britain. See JR Brown, '44.1 Ways to Prove Foreign Law' (1984) 9 *Maritime Lawyer* 179, 183–84.

[263] *Decision of the Federal Court of Justice from 30 April 1992* (BGH, IX. Zivilsenat) IX ZR 233/90, BGHZ 118, 151, 163.

[264] Schack, *Internationales Zivilverfahrensrecht* (n 7), para 756; Geimer (n 51), para 2579.

[265] Junker (n 51), § 11 para 3.

[266] *Decision of the Federal Court of Justice from 30 March 1976* (BGH, VI. Zivilsenat) VI ZR 143/74, NJW 1976, 1581, 1582–83; *Decision of the Federal Court of Justice from 20 December 2017* (BGH, XII. Zivilsenat) XII ZB 333/17, BGHZ 217, 165, 174; *Decision of the Federal Court of Justice from 18 March 2020* (BGH, IV. Zivilsenat) IV ZR 62/19, NJW-RR 2020, 802, 804. The possibility for the German

obtain knowledge of foreign law.[267] When investigating the content of foreign law, the German judge is not bound by the rules of evidence generally applicable in terms of the German Code of Civil Procedure.[268] The German judge may and must use all accessible sources of information.[269] This freedom is known in German law as the principle of *Freibeweis*[270] (ie free from the rules of evidence), as opposed to *Strengbeweis*[271] (ie strict application of the rules of evidence). The German court can draw on previously published opinions,[272] refer to any academic sources available, and, in so doing, conduct its investigation of foreign law in a similar manner to how it would research an area of domestic law.[273]

The demands of the German judge's investigative obligations increase consonant with the complexity of the applicable foreign law and the extent of the difference between it and the relevant German law.[274] The German court should take account of foreign academic discourse and case law to understand how the relevant foreign law is actually applied,[275] with the option to make reference to

appeal court to review how foreign law has been investigated by the lower instance court is considered in detail in due course.

[267] *Decision of the Federal Court of Justice from 30 January 2001* (BGH, XI. Zivilsenat) XI ZR 357/99, NJOZ 2001, 1, 2; *Decision of the Federal Court of Justice from 30 March 1976* (BGH, VI. Zivilsenat) VI ZR 143/74, NJW 1976, 1581, 1583; *Decision of the Federal Court of Justice from 17 May 2018* (BGH, IX. Zivilsenat) IX ZB 26/17, IWRZ 2019, 80, 80–81; Junker (n 51), § 11 para 4; Geimer (n 51), para 2581.

[268] *Decision of the Federal Court of Justice from 24 November 1960* (BGH, II. Zivilsenat) II ZR 9/60, NJW 1961, 410, 411.

[269] Junker (n 51), § 11 para 7.

[270] *Decision of the Federal Court of Justice from 24 November 1960* (BGH, II. Zivilsenat) II ZR 9/60, NJW 1961, 410, 411; *Decision of the Federal Court of Justice from 20 December 2017* (BGH, XII. Zivilsenat) XII ZB 333/17, BGHZ 217, 165, 174; Junker (n 51), § 11 para 7; Geimer (n 51), para 2585; R Hüßtege, 'Zur Ermittlung ausländischen Rechts: Wie man in den Wald hineinruft, so hallt es auch zurück' (2002) *Praxis des Internationalen Privat- und Verfahrensrechts* 292, 293.

[271] *Decision of the Federal Court of Justice from 24 November 1960* (BGH, II. Zivilsenat) II ZR 9/60, NJW 1961, 410, 411; Junker (n 51), § 11 para 7.

[272] For example, the Max Planck Institute for Comparative and International Private Law has a number of publications, which are conveniently listed on its website. See Max Planck Institute for Comparative and International Private Law, 'Institute Publications', www.mpipriv.de/1158123/Institutspublikationen. Many published opinions are contained in the journal *Gutachten zum internationalen und ausländischen Privatrecht* (IPG), which has been in operation since 1965. It is stated that the opinions 'show the extremely broad spectrum of cases in this field and serve not only to facilitate legal practice but also to enrich scholarship in the field of conflict of laws.' See Max Planck Institute for Comparative and International Private Law, 'Gutachten zum internationalen und ausländischen Privatrecht', www.mpipriv.de/1158829/Gutachten.

[273] Prütting, '§ 293' (n 6), para 24.

[274] *Decision of the Federal Court of Justice from 30 April 1992* (BGH, IX. Zivilsenat) IX ZR 233/90, BGHZ 118, 151, 163; *Decision of the Federal Court of Justice from 20 December 2017* (BGH, XII. Zivilsenat) XII ZB 333/17, BGHZ 217, 165, 174; *Decision of the Federal Court of Justice from 18 March 2020* (BGH, IV. Zivilsenat) IV ZR 62/19, NJW-RR 2020, 802, 804; Geimer (n 51), para 2581; Bacher (n 151), para 18; I Saenger, *Zivilprozessordnung*, 9th edn (Nomos 2021), § 293 para 13.

[275] *Decision of the Federal Court of Justice from 23 June 2003* (BGH, II. Zivilsenat) II ZR 305/01, NJW 2003, 2685, 2686; *Decision of the Federal Court of Justice from 30 January 2001* (BGH, XI. Zivilsenat) XI ZR 357/99, NJOZ 2001, 1, 2; *Decision of the Federal Court of Justice from 30 March 1976* (BGH, VI. Zivilsenat) VI ZR 143/74, NJW 1976, 1581, 1583. There is case law suggesting that the German court should ignore the clear text of a foreign statute where the highest instance courts of the relevant country have done so. See Hübner (n 66), 202, which discusses *Decision of the Hamm Court of Appeal from 6 June 2000* (OLG Hamm) 2 UF 36/00, NJWE–FER 2000, 306.

detailed, existing German language sources covering the content of foreign legal systems.[276] Reliance on statutory provisions alone will often be insufficient,[277] although it is going too far to suggest that it will never be enough.[278] Where a party calls a specific matter into doubt, even if it has been considered by an expert, the court should consider undertaking further investigation of that matter.[279] This is especially the case where the parties make detailed and conflicting submissions.[280] Where the foreign court is bound by the doctrine of precedent, the German court is equally so bound.[281] The German court is required to exhaust all available sources of the applicable foreign law.[282]

Based on the wording of § 293 of the Code of Civil Procedure alone,[283] the German judge can proceed solely on the basis of his own knowledge, although this seems very unlikely in most cases, which will require independent research or an expert opinion.[284] Even if a German judge were familiar with a point of foreign

[276] See, for example, C von Bar (ed), *Ausländisches Privat- und Privatverfahrensrecht in deutscher Sprache*, 10th edn (Otto Schmidt, 2017); A Bergmann, M Ferid and D Henrich (eds), *Internationales Ehe- und Kindschaftsrecht*, Loose-leaf-collection of approximately 18,000 pages in 23 folders (2021); M Ferid and others (eds), *Internationales Erbrecht*, 116th edn (Loose-leaf-collection of 21,550 pages in 9 folders) (2021). These sources have been described as important aids that can often be sufficiently illuminating in and of themselves. Schack, *Internationales Zivilverfahrensrecht* (n 7), para 759.

[277] See, for example, the *Decision of the Federal Court of Justice from 18 March 2020* (BGH, IV. Zivilsenat) IV ZR 62/19, NJW-RR 2020, 802, 805, which is discussed in R Hüßtege, 'Internetrecherche contra Sachverständigengutachten – Zur Ermittlung ausländischen Rechts durch deutsche Gerichte' (2021) *Praxis des Internationalen Privat- und Verfahrensrechts* 261.

[278] The suggestion in Hüßtege, 'Zur Ermittlung ausländischen Rechts: Wie man in den Wald hineinruft, so hallt es auch zurück' (n 270), 393, with reference to the *Decision of the Federal Court of Justice from 30 January 2001* (BGH, XI. Zivilsenat) XI ZR 357/99, NJOZ 2001, 1, 2, is that reference to statute law alone will never be enough. However, it has been said that 'hard cases make bad law' and there may be relatively straightforward cases where reference to statute law alone will be enough, eg the age of testamentary capacity in English law under the Wills Act 1837, s 7: 'No will made by any person under the age of eighteen years shall be valid.' (Although this seemingly straightforward rule does have some exceptions, eg soldiers in active military service, under the Wills (Soldiers and Sailors) Act 1918, s 1.) The court should take account of the overall circumstances and whether the position is sufficiently clear from the relevant statutory provisions. Kegel and Schurig argue that statutory provisions alone will be sufficient where they are clear and comprehensive. Kegel and Schurig (n 3), 501.

[279] *Decision of the Federal Court of Justice from 23 June 2003* (BGH, II. Zivilsenat) II ZR 305/01, NJW 2003, 2685, 2086.

[280] *Decision of the Federal Court of Justice from 30 April 1992* (BGH, IX. Zivilsenat) IX ZR 233/90, BGHZ 118, 151, 164; *Decision of the Federal Court of Justice from 18 March 2020* (BGH, IV. Zivilsenat) IV ZR 62/19, NJW-RR 2020, 802, 805.

[281] Junker (n 51), § 11 para 6.

[282] *Decision of the Federal Court of Justice from 14 January 2014* (BGH, II. Zivilsenat) II ZR 192/13, NJW 2014, 1244, 1245; *Decision of the Federal Court of Justice from 17 May 2018* (BGH, IX. Zivilsenat) IX ZB 26/17, IWRZ 2019, 80, 81; *Decision of the Federal Court of Justice from 18 March 2020* (BGH, IV. Zivilsenat) IV ZR 62/19, NJW-RR 2020, 802, 804.

[283] The requirement for evidence as to the content of foreign laws exists only 'als sie dem Gericht unbekannt sind' ('in so far as the court is not aware of them') [Translation by Schöning (n 243), § 293].

[284] Thomas Pfeiffer, a German academic with extensive judicial experience, suggests that it is both usual and helpful for the German judge to carry out independent research initially, as it both assists when framing questions to the expert and assists with the ongoing discourse: see T Pfeiffer, 'Methoden der Ermittlung ausländischen Rechts' in R Stürner and others (eds), *Festschrift für Dieter Leipold zum 70 Geburtstag* (Mohr Siebeck, 2009), 286. The risk of duplication of effort and wasted time is noted at 287 of the same article.

law, he would surely seek to refresh his memory using any available sources. Any appeal court reviewing his decision would doubtless seek to understand the basis of any conclusions made.[285] It has been held:

> Where the contested decision does not provide information that the trial judge fulfilled his duty to investigate foreign law, it must be assumed that adequate research into the foreign law was not conducted as procedurally necessary. [Translation by author][286]

Moreover, it is questionable whether a German court can effectively undertake its own research when considering anything other than straightforward points of foreign law,[287] with the risk of mistake being unacceptably high in more complicated cases.[288] The point at which the German judge should order an expert opinion is difficult to identify. Evidence suggests that German judges typically avoid doing so,[289] but one is left wondering if foreign law is, in fact, being correctly applied in many cases where no expert opinion is ordered, at least where the applicable foreign law is complicated. However, it is welcome that § 293 of the Code of Civil Procedure offers flexibility in those circumstances where the German judge does have sufficient knowledge, through experience or study, of a foreign legal system, especially where the system is closely related to the German legal system.[290]

[285] ibid, 286. The matter of appeals is considered in more detail in due course.

[286] *Decision of the Federal Court of Justice from 30 April 2013* (BGH, VII. Zivilsenat) VII ZB 22/12, NZI 2013, 763, 765: 'Gibt die angefochtene Entscheidung keinen Aufschluss darüber, dass der Tatrichter seiner Pflicht nachgekommen ist, ausländisches Recht zu ermitteln, ist davon auszugehen, dass eine ausreichende Erforschung des ausländischen Rechts verfahrensfehlerhaft unterblieben ist.' See also *Decision of the Federal Court of Justice from 23 April 2002* (BGH, XI. Zivilsenat) XI ZR 136/01, NJW-RR 2002, 1359, 1360.

[287] See Schack, *Internationales Zivilverfahrensrecht* (n 7), para 761. While Schack advocates the use of official websites for research purposes, these can be of poor quality or, at least, insufficiently detailed for professional use. It would be extremely difficult to accurately investigate and determine the law on a complicated matter of English (or Scots) law with reference only to freely accessible sources, eg legislation.gov.uk. See also the analysis in respect of the European Judicial Network at section II.B.(iv)(b), and a discussion of some sources freely available on the internet at Chapter four at section II.A. at fn 81. The temptations and dangers of conducting internet research are discussed in Hüßtege, 'Internetrecherche contra Sachverständigengutachten – Zur Ermittlung ausländischen Rechts durch deutsche Gerichte' (n 277), 262, where it is pointed out that unfamiliar legal terminology and concepts raise high barriers to successfully establishing the content of foreign law through internet research. Hüßtege concludes, at 264, that the possibilities for research offered by the internet are not sufficient to avoid the requirement to instruct expert opinions.

[288] Even those German writers who seem to strongly countenance the merits of the judge's internal investigation accept that the court should be careful in rejecting any demand of the parties that an expert opinion be instructed. See Prütting, '§ 293' (n 6), para 24.

[289] M Stürner and F Krauß, *Ausländisches Recht in deutschen Zivilverfahren: Eine rechtstatsächliche Untersuchung* (Nomos, 2018), paras 197–202. In a series of interviews, one lower instance judge commented: 'Ich habe auch noch nie ein Gutachten vom Max-Planck-Institut eingeholt. Das wäre ja der letzte Rettungsanker' ('I have also never obtained an expert opinion from the Max Planck Institute. That would really be the last lifeline') [Translation by author]. This appears to be the sentiment of the other judges interviewed.

[290] The Federal Court of Justice (BGH) has acknowledged that the extent of the investigation required is lower where the applicable law is closely related to German law and the relevant legal provisions at issue are clear. See *Decision of the Federal Court of Justice from 20 December 2017* (BGH, XII. Zivilsenat) XII ZB 333/17, BGHZ 217, 165, 174. See also Geimer (n 51), para 2581.

The duties of the judge in respect of the investigation of the content of the *lex causae* are an area where the German and British courts decisively differ. The British judge has no duty to investigate the content of foreign law and, indeed, his duty lies in refraining from doing so,[291] especially where the parties are in agreement.[292] These propositions derive from the fact approach, which prima facie restricts the British judge to an assessment of the evidence on the balance of probabilities.[293] The British judge's traditional role, which manifests itself in this context, has been summarised by the House of Lords:

> We have rejected inquisitorial methods and prefer to regard our Judges as entirely independent. Like referees at boxing contests, they see that the rules are kept and count the points.[294]

Where documents pertaining to the content of the applicable foreign law have been lodged by parties but not spoken to by expert witnesses, it has traditionally been the position that the British judge may not consider them:[295]

> The Italian law materials that the claimant placed in the trial bundle, and to which I have been referred, have enabled me to see the general shape of the claimant's case, but they are not admissible evidence of the foreign law relied on. The English court will not conduct its own researches into foreign law.[296]

The British judge has therefore almost entirely been restricted to evidence spoken to by expert witnesses.[297] The strictures of this rule have been applied in respect

[291] *Bumper Development Corporation v Metropolitan Police Commissioner* [1991] 1 WLR 1362, 1371. Briggs (n 106), 10: 'But the notion that the judge may go off on a frolic of his own and conduct a personal inquiry into foreign law has no place in an English court.'

[292] *Roberts v Soldiers, Sailors, Airmen and Families Association* [2020] EWHC 994 (QB), [190]. An argument suggesting the contrary was firmly rejected in *Brownlie v Four Seasons Holdings Inc* [2015] EWCA Civ 665, [89].

[293] A Zuckerman, *Zuckerman on Civil Procedure: Principles of Practice*, 4th edn (Sweet & Maxwell, 2021), para 22.39ff.

[294] *Thomson v Glasgow Corp* 1962 SC (HL) 36, 52. See comments from the English Court of Appeal regarding the English court's limited interventive function in *Mensah v East Hertfordshire NHS Trust* [1998] EWCA Civ 954, 1998 WL 1042510, and from the Employment Appeal Tribunal in *Joseph v Brighton & Sussex University Hospitals NHS Trust* EAT, 17 April 2015, 2015 WL 3750910, [32]–[38]. The matter was discussed, in the context of the Civil Procedure Rules 1998, in more detail in the introduction to this chapter.

[295] The rule is long-standing. See Chapter two, section I.B. regarding the development of the rule in England. The rule has also long been recognised in Scotland. See *Kolbin & Sons v Kinnear & Co Ltd* 1930 SC 724, 737.

[296] *Bianco v Bennett* [2015] EWHC 626 (QB), [22]. See also *Roberts v Soldiers, Sailors, Airmen and Families Association* [2020] EWHC 994 (QB), [190].

[297] *Re Cohn* [1945] Ch 5 is an odd case as no expert evidence appears to have been led regarding the content of German testamentary law, although the fact that England and Germany were at war when judgment was given would have made sourcing an expert opinion almost impossible. This same approach then seems to have been taken by the English court in other cases of the same era. A surprising example is *F & K Jabbour v Custodian of Israeli Absentee Property* [1954] 1 WLR 139, where the English judge was applying Israeli law without expert evidence, but with the consent of the parties, and gave a strong hint that he was struggling with the task. The reliance on *Re Cohn* (1945) in the case, at 147, is notable. The fact that *Re Cohn* (1945) was heard during World War 2 does not appear to have

of any foreign law,[298] and even where the Scottish court is applying English law[299] (and vice versa).[300] It has applied, in principle at least, regardless of whether the English judge is also professionally qualified in Scots law, or has dual-qualified barristers appearing before him.[301] To this extent, the rule can lead to absurd outcomes, if applied rigidly, and more flexibility, as is offered under § 293 of the German Code of Civil Procedure, would be preferable. It is presumably for this reason that Lord Leggett suggested in *FS Cairo (Nile Plaza)* (2021) that:

> The old notion that foreign legal materials can only ever be brought before the court as part of the evidence of an expert witness is outdated. Whether the court will require evidence from an expert witness should depend on the nature of the issue and of the relevant foreign law.[302]

The practical implications of Lord Leggett's reasoning in this regard have yet to become fully clear, although Mr Justice Warby's reasoning in *Soriano* (2021) suggests that it is already having an impact in (further) relaxing the traditional rules in respect of referring to foreign law without expert evidence.[303] It is not clear whether the Scottish courts will follow Lord Leggett's reasoning given in what was ultimately an English appeal.[304] While Lord Leggett's reasoning may go some way to relaxing the strictures of proof, at least in England, in respect of establishing the content of foreign law, it nonetheless presumably remains the case that the British judge has no investigative function. However, British judges do have some relevant functions. First, as will be discussed, there are some tools available, in theory at least, to the British judge to assist with ascertaining the content of a foreign law. Second, the British judge does have an important case management role.[305] For example, parties are required in the English courts to seek permission

been given significance in any later cases or academic texts. In Fentiman, *Foreign Law in English Courts* (n 70), 260–61, other contemporaneous examples drawing on *Re Cohn* (1945) are given. Even if the approach in these cases may have been justified on the facts, this work takes the view that these cases do not represent current law in either England or Scotland, which, as matters stand, requires evidence spoken to by expert witnesses.

[298] *Brownlie v Four Seasons Holdings Inc* [2015] EWCA Civ 665, [89]: 'In a common law system, such as that in England and Wales, the court does not have any inquisitorial function and cannot therefore conduct an inquiry itself as to foreign law.'

[299] *McGowan v Summit at Lloyds* 2002 SC 638, 644.

[300] *Re X (A Child) and Y (A Child) (Jurisdiction: Secure Accommodation)* [2016] EWHC 2271 (Fam), [12].

[301] There is evidence that the fullest strictures of the fact approach are not always applied in practice. See in *Re A (Children) (Adoption: Scottish Permanence Orders)* [2018] Fam 177, in particular [38], where a dual-qualified barrister assisted the English court with matters of Scots law.

[302] *FS Cairo (Nile Plaza) LLC v Lady Brownlie* [2021] UKSC 45, [148].

[303] *Soriano v Forensic News LLC* [2021] EWCA Civ 1952, [62].

[304] This is doubted in B Heaney, 'International private law – the default rule and presumption of similarity' (2021) 162 *Civil Practice Bulletin* 6, which also points out that most practitioners will be reluctant to rely only on research conducted on the internet.

[305] The English judge has significantly more case management powers than the Scottish judge, although the Scottish judge's powers in this respect continue to increase. See the discussion at section II, fn 10–21.

to lead expert evidence.[306] At the point of considering an application to lead expert evidence, the English judge can, for example, prevent parties leading evidence on irrelevant points or offer his opinion as to the suitability of experts.[307] Third, where an expert's opinion is obviously inconsistent with the materials presented, or otherwise not properly justified, the judge can reject it,[308] but subject to the restriction that the judge cannot adopt an interpretation wholly unsupported by any expert.[309] Fourth, where the experts conflict, there is some scope for the judge to look independently at the materials referred to by the experts when deciding what the position under the applicable foreign law is.[310] However, it is accepted that such judicial responsibilities pale in their significance when compared to the responsibilities of a German judge investigating the content of foreign law.

(iv) Seeking Information from Foreign Authorities and Courts

(a) 1968 European Convention on Information on Foreign Law

The 1968 European Convention on Information on Foreign Law (commonly known as the 'London Convention'), a Council of Europe treaty, has been ratified[311] both by Germany and the UK.[312] The London Convention is of little practical

[306] CPR 35.4(1). As matters stand, Scottish procedural rules do not require parties to seek permission to lead expert witness evidence.

[307] The importance of case management generally is made clear by the court in *BB Energy (Gulf) DMCC v Al Amoudi* [2018] EWHC 2595 (Comm), [49].

[308] *Roberts v Soldiers, Sailors, Airmen and Families Association* [2020] EWHC 994 (QB), [190].

[309] *Bumper Development Corporation v Metropolitan Police Commissioner* [1991] 1 WLR 1362, 1371. In particular, the judge cannot carry out independent research on a point, even if he thinks the experts are wrong, by searching for materials which have not been referred to by them.

[310] *Roberts v Soldiers, Sailors, Airmen and Families Association* [2020] EWHC 994 (QB), [190]. It is argued in Collins (Lord Collins of Mapesbury) and Harris (eds) (n 112), at para 9-015 – a proposition to which the judge in *Roberts* (2020) refers – that the judge is restricted entirely to the evidence presented, eg the specific part of a foreign legal text or code, and he may not look at any other part of the text or code. This seems fairly artificial, with the proposition drawing on quite old authority. It is likely that a judge would reject this restriction today in certain circumstances, eg where the following page of the text suggested that the preceding analysis was a minority view or suggested something contradictory. The Scottish Inner House of the Court of Session suggested in *Ted Jacob Engineering Group Inc v Morrison* 2019 SC 487, at 492, when making clear that the role of the expert is to assist the court, that the court 'may obviously have regard to the primary sources of foreign law that are made available to it', the implication being that the court should not be slavishly bound to the particular parts of whichever statute or code is referred to by the expert. The question of how the judge should reach a determination is considered in more detail at section II.B.(vii).

[311] For more information on the meaning of ratification in public international law, see, in German, W Vitzthum, 'Begriff, Geschichte und Rechtsquellen des Völkerrechts' in W Vitzthum and A Proelß (eds), *Völkerrecht*, 7th edn (De Gruyter, 2016), para 117, or, in English, F Berman and D Bentley, 'Treaties and other International Instruments: Ratification, Accession, Acceptance and Approval, Treaty Succession' in I Roberts (ed), *Satow's Diplomatic Practice*, 7th edn (Oxford University Press, 2016), at 34.3ff of Book VII (Treaties and Treaty-Making).

[312] Council of Europe, 'Chart of signatures and ratifications of Treaty 062 – European Convention on Information on Foreign Law', www.coe.int/en/web/conventions/full-list/-/conventions/treaty/062/signatures?p_auth=3u9aAJ7p.

significance in Germany and of virtually no significance in the UK.[313] The terms of the London Convention have been considered in detail in other works, and it is not necessary to extensively rehearse its provisions here.[314] However, brief consideration of the London Convention is justified as it provides an important example of how information on foreign law can be exchanged between states. It is the only significant example of its species in force in the relevant jurisdictions.[315]

The signatories of the London Convention have obliged themselves to provide information on their law and procedure in civil and commercial fields, as well as on their judicial organisation, on a reciprocal basis.[316] A court in a signatory state may pass a request for information through its appointed agency to the appointed agency in the receiving signatory state.[317] A request for information must always emanate from a judicial authority, eg a court, even where the request has not been drawn up by that authority. Court proceedings must have been initiated.[318] Thus, requests may not be abstract requests for information on foreign law. States receiving requests have a duty to respond.[319] The response must be given as quickly as possible.[320] The appointed agency in the receiving state may deal with the request itself or instruct a qualified lawyer to deal with it.[321] Approval for incurring costs must be sought from the state requesting the information in advance; otherwise no charge may be made.[322] This would seem to be particularly important where external lawyers are instructed. The response must be impartial and objective, with reference to any necessary authority.[323]

There is, however, no evidence that the London Convention has ever been used by a British court to seek information on a foreign legal system, and there is no UK implementing legislation. There is no reference to the London Convention in either the English or Scottish court rules. There is no information available on the London Convention on the websites of the UK Foreign, Commonwealth & Development Office[324] or Ministry of Justice.[325] Accordingly, it would be very difficult for a British court to seek information on foreign law by means of the London

[313] Schack, *Internationales Zivilverfahrensrecht* (n 7), para 762.

[314] Hübner (n 66), 243ff; Fentiman, *Foreign Law in English Courts* (n 70), 239ff.

[315] For example, there is a treaty in force between Germany and Morocco to facilitate the exchange of information on foreign law, however, it is modelled on the London Convention. See Otto (n 261), 303, and Prütting, '§ 293' (n 6), para 27. It is not clear why this treaty is necessary, as Morocco is listed as a non-member signatory of the London Convention. See Council of Europe (n 312).

[316] European Convention on Information on Foreign Law, 7 June 1968 (Council of Europe), Art 1(1).

[317] ibid, Art 2.

[318] ibid, Art 3(1).

[319] ibid, Art 10.

[320] ibid, Art 12.

[321] ibid, Art 6.

[322] ibid, Art 6(3).

[323] ibid, Art 7.

[324] 'Foreign, Commonwealth & Development Office', www.gov.uk/government/organisations/foreign-commonwealth-development-office.

[325] 'Ministry of Justice', www.gov.uk/government/organisations/ministry-of-justice.

Convention. As litigation is generally party driven in the British courts, it would probably require the parties to suggest using the London Convention to the court. This is unlikely to ever happen. First, most British lawyers are unlikely to have ever heard of the London Convention. Second, in the absence of any implementing legislation, it is unclear how a request would work. Third, as the request may or may not be successful, the court (and the parties!) would be reluctant to leave the action *in stasis* while a request is made, particularly as the format for doing so is so unclear. It does appear that some requests are received by the Foreign, Commonwealth & Development Office from other states. For example, in a 2014 appeal, which came before the German Federal Court of Justice, the Foreign and Commonwealth Office had received a request from Germany under the London Convention for information regarding the scope of a bankruptcy discharge, under the Insolvency Act 1986.[326] The UK Department for Business, Innovation and Skills appears to have been given responsibility for dealing with the request.[327]

There is domestic legislation facilitating the use of the London Convention in German law,[328] and there is evidence that the London Convention is used by German courts in up to 30 cases per year,[329] with reported cases of it having been used.[330] However, the London Convention's importance in Germany remains questionable, despite this limited evidence of its use. This is for several reasons. One reason must surely be ignorance of its existence and potential benefits. Another is that lower instance decisions have been overturned by appeal courts on several occasions on the basis that it has been considered insufficient to rely on the response given under the London Convention alone.[331] It thus seems pointless to instruct a foreign authority to provide a response when the answer is unlikely to

[326] *Decision of the Federal Court of Justice from 14 January 2014* (BGH, II. Zivilsenat) II ZR 192/13, NJW 2014, 1244, 1244.

[327] *Decision of the Federal Court of Justice from 14 January 2014* (BGH, II. Zivilsenat) II ZR 192/13, NJW 2014, 1244, 1244.

[328] Gesetz zur Ausführung des Europäischen Übereinkommens betreffend Auskünfte über ausländisches Recht und seines Zusatzprotokolls (AuRAG) (Act implementing the European Convention on Information on Foreign Law of 5 July 1974).

[329] Federal Republic of Germany, 'Germany's responses to the questionnaire on the treatment of foreign law' (2008), assets.hcch.net/upload/wop/genaff_pd09de.pdf.

[330] For example, *Decision of the Federal Court of Justice from 29 June 1987* (BGH, II. Zivilsenat) II ZR 6/87, NJW 1988, 647.

[331] See the *Decision of the Federal Court of Justice from 30 January 2001* (BGH, XI. Zivilsenat) XI ZR 357/99, NJOZ 2001, 1, in which two requests were made under the London Convention for information on the relevant Spanish law. The response from the Spanish justice ministry appears to have simply set out the relevant legislative authority, without reference to relevant case law or an explanation of relevant practice. The Federal Court of Justice allowed the appeal and returned the case to the lower court to seek further evidence such as an opinion from a Spanish court or Spanish professor of civil procedure. See also the *Decision of the Federal Court of Justice from 29 June 1987* (BGH, II. Zivilsenat) II ZR 6/87, NJW 1988, 647, 648, and the *Decision of the Federal Court of Justice from 14 January 2014* (BGH, II. Zivilsenat) II ZR 192/13, NJW 2014, 1244, 1245. In the latter decision, the Federal Court of Justice suggested requesting further clarification from the UK Foreign & Commonwealth Office, failing which, an expert opinion should be instructed.

be acceptable on its own,[332] which will often be the case as the London Convention essentially permits only abstract questions,[333] which will be difficult to formulate concisely, together with limited additional information,[334] and is thus unlikely to deliver the precise answer that the domestic court is looking for.[335] It is unfortunate that a dialogue between the court making the request and the state providing the information does not seem possible under the London Convention.[336] The timescales involved can also be significant. Germany has provided information that, on average, requests take three weeks for them to deal with, but it takes, on average, 20 weeks for foreign states to respond to its requests.[337] The prospect of such a long delay is likely to be another reason why German courts are reluctant to make requests under the London Convention.

Academics have been generally critical of the London Convention. Schack points to the fact that whoever is considering the request will not have sight of the court file and will have an incomplete understanding of what the court making the request is looking for.[338] He draws attention to the abstract nature of requests under the London Convention when concluding that the risk of misunderstanding seems extraordinarily great.[339] This must be correct. The result of a request made under the London Convention may be a long wait and an answer that raises more questions than it answers. The mechanism does not provide the same opportunity for discourse as with an expert instructed in the normal course of proceedings. Fentiman persuasively argues that the London Convention has clear disadvantages from the point of view of the British adversarial system.[340] He questions the value of the procedure, as the parties are likely to have their own experts, and argues that, even if the London Convention were used to the exclusion of expert evidence, it could not stand alone as a fair or effective mechanism for establishing the content of foreign law.[341]

It is unclear what the consequences are if incorrect advice is tendered following a request under the London Convention. If the advice has been tendered by a

[332] Pfeiffer anecdotally notes that he has only seen cases where a request under the London Convention has been made by the German court, but this has failed to produce a satisfactory result. Pfeiffer (n 284), 288.

[333] Stürner and Krauß (n 289), para 44.

[334] The requirements are set out in Article 4 of the European Convention on Information on Foreign Law (n 316). A request 'shall specify as exactly as possible the questions on which information concerning the law of the requested State is desired, and where there is more than one legal system in the requested State, the system of the law on which information is requested' and 'shall also state the facts necessary both for its proper understanding and for the formulation of an exact and precise reply. Copies of documents may be attached where necessary to clarify the scope of the request.'

[335] Pfeiffer notes that the information provided by the UK authorities on English contract law generally refers only to the relevant contract and not to English contract law itself. Pfeiffer (n 284), 288.

[336] Stürner and Krauß (n 289), para 44.

[337] Federal Republic of Germany (n 329), 2.

[338] Schack, *Internationales Zivilverfahrensrecht* (n 7), para 762.

[339] ibid, para 762.

[340] Fentiman, *Foreign Law in English Courts* (n 70), 242.

[341] ibid, 242.

foreign state, it would likely have immunity[342] in respect of that advice in domestic courts. Where foreign states do pass requests to practising lawyers, who will want to charge for their services, perhaps it would be best to cut out the middleman and for suitable experts to be instructed directly. Indeed, courts (and parties) may be reluctant to have important parts of a case handled by a person not of their choosing. It has been pointed out that the individual dealing with a request made under the London Convention could be a research assistant at a foreign law institute, who would not be considered an expert in terms of English law.[343]

Nonetheless, the London Convention does offer potential benefits in more straightforward cases, especially where the parties are not well-funded. Although Fentiman's criticism of the London Convention is well-made, if the parties are not of sufficient means to pay for an expert opinion then the London Convention, or a similar mechanism, offers the court a practical means of obtaining information on foreign law. Perhaps the fact that British courts are effectively unable to seek information under the London Convention should be viewed with some regret.

(b) European Judicial Network

The European Judicial Network in civil and commercial matters (EJN)[344] was created by Council Decision 2001/470/EC[345] to 'improve, simplify and expedite effective judicial cooperation between the Member States'.[346] This legislation was substantially amended by Decision No 568/2009/EC.[347] These more recent modifications were made, in part, as a result of a report presented to the Commission in May 2006 arguing that, although the EJN had generally met its objectives set in 2001, it was still a long way from developing its full potential.[348] The UK explicitly indicated its wish to take part in the modified Decision,[349] as was necessary in terms of its opt-in in matters of private international law.[350] The EJN is a

[342] See, for an explanation of the concept in British law, Beaumont and McEleavy, *Anton's Private International Law* (n 133), para 6.21ff, and, in German law, M Kau, 'Der Staat und der Einzelne als Völkerrechtssubjekte' in W Vitzthum and A Proelß (eds), *Völkerrecht*, 7th edn (De Gruyter, 2016), para 90ff.

[343] Fentiman, *Foreign Law in English Courts* (n 70), 243. The qualifications required for a witness to be considered an expert in the eyes of the British courts are considered at section IV.B below.

[344] European Judicial Network in civil and commercial matters, 'About the network', e-justice.europa.eu/content_about_the_network-431-en.do?clang=en.

[345] Council Decision No 2001/470/EC of 28 May 2001 establishing a European Judicial Network in civil and commercial matters (Decision No 2001/470/EC).

[346] ibid, Recital (6).

[347] Decision No 568/2009/EC of the European Parliament and of the Council of 18 June 2009 amending Council Decision 2001/470/EC establishing a European Judicial Network in civil and commercial matters (Decision No 568/2009/EC).

[348] ibid, Recital (3).

[349] ibid, Recital (20). The UK had opted-in to Decision No 2001/470/EC (n 345), under Recital (18) of that instrument.

[350] Protocol (No 21) to the TFEU on the Position of the United Kingdom and Ireland in respect of the area of Freedom, Security and Justice (2016) OJ C 202/295, Art 3(1) (Protocol (No 21)).

mechanism from which the UK has now withdrawn as a result of Brexit, considering that its legal foundations rest entirely on provisions of EU law.

A mechanism for the exchange of information between judicial authorities is provided by the EJN. All Member States must designate a contact point, or several, where this is necessary.[351] An amendment introduced by Decision No 568/2009/EC was that each contact point must be associated with a judge.[352] Information is provided on the EJN's website as to what the contact points in the Member States are, although, the information is kept in vague terms, presumably to discourage members of the public from seeking to approach the contact points themselves. For example, the listed contact point for England was the UK Ministry of Justice,[353] which is a vast organisation. There is a form available for making requests to contact points on the EJN website, which is stated to be for use by judicial authorities only.[354] A further, relevant amendment introduced by Decision No 568/2009/EC states that national contact points are required to:

> Supply any information to facilitate the application of the law of another Member State that is applicable under a Community or international instrument.[355]

Requests should be dealt with within 15 days, failing which, 30 days,[356] but it is unclear what form such requests or any answers given should take. It is very likely that requests should be in a similar form, with all the associated problems, to those made under the previously considered London Convention, ie abstract requests for information on foreign law. Despite legislative provision for the furnishing of statistics,[357] there appears, as of July 2022, to be no publicly available evidence of the number of requests having been exchanged under the EJN mechanism.[358]

[351] Decision No 2001/470/EC (n 345), as amended by Decision No 568/2009/EC (n 347), Art 2(2). Reasons listed making it necessary are the existence of separate legal systems, the domestic distribution of jurisdiction, the tasks to be entrusted to the contact points or in order to associate judicial bodies that frequently deal with cross-border litigation directly with the activities of the contact points.

[352] Decision No 568/2009/EC (n 347), Article 1(1).

[353] European Judicial Network in civil and commercial matters, 'About the network – England and Wales', e-justice.europa.eu/content_about_the_network-431-ew-en.do?member=1.

[354] European Judicial Network in civil and commercial matters, 'Would you like to contact an EJN-civil Contact Point from your country?', e-justice.europa.eu/contactPoint.do.

[355] Decision No 568/2009/EC (n 347), Art 1(3), which amended Decision No 2001/470/EC (n 345), Article 5(2)(c).

[356] Decision No 2001/470/EC (n 345), as amended, Art 8(1).

[357] ibid, as amended, Art 8(3).

[358] The EJN seems most active in terms of general judicial cooperation, which is recognised in a report on the activities of the EJN published in 2014. Publications Office of the European Union, 'Evaluation of the activities of the European Judicial Network in civil and commercial matters' (2015), op.europa.eu/en/publication-detail/-/publication/a877dc52-3f93-472b-a81f-9b7c5d810718. See also the most recently published 2012 Annual Report on International Family Justice from the Office of the Head of International Family Justice for England and Wales, 'Annual Report 2012', www.judiciary.uk/wp-content/uploads/JCO/Documents/Reports/international_family_justice_2013.pdf, which at fn 10 states: 'The use of the EJN, both formally and through these network judges is commonplace in international family proceedings and, indeed, is encouraged in part X of the Good Practice Guide to Regulation EC 2201/2203 (Brussels II revised) produced by the European Commission.' It was observed in *Mercredi v Chaffe* [2011] EWCA Civ 272, [89]: 'Judicial collaboration in cross-border

However, under a recent implementing decision of the Commission dated July 2019,[359] there is evidence of legislative activity to progress matters by means of the Internal Market Information System.[360] Considering that this comes 10 years after Decision No 568/2009/EC, it is likely that progress will continue to be slow. The EJN equivalent, as it addresses criminal matters, appears to be significantly more developed,[361] suggesting that the potential exists for further development in the civil and commercial sphere.

A further role of the EJN, in the civil and commercial sphere, is the provision of publicly available information on Member State legal systems.[362] However, the EJN's website, as it concerns civil and commercial matters,[363] is limited, containing only basic information on the laws of the respective Member States.[364] While the topic-based outlines do contain references to the underlying statutory provisions, there is insufficient detail and reference to case law generally.[365] While the EJN database is no doubt a useful starting point for members of the public, it would appear to be inappropriate and irresponsible for legal professionals to rely on the information provided.[366]

(c) Exchange of Information between Judges

There is the possibility of judges communicating amongst themselves to investigate the content of foreign law. The mechanism used may be informal, eg a

family disputes within the European Union is, as is now well known, at a stage of advanced development. There are regular meetings of the EJN devoted to family law and practice.' There is no published information of meetings or events having taken place since 2017, and it would be helpful if there were more recent information about its ongoing work. European Judicial Network in civil and commercial matters, 'Events/news', e-justice.europa.eu/content_eventsnews-438-en.do?clang=en.

[359] Commission implementing Decision (EU) 2019/1253 of 22 July 2019 on a pilot project to implement the administrative cooperation provisions set out in Council Decision 2001/470/EC establishing a European Judicial Network in civil and commercial matters by means of the Internal Market Information System.

[360] European Commission, 'About IMI', ec.europa.eu/internal_market/imi-net/about/index_en.htm.

[361] See, for example, European Judicial Network, 'Report on Activities and Management: 2013–14', www.ejn-crimjust.europa.eu/ejnupload/StaticPages/EJN%20Report%20on%20activities%20and%20management_2013-2014_EN.pdf.

[362] Council Decision 2001/470/EC, as amended, Arts 13–15.

[363] 'European Judicial Network in civil and commercial matters', e-justice.europa.eu/content_european_judicial_network_in_civil_and_commercial_matters-21-en.do.

[364] European Judicial Network in civil and commercial matters, 'Information on national law (information sheets)', e-justice.europa.eu/content_information_on_national_law_information_sheets-439-en.do?clang=en. As of May 2021, information is still provided on the website in respect of the UK legal systems with a notice that 'In the field of civil justice, pending procedures and proceedings initiated before the end of the transition period will continue under EU law. The e-Justice Portal, on the basis of a mutual agreement with the UK, will maintain the relevant information related to the United Kingdom until the end of 2022.'

[365] See, for example, European Judicial Network in civil and commercial matters, 'Divorce – Scotland', e-justice.europa.eu/content_divorce-45-sc-en.do?member=1.

[366] Hüßtege considers that the EJN database can only be considered an '*Einstieg*' (Starting point). Hüßtege, 'Internetrecherche contra Sachverständigengutachten – Zur Ermittlung ausländischen Rechts durch deutsche Gerichte' (n 277), 262.

question asked by e-mail, perhaps based on an existing professional connection. Such an approach is significantly more likely to be taken in Germany, which, as demonstrated, provides the judge with greater scope for personally investigating the applicable foreign law.

The exchange of information between judges on a more informal basis is not without infrastructure. In addition to the possibility of building contacts through the EJN[367] and other available networking possibilities, the Network of the Presidents of the European Supreme Courts was created in 2004 to help facilitate the better exchange of information between EU Member State courts.[368] It has been argued that:

> An informal approach within the terms of the network seems preferable in comparison to a laborious and expensive reference procedure. [Translation by author][369]

While it is accepted that the informal exchange of information between judges has the potential to be cheaper and quicker than other possible means, especially in urgent cases, where the domestic court is likely to be working with incomplete information, caution is warranted. First, even an esteemed foreign judge cannot be an expert in all areas of the law but may nonetheless feel obliged to provide an answer. Second, decisions given in respect of domestic law are carefully considered, with judgments issued explaining the reasoning of the court. This is unlikely to be the case where there is an exchange of e-mails. Third, domestic judges are held to account by their colleagues and practitioners, with the possibility of an appeal. An exchange of e-mails manifestly lacks the requisite level of transparency and accountability. Indeed, the mere exchange of correspondence regarding the foreign law applicable to an ongoing case, especially where there is little involvement of the parties in framing the questions, is likely to infringe on requirements of due process. In short, while discourse between judges of different countries is to be encouraged, such discourse should not, other than in exceptional circumstances, extend to the resolution of ongoing court actions.

(d) Foreign Embassies

There is some evidence of German courts seeking information on foreign law from foreign embassies.[370] Such approaches appear to fall outwith the scope of any treaty

[367] See, under Decision No 2001/470/EC (n 345), Art 11(1): 'Meetings open to all members of the Network shall be held to enable them to get to know each other and exchange experience, to provide a platform for discussion of practical and legal problems met and to deal with specific questions.' As briefly discussed in n 358 above, this seems to be the area that the EJN is most active in.

[368] 'Network of the Presidents of the European Supreme Courts', network-presidents.eu/. The UK was still listed on the website as a member in May 2021, but this is presumably because the website hasn't been updated since the transition period ended. The UK may become an observer in due course.

[369] Hübner (n 66), 262: 'Das formlose Vorgehen im Rahmen des Netzwerks erscheint auch gegenüber einem aufwendigen und teuren Vorlageverfahren vorzugswürdig.'

[370] *Decision of the Federal Court of Justice from 24 November 1960* (BGH, II. Zivilsenat) II ZR 9/60, NJW 1961, 410, 411. There are two examples given of German authorities seeking information on

and can operate in two ways. First, a foreign embassy based in Germany could be asked a question directly. Second, a German embassy based abroad could conduct a locally-based investigation, eg the German embassy in Kabul could seek information on the content of Afghan law from official sources based there.[371] German academics appear to favour such an approach where the question is clear and short, but caution against seeking information through this means where the question is more complicated.[372] While foreign embassies are a potential avenue for obtaining information on foreign law, the same, if not more, caution is warranted as when approaching foreign judges directly. A response given by a foreign embassy will not have the required level of transparency and accountability that parties can legitimately expect. Embassy staff are unlikely to be legally qualified,[373] and, even if so qualified, are unlikely to possess expertise with regards to matters of civil and commercial law. Where the investigation requires to be carried out locally, this is likely to be resource-intensive and create a cumbersome information chain stretching all the way back to the domestic court. It is likely that the involvement of diplomatic channels was more relevant in the past, when it would have been more difficult to get in touch with lawyers based in foreign jurisdictions directly. In the twenty-first century, it is respectfully suggested that there are more effective means of sourcing the necessary information. There is no evidence that the Foreign, Commonwealth & Development Office is prepared to involve itself with investigations into the content of foreign law,[374] even if that were desired by the British court.

(v) References to Foreign Courts

In this and the subsequent section, mechanisms are considered which allow the domestic court to 'contract out' part of its responsibility for the process of investigating and determining the applicable foreign law. In this context, while it is recognised that the domestic court will always have the final say as to whether to accept an opinion issued by, for example, a foreign court, this and section B.(vi) consider scenarios where any opinion obtained will almost certainly be followed.

foreign law from foreign embassies in Otto (n 261), 302. First, information was obtained from the German embassy in Rome in relation to the use of names by married women under Italian law and, second, information was obtained from the German embassy in Manila in relation to the validity of a marriage under Philippine law. Otto suggests that a German expert would not have been in a position to provide this wealth of information. The merits of various forms of expert are considered at section IV.B below.

[371] *Decision of the Federal Court of Justice from 24 November 1960* (BGH, II. Zivilsenat) II ZR 9/60, NJW 1961, 410.

[372] Schack, *Internationales Zivilverfahrensrecht* (n 7), para 761; Prütting, '§ 293' (n 6), para 26.

[373] Otto (n 261), 302.

[374] In respect of civil proceedings, the Foreign, Commonwealth & Development Office does assist with the service of documents and the taking of evidence. See UK Government, 'Service of documents and taking of evidence', www.gov.uk/guidance/service-of-documents-and-taking-of-evidence.

There is a conceptual difference between mechanisms allowing a court to refer[375] a case to a foreign court for an opinion to be given by it on the content of the *lex causae*, and providing courts with a mechanism to seek information from authorities abroad, generally by means of asking questions. Examples of the latter mechanism were considered in section B.(iv). In terms of the mechanism for reference, there is also a distinction between whether the domestic court itself initiates the reference (eg by passing (part of) the court file to the foreign court) or whether the parties are directed to initiate proceedings in the foreign court themselves, usually to resolve a discrete point.

For example, a mechanism in place in respect of the courts of New South Wales and Singapore clearly puts the onus on the parties to raise additional proceedings in the foreign court to seek its opinion on the content of the *lex causae*:

> If an issue in proceedings before one Party is governed by the law of the other Party, each Party will give consideration, in accordance with its rules and procedures, to directing the parties in the proceedings to take steps to have any contested issue of law determined by the courts of the Party of the governing law.[376]

In other words, there is no direct interaction between the New South Wales court and the Singaporean court. It is important to note that the preamble to the agreement between New South Wales and Singapore refers[377] to the English case of *Westacre* (2008),[378] which will be considered in more detail below, when this work addresses the potential role of the parties in the investigation of the content of the applicable foreign law. *Westacre* (2008) was very much a situation where the parties were left with responsibility for raising further proceedings in the English courts.[379] On the other hand, the Memorandum of Understanding between the Chief Justice of New South Wales and the Chief Judge of the State of New York on references of questions of law appears, at least on the face of it, to provide for a reference procedure:

> If a substantial legal issue in proceedings before one Court is governed by the law of the other Court, each Party shall give consideration, in accordance with its rules and

[375] In some British authorities, the term remit is used to describe what might otherwise be described as a reference. In this work, the words reference and remit are treated as synonyms, with remit being used in relation to English and Scots law, and reference more generally.

[376] 'Memorandum of Understanding between the Supreme Court of Singapore and the Supreme Court of New South Wales on references of questions of law', www.supremecourt.justice.nsw.gov.au/Pages/sco2_practiceprocedure/sco2_internationaljudicialcooperation/SCO2_agreement_singapore.aspx, Art 1.

[377] ibid, preamble: 'ACKNOWLEDGING the innovative procedure adopted by the Supreme Court of Singapore by referring a question of foreign law to the High Court of Justice of England and Wales in Westacre Investments Inc v The State-Owned Company Yugoimport SDPR (also known as Jugoimport-SDPR) [2009] 2 SLR(R) 166 and Westacre Investments Inc v Yugoimport SDPR [2008] EWHC 801 (Comm).'

[378] *Westacre Investments Inc v The State-Owned Company Yugoimport SDPR* [2008] EWHC 801 (Comm).

[379] *Westacre Investments Inc v The State-Owned Company Yugoimport SDPR* [2008] EWHC 801 (Comm), [2].

> procedures, to taking steps to have any contested issue of law referred to the Party of the governing law for an answer to be provided in accordance with the procedures of the requested jurisdiction.[380]

Being clear as to how exactly the mechanism is supposed to operate in practice is essential. Otherwise, parties and courts are left confused as to how the case should proceed, adding cost, wasting time, and undermining the effectiveness of the mechanism provided. There appear to be no mechanisms in German law facilitating a direct reference to a foreign court for an opinion to be given. Thus, the mechanisms available to the German court appear to facilitate the seeking of information only, such mechanisms having been considered in the previous section.

The British Law Ascertainment Act 1859 ('the 1859 Act') was passed during the zenith of the British Empire and sought to improve the mechanisms underlying the application of foreign law throughout the courts of the British Empire.[381] The principle underlying the 1859 Act was that a case setting out the facts, together with relevant questions of law to be answered, could be prepared and sent to any court located within the British Empire for an opinion to be given as to the law applicable to those facts.[382] Despite some academics suggesting otherwise,[383] the 1859 Act will only be applied by the British court if the foreign law has been pleaded by either of the parties, as required in terms of the fact approach.

[380] 'Memorandum of Understanding between the Chief Justice of New South Wales and the Chief Judge of the state of New York on references of questions of law', www.supremecourt.justice.nsw.gov.au/Pages/sco2_practiceprocedure/sco2_internationaljudicialcooperation/SCO2_agreement_newyork.aspx, Art 1.

[381] The original legislation, as at 13 August 1859, contained the following introductory text: 'Whereas great Improvement in the Administration of the Law would ensue if Facilities were afforded for more certainly ascertaining the Law administered in one Part of Her Majesty's Dominions when pleaded in the Courts of another Part thereof.' See legislation.gov.uk, 'British Law Ascertainment Act 1859 (as enacted)', www.legislation.gov.uk/ukpga/Vict/22-23/63/introduction/enacted.

[382] It is not clear how the mechanism was supposed to work in practice. A summary of the lengthy terms of s 1 of 1859 Act is that where an action is depending within one of 'Her Majesty's dominions' (which includes the UK), the court can direct that a case be prepared for an opinion to be given by a foreign court, providing that court is also located within one of 'Her Majesty's dominions', setting out the facts and those questions of law arising out of the same which require to be answered, either by agreement or by jury (!), or by such other person appointed by the court for that purpose, in the event of the parties not agreeing, subject to the approval of the court.

[383] It has been suggested that the 1859 Act cuts through the usual principles underlying the fact approach. Fentiman mentions this possibility both in the introduction to his 1998 text, *Foreign Law in English Courts* (n 70), 4, and more substantively at 134: 'The effect is that the application of foreign law is required and, in effect, to render any given choice of law rule mandatory for the purposes of the case in hand.' This point is drawn on in Trautmann (n 112), 69. Especially considering its terms, as referenced above, and the long title of the 1859 Act: 'An Act to afford Facilities for the more certain Ascertainment of the Law administered in one Part of Her Majesty's Dominions when pleaded in the Courts of another Part thereof,' there is no evidence that the 1859 Act was intended to usurp the usual position requiring that foreign law be pled in British cases. In the substantive analysis in Fentiman, *Foreign Law in English Courts* (n 70), 134, Fentiman's own footnote casts doubt on his proposition, in part, because his only authority is *Topham v The Duke of Portland* (1863) 1 De GJ & S 517; 46 ER 205, and, in part, because the judgment in *Topham* (1863) is extremely unclear, a fact which Fentiman acknowledges.

The 1859 Act was not the only statute passed during the mid-nineteenth century by the UK Parliament addressing the difficulties posed to courts investigating the content of foreign law,[384] but it is the only statute that remains in force. If the provision of relevant legislation is to be taken as an indication, it is notable that the UK Parliament was more conscious 160 years ago of the difficulties involved in the investigation of foreign law than it appears to be today.

The 1859 Act provides for the foreign court to hear the parties and their representatives, or to decide a case on the basis of the information presented, following which an opinion should be given and certified by the foreign court.[385] Parties are then required to lodge the opinion with the domestic court (ie the foreign court does not itself send the opinion to the referring court) and, if so advised, to move the domestic court to implement the terms of the opinion.[386] However, the opinion of the foreign court is not necessarily the final word on the matter. Thus, the UK Supreme Court or the Judicial Committee of the Privy Council may adopt or reject the opinion, subject to the important restriction that an appeal to the UK Supreme Court or the Judicial Committee of the Privy Council is only possible where such opinions are reviewable by either of those courts.[387] Where no appeal lies from the foreign court to either of those courts – usually because the possibility has been abolished[388] – then the opinion may, it seems, not be reviewed by either court, under the 1859 Act.

Even though the 1859 Act remains British law, the scope for its use is extremely limited. First, the 1859 Act works on the basis of reciprocity, ie both the sending and receiving court must be bound by its terms. There is little evidence that most Commonwealth countries still consider themselves bound by its terms. It does appear to be in force in the State of the Australian Capital Territory,[389] but most former parts of the British Empire, including India,[390] have repealed it. Second, it is questionable whether a reference by a British court is competent under the 1859 Act. Thus, can a British court refer a case to the courts of the Australian

[384] The Foreign Law Ascertainment Act 1861 provided a mechanism for references to be made to foreign courts to ascertain the content of foreign law. However, the 1861 Act was never used in practice as no reciprocal convention was ever entered into by the UK to implement its terms. The 1861 Act was repealed in 1973. See in this regard: Fentiman, *Foreign Law in English Courts* (n 70), 141. The 1861 Act does appear to still be on the Irish statute book according to the electronic Irish Statute Book (eISB). See 'Foreign Law Ascertainment Act 1861 (Ireland)', www.irishstatutebook.ie/eli/1861/act/11/enacted/en/html.

[385] British Law Ascertainment Act 1859, s 1.

[386] British Law Ascertainment Act 1859, s 2.

[387] British Law Ascertainment Act 1859, s 4. The act refers to her 'Her Majesty in Council', which is also known as the Judicial Committee of the Privy Council. See The Privy Council Office, 'Judicial Committee', privycouncil.independent.gov.uk/privy-council/judicial-committee/#:~:text=The%20Judicial%20Committee%20of%20the,Republics%2C%20to%20the%20Judicial%20Committee.

[388] See, for example, in relation to New Zealand, the Supreme Court Act 2003, s 42.

[389] 'British Law Ascertainment Act 1859 (22 and 23 Vic c 63)', www.legislation.act.gov.au/DownloadFile/a/db_1786/19870112-2269/PDF/db_1786.pdf.

[390] 'The British Statutes (Repeal) Act 2004', www.prsindia.org/sites/default/files/1167484943_THE_BRITISH_STATUTES.pdf.

Capital Territory in view of the fact that the 1859 Act appears to remain on the statute books of the Australian Capital Territory? If a literal approach[391] is taken to the wording of section 1 of the 1859 Act then the answer is no. A reference, in terms of the 1859 Act, may only be made to one of 'Her Majesty's Dominions',[392] a status which Australia no longer holds. On the other hand, it is arguable that a purposive interpretation,[393] together with the possibility of reciprocity with courts of the Australian Capital Territory, may allow a reference under the 1859 Act. A British court would likely have to be satisfied that the courts of the Australian Capital Territory would be prepared to deal with the reference, presumably by means of confirmation from them, before allowing recourse to the 1859 Act. However, a British court may be discouraged by the fact that no appeal would lie, in terms of the opinion given, to the Judicial Committee of the Privy Council, as no appeal lies from an Australian court to that court.[394] Third, there is no evidence that the 1859 Act has ever been used extensively in practice. Indeed, it appears to have been overlooked that every reported British case[395] in which the 1859 Act was used[396] was one which involved the English and Scottish courts only, ie the reference was requested by the Scottish court in respect of English law or vice versa.[397] Thus, there does not appear to be a reported British case where a case was sent, under the 1859 Act, to anywhere in the wider British Empire for an opinion to be given,[398] although this cannot be completely ruled out.

[391] See J Boylan-Kemp, *English Legal System: The Fundamentals* (Sweet & Maxwell, 2018), para 2-049, citing *R v City of London Court Judge* [1892] 1 QB 273.

[392] The term dominion had largely lost its significance by the 1940s. See FR Scott, 'The End of Dominion Status' (1944) 38 *The American Journal of International Law* 34, 45–46. While the other former dominions appear to have dispensed with the term, the term still appears to form part of the formal title of Canada, see the Constitution Act 1867, s 3, and, for some background, The Canadian Encyclopedia, 'Dominion of Canada' (7 November 2019), www.thecanadianencyclopedia.ca/en/article/dominion: 'Dominion of Canada is the country's formal title, though it is rarely used.'

[393] See Boylan-Kemp (n 391), para 2-055, citing *R v Registrar General, Ex parte Smith* [1991] 2 QB 393.

[394] Australia Act 1986, s 11.

[395] Collins (Lord Collins of Mapesbury) and Harris (eds) (n 112), para 9-003; Trautmann (n 112), 69; T Rogoz, *Ausländisches Recht im deutschen und englischen Zivilprozess* (Mohr Siebeck, 2008), 109; Fentiman, *Foreign Law in English Courts* (n 70), 134–35.

[396] Cases from the nineteenth century that involved the 1859 Act include *Topham v The Duke of Portland* (1863) 1 De GJ & S 517; 46 ER 205; *Lord v Colvin* (1860) 1 Drew & Sm 24; 62 ER 287 and *Earl of Eglinton v Lamb* (1867) 15 LT 657. Those cases from the twentieth century are considered in the next footnote. In *Colvin* (1860), the English court rejected the submissions of the plaintiff, 'argued at great length', that the Court should decide 'on the evidence of Scotch lawyers before it'. The judge held 'that I ought to avail myself of the power which the Legislature has given me to refer the points of Scotch law here raised, to be decided by a Scotch Court'. The judge then spelled out the benefits of doing so, as against seeking expert evidence from Scottish lawyers.

[397] It is suggested in Trautmann (n 112), 70, that there have been no cases under the 1859 Act since the nineteenth century. This appears not to be the case. In *Duke of Wellington's Executor* 1946 SC 32, the Scottish court considered a remit from Mr Justice Cohen, a judge of the Chancery Division of the English High Court at that time. Moreover, the 1859 Act is referred to in *Stirling v Stirling* [1908] 2 Ch 344 as the 'proper course' where evidence is required as to the content of Scots law, and there is a further reported Scottish case from the twentieth century, namely, *Macomish's Executors v Jones* 1932 SC 108, in which the 1859 Act was applied to remit a case to England.

[398] That is certainly not to suggest that such a step was never competent. In *MacDougall v Chitnavis* 1937 SC 390, the Scottish Inner House of the Court of Session declined to refer a case to the Indian

Despite its limited application in practice, the mechanism contained in the 1859 Act had some potential to facilitate the effective application of foreign law in the courts to which it applied. Thus, Fentiman goes too far in arguing that a reference to a foreign court under the 1859 Act is necessarily more expensive and time-consuming than relying on expert evidence.[399] Where there is recourse to oral expert evidence in British court proceedings, it can take many days of court time to tease out each expert's evidence,[400] and, where there are conflicting views, can leave the judge still having to make a difficult assessment of the content of the applicable foreign law.[401] It is unclear why, according to Fentiman, having a foreign court consider a case necessarily introduces:

> An unacceptable degree of risk, unpredictability and delay into the process.[402]

It is submitted that having a judge consider a foreign law that he has never studied, and of which he may have no previous experience is equally susceptible to risk, unpredictability, and delay. It is true that expense will be incurred in having the parties engage with foreign court proceedings, but it is questionable whether this will necessarily amount to more than the costs involved in leading expert witness evidence. Reference to a foreign court seems very likely to produce an accurate decision regarding the content of the applicable foreign law. In short, issue is taken with Fentiman's position, who argues that the 1859 Act is:

> An object lesson perhaps in how not to design a mechanism for obtaining proof of foreign law, an indicator of the pragmatism and cost-consciousness of litigants and their advisers.[403]

The 1859 Act's flaws are that it is outdated and obscure, with no clear mechanism for implementing its terms. In view of the paucity of its use to date, and its

court, which appears to be the closest a British court actually got to referring a case to a court outwith the UK under the 1859 Act. The test was set out by Lord President Normand at 400: 'Before we can remit this question to the Indian Court we have to be reasonably satisfied that a remit is necessary or expedient for the proper disposal of the present action.'

[399] Fentiman, *Foreign Law in English Courts* (n 70), 239. It is interesting to note that the Scottish judge Lord Hunter commented in 1932, in relation to the 1859 Act, in *Macomish's Executors v Jones* 1932 SC 108, 112–13: 'Manifestly the intention was to save parties the expense of having a proof upon the question of law which might arise. The simple procedure was allowed, under statute, of remitting to a Court in England to give an expression of opinion of what the law is.' In *Lord v Colvin* (1860) 1 Drew & Sm 24; 62 ER 287, expense appears to have been an issue raised by the Plaintiff's counsel, who had argued at great length to prevent the case being referred to the Scottish court. However, the court held, at 287, 'With regard, however, to the expense, I do not see that it would be so great as has been stated; because I must state all the facts of the case for the Scotch Court, and that Court will only have to decide the questions of law.'

[400] For example, see *Macmillan Inc v Bishopsgate Investment Trust Plc (No 3)* [1995] 1 WLR 978, the first instance trial of which appears to have taken well over a year to reach a conclusion.

[401] *Bumper Development Corporation v Metropolitan Police Commissioner* [1991] 1 WLR 1362, 1368: 'It is however the duty of the judge when faced with conflicting evidence from witnesses about a foreign law to resolve those differences in the same way as he must in the case of other conflicting evidence as to facts.'

[402] Fentiman, *Foreign Law in English Courts* (n 70), 239.

[403] ibid, 239.

very limited scope of application, there is little doubt that the 1859 Act should be repealed. However, there is little that is inherent in the 1859 Act that means it could not have assisted with the effective disposal of cases in the past. In short, it is unfortunate that the mechanism provided by the 1859 Act has played such a limited role since its introduction.

(vi) References to Foreign Lawyers

There are some nineteenth-century[404] Scottish authorities suggesting that a case may be remitted by the Scottish court to a foreign lawyer for a determination to be made by him as to the content of the applicable foreign law.[405] The precise workings of the mechanism are unclear, with cases rather contradictory, although the following seeks to set out the principles as coherently as possible. Thus, these nineteenth-century cases appear to have been remitted to a foreign lawyer by the Scottish court itself,[406] albeit usually with the parties' assistance in preparing the case,[407] whereas, in the normal course of proceedings today, it is the parties in Scottish proceedings who instruct their experts directly, without the involvement of the court.[408] These nineteenth-century cases probably find their origin in some of the cases examined in Chapter two, the historical chapter of this work, eg *Johnson* (1776), where a case was made up for the opinion of Dutch counsel.[409] There is suggestion in contemporary academic texts on Scottish private international law that the possibility of remit by the Scottish court to a foreign lawyer – it is said only with the parties' consent[410] – continues to exist as a mechanism to prove the content of foreign law in contemporary Scots law.[411] This is the reason why the mechanism is considered in this section of this work.

[404] The only reference to the procedure to be found in a twentieth-century Scottish case is *Higgins v Ewing's Trustees* 1925 SC 440, where the appeal court ordered a proof (trial) and acknowledged at 449, with reference to *Welsh v Milne* (1844) 7 D 213, that 'remit of consent to foreign counsel' was an option available to the Scottish court for proving the content of foreign law.

[405] See, for example: *Bank of Scotland v Broughton and Weston* (1830) 8 S 424, where a joint case was prepared for English counsel and the opinion applied; *Welsh v Milne* (1844) 7 D 213; *Fyffe v Fyffe* (1840) 2 D 1001; *Williamson v Taylor* (1845) 8 D 156; *Goetze & Sohn v Aders, Preyer & Co* (1874) 2 R 150.

[406] *Goetze & Sohn v Aders, Preyer & Co* (1874) 2 R 150.

[407] It is unclear whether the parties themselves were responsible for making up the case for the court's approval, as would seem normal, although *Williamson v Taylor* (1845) 8 D 156, 157, explicitly states that the case was prepared for remit by the court, suggesting that they were not involved in the preparation of every case.

[408] This is not the case in England, where permission is required, at least if the parties want to lead the evidence in court or recover expenses. See CPR 35.5(1).

[409] *Johnson v Crawford and Mason* [1776] Mor in Arbitration, Appendix, Part I, No 4, 5.

[410] Beaumont and McEleavy, *Anton's Private International Law* (n 133), para 27.183. The requirement for consent is suggested in *Higgins v Ewing's Trustees* 1925 SC 440, 449, but in *Goetze & Sohn v Aders, Preyer & Co* (1874) 2 R 150, 152, the suggestion is that the Scottish court ordered the remit as the parties were unable to agree their respective rights under the law of Saxony.

[411] Beaumont and McEleavy, *Anton's Private International Law* (n 133), para 27.183; Crawford and Carruthers (n 78), para 8-28.

It might be thought that a remit to a foreign lawyer made by the court is the same as the instruction of an expert opinion, a thought that would find especially strong resonance in Germany, where expert opinions (*Gutachten*) are, as a rule, sought directly by the German court.[412] However, despite a prima facie similarity, the remit procedure discussed here is of a different character. First, although this work takes the view that the Scottish court has always retained residual discretion as to whether to accept the opinion of a foreign lawyer instructed on a remit basis, there is strong suggestion in the early authorities that the opinion of the foreign lawyer instructed on a remit basis was, in effect, binding.[413] This far exceeds the authority given to expert opinions in German court proceedings, where there is no suggestion that the opinion binds the judge or absolves him of his responsibility to investigate the content of the applicable foreign law.[414] Moreover, as will be discussed in due course, the formal instruction of an expert by the German court is recognised as falling within the rules applying to expert evidence generally, including affording the opportunity for the parties to put questions to the expert in oral proceedings.[415] This opportunity to ask questions does not appear to be a feature of the Scottish remit procedure. These differences distinguish the Scottish remit procedure from the direct instruction of experts by the German court. Significantly more detail is given as to the role of experts in section IV below.

In those Scottish cases where a remit was made to a foreign lawyer, with the exception of *Goetze* (1874),[416] and in common with those cases remitted to courts furth (outside) of the respective jurisdiction by English and Scottish courts under the 1859 Act,[417] all cases remitted to foreign lawyers by the Scottish courts were to English counsel on points of English law.[418]

In *Goetze* (1874), where the law of Saxony was applied, the remit procedure appears to have provided the Scottish court with a particularly effective means to resolve the dispute. The court commented that it had:

> found it impossible to decide without knowing what their rights were under the Saxon sequestration. We were in hopes that the parties would lay before us a statement of what their rights were under the Saxon law. This led to considerable delay, and when it was found that the parties could not agree, it became necessary to have a case prepared for the opinion of German lawyers. We have now a very excellent and clear opinion of Professor Endemann.[419]

[412] Prütting, '§ 293' (n 6), para 29.

[413] *Welsh v Milne* (1844) 7 D 213, 214. The logical distinction between an opinion provided by a foreign government as to its law being (highly) persuasive and being 'binding, if reasonable' was recently considered by the US Supreme Court in *Animal Science Products Inc v Hebei Welcome Pharmaceutical Co Ltd* (2018) 585 US ___ (Slip Opinion).

[414] Schack, *Internationales Zivilverfahrensrecht* (n 7), para 760.

[415] ibid, para 766.

[416] *Goetze & Sohn v Aders, Preyer & Co* (1874) 2 R 150.

[417] See section II.B.(v), text to nn 395–398 above.

[418] *Cranstoun v Cuninghame* (1839) 1 D 521; *Fyffe v Fyffe* (1840) 2 D 1001; *Williamson v Taylor* (1845) 8 D 156; *Stiven v Myer* (1868) 6 M 885.

[419] *Goetze & Sohn v Aders, Preyer & Co* (1874) 2 R 150, 152. The author of the opinion, Professor Endemann, who appears to have been a professor in the city of Jena, Thuringia, and the author, for

Despite the remit procedure providing the Scottish court with a mechanism to effectively investigate and determine the content of foreign law in some cases, there is evidence that justice was not always served by the procedure. In the leading case of *Welsh* (1844), an opinion was sought from New York lawyers as to the law of South Carolina, which opinion was said to have been obtained with 'no irregularity or mistake.'[420] However, the decision is odd in so far that it is questionable what knowledge lawyers from the State of New York would have had of the law of the State of South Carolina. The reclaimer (appellant) sought that an opinion be obtained from lawyers versed in the law of South Carolina, but this was refused by the appeal court.[421]

It is highly questionable whether a Scottish court today would be prepared to use the remit procedure, especially considering the antiquity of the last remit to a foreign lawyer. There is no mention in the Scottish court rules of the remit procedure discussed here. Moreover, in view of the binding nature of the resulting opinion, it is very unlikely that the parties would agree to the remit, especially where the point concerned an important element of the case.

There is no evidence that the English courts ever remitted cases to foreign lawyers in the same manner as the Scottish courts. There is nonetheless similarity between the Scottish remit procedure and the instruction of a single joint expert, as is possible under the English Civil Procedure Rules,[422] with this instruction falling within the sanction and direction of the English court.[423] However, first, single joint expert appointments appear to be unusual in the context of proving foreign law; second, there is no question of the opinion binding the court; and, third, the instruction is jointly made by *the parties*.

While there does not appear to be evidence of German courts ever having remitted cases to foreign lawyers (ie furth of the territory that came to constitute Germany in 1871), there existed a well-established practice into the early nineteenth century of courts remitting cases to German universities for their opinion on the law applicable to the facts of the case. Known as *Aktenversendung*,[424] this mechanism was more commonly employed in complicated cases.[425] For example, opinions were produced by academics at the University of Tübingen from as early as 1495, and, in 1805, as many as 160 cases were dealt with by academics based at the university.[426] While the choice of which law faculty to send the case

example, of W Endemann, *Das Deutsche Civilprozeßrecht* (Bangel & Schmitt, 1868), received high praise from the court. Lord Deas commented, at 155, that he had 'never seen an opinion by foreign counsel better calculated to be useful to the Court.'

420 *Welsh v Milne* (1844) 7 D 213, 214.

421 *Welsh v Milne* (1844) 7 D 213, 214.

422 CPR 35.7–8.

423 CPR 35.7–8. See, for commentary, S Cunningham-Hill and K Elder, *Civil Litigation: 2018–2019*, 11th edn (Oxford University Press, 2018), para 18.8.4.

424 E Klugkist, 'Die Aktenversendung an Juristenfakultäten: Ein gemeinsames Kapitel aus der Geschichte des deutschen Prozeßrechts und der deutschen Universitäten' (1967) 22 *Juristenzeitung* 155.

425 ibid, 156.

426 ibid, 157.

to ultimately lay with the court, the parties were afforded the opportunity to view the court process and to suggest three law faculties to which the case could be sent.[427] An unusual feature of the mechanism, when one considers German procedure today, was that the court would generally adopt the terms of the opinion in full.[428] However, in common with Scotland's approach to remits to foreign lawyers, the practice does not exist today in German civil procedure, with steps having been taken by various pre-unification States in the nineteenth century to ban the practice, eg by Württemberg in 1819.[429]

(vii) Determination of the Content of the Applicable Foreign Law

The determination of the content of the applicable foreign law is a difficult and skilled task, requiring the domestic judge to be clear in his mind as to what he is seeking to find in the applicable foreign law. The judge may be faced with irrelevant information;[430] with conflicting and inconclusive authorities;[431] or with conflicting accounts of the content of the foreign law.[432] It has been said:

> There are many cases in which the judge has had to pick his way through baffling and contradictory evidence of foreign law, with the result that one may applaud the effort yet still lack confidence in the outcome ...[433]

It has been stated previously that the British judge is required to apply the law as it is applied in the foreign state,[434] which is a long-standing principle:

> The Court sitting here decides from the evidence of persons skilled in that law, and decides as it would if sitting in Belgium.[435]

[427] ibid, 155.
[428] ibid, 155.
[429] ibid, 157.
[430] *Exportadora de Sal SA de CV v Corretaje Maritimo Sud-Americano Inc* [2018] EWHC 224 (Comm), [29].
[431] *Re Duke of Wellington* [1947] Ch 506, 515: 'The task of an English judge, who is faced with the duty of finding as a fact what is the relevant foreign law, in a case involving the application of foreign law, as it would be expounded in the foreign court, for that purpose notionally sitting in that court, is frequently a hard one; but it would be difficult to imagine a harder task than that which faces me, namely, of expounding for the first time either in this country or in Spain the relevant law of Spain as it would be expounded by the Supreme Court of Spain, which up to the present time has made no pronouncement on the subject, and having to base that exposition on evidence which satisfies me that on this subject there exists a profound cleavage of legal opinion in Spain, and two conflicting decisions of courts of inferior jurisdiction.'
[432] *Bumper Development Corporation v Metropolitan Police Commissioner* [1991] 1 WLR 1362, 1368. A good example is provided by the case of *Scottish National Orchestra Society Ltd v Thomson's Executor* 1969 SLT 325, where the Scottish judge was confronted with four experts on Swedish law, two on each side of the argument. It is often the case in British cases that the parties agree on a number of points, leaving the contested issues to then be decided by the judge. See, for example, *Roberts v Soldiers, Sailors, Airmen and Families Association* [2020] EWHC 994 (QB), [197], and *PJSC VTB Bank v Laptev* [2020] EWHC 321 (Ch), [17]–[19].
[433] Briggs (n 106), 10.
[434] See *Dexia Crediop SPA v Comune di Prato* [2017] EWCA Civ 428, [34].
[435] *Collier v Rivaz* (1841) 2 Curteis 855, 863; 163 ER 608.

The English case of *Exportadora de Sal SA de CV* (2018)[436] is instructive as to the difficulties involved in determining the content of the applicable foreign law. The parties, ESSA and CMSA, entered into a shipbuilding contract on 3 July 2014, which was terminated on 27 May 2015, leaving a significant outstanding balance due to CMSA.[437] The case proceeded to arbitration and CMSA was awarded the outstanding balance by the arbitrator.[438] ESSA, ownership of which lay 51 per cent in the hands of the Mexican Federal Government,[439] argued in the High Court that it was subject to provisions of Mexican administrative law regarding a requirement to properly tender contracts.[440] The requirements had not been fulfilled.[441] It was argued that the failure to properly tender rendered the contract (including the arbitration agreement) a nullity on the basis that ESSA had had no capacity to contract in July 2014.[442] Evidence was tendered by two experts on Mexican law.[443] The judge stated that he was:

> Confident both experts gave me their honest, considered and unbiased opinions on Mexican law.[444]

However, the judge also made clear that much of the evidence given on Mexican law was not on point.[445] By way of example, the judge stated:

> Sr. López Melih offered a brief analysis of whether ESSA should have raised its jurisdiction objection earlier than it did, which was not a matter for him at all, and Sra. Azar-Manzur offered a wide-ranging discussion of matters of Mexican law mostly not relevant to the narrow claim pursued by ESSA.[446]

The judge also had to deal with difficulties in the quality and consistency of the evidence provided by the expert witnesses:

> Not least because that was Sra. Azar-Manzur's analysis of the applicable Mexican law, I found it elusive to discern from her written evidence or her explanations in

[436] *Exportadora de Sal SA de CV v Corretaje Maritimo Sud-Americano Inc* [2018] EWHC 224 (Comm).
[437] *Exportadora de Sal SA de CV v Corretaje Maritimo Sud-Americano Inc* [2018] EWHC 224 (Comm), [1].
[438] *Exportadora de Sal SA de CV v Corretaje Maritimo Sud-Americano Inc* [2018] EWHC 224 (Comm), [1].
[439] *Exportadora de Sal SA de CV v Corretaje Maritimo Sud-Americano Inc* [2018] EWHC 224 (Comm), [4].
[440] *Exportadora de Sal SA de CV v Corretaje Maritimo Sud-Americano Inc* [2018] EWHC 224 (Comm), [4].
[441] *Exportadora de Sal SA de CV v Corretaje Maritimo Sud-Americano Inc* [2018] EWHC 224 (Comm), [5].
[442] *Exportadora de Sal SA de CV v Corretaje Maritimo Sud-Americano Inc* [2018] EWHC 224 (Comm), [5]. Important issues in the case included whether the arbitral tribunal had had jurisdiction and whether it was appropriate for the High Court to review the arbitral award, notwithstanding the alleged nullity, but such matters do not need to be discussed here.
[443] *Exportadora de Sal SA de CV v Corretaje Maritimo Sud-Americano Inc* [2018] EWHC 224 (Comm), [28].
[444] *Exportadora de Sal SA de CV v Corretaje Maritimo Sud-Americano Inc* [2018] EWHC 224 (Comm), [29].
[445] *Exportadora de Sal SA de CV v Corretaje Maritimo Sud-Americano Inc* [2018] EWHC 224 (Comm), [29].
[446] *Exportadora de Sal SA de CV v Corretaje Maritimo Sud-Americano Inc* [2018] EWHC 224 (Comm), [29].

> cross-examination whether she held an opinion capable of supporting the claim actually advanced by ESSA.[447]

The situation of experts disagreeing as to the position under the applicable foreign law is not uncommon,[448] and presents a situation of extreme complexity. It has been said, in respect of the British courts, that where there is conflicting evidence the court should approach the conflict as it would any other conflict of fact.[449] Thus, the judge has a duty to take a view and make a relevant finding.[450] It is the judge himself who must independently determine the content of the applicable foreign law.[451] In doing so he:

> Must test the evidence against the relevant documents and the probabilities and take account of any views which he forms as to the independence and impartiality of the witness.[452]

Moreover, despite foreign law being a question of fact, the British judge is entitled to bring his legal experience to bear on matters,[453] a task that will be easier when the case involves a familiar legal system, eg the law of New York.[454] Where the applicable foreign law is in a codified form, the British court is required to look independently at the written materials when reaching its determination,[455] although always with strict reference to the expert evidence given.[456]

A further important issue arises regarding the true objective of the British court when seeking to determine the position under the applicable foreign law, when viewed in the context of the fact approach and the British adversarial system. Although, as stated previously, the British courts seek to apply foreign law as the

[447] *Exportadora de Sal SA de CV v Corretaje Maritimo Sud-Americano Inc* [2018] EWHC 224 (Comm), [37].

[448] See, for example, *Morgan Grenfell & Co Ltd v SACE Istituto per i Servizi Assicurativi del Commercio* [2001] EWCA Civ 1932, [44]: 'It is plain from the above that there were a number of issues of Italian law which the judge had to resolve. The resolution of those issues involved detailed consideration of starkly conflicting evidence given by Professor Gambino for SACE and Avv Gioscia for MG.'

[449] *Bumper Development Corporation v Metropolitan Police Commissioner* [1991] 1 WLR 1362, 1368.

[450] *Kolbin & Sons v Kinnear & Co Ltd* 1930 SC 724, 737: 'I do not apprehend that, merely because the expert evidence is conflicting – as is not quite unknown in Practice – the Court must necessarily throw up its hands in despair, and refuse to attempt to solve the problem submitted to it.'

[451] *Ted Jacob Engineering Group Inc v Morrison* 2019 SC 487, 492: 'The question is what the relevant foreign law is, and that is an issue that must ultimately be decided by the court, not the experts.'

[452] *Morgan Grenfell & Co Limited v SACE Istituto per i Servizi Assicurativi del Commercio* [2001] EWCA Civ 1932, [48].

[453] *Morgan Grenfell & Co Limited v SACE Istituto per i Servizi Assicurativi del Commercio* [2001] EWCA Civ 1932, [49]. See also *Allen v Depuy International Limited* [2015] EWHC 926 (QB), [11], where the judge considered himself 'both entitled and indeed bound to bring to bear [his] own judgement in reaching conclusions' as to the content of the applicable foreign law.

[454] *Morgan Grenfell & Co Limited v SACE Istituto per i Servizi Assicurativi del Commercio* [2001] EWCA Civ 1932, [50].

[455] *DNO Oman Ltd v Clouston* 2019 SLT 395, 407.

[456] *Kolbin & Sons v Kinnear & Co Ltd* 1930 SC 724, 737: 'I think the sound view is that the Court must construe foreign written law with the assistance of the expert evidence adduced. The Court is not entitled to construe that law for itself without any assistance at all. The law might … have been repealed or otherwise overruled, and the Court therefore must be advised as to its applicability.'

foreign judge would, it should not be forgotten that the adversarial process places a fundamental restriction on how far the British judge may go when considering the evidence before him, and he must be very careful not to overstep the mark:

> It is an essential feature of the Judge's function to see that the litigation is carried on fairly between the parties. Judges sometimes flatter themselves by thinking that their function is the ascertainment of truth. This is so only in a very limited sense. Our system of administering justice in civil affairs proceeds on the footing that each side, working at arm's length, selects its own evidence.[457]

The German court is tasked with determining and applying the applicable foreign law as it actually stands,[458] and the court is not hindered in its task by the adversarial process. The German judge is said to be bound by case law in the same way as the foreign judge would be.[459] Where such a possibility for review exists under the applicable foreign law, it has been argued that the German judge should go as far as considering whether the relevant legal provisions are constitutional, in terms of the constitutional law of the *lex causae*,[460] which undoubtedly places an onerous burden on the German judge.

Moreover, where the *lex causae* does not provide a solution, it is said that the German court should consider whether the *lex causae* can be developed in such a way as to solve the case,[461] which permits the law to be developed in a way which will be familiar to a British judge.[462] While such an argument no doubt has theoretical strength, two points should be borne firmly in mind if a German court is applying English (or Scots) law. First, it is questionable to speak of development (*Rechtsfortbildung*) of the *lex causae*, as decisions of German courts on points of English law are very unlikely to directly influence the development of English law itself,[463] although decisions by foreign courts on English (or Scots) domestic law may certainly be noted with interest.[464] Second, German courts should avoid treading too far into the creative sphere, as such an exercise is only cautiously

[457] *Thomson v Glasgow Corp* 1962 SC (HL) 36, 51–52.

[458] *Decision of the Federal Court of Justice from 7 June 2016* (BGH, Kartellsenat) KZR 6/15, BGHZ 210, 292, 320.

[459] Schack, *Internationales Zivilverfahrensrecht* (n 7), para 758; Geimer (n 51), para 2604.

[460] Schack, *Internationales Zivilverfahrensrecht* (n 7), para 758; KH Neumayer, 'Fremdes Recht und Normenkontrolle' (1958) 23 *Rabels Zeitschrift für Ausländisches und Internationales Privatrecht (Festgabe für Alexander N Makarov)* 573, 589ff; Kropholler (n 5), 214.

[461] Schack, *Internationales Zivilverfahrensrecht* (n 7), para 758; Geimer (n 51), para 2605.

[462] An excellent example of how the UK House of Lords developed English law was *White v Jones* [1995] 2 AC 207, in which it was held that a solicitor owes disappointed beneficiaries a duty of care when taking instructions to draft a will.

[463] In *Iran v Berend* [2007] EWHC 132 (QB), [47], when considering the content of French law, the English court expressed scepticism of such a notion. The court noted that a French court would read an opinion of the English court on French law 'with interest', but the court was clear 'that an English judge would in no way be making a decision of French law or intruding upon the French jurisdiction. It would simply be a decision *about* French law.'

[464] In *A v XY Limited* [2021] CSOH 21, [53], Lord Woolman noted that he had studied an English decision on the Scots law of limitation 'with interest and profit'.

undertaken even by English courts.[465] Thus, while potentially necessary in certain circumstances, it is correct to argue that reticence and significant caution are required.[466]

The English court has recognised that it may be necessary to rule on an issue that has not come before the courts (or a sufficiently authoritative court) of the *lex causae*.[467] However, the English court is likely to shy away from any suggestion of developing foreign law,[468] especially if such development requires the English court to implement a policy change:

> I should not anticipate any such changes, since not only would that be presumptuous, but I should be exceeding my function – which is to determine, on the evidence, the relevant law of France *as it stands*.[469]

III. The Parties

A. Role in the Introduction of Choice of Law Rules

As a general proposition, parties in German court proceedings have no direct role to play as to whether a choice of law rule is introduced and applied, a responsibility that rests firmly with the German court.[470] Nonetheless, as previously discussed, parties in German court proceedings do have some influence over the choice of

[465] Although Lord Denning, and to a lesser extent, Lord Diplock, are seen to have been more prone to a touch of judicial creativity than some of their judicial peers. Lord Denning MR's judgment in *Boys v Chaplin* [1968] 2 QB 1, considered in Chapter one, is a fine example of such judicial creativity, especially at 20, where he states: 'I will show how the English authorities can be fitted in so as to achieve this result.' See Chapter one, section I.B of this work. However, see B Dickson, 'The Contribution of Lord Diplock to the General Law of Contract' (1989) 9 *Oxford Journal of Legal Studies* 441, 461–62, which (Lord Denning excepted) concludes that there is not strong evidence of judicial creativity among judges, especially Lord Diplock. However, see, for an important, recent analysis, P Hodge (Lord Hodge), 'The Scope of Judicial Law-Making in the Common Law Tradition' (2020) 84 *Rabels Zeitschrift für Ausländisches und Internationales Privatrecht* 211. At 212–13, Lord Hodge considers several significant fields, such as contract and tort law, as being essentially judge-made. At 213, he reasons that 'the myth that judges discover the law rather than make law has long been recognised.' Later, at 216, he refers to the contribution of Lord Mansfield, who has featured prominently in this work elsewhere. However, he acknowledges a number of constraints on judicial law-making, from 223–27, having acknowledged, at 222, that there is 'no consensus' as to the 'boundary to judicial law-making'.

[466] Prütting, '§ 293' (n 6), para 58.

[467] *Iran v Berend* [2007] EWHC 132 (QB), [48]: 'If the evidence (including that of the experts) points clearly to a particular outcome according to French principles and methods of application, an English judge should not necessarily feel inhibited by the fact that no French judge happens to have reached such a conclusion in the past. The particular question, or the particular factual circumstances, may simply not have arisen hitherto.'

[468] *Iran v Berend* [2007] EWHC 132 (QB), [48]: 'On the other hand, an English judge must tread with care when it appears that a particular result would not only be unprecedented but also involve the application of new principles, or a judicial development of French law, by the hypothetical French judge.'

[469] *Iran v Berend* [2007] EWHC 132 (QB), [49].

[470] Schack, *Internationales Zivilverfahrensrecht* (n 7), para 752.

law process.[471] First, where permitted, the parties may agree a choice of law during the proceedings in favour of the *lex fori* (or any other permitted legal system) thus negating the need for foreign law to be applied in the case. Second, the parties do have a limited role to play in so far as they have responsibility in the normal course of civil proceedings for the introduction of facts. Thus, it is conceivable, though unlikely, that the parties could intentionally refrain from introducing any fact which would require the application of a choice of law rule. Third, there is authority, particularly in the contractual context, that the parties can tacitly (*stillschweigend*) consent to the application of the *lex fori* through a failure to make any reference to foreign law throughout the duration of the proceedings. Fourth, the parties have some influence over whether foreign law is applied by the court through their conduct. Thus, agitating for the application of foreign law in a case is likely to draw the court's attention to the issue, leading to the introduction and application of a choice of law rule.

In Great Britain, the traditional or voluntary choice of law approach is that the parties decide whether they wish to rely on a rule of foreign law; otherwise, the relevant choice of law rule will not be applied by the British court *ex proprio motu* and the *lex fori* will apply. By pleading the relevant foreign law, British parties thus, either explicitly or impliedly, introduce the choice of law rule into the proceedings. A party is only likely to plead the relevant foreign law if they consider that it is to their benefit to have foreign law applied in the case. In England, this generally involves setting out the relevant rule in the particulars of claim,[472] which accompanies the claim form initiating the action. In Scotland, foreign law is also introduced by pleading the relevant foreign law, for example, in the initial writ.[473] A failure to plead the relevant foreign law is an indication by the parties that they do not seek to rely on it.

British academics generally take the view that it is appropriate in most cases for the decision as to whether to plead foreign law, and so engage choice of law rules, to lie in the hands of the parties. In an article written in 1996 in the context of the Rome Convention, Trevor Hartley argued:

> Since this is meant to be for the benefit of the parties, it would seem perverse for a court to apply foreign law when neither of them wanted it to do so.[474]

Paul Beaumont recently argued that if parties:

> do not want to invest resources in using those applicable law rules, then why should the State compel them to do so or instead pay for it itself through legal aid or through the time of its judges.[475]

[471] See section II.A.(i)(a).
[472] CPR, Part 16.
[473] See Cubie (ed) (n 120), para 9.19.
[474] Hartley (n 165), 291.
[475] PR Beaumont, 'When should EU private international law require that foreign law be applied?' in J von Hein, E-M Kieninger and G Rühl (eds), *How European is European Private International Law?* (Intersentia, 2019) 179.

A similar approach was advocated by the German academic Axel Flessner, as one of the few German academics supporting voluntary choice of law:

> If we only apply choice of law rules which lead to the application of foreign law at the request of a party, this is in the interests of the parties. [Translation by author][476]

As previously discussed, the law appears to have been settled beyond doubt by the UK Supreme Court in *FS Cairo (Nile Plaza) LLC* (2021),[477] and there is no doubt strength in the argument that it could be time-consuming, pointless, and wasteful, in certain circumstances, if the British court were to insist that foreign law be investigated and applied, where neither party desires this.

However, a question which arises in the context of British civil procedure is whether lawyers involved in civil litigation in the British courts have any obligation whatsoever to bring the applicable choice of law rules to the court's attention notwithstanding that they don't seek to rely on a rule of foreign law.[478] It has long been recognised that advocates before British courts not only have a duty not to deceive the court in respect of points of law, but also have a positive duty to make full disclosure of the law relevant to the facts of the case.[479] Lord Chancellor Birkenhead stated, in *Glebe Sugar Refining Co* (1921), a Scottish appeal to the House of Lords:

> But, as a point of very considerable general importance has arisen, I think it right to make this observation at once. It is not, of course, in cases of complication possible for their Lordships to be aware of all the authorities, statutory or otherwise, which may be relevant to the issues which in the particular case require decision. Their Lordships are therefore very much in the hands of counsel, and those who instruct counsel, in these matters, and this House expects, and indeed insists, that authorities which bear one way or the other upon matters under debate shall be brought to the attention of their Lordships by those who are aware of those authorities. This observation is quite irrespective of whether or not the particular authority assists the party which is so aware of it.[480]

The duty has been framed in particularly onerous terms in so far that the Scottish court has indicated not only that unreported English decisions can be drawn to the Scottish court's attention, but that advocates actually have an obligation to draw such decisions to the court's attention, if known to them.[481] Based on established practice, it does not appear that lawyers are misleading British courts by failing to draw the court's attention to an applicable choice of law rule, although

[476] Flessner (n 103), 583: 'Wenn wir den kollisionsrechtlichen Verweisungen auf fremdes Recht nur auf Antrag einer Partei Folge leisten, so geschieht dies im Interesse der Parteien.'

[477] *FS Cairo (Nile Plaza) LLC v Lady Brownlie* [2021] UKSC 45, [113]–[114].

[478] The point has been considered in the context of US law. See Sprankling and Lanyi (n 106), 13.

[479] A Paterson, 'Duties to the Court', *Strathprints* (University of Strathclyde Glasgow, 2007), strathprints.strath.ac.uk/4793/, accessed 9 May 2022.

[480] *Glebe Sugar Refining Co v Greenock Harbour Trustees* 1921 SC (HL) 72, 73–74.

[481] *Leighton v Harland & Wolff Limited* 1953 SLT (Notes) 34, 35–36.

this somewhat anomalous situation is questionable, especially in the context of ex parte applications. In the general context of ex parte applications, it has been held that the applicant:

> must disclose all facts which reasonably could or would be taken into account by the judge in deciding whether to grant the application. It is no excuse for an applicant to say that he was not aware of the importance of matters he has omitted to state. If the duty of full and fair disclosure is not observed the court may discharge the injunction even if after full inquiry the view is taken that the order made was just and convenient and would probably have been made even if there had been full disclosure.[482]

This reasoning has been applied with reference to an ex parte application that was granted without the judge's attention having been drawn to the potential impact of Russian law in the case.[483] In subsequently discharging the worldwide freezing injunction on the grounds of material non-disclosure,[484] Mr Andrew Sutcliffe KC, sitting as a judge of the English High Court, held:

> In my judgment, Holding's failure to disclose to Sales J the potential impact of Russian law and the possible defences under Russian law was a breach of its duty of full and fair disclosure on the without notice application. It ought to have been possible for Holding to produce an expert report as to Russian law for the purposes of the without notice hearing and, in fulfilling his duty to the court, that expert ought to have identified the potential difficulties facing Holding's claim as a matter of Russian law.[485]

In relevant circumstances, perhaps the safest course of action is for the advocate to acknowledge that foreign law may be applicable to the facts of the case under an applicable choice of law rule, but state that no attempt will be made to rely on, or lead evidence in respect of, any rule of the nominally applicable foreign law. The responsibility then lies with the judge, or the other party, if present, to raise an objection to this proposed course of action. Moreover, in an ex parte application, a party should be advised that there is a risk, at least, of damages later being awarded against them if, despite foreign law being applicable, foreign law is not addressed in an ex parte application and it ends up determining the dispute.[486]

A further question which arises in this connection is whether a lawyer can be held professionally negligent for failing to advise that a choice of law rule is applicable to the facts of the case. Choice of law rules are, after all, part of domestic law,

[482] *Siporex Trade SA v Comdel Commodities Ltd* [1986] 2 Lloyd's Rep 428, 437.
[483] *OJSC TNK-BP Holding v Beppler & Jacobson Ltd* [2012] EWHC 3286 (Ch), [320]–[323].
[484] *OJSC TNK-BP Holding v Beppler & Jacobson Ltd* [2012] EWHC 3286 (Ch), [334.4].
[485] *OJSC TNK-BP Holding v Beppler & Jacobson Ltd* [2012] EWHC 3286 (Ch), [328].
[486] A cross-undertaking in damages must be given by the applicant in their application for an interim injunction. See, for a summary, Bean, Parry and Burns (n 203), 5–10, which describes this as the 'usual undertaking'. See, for a detailed, although somewhat dated, analysis of the position regarding cross-undertakings in ex parte applications under English law: A Zuckerman, 'The Undertaking in Damages: Substantive and Procedural Dimensions' (1994) 53 *CLJ* 546. For a summary regarding the risk of damages for wrongful interdict in Scotland, and the presumption of entitlement to summary decree for the defender where the interdict is recalled, see *Aird Geomatics Ltd v Stevenson* 2015 SLT 329, 332.

and lawyers have a duty to know the content of all relevant domestic law that they are advising upon.[487] There are no decisions on point in Great Britain; however, it seems likely that a failure to advise that a foreign law is applicable under a relevant choice of law rule could constitute professional negligence. In Germany, the position is clear that a lawyer can be held liable for a failure to advise that a choice of law rule is applicable to the facts of the case.[488]

B. Role in Investigating the Content of the Applicable Foreign Law

(i) Obligations on the Parties

It has been held that no party involved in civil proceedings in Germany bears a burden of proof as regards the content of the applicable foreign law.[489] Moreover, it has been argued that no obligations should be placed by the German court on a party to prove the content of the applicable foreign law.[490] This logic, taken to its fullest extent, would suggest that the parties may sit on their hands and wait for the German court to investigate the content of the applicable foreign law. However, it is not as simple as that. The parties are, in fact, required to support the German

[487] A detailed discussion of professional negligence would exceed the scope of this work. However, for relevant discussion of the standard of care required in England (or what constitutes a breach thereof), see C Walton, P Kramer and R Cooper (eds), *Charlesworth & Percy on Negligence*, 14th edn (Sweet & Maxwell, 2018), para 10-104ff (in relation to barristers) and para 10-250ff (in relation to solicitors); M Cannon, H Evans and R Stewart (eds), *Jackson and Powell on Professional Liability*, 9th edn (2021), para 11-158ff (in relation to solicitors) and para 12-026ff (in relation to barristers). The English authorities in this area are probably applicable in full in Scotland. See WJ Stewart and D Brodie (eds), *Reparation: Liability for Delict*, 33rd Release (W Green, 2020), para A18-011, which makes the point that the question as to whether a higher duty of care is required of a legal professional holding themselves out to be an expert in a particular area is as yet unresolved, but the 'direction of travel … undoubtedly suggests that the law expects more of a specialist.' Note that the civil immunity that protected legal professionals from professional negligence claims in the conduct of legal actions was effectively abolished by the House of Lords in *Arthur JS Hall & Co v Simons* [2002] 1 AC 615. See a brief comment in this regard in Hodge (Lord Hodge) 'The Scope of Judicial Law-Making' (n 465), 218. The measure of any loss (quantum) is, of course, an entirely separate question. This would require a complicated assessment of what the claimant would have been awarded under the applicable foreign law.

[488] See J Gruber, 'Rechtsprechung: Anwaltshaftung bei Anwendung ausländischen Rechts' (1997) 7(11) *Deutsche Zeitschrift für Wirtschafts- und Insolvenzrecht* 460, which comments on the *Decision of the Hamm Court of Appeal from 14 March 1995* (OLG Hamm) 28 U 104/94, BeckRS 1995, 04287. Gruber argues, at 461, 'Das deutsche Kollisionsrecht ist haftungsrechtlich somit wie das materielle deutsche Recht zu behandeln' ('German choice of law rules must therefore be treated, in terms of liability for professional negligence, in the same way as German substantive law') [Translation by author]. See also Schack, *Internationales Zivilverfahrensrecht* (n 7), para 753.

[489] *Decision of the Federal Court of Justice from 24 November 1960* (BGH, II. Zivilsenat) II ZR 9/60, NJW 1961, 410, 410; *Decision of the Federal Labour Court from 7 May 2020* (BAG, II. Senat) 2 AZR 692/19, NZA 2021, 225, 231. See also Prütting, '§ 293' (n 6), para 14; Rühl (n 238), 568–69.

[490] See Junker (n 51), § 11 para 11, which argues that no *Beweislastentscheidung* affecting the burden of proof may be made, a position shared by Huzel. See Huzel (n 261), 81. See also, regarding a *Beweislastentscheidung*, H Prütting, '§ 286' in W Krüger and T Rauscher (eds), *Münchener Kommentar zur Zivilprozessordnung: Band 1 (§§ 1–354)*, 6th edn (CH Beck, 2020), para 97.

court in its investigation.[491] Where a party can access the relevant foreign sources of law without difficulty, there is an expectation that they will furnish the court with detailed information and evidence.[492]

The precise extent and basis of the responsibilities placed on the parties is controversial.[493] Schack cautions that an order that the parties arrange an expert opinion, made under § 273 of the German Code of Civil Procedure, which allows for case management and directions orders generally, is not permissible.[494] On the other hand, it appears to be legitimate for the court to require that evidence of foreign law be procured by a party under § 293;[495] otherwise, in effect, an adverse inference will be made.[496] This is likely to be the case where, for example, a party is basing their case on an obscure proposition of foreign law about which the German court is unable to draw any definitive conclusions. Where a party draws the German court's attention to a potentially important case, but then fails to assist the court in sourcing that case, the court is not required to follow up the lead, where it has otherwise carried out a satisfactory investigation.[497] It is evident from the case law and academic material that the matter is a grey area, with, on one hand, the clear principle that the investigation of the content of foreign law is a matter for the German court,[498] and, on the other, the pragmatic acceptance that for reasons of due process,[499] the parties ought to be involved in the often complicated and difficult investigative process. Indeed, the Federal Court of Justice has rebuked the rejection without justification of an expert opinion sourced by the parties.[500]

In terms of the investigation into the content of the applicable foreign law, it appears that British advocates have little obligation to do anything, other than comply with court orders and represent their clients' interests. As foreign law

[491] *Decision of the Federal Court of Justice from 24 November 1960* (BGH, II. Zivilsenat) II ZR 9/60, NJW 1961, 410, 410; Junker (n 51), § 11 para 10; Saenger (n 274), § 293 para 21.

[492] *Decision of the Federal Court of Justice from 30 April 1992* (BGH, IX. Zivilsenat) IX ZR 233/90, BGHZ 118, 151, 164. See also Geimer (n 51), para 2589.

[493] Huzel (n 261). See also Rühl (n 238), 571, which questions whether it is even possible to talk in such terms.

[494] Schack, *Internationales Zivilverfahrensrecht* (n 7), para 760.

[495] This does not appear to be a uniformly accepted view. See Prütting, '§ 293' (n 6), para 53.

[496] Huzel (n 261), 81. Huzel speaks in terms of possible disadvantage. It is important not to frame any responsibility placed on the parties in terms of obligations, as this is not the approach taken in the German courts. Rühl argues that the majority opinion favours the court where a party fails to produce evidence, proceeding on the assumption that any further investigation will not bring any further results. Rühl (n 238), 571. See, for a similar viewpoint, Geimer (n 51), para 2590. While Junker does use the word obligation (*Obliegenheit*), it is perhaps not in the context that a British lawyer would be familiar with. Junker (n 51), § 11 para 10.

[497] *Decision of the Federal Court of Justice from 30 March 1976* (BGH, VI. Zivilsenat) VI ZR 143/74, NJW 1976, 1581, 1583.

[498] Schack, *Internationales Zivilverfahrensrecht* (n 7), para 760.

[499] Prütting, '§ 293' (n 6), para 51, and Geimer (n 51), para 2591. Thus, the court may not ignore the parties' submissions and evidence relating to the content of the applicable foreign law.

[500] *Decision of the Federal Court of Justice from 21 January 1991* (BGH, II. Zivilsenat) II ZR 49/90, NJW-RR 1991, 1211, 1212.

is a question of fact in British proceedings,[501] it seems that British court advocates have no general duty to bring any specific rules of foreign law to the court's attention.[502] The question as to whether British court advocates are required to introduce choice of law rules has been discussed previously.[503]

It is likely that the duties owed by British lawyers to their clients extend to recommending the investigation of the content of the applicable foreign law, where this will potentially serve the client's interests, as well as recommending its introduction into a case if it offers a favourable outcome.[504] For example, where an accident has taken place abroad, it might be that the *lex loci delicti* affords substantially more damages than the *lex fori*. British lawyers should advise about this possibility; otherwise, they may be liable in damages for professional negligence. It seems very unlikely that a British lawyer is expected to research the content of foreign law themselves. Indeed, it is likely to be considered professionally negligent to do so. The position as to whether a German lawyer is expected to carry out research on, and advise about, the content of foreign law is not entirely clear, although weight appears to be placed on how complicated the matter is to research.[505] A sensible distinction appears to be drawn between a specialist lawyer, especially one who holds themselves out to be qualified in a particular legal system, and a generalist lawyer who does not – a distinction that would likely be equally valid in Great Britain.[506] However, it might be that all German lawyers are expected to research simple, easily established points of foreign law, but it is difficult to say with certainty. Probably the matter would turn on the facts and circumstances of the case.

[501] The matter has been discussed previously. See, for example, *Dexia Crediop SPA v Comune di Prato* [2017] EWCA Civ 428, [34].

[502] See Paterson (n 479), 14, in relation to facts generally. Foreign illegality and the sphere of criminal law are probable exceptions for the same reasons discussed in respect of choice of law rules at section II.A.(ii)(e) above.

[503] See section III.A. above.

[504] The question as to whether an applicable choice of law rule should be brought to the client's attention has been discussed previously. See section III.A. at fn 487. Note the clear distinction between whether a lawyer is required to advise on an applicable choice of law rule – a part of domestic law – and whether a lawyer is required to investigate, and advise on, the content of foreign law.

[505] See *Decision of the Hamm Court of Appeal from 14 March 1995* (OLG Hamm) 28 U 104/94, BeckRS 1995, 04287: 'Den Beklagten entlastet nicht, daß es sich hierbei um eine Rechtsvorschrift des italienischen Rechts handelt … Hier war dem Beklagten die Beschaffung der notwendigen Gesetzeskenntnisse über die in Betracht kommenden Anfechtungsfristen nach italienischem Recht möglich, weil die Regelungen des Codice Civile auch in deutscher Sprache veröffentlicht sind' ('The fact that the case relates to a provision of Italian law does not relieve the defendant of liability … In this case, it was possible for the defendant to acquire the necessary legal knowledge of the relevant time bar for contesting a decision under Italian law because the provisions of the Codice Civile are also published in German') [Translation by author]. For a concise discussion of the competing positions, see Gruber, 'Rechtsprechung' (n 488), 462–63. It is notable that the German Notarisation Act (*Beurkundungsgesetz*) explicitly requires, at § 17(3), that the German notary draw attention to the fact that foreign law is (or is potentially) applicable but does not require him to advise as to the content of any applicable foreign law. See, for critical discussion of this provision, O Meyer, 'Die Belehrungspflichten des Notars bei Auslandssachverhalten' (2018) *Deutsche Notar-Zeitschrift* 726.

[506] Gruber, 'Rechtsprechung' (n 488), 462.

(ii) Deferral to the Parties

It follows from the foregoing that German procedural law militates strongly against deferral to the parties in respect of the investigation into the content of foreign law, although, as noted, parties may essentially be required by the court to take specific steps. Moreover, it is expected that the German court will carry out a more extensive investigation where the parties make detailed and conflicting submissions in respect of the content of the applicable foreign law.[507] Anything that a party does bring to the court's attention – for example, a privately instructed expert opinion – should be considered.[508] However, Schack warns specifically against reliance on the parties' evidence on the basis that it cannot be expected that the parties will investigate unfavourable elements of the applicable foreign law to the same extent as favourable elements.[509]

In ordinary civil proceedings, it appears that the parties may not bind the German court through admission of the content of foreign law or absolve the court thereby of its responsibility to carry out an investigation.[510] However, there is conflicting authority regarding admission of such content between the Federal Court of Justice (BGH), which is the final German court of appeal in civil matters, and the Federal Labour Court (BAG), which is the final German court of appeal in employment matters. Thus, where American parties were agreed as to the position under US law, the Federal Labour Court considered that this agreement created a strong presumption, which gave the lower instance judge the opportunity to forgo any further investigation on the basis that foreign parties ought to know their own law:

> The question of the proof of foreign law is a question of judicial conviction; such a conviction can derive from consistent submissions by the foreign parties – who 'ought to know.' [Translation by author][511]

While such reliance on the parties, at least from the British viewpoint, has much to commend it, the approach of the Federal Labour Court is difficult to align with

[507] *Decision of the Federal Court of Justice from 30 April 1992* (BGH, IX. Zivilsenat) IX ZR 233/90, BGHZ 118, 151, 164. The ability of the parties to impact on the extent of the investigation required was recently reaffirmed in the *Decision of the Federal Court of Justice from 18 March 2020* (BGH, IV. Zivilsenat) IV ZR 62/19, NJW-RR 2020, 802, 805, and in the *Decision of the Federal Labour Court from 7 May 2020* (BAG, II. Senat) 2 AZR 692/19, NZA 2021, 225, 231.

[508] *Decision of the Federal Court of Justice from 30 April 1992* (BGH, IX. Zivilsenat) IX ZR 233/90, BGHZ 118, 151.

[509] Schack, *Internationales Zivilverfahrensrecht* (n 7), para 760. This necessarily flows from the adversarial process within which the parties are not committed to a genuine search for the truth. See C Menkel-Meadow, 'The Trouble with the Adversary System in a Postmodern, Multicultural World' (1996) 38 *William and Mary Law Review* 5, 13.

[510] Schack, *Internationales Zivilverfahrensrecht* (n 7), para 756; Prütting, '§ 293' (n 6), para 14; Otto (n 261), 302.

[511] *Decision of the Federal Labour Court from 10 April 1975* (BAG, II. Senat) 2 AZR 128/74, BAGE 27, 99: 'Die Frage des Beweises ausländischen Rechts ist eine Frage der richterlichen Überzeugung; eine solche Überzeugung kann sich aus dem übereinstimmenden Vortrag der ausländischen Parteien – die es "eigentlich wissen müßten" – ergeben.'

the jurisprudence of the Federal Court of Justice, which insists on an independent investigation by the German judge.[512]

Where a party in British court proceedings chooses to rely on a rule of foreign law, they are responsible for pleading the substance of the foreign rule on which they found (rely), why it is in point, and its effect in respect of the facts of the case,[513] as well as for proving the content of that law to the satisfaction of the court.[514] This follows from the treatment of foreign law as a matter of fact. Moreover, it is not permissible for parties to simply lodge materials on the applicable foreign law, eg cases and textbooks, and draw on them when making their submissions.[515] As held by Lord Blackburn in the House of Lords in *Mackonochie* (1881), a crucial difference between foreign and domestic law is that foreign law must be proven by experts, whereas domestic law is ascertained by argument founded on legal principles and authorities.[516]

This means that the main responsibilities of the parties are to source experts on foreign law, arrange for their expert opinion, and lead their evidence at trial. However, the parties' control of expert evidence is lessening. As will be discussed in due course, the English courts have moved towards much firmer control of what expert evidence is led than in the past,[517] though there is evidence that permission is not always sought as required.[518]

Though proposals for the ongoing rewrite of the Scottish civil procedure rules are not currently suggesting that parties will have to seek permission to lead expert evidence in Scottish proceedings,[519] Scottish judges are likely to have more control over expert evidence in the future.[520] The role and responsibility of the experts themselves is considered in section IV.C below.

[512] It is implied in Geimer (n 51), para 2588, that the approach taken by the Federal Labour Court (BAG) in respect of parties from the relevant foreign country is applicable to other civil proceedings generally, and in Hüßtege, 'Internetrecherche contra Sachverständigengutachten – Zur Ermittlung ausländischen Rechts durch deutsche Gerichte' (n 277), 262, it is suggested that concurring positions from the parties regarding the content of the applicable foreign law may, as a rule, be adopted by the German court as correct. Other writers do not mention the general applicability of this exception, and it appears that the Federal Court of Justice requires an independent investigation by the court regardless of the background of the parties. However, there is some suggestion in *Decision of the Federal Court of Justice from 30 April 1992* (BGH, IX. Zivilsenat) IX ZR 233/90, BGHZ 118, 151, 164, which refers to *Decision of the Federal Labour Court from 10 April 1975* (BAG, II. Senat) 2 AZR 128/74, BAGE 27, 99, that where the parties are in agreement, the Federal Court of Justice does not require as detailed an analysis of the applicable foreign law as it would otherwise.

[513] Beaumont and McEleavy, *Anton's Private International Law* (n 133), para 27.174. See also Crawford and Carruthers (n 78), para 8-28, and Collins (Lord Collins of Mapesbury) and Harris (eds) (n 112), para 9-003.

[514] Beaumont and McEleavy, *Anton's Private International Law* (n 133), para 27.178; Crawford and Carruthers (n 78), para 8-28; Collins (Lord Collins of Mapesbury) and Harris (eds) (n 112), para 9-004.

[515] *Bianco v Bennett* [2015] EWHC 626 (QB), [22].

[516] *Mackonochie v Lord Penzance and Martin* (1880–81) LR 6 App Cas 424, 446. As discussed in n 297 above, there are a few English cases that seem to contradict the rule, eg *Re Cohn* [1945] Ch 5.

[517] CPR, Part 35, places onerous duties on the court and the parties in respect of expert evidence. Under CPR 35.4(1): 'No party may call an expert or put in evidence an expert's report without the court's permission.'

[518] *BB Energy (Gulf) DMCC v Al Amoudi* [2018] EWHC 2595 (Comm), [49]–[50].

[519] Scottish Civil Justice Council, 'The New Civil Procedure Rules: First Report' (n 24), 41.

[520] ibid, 43–45.

(iii) Party References to Foreign Courts

There exists in all the relevant jurisdictions, under Article 15 of the Hague Child Abduction Convention, a procedure to facilitate a party-driven reference to the authorities[521] of the state of the habitual residence of the child (the requesting state) for a determination that the removal or retention was wrongful,[522] although the fact that the procedure has developed as such was not necessarily expected.[523]

The overall effectiveness of the Article 15 procedure has been questioned, being described as 'bedevilled by practical complexities'.[524] There are authorities supporting the propositions that the domestic court seised with the return application is not required to facilitate this procedure if it is not considered to be in the interests of justice to do so;[525] that requests made by parties to the courts of the requesting state, although legitimate,[526] can be deemed inappropriate if not made for a 'proper purpose';[527] and that the court is not necessarily obliged to accept the

[521] This should sensibly be interpreted to mean court, which would be the authority involved in most contracting states. See R Schuz, *The Hague Child Abduction Convention: A Critical Analysis* (Hart Publishing, 2013) 448.

[522] Article 15 determinations should not normally be required. The application for a return should contain a certificate or an affidavit from a qualified person, eg, a solicitor, a barrister, or a research institution, speaking to the law of the requesting state under Art 8(f) of the Convention, which should suffice in most cases. See E Pérez-Vera, 'Explanatory Report on the Convention on the Civil Aspects of International Child Abduction' (1982), assets.hcch.net/upload/expl28.pdf, para 101. As previously discussed in the context of judicial notice, Art 14 of the Convention also relaxes the usual requirements of proof in respect of the law of the requesting state, which should further expedite matters. See also Beaumont and McEleavy, *The Hague Convention on International Child Abduction* (n 255), 63–64.

[523] The fact that applicants have tended to seek a declaration on their own initiative or have been instructed to do so was described in 1999 as a 'worrying' trend. Beaumont and McEleavy, *The Hague Convention on International Child Abduction* (n 255) 63–65. See also Schuz (n 521) 155: 'Article 15 clearly envisages that the court of the requested State will request the declaration.'

[524] Beaumont and McEleavy, *Anton's Private International Law* (n 133), para 17.71.

[525] See *Decision of the Karlsruhe Court of Appeal from 23 February 2006* (OLG Karlsruhe) UF 2/06, NJOZ 2006, 1374, 1376. The court also made clear that it may not make the reference itself. The Canadian court was not prepared to countenance making an Art 15 reference as it would cause unnecessary delay in *BSP v CM* 2017 SKQB 179 (INCADAT Cite: HC/E/CA 1438), [41].

[526] See, for the domestic legislation permitting a request to be made to the respective courts in the relevant jurisdictions, s 8 of the Child Abduction and Custody Act 1985 and § 41 of the IntFamRVG. An example from Germany is the *Decision of the Berlin Court of Appeal from 4 June 2021* (KG) 16 UF 40/21, NJW-RR 2021, 1089, where the father had sought a determination under Article 15 of the Hague Child Abduction Convention (n 255) that the removals to Russia from Germany were wrongful. For relevant English authority see *Re P (Abduction: Declaration)* [1995] 1 FLR 831 (INCADAT Cite: HC/E/US 9), 840, which was followed, in Scotland, by the Inner House of the Court of Session in *AJ v FJ* 2005 1 SC 428 (INCADAT Cite: HC/E/US 803).

[527] *Re P (Abduction: Declaration)* [1995] 1 FLR 831 (INCADAT Cite: HC/E/US 9), 840, where a proper purpose was found to be established. A proper purpose was also found established in both *Re L (Children) (Abduction: Declaration)* [2001] 2 FCR 1 and *A v B (Abduction: Declaration)* [2009] 1 FLR 1253 (INCADAT Cite: HC/E/FR 1056). See also the instructive decision of the Supreme Court of Israel in *Plonit v Ploni* Family Appeal Motion 1930/14 (2014) (INCADAT Cite: HC/E/IL 1317) (Translation provided by the Central Authority of Israel). While the court acknowledged that a party has the right to petition for a declaration under Art 15, not every such petition should be adjudicated on its substance, and the court ought to exercise discretion in deciding whether its terms are consistent with the purpose of the Hague Child Abduction Convention (n 255).

ruling of the court of the requesting state as to whether the removal or retention was wrongful under its law, as the concept should be interpreted under Article 3 of the Hague Child Abduction Convention. However, in the absence of grave procedural irregularities, such a ruling *is* likely to be conclusive, at least, in terms of the parties' rights under the law of the requesting state:

> Save in exceptional circumstances, for example where the ruling has been obtained by fraud or in breach of the rules of natural justice, it must be conclusive as to the parties' rights under the law of the requesting state … The foreign court is much better placed than the English to understand the true meaning and effect of its own laws in Convention terms. Only if its characterisation of the parent's rights is clearly out of line with the international understanding of the Convention's terms, as may well have been the case in *Hunter v Murrow*, should the court in the requested state decline to follow it.[528]

Other than the Article 15 procedure, there do not appear to be any formal mechanisms in the relevant jurisdictions facilitating party-driven references to foreign courts. However, in *Westacre* (2008), the English court was faced with an application for declaratory relief, in respect of ongoing proceedings in Singapore, seeking determination as to whether an English judgment was still enforceable under English law.[529] The court commented:

> In one sense there is no lis pending between the two parties of which this court is seised, and the court is on that footing being asked to determine a hypothetical question. This court is of course always anxious to respond so far as properly it can to a request for assistance from an overseas court.[530]

As the English court recognised in its judgment, while the question could be framed as a hypothetical one as far as the English court was concerned, it was also necessary for the question to be answered in order that proceedings could continue in Singapore. It is hardly surprising that the English court was prepared

[528] *In re D (A Child) (Abduction: Rights of Custody)* [2007] 1 AC 619 (INCADAT Cite: HC/E/UKe 880), at 637–38 (Baroness Hale). As noted in Baroness Hale's judgment, a particularly restrictive approach was taken by the English Court of Appeal in *Hunter v Murrow* [2005] EWCA Civ 976 (INCADAT Cite: HC/E/UKe 809), which was cited approvingly by the New Zealand Court of Appeal in *Fairfax v Ireton* [2009] 3 NZLR 289 (INCADAT Cite: HC/E/AU 1018). As the authors note in their practice note in M Hausleiter and B Schramm, 'Beschwerde gegen Widerrechtlichkeitsbescheinigung nach dem HKÜ' (2021) *Neue Juristische Wochenschrift-Spezial* 549, there are also competing decisions from the German-speaking jurisdictions. After some to and fro, including input from several professors, the Art 15 determinations of the Italian authority appear to have been ultimately ignored in the *Decision of the Celle Court of Appeal from 24 May 2007* (OLG Celle, 17. Zivilsenat) 17 UF 72/07, BeckRS 2008, 2605, FamRZ 2007, 1587; however, the court in the *Decision of the Hamm Court of Appeal from 2 March 1999* (OLG Hamm) 7 UF 43/99, BeckRS 1999, 31160317, FamRZ 2000, 370 approved of an anaylsis that an Art 15 determination is binding unless there is '*greifbarer Gesetzeswidrigkeit*' (tangible illegality), which is similar to Baroness Hale's reasoning in the House of Lords.

[529] *Westacre Investments Inc v The State-Owned Company Yugoimport SDPR* [2008] EWHC 801 (Comm).

[530] *Westacre Investments Inc v The State-Owned Company Yugoimport SDPR* [2008] EWHC 801 (Comm), [2].

to deal with the application in the case. First, the parties had paid the court fees and instructed lawyers to attend court. It would have been harsh not to deal with the application. Second, the Singaporean court had directed the claimant to seek a decision from the English court, with judicial comity essentially demanding that the application be dealt with. Third, answering the question was directly relevant to an ongoing case in Singapore.

Two questions that follow from *Westacre* (2008), neither of which can be answered on the basis of current authority, are, first, whether the English courts, in the absence of a treaty,[531] are, as a rule, prepared to answer questions from foreign courts where a matter is governed by English law, and, second, whether an English court might be prepared to do the same as the Singaporean court in *Westacre* (2008) in reverse. It is submitted that *Westacre* (2008) does not provide a firm basis for future cases. In the case, the Singaporean court seems to have said to the claimant, in essence: obtain a declaratory judgment from the English court or your English judgment will not be recognised in this jurisdiction. Thus, the responsibility lay on the claimant to start fresh proceedings in England. The English court could have refused to deal with the case, causing wasted expense and time, potentially leaving the claimant with no possibility to enforce their judgment. Mere reliance on judicial comity, on a case-by-case basis, as in *Westacre* (2008), cannot be the driving force behind references between courts. Instead, there should be infrastructure facilitating such references.

IV. Experts

A. Procedural Background

The rules in the relevant jurisdictions in respect of the introduction of expert evidence generally are detailed and complicated. All that can realistically be given here is a summary of the relevant provisions, but these rules do have relevance to the question of how foreign law is investigated and determined.[532]

[531] There also exists the potential for more informal mechanisms such as the previously mentioned memoranda of understanding in respect of New South Wales, Singapore, and New York. A further example of international cooperation between judges is given by the UK–Pakistan Judicial Protocol on Children Matters. See Foreign, Commonwealth & Development Office, 'Pakistan: Child Abduction' (2021), www.gov.uk/government/publications/pakistan-child-abduction/pakistan-child-abduction#:~:text=In%20January%202003%20judges%20from,or%20religion%20of%20the%20parents.

[532] The procedural rules applicable to expert evidence are always the procedural rules of the *lex fori*, regardless of the substantive applicable law. In *Wall v Mutuelle de Poitiers Assurances* [2014] 1 WLR 4263, a personal injury action governed by French law under the Rome II Regulation (n 79), the defendants sought to argue that a French-style medico-legal expert opinion should be ordered by the English court to properly calculate the damages a French court would award. At 4269, the court held: 'It cannot be the case that the Regulation envisages that the law of the place where the damage occurs should govern the way in which evidence of fact or opinion is to be given to the court which has to

In Germany, there is some debate as to whether the instruction of experts in respect of the investigation of foreign law necessarily takes place on the basis of the strict rules applying to expert witness evidence generally, ie those rules found in § 402ff of the Code of Civil Procedure (ZPO), or whether such instruction may take place on an informal basis outwith the scope of these rules.[533] The distinction appears to be best framed in terms of whether the German court has instructed an expert to provide an opinion, or whether the judge is simply asking questions to further his own independent investigation. Thus, where the German judge decides to seek information on foreign law informally, eg through e-mail correspondence with a foreign lawyer, then such enquiries cannot be said to constitute the formal instruction of an expert. The extent to which the use of such informal mechanisms is a valid way of investigating foreign law is a question which has previously been considered, but it is likely that such mechanisms become increasingly inappropriate commensurately with the complexity of the case at hand.[534] Where the German court decides that an expert opinion is necessary to resolve the case, and makes a formal order (*Beweisbeschluss*) for an expert opinion to be obtained, there is little doubt that the relevant rules applying to experts[535] are applicable to their full extent.[536]

English law is taking an increasingly strict line with regard to the use of expert evidence in civil proceedings. Expert evidence is only allowed with the court's permission,[537] and English courts have been recently critical of parties who have proceeded to obtain expert opinions of their own volition, particularly where parties have adduced expert evidence without permission in interim applications.[538] The emphasis of the rules is on giving the English court control to prevent irrelevant evidence being led, which wastes both time and expense.

The detailed rules applying to expert evidence in civil proceedings in English law generally are found in Part 35 of the Civil Procedure Rules. For example, subject to the court's direction, the expert's evidence must first be given in a written

determine the case. An English court is ill-equipped to receive expert evidence given in the French manner.'

[533] Prütting, '§ 293' (n 6), para 28.

[534] It has been made clear by the Federal Court of Justice that the necessary depth of the investigation increases commensurately with the detail and controversy of the case. See *Decision of the Federal Court of Justice from 23 April 2002* (BGH, XI. Zivilsenat) XI ZR 136/01, NJW-RR 2002, 1359, 1360.

[535] The rules applicable to expert witness evidence in German civil proceedings are found in ZPO § 402 ff; however, other rules applicable to witnesses generally are also applicable to expert witnesses under ZPO § 402.

[536] *Decision of the Federal Court of Justice from 10 July 1975* (BGH, II. Zivilsenat) II ZR 174/74, NJW 1975, 2142, 2143; *Decision of the Federal Court of Justice from 15 June 1994* (BGH, VIII. Zivilsenat) VIII ZR 237/93, NJW 1994, 2959, 2960.

[537] CPR 35.4(1).

[538] See *BNP Paribas SA v Trattamento Rifiuti Metropolitani SPA* [2018] EWHC 1670 (Comm), [50]; *Gulf International Bank BSC v Aldwood* [2019] EWHC 1666 (QB), [9]; and *BB Energy (Gulf) DMCC v Al Amoudi* [2018] EWHC 2595 (Comm), [49]: 'permission being required for interlocutory hearings as much as for trials.'

report,[539] which is produced in almost every civil case where expert evidence is led.[540] A potentially important rule contained in the Civil Procedure Rules is that in respect of the use of single joint experts:

> Where two or more parties wish to submit expert evidence on a particular issue, the court may direct that the evidence on that issue is to be given by a single joint expert.[541]

This innovation was a significant one in England,[542] moving its approach as regards experts away from the strictly adversarial approach traditionally taken,[543] although, as stated previously,[544] there is little evidence that single joint experts are regularly instructed in English cases where foreign law requires to be proven.[545] Perhaps single joint experts offer a cost-effective means of proving foreign law in low-value actions. In those cases where parties cannot agree as to which expert should be instructed, the court is entitled to decide for them.[546]

In comparison with England and Germany, the Scottish procedural rules relating to the use of expert evidence are relatively bare, although particularly important general guidance in respect of Scots law was provided by the UK Supreme Court in *Kennedy* (2016).[547] Moreover, the Scottish court has control of expert evidence in so far that it is a matter for the court whether a person is certified as an expert for whom expenses may be recoverable.[548] However, unlike the English Civil Procedure Rules[549] and Family Procedure Rules,[550] neither the Scottish sheriff court rules nor the Rules of the Court of Session provide any specific section addressing expert evidence, and, notwithstanding the possibility of a party making an objection during the proceedings, the control which the Scottish court can exert over an expert's evidence is comparatively limited.[551]

[539] CPR 35.5(1). Note that the Family Procedure Rules (FPR), which apply in English family proceedings, have broadly similar provisions.

[540] T Hodgkinson and M James, *Expert Evidence: Law and Practice*, 5th edn (Thomson Reuters (Professional) UK Limited, 2020), para 8-012.

[541] CPR 35.7(1).

[542] The change came with the introduction of the Civil Procedure Rules 1998. Part 35 of the legislation, as made, can be found at legislation.gov.uk, 'The Civil Procedure Rules 1998, Part 35 (as made)', www.legislation.gov.uk/uksi/1998/3132/part/35/made.

[543] Zuckerman, 'Lord Woolf's Access to Justice' (n 11).

[544] See section II.B.(vi), text to nn 422 and 423.

[545] Examples of cases where an expert report was jointly instructed are *Re F (A Child) (Abduction: Refusal to Order Summary Return)* [2009] EWCA Civ 416 and *JXJ v Province of Great Britain of the Institute of Brothers of the Christian Schools* [2020] EWHC 1914 (QB).

[546] CPR 35.7(2).

[547] *Kennedy v Cordia (Services) LLP* [2016] UKSC 6. See also, for brief discussion, Cubie (ed) (n 120), para 15.17.

[548] See r 5.3 of the Taxation of Judicial Expenses Rules 2019. Certification must usually be sought in advance, unless on cause shown. Certification will only be granted if the court is satisfied that the person is a skilled (expert) person and it is, or was, reasonable and proportionate that the person should be employed.

[549] CPR, Part 35.

[550] FPR, Part 25.

[551] An objection can be made on the ground that the evidence is inadmissible. Thus, in *Kennedy v Cordia (Services) LLP* [2016] UKSC 6, [44], the court considered that there are 'four considerations

B. Qualifications

There is wide variance between the British and German courts in terms of the qualifications required for a lawyer to be considered suitable to give an expert opinion on foreign law. German legal academics, working either at universities or research institutions, are the most likely to be chosen by German courts to provide opinions on foreign law.[552] Thus, there is a strong preference in Germany for locally-based experts to whom the court process (or file) can be sent.[553] Having the opportunity to study the court process enables the locally-based expert to understand the wider circumstances of the case and so better tailor their opinion to the specifics of the case.[554] Moreover, other important considerations militating in favour of a locally-based expert are geographical distance from the court, and the ability of the chosen expert to give evidence on the relevant foreign law not only in the German language, but in the technical, legal language familiar to the court.[555] This means that experts instructed by the German courts are unlikely to be considered experts in the eyes of the applicable law itself, ie they will not usually be a respected practitioner in that legal system.

The suitability of locally-based experts to provide evidence to the German court on foreign law is not beyond question. Notable criticism as to the suitability of academic institutions to provide German courts with expert opinions on foreign law came from the Federal Court of Justice in the *Ventuari* (1991) case.[556] The Federal Court of Justice rejected, on grounds of inadequacy, the expert opinion provided by the well-regarded Max Planck Institute for Comparative and International Private Law ('Max Planck Institute')[557] on the basis that the academic drafting the opinion did not have specialist knowledge of Venezuelan law.[558] The Federal Court of Justice criticised what it perceived to be textbook research, with too much emphasis on literature and statute law, and too little on case law.[559] In favouring a foreign expert, the court stated:

> It is obvious that, for example, professors of the Central University of Venezuela, who are familiar with Venezuelan doctrine and legal practice, rather than the Court of

which govern the admissibility of skilled evidence: (i) whether the proposed skilled evidence will assist the court in its task; (ii) whether the witness has the necessary knowledge and experience; (iii) whether the witness is impartial in his or her presentation and assessment of the evidence; and (iv) whether there is a reliable body of knowledge or experience to underpin the expert's evidence.'

[552] Pfeiffer (n 284), 284; Schack, *Internationales Zivilverfahrensrecht* (n 7), para 763.

[553] Schack, *Internationales Zivilverfahrensrecht* (n 7), para 763.

[554] ibid, para 764.

[555] Prütting, '§ 293' (n 6), para 30.

[556] *Decision of the Federal Court of Justice from 21 January 1991* (BGH, II. Zivilsenat) II ZR 49/90, NJW-RR 1991, 1211.

[557] See Max Planck Institute for Comparative and International Private Law, 'About Us', www.mpipriv.de/1040131/ueber-uns.

[558] *Decision of the Federal Court of Justice from 21 January 1991* (BGH, II. Zivilsenat) II ZR 49/90, NJW-RR 1991, 1211, 1212.

[559] *Decision of the Federal Court of Justice from 21 January 1991* (BGH, II. Zivilsenat) II ZR 49/90, NJW-RR 1991, 1211.

> Appeal or the academics of the Max Planck Institute, possess the specialised knowledge and sources necessary to determine the scope of application and extent of a clear positive rule of the Venezuelan legal system. [Translation by author][560]

In an important contribution to the debate shortly following the decision, Jürgen Samtleben, who was an expert working at the Max Planck Institute at the time,[561] explained that the opinion produced by the institution had been mischaracterised by the Federal Court of Justice and other German academics.[562] He drew attention to the fact that 140 hours had been invested in the opinion, and argued that the institution had produced a comprehensive, peer-reviewed opinion written by an expert on the law of the sea (albeit not Venezuelan law specifically). According to Samtleben, the Federal Court of Justice had misrepresented the circumstances of the first instance decision in so far as four expert opinions drafted by experts in the Venezuelan law of the sea had been presented to the court, two of whom concurred with the Max Planck Institute's opinion. According to Samtleben:

> The investigator had also studied and dealt thoroughly with the controversial opinions submitted by Venezuelan experts. What else should he have done? [Translation by author][563]

He commented further:

> It would, however, be utopian to assume that, in a German institute, there is a specialist expert for every legal system and specialist area. [Translation by author][564]

The basic difficulty from the British perspective is that the individual producing the report in *Ventuari* (1991), regardless of their qualifications in comparative law and the subject matter generally, would be unlikely to have been considered an expert in the eyes of the British court, which generally places the greatest emphasis

[560] *Decision of the Federal Court of Justice from 21 January 1991* (BGH, II. Zivilsenat) II ZR 49/90, NJW-RR 1991, 1211: 'Es liegt auf der Hand, daß z.B. die mit der venezolanischen Lehre und Rechtspraxis vertrauten Professoren der Zentraluniversität in Caracas eher als das Berufungsgericht oder der Gutachter des Max-Planck Instituts über die Spezialkenntnisse und Erkenntnisquellen verfügen, die erforderlich sind, um den Anwendungsbereich und die Tragweite eines der klaren positiv-rechtlichen Regelung entbehrenden venezolanischen Rechtsinstituts zu ermessen.'

[561] J Samtleben, 'Der unfähige Gutachter und die ausländische Rechtspraxis' (1992) *Neue Juristische Wochenschrift* 3057. Though he did not work on the expert opinion for the *Ventuari* (1991) case, Samtleben was a colleague of the academic at the Max Planck Institute who did. Samtleben was an expert on the law of Latin American countries at the Max Planck Institute from 1971 to 2002. See Max Planck Institute for Comparative and International Private Law, 'Dr. iur. Jürgen Samtleben', www.mpipriv.de/898048/samtleben-juergen.

[562] Samtleben is particularly scathing of a contribution by Schütze in R Schütze, 'Der Abschied von der Nichtrevisibilität ausländischen Rechts?' (1991) *Europäisches Wirtschafts- und Steuerrecht* 372, whom Samtleben described as an *ahnungloser Kommentator* (clueless commentator). See Samtleben (n 561), 3062.

[563] Samtleben (n 561), 3059: 'Hatte der Bearbeiter darüber hinaus die im Rechtstreit von venezolanischen Experten vorgelegten kontroversen Gutachten studiert und sich eingehend mit ihnen auseinandergesetzt. Was hätte er außerdem tun sollen?'.

[564] ibid, 3059: 'Es wäre aber utopisch anzunehmen, daß in einem deutschen Institut für jede entfernte Rechtsordnung und Spezialmaterie ein besonderer Experte vorhanden ist.'

on the expert witness having practical experience of the given foreign legal system. Thus, the general principle has been stated:

> That no person is a competent witness unless he is a practising lawyer in the particular legal system in question, or unless he occupies a position or follows a calling in which he must necessarily acquire a practical working knowledge of the foreign law. In other words, practical experience is a sufficient qualification.[565]

Samtleben himself critically draws attention to the well-known English case of *Bristow* (1850), where Judge Alderson commented during proceedings:

> If a man who has studied law in Saxony, and never practised in Prussia, is a competent witness to prove the law of Prussia, why may not a Frenchman, who has read books relating to Chinese law, prove what the law of China is?[566]

However, it is important not to mischaracterise or oversimplify the current English (or Scottish)[567] position, which offers more flexibility than either of the above quotes would suggest. Thus, while there is, no doubt, an emphasis in England on the expert witness having practical experience of the given legal system, recent decisions[568] suggest that the suitability of an expert is very much left to the discretion of the court,[569] with the purist position propounded by *Bristow* (1850) having diminished in subsequent decisions,[570] and further diminished by the passing of

[565] Fawcett and Torremans (eds) (n 158), 110.

[566] *Bristow v Sequeville* (1850) 5 Exch 275, 276–77; 155 ER 118, 119.

[567] There are precious few Scottish cases. See, on this point, but written in 2011, Beaumont and McEleavy, *Anton's Private International Law* (n 133), para 27.184: 'The Scottish cases give little guidance as to what qualifies a witness to give evidence as to foreign law.' However, in the 2018 case of *Ted Jacob Engineering Group Inc v Morrison and Thompson* [2018] CSOH 51, the Scottish court repelled an objection to the competency of an expert witness and commented, in respect of the test of whether a person is an expert, at [18]: 'The question is did he have the relevant knowledge and experience to give expert evidence?'

[568] See the analysis of Mr Justice Moore-Bick, who carefully weighs up the merits of the various experts on Fujairah law, in *Glencore International AG v Metro Trading International Inc* [2001] CLC 1732, 1750–51. See also *Pt Royal Bali Leisure v Hutchinson & Co Trust Company Ltd* [2004] EWHC 1014 (Ch), [107], which is considered below. Nonetheless, most expert witnesses on foreign law in the English courts are practising lawyers in the relevant legal system. See, for example, *PJSC VTB Bank v Laptev* [2020] EWHC 321 (Ch), [14]–[15], and *Roberts v Soldiers, Sailors, Airmen and Families Association* [2020] EWHC 994 (QB), [188].

[569] This is the view of the English authorities taken in Beaumont and McEleavy, *Anton's Private International Law* (n 133), para 27.185: 'The English cases are conflicting but seem to establish that while the expert called need not necessarily be a barrister or even a practising lawyer, he must have some claim to expertise in the domain of law in question.' This passage was cited by the Scottish court approvingly in *Ted Jacob Engineering Group Inc v Morrison and Thompson* [2018] CSOH 51, [16].

[570] The *Bristow* decision was followed, albeit reluctantly, in *In the Goods of Bonelli* [1875] 1 PD 69: 'I was anxious, if possible, to allow administration to go on this evidence, but it has been decided in the case of *Bristow v. Sequeville* that the law of a foreign country cannot be proved even by a juris consult, if his knowledge of it be derived solely from his having studied at a university in another country.' However, as early as the late-nineteenth-century, cases were being decided that undermined any suggestion that the rule in *Bristow v Sequeville* (1850) 5 Exch 275; 155 ER 118 was an absolute one. With hesitation, the English court accepted the evidence of a notary who had neither practised nor was qualified in (the courts of) Chile in *In the Goods of Whitelegg* [1899] P 267, 269–70. In *Cooper-King v Cooper-King* [1900] P 65, the English court accepted affidavit evidence of the former Governor of

the Civil Evidence Act 1972, under which a 'suitably qualified' person is entitled to give evidence on foreign law 'irrespective of whether he has acted or is entitled to act as a legal practitioner there'.[571] The full extent of the shift from the mid-nineteenth-century position to the current, much more flexible position was made clear in *Pt Royal Bali Leisure* (2004).[572] In the case, a senior researcher based at the University of Leiden was accepted by the English court, despite objections, as being a suitable expert on Indonesian land law on the basis of his extensive, specialist academic knowledge of it.[573] Indeed, the court considered that the academic had the greater understanding of Indonesian land law as compared the other party's expert, who was a legal practitioner in that jurisdiction.[574] The factor that seems most important to the British court is the expert's specific and demonstrable existing knowledge of the applicable law.[575] Thus, it would not be enough for the British court that the expert had acquired knowledge of the legal system concerned only for the purposes of the case at hand, something that is much more likely to be accepted by a German court.

C. Role and Duties

Both English and Scottish procedural law are clear that the expert's duty is to the court,[576] with this duty overriding any duty owed to the parties. In *MCC Proceeds*

Hong Kong as to the law of that then British colony. While the existence of a general rule requiring experience of practice was recognised in *Wilson v Wilson* [1903] P 157, the court was clear that it could be deviated from in exceptional cases. The flexibility of English courts on the point was made clear in *Brailey v Rhodesia Consolidated Ltd* [1910] 2 Ch 95, 102–3: 'The expert who was called on Rhodesian law was in my opinion a sufficient expert to prove that fact. It is quite true he is not actually practising in Rhodesia, but he is the Reader in Roman-Dutch Law for the Incorporated Council of Legal Education; he has made a special study of Roman-Dutch law as applicable to our Colonies for the purpose of instructing in that law the students here who will practise in those Colonies, and I think his position as an expert was quite sufficiently proved.'

[571] Civil Evidence Act 1972, s 4(1).

[572] *Pt Royal Bali Leisure v Hutchinson & Co Trust Company Ltd* [2004] EWHC 1014 (Ch). A more recent example is provided by *Bazhanov v Fosman* [2017] EWHC 3404 (Comm), [7], where two law professors were held to be 'eminently qualified to assist the court' with regard to Russian law, although, judging from their website biographies, both have experience of practice as well. Birkbeck University of London, 'Professor Bill Bowring', www.bbk.ac.uk/law/our-staff/bowring/biography, and Centre for EU–Russia Studies (CEURUS), 'Professor William Simons', ceurus.ut.ee/home/people-archived/associated-scholars/prof-william-simons/.

[573] *Pt Royal Bali Leisure v Hutchinson & Co Trust Company Ltd* [2004] EWHC 1014 (Ch), [107].

[574] *Pt Royal Bali Leisure v Hutchinson & Co Trust Company Ltd* [2004] EWHC 1014 (Ch), [107].

[575] It is notable that one of the experts in *FS Cairo (Nile Plaza) LLC v Brownlie* [2020] EWCA Civ 996 was described, at [98], as 'a barrister practising at the English Bar and a well-known expert on the laws of Middle Eastern countries, and in particular Egypt, who has taught at the School of Oriental and African Studies for many years and published extensively in that field.' While the court noted that the expert had particular experience in Egyptian law, which was applicable in the case, it is questionable whether the traditional conception of the required expertise in the English courts was satisfied, and this recent case seems to be further evidence of a movement away from the rigid requirements of the past.

[576] The English provisions are set out in the relevant procedure rules: see the CPR 35.3; FPR 25.3. Although there are no statutory rules in Scots law, in the Scottish appeal of *Kennedy v Cordia (Services)*

Inc (1999), the court stated that the role of an expert witness in English proceedings in respect of foreign law is:

> (1) to inform the court of the relevant contents of the foreign law; identifying statutes or other legislation and explaining where necessary the foreign court's approach to their construction;
>
> (2) to identify judgments or other authorities, explaining what status they have as sources of the foreign law; and
>
> (3) where there is no authority directly in point, to assist the English judge in making a finding as to what the foreign court's ruling would be if the issue was to arise for decision there.[577]

In other words, the expert's role is to inform the court of the content of the applicable foreign law. He is required to identify relevant statutes and judgments,[578] together with any relevant academic discussion, always highlighting their relative significance under the applicable law, and, even where there is an absence of authority on a given point, to assist the court to reach a similar decision to that which the foreign court would reach. Separately, the expert witness must ensure that he does not present an account of the law that he personally favours; ie he should not seek to develop the applicable foreign law on the basis of a theory he advocates, but rather should predict the most likely decision of the foreign court.[579]

The rules of German civil procedure do not appear to specifically set out an overriding duty of the expert to the court, although such a duty is clearly recognised in so far as there is consensus that the role of the expert is to assist the court.[580] Perhaps the lack of such an explicit duty in the German Code of Civil Procedure is due to the fact that it is the German court which normally instructs the expert, rather than the parties, leaving no doubt as to whom a duty is ultimately owed. Many of the specific duties on experts instructed by the German courts have been

LLP [2016] UKSC 6, at [52]–[53], the UK Supreme Court referred favourably to the reasoning of Mr Justice Cresswell in *National Justice Cia Naviera SA v Prudential Assurance Co Ltd (The 'Ikarian Reefer')* [1993] FSR 563, 565, where he said, inter alia: 'Expert evidence presented to the court should be, and should be seen to be, the independent product of the expert uninfluenced as to form or content by the exigencies of litigation.' See also Law Society of Scotland, 'Expert witness code of practice', www.lawscot.org.uk/members/business-support/expert-witness/expert-witness-code-of-practice/.

[577] *MCC Proceeds Inc v Bishopsgate Investment Trust plc* [1999] CLC 417, 424. There is no reason why this authority would not be followed in Scotland, and the case was referred to by parties in *DNO Oman Ltd v Clouston* 2019 SLT 395.

[578] In *Wall v Mutuelle de Poitiers Assurances* [2014] 1 WLR 4263, 4272, the English Court of Appeal made clear that the court can take account of any relevant guidelines: 'No doubt one can call this "soft law" rather than "hard law" but it is law nevertheless. Any foreign judge having to apply English law on the assessment of damages would find the Judicial College guidelines helpful as a starting point. If, therefore, French law had the equivalent of these guidelines, I would hold that the master could permit evidence of them to be given by an English court.' Accordingly, the expert should draw any such guidelines to the court's attention when giving their evidence.

[579] *MCC Proceeds Inc v Bishopsgate Investment Trust plc* [1999] CLC 417, 424–25.

[580] Musielak and Voit, *Grundkurs ZPO* (n 149), para 788; W Lüke, *Zivilprozessrecht*, 10th edn (CH Beck, 2011), para 304.

codified,[581] for example, that the expert must decide at the point of instruction whether he has the requisite knowledge to provide an expert opinion on the relevant issue.[582] In terms of the expert's specific role with regard to the investigation of the content of foreign law, the relevant German literature appears to be remarkably sparse, with matters framed entirely in terms of the German judge's duties.[583] However, it is likely that the expert's role in German civil proceedings is very similar to that of the expert in British proceedings, which was discussed above.

D. The Interaction between the Court, the Parties, and the Experts

The fact that the expert is usually instructed by the German court means that the interaction takes place primarily between the court and the expert, although there always remains the possibility for a party to instruct an expert on a private basis.[584] The quality of the interaction between the German court and the expert is likely to be aided by the preference in Germany for a locally-based expert.[585] Thus, the expert chosen in German civil proceedings will be proficient not only in the German language, but also in the procedural options open to the court.[586] It is clear that a locally-based expert may be sent the court file.[587] The parties are entitled to insist upon an opportunity to put questions to the expert orally,[588] although it may be uneconomical for the expert to actually appear in court.[589] More economical are said to be written follow-up questions to the expert's written opinion, which are, in any case, more likely to provide a satisfactory answer.[590]

As compared with Germany, the basic position is almost entirely reversed in British proceedings, where it is the parties who instruct the experts. In terms of the

[581] ZPO § 407a. See, for explanation, W Zimmermann, '§ 407a' in W Krüger and T Rauscher (eds), *Münchener Kommentar zur Zivilprozessordnung: Band 2 (§§ 355–945b)*, 6th edn (CH Beck, 2020).

[582] ZPO § 407a(1); ibid, para 2ff.

[583] Such duties are extensive and were considered previously. See section II.B.(iii).

[584] There is authority that the German court is required to consider an expert opinion instructed on a private basis, if produced by a party. See *Decision of the Federal Court of Justice from 30 April 1992* (BGH, IX. Zivilsenat) IX ZR 233/90, BGHZ 118, 151, 164.

[585] Prütting, '§ 293' (n 6), para 30. The advantages and disadvantages of foreign, as opposed to local experts, in German cases were concisely discussed by Pfeiffer. See Pfeiffer (n 284), 297ff.

[586] Schack, *Internationales Zivilverfahrensrecht* (n 7), para 764.

[587] ibid, para 764; Prütting, '§ 293' (n 6), para 30; Hüßtege, 'Internetrecherche contra Sachverständigengutachten – Zur Ermittlung ausländischen Rechts durch deutsche Gerichte' (n 277), 264. In view of the availability of instantaneous modern communication possibilities, it is not entirely clear why Hüßtege suggests that a local expert is quicker to contact, although perhaps different time zones could create some difficulty.

[588] Schack, *Internationales Zivilverfahrensrecht* (n 7), para 766; *Decision of the Federal Court of Justice from 15 June 1994* (BGH, VIII. Zivilsenat) VIII ZR 237/93, NJW 1994, 2959, 2960.

[589] Schack, *Internationales Zivilverfahrensrecht* (n 7), para 767. The possibility of appearing by video link may reduce some of the cost, see Hüßtege, 'Internetrecherche contra Sachverständigengutachten – Zur Ermittlung ausländischen Rechts durch deutsche Gerichte' (n 277), 264.

[590] Schack, *Internationales Zivilverfahrensrecht* (n 7), para 767.

relationship between the party and their expert, the English rules of procedure do not specifically regulate this essentially contractual relationship, although parties and experts should be careful to avoid any potential allegation of bias. Indeed, the specific instructions given to the professional expert by their instructing party must be acknowledged by the expert in their written report,[591] and, in certain situations, orders can be made by the court for disclosure of any instructions given.[592] Professional witnesses, whose reputations are at stake, are not necessarily susceptible to bias simply on the basis that the instruction comes directly from a party,[593] although there is undoubtedly a risk of parties shopping around possible experts for a viewpoint that favours their case. In terms of possible interaction between a party and the opposing side's expert, while this is obviously limited, there is provision in the English civil procedure rules to allow for questions to be put to the opposing side's expert following disclosure of their expert opinion.[594] Questions may only be put once, must be put within 28 days of service of the expert's report, and must be for the purposes of clarification.[595]

In terms of the interaction between the British judge and the expert, it is generally not appropriate for the judge in British court proceedings to correspond directly with party experts, although it may potentially happen if the judge needs to clarify a particular point following trial.[596] Any questions put by the British judge to the expert at trial are usually limited to clarification, with parties taking responsibility for the vast majority of questions put to experts:

> Judges on the whole should leave the examination of witnesses to counsel and only themselves ask questions if they need clarification.[597]

[591] CPR 35.10(3).

[592] CPR 35.10(4).

[593] This is not the position advocated by Schack, who appears to suggest that party-instructed expert opinions are inherently biased. See Schack, *Internationales Zivilverfahrensrecht* (n 7), para 760. Pfeiffer takes a less critical view, pointing out that while there is risk of preference for one side or the other, professional experts are not likely to tarnish their reputations by taking a viewpoint that is not justifiable. There are also potential criminal and professional consequences for giving false testimony to a court. See Pfeiffer (n 284), 291–92. Moreover, a scathing opinion of an expert in a published judgment is likely to mean that the expert is not instructed in any further cases, and there is equally a risk of a court-instructed expert going on a frolic by representing an opinion that is held only by a minority of lawyers. However, concerns of risk of potential bias are justified. See the analysis of Circuit Judge Posner *Bodum USA v La Cafetiere* 621 F 3d 624 (2010), 633: 'Lawyers who testify to the meaning of foreign law, whether they are practitioners or professors, are paid for their testimony and selected on the basis of the convergence of their views with the litigating position of the client, or their willingness to fall in with the views urged upon them by the client. These are the banes of expert testimony.' There is a similar analysis from the same judge in *Sunstar Inc v Alberto-Culver Co* 586 F 3d 487 (2009), 495–96.

[594] CPR 35.6.

[595] CPR 35.6(2).

[596] This would only happen if the parties were aware and were copied into any correspondence.

[597] *Manning v King's College Hospital NHS Trust* [2009] EWCA Civ 832, [16]. See also *Jones v National Coal Board* [1957] 2 QB 55, 63: 'In the system of trial which we have evolved in this country, the judge sits to hear and determine the issues raised by the parties, not to conduct an investigation or examination on behalf of society at large, as happens, we believe, in some foreign countries.' However, the court in *Jones* (1957), at 65, was equally clear that the judge may clarify matters with witnesses: 'Now, it cannot, of course, be doubted that a judge is not only entitled but is, indeed, bound to intervene at

Experts themselves are entitled to ask the court for directions.[598]

An important innovation in England is the provision for joint meetings between the opposing sides' experts.[599] At such meetings, the experts should work to identify the relevant issues and determine those matters on which they agree.[600] In circumstances where the court orders an agreed statement to be made by the experts,[601] those matters on which they disagree should be justified by reasons.[602] This appears to be a particularly effective means of narrowing the issues in dispute and reducing the time spent at trial hearing expert evidence. The way in which the expert's evidence is taken at trial, if required,[603] will also have an impact on how the expert evidence is presented, and the extent to which the judge will be able to ask questions.

The traditional method in British proceedings is that each party asks their expert witness questions (examination-in-chief), with the opposing side following with cross-examination,[604] although more novel methods finding their way into English and Scottish civil procedure include hot-tubbing.[605] This is where experts

any stage of a witness's evidence if he feels that, by reason of the technical nature of the evidence or otherwise, it is only by putting questions of his own that he can properly follow and appreciate what the witness is saying.'

[598] CPR 35.14.

[599] The change came with the introduction of the Civil Procedure Rules 1998. Part 35 of the legislation, as made, can be found at legislation.gov.uk/uksi/1998/3132/part/35/made (n 542).

[600] CPR 35.12(1).

[601] This may be framed in terms of a joint report or memorandum, which is likely to be particularly helpful. See *Roberts v Soldiers, Sailors, Airmen and Families Association* [2020] EWHC 994 (QB), [188]–[189], and *PJSC VTB Bank v Laptev* [2020] EWHC 321 (Ch), [17].

[602] CPR 35.12(3)(b).

[603] In *Committeri v Club Mediterranee SA* [2016] EWHC 1510 (QB), it was noted, at [13], that as the written expert opinions on French law had 'common ground on almost all of the issues', there was neither any necessity for the experts to meet pre-trial nor for them to attend trial to give evidence. Thus, the experts' written reports stood as their evidence, and the judge drew his conclusions based on them. It is increasingly common, in England at least, that all expert evidence is given only by written report. Hodgkinson and James (n 540), para 8-012. It might also be speculated that evidence given by experts by video conference will also become increasingly common, which has the potential to further reduce costs and wasted time.

[604] It is increasingly the case, in England at least, that 'the bulk of the expert's time in the witness box is usually taken up with cross-examination.' Hodgkinson and James (n 540), para 8-012. Re-examination will usually also be possible: *Wall v Mutuelle de Poitiers Assurances* [2014] 1 WLR 4263, 4269. Pfeiffer recognises the benefits of this process, although there are risks, including good rhetoric (or lack thereof) being given too high a value. Pfeiffer (n 284), 292. Fentiman is a particularly keen advocate of the benefits of expert evidence and cross-examination. See, briefly, R Fentiman, 'Foreign Law in National Courts: A Common Law Perspective' in M Andenas and D Fairgrieve (eds), *Courts and Comparative Law* (Oxford University Press, 2015), 81, and more extensively, Fentiman, *Foreign Law in English Courts* (n 70), 299–300.

[605] Provision was made for this in CPR, Practice Direction 35, para 11, introduced on 1 April 2013, which is headed 'Concurrent witness evidence'. Hodgkinson and James (n 540), para 8-009. It has only been rarely used in Scotland, but see the positive comments of Lord Woolman in *SSE Generation Ltd v Hochtief Solutions AG* [2016] CSOH 177, [156]: 'There were several sessions in the proof where I heard concurrent evidence from the experts. This procedure, known colloquially as "hot-tubbing", involved several experts being present in court at the same time. I chaired a discussion between them with a view to crystallising their respective positions. I found it a valuable way of focussing on the main issues and assessing the quality of their contributions.'

are subject to simultaneous cross-examination, with the judge having the right to ask questions in the first instance.[606] However, regardless of the specific form taken, having both experts attend trial to give evidence is likely to be expensive.[607]

E. Costs

The adversarial approach in the British courts towards the proof of foreign law as a point to be won or lost, with responsibility for proof falling on the party relying on provisions of foreign law, appears to be reflected in the costs position.[608] In *Strickland* (2017), an appeal to the English High Court from the Employment Appeal Tribunal,[609] the costs of the expert opinion on Dubai law had been ordered by the tribunal to be split on a joint basis.[610] The appellant drew on the principle that a party relying on foreign law must prove it,[611] and relied on two well-known works,[612] as well as a case previously referred to in this work.[613] The court agreed that the appellant was entitled to rely on the presumption that Dubai law is the same as English law.[614] If the respondent wished to contest this, it was his responsibility to adduce the necessary evidence.[615] The court held:

> In those circumstances, in my judgment, it is not for the Claimant to produce evidence at this stage, still less for him to be ordered to pay half of the cost of providing that evidence, whether it is to be produced by Herbert Smith Freehills or some other law firm. It follows that, in ordering that he do so, alternatively that a firm of the Tribunal's choosing be instructed on a joint basis, I consider that the Tribunal made an error of law.[616]

[606] Hodgkinson and James (n 540), para 8-009. See, for an optimistic Singaporean view of hot-tubbing in the context of proving foreign law, D Xu, 'Proving foreign law in domestic proceedings – the futility of the "expert" advocate and some more sensible procedural solutions: Re Harish Salve [2018] SGCA 6' (2018) 37 *CJQ* 319, 331.

[607] Although the bulk of the costs may already have been incurred by the point the case goes to trial. See Hodgkinson and James (n 540), para 8-009.

[608] The law underlying costs generally (known as expenses in Scotland) is extremely complicated, with various possible modifications depending on, inter alia, conduct and any offers made. See briefly, with regard to English law, Cunningham-Hill and Elder (n 423), para 4.2ff and, with regard to Scots law, Cubie (ed) (n 120), para 19.10ff. A British court would never meet the costs of investigating the content of foreign law, although it is possible that public funding through legal aid may do so.

[609] *Strickland v Kier Ltd* 2017 WL 5760129.

[610] *Strickland v Kier Ltd* 2017 WL 5760129, [6].

[611] *Strickland v Kier Ltd* 2017 WL 5760129, [13].

[612] Collins (Lord Collins of Mapesbury) and Harris (eds) (n 112), under Dicey's rule 25 and the related analysis in chapter 9, and Fentiman, *Foreign Law in English Courts* (n 70).

[613] *Podgorica v Bishopscourt (BB&Co) Ltd* [2002] EWCA Civ 1468. The case concerned an application for summary judgment. The court held that there is no reason why a claimant should be in a different position in a summary judgment application to that they would be in at trial.

[614] *Strickland v Kier Limited* 2017 WL 5760129, [14].

[615] *Strickland v Kier Limited* 2017 WL 5760129, [14].

[616] *Strickland v Kier Limited* 2017 WL 5760129, [15].

The question as to whether the costs involved in the investigation of foreign law should be passed on to the parties appears to be a contested one in Germany. The source of the controversy appears to derive from the ongoing dispute as to whether foreign law is indeed a matter of law essentially equivalent to domestic law. Thus, Geimer suggests that a party should not be made to pay the costs of instructing experts on the ground that, at issue, is essentially a matter of law.[617] However, this seems to contradict majority opinion, in terms of which, any costs incurred by the German court in instructing an expert opinion should ultimately be borne by the parties on the normal 'loser pays' basis.[618] Where the successful party has privately instructed an expert, which is considered to have been necessary to progress the action, that is said to be recoverable from the losing party.[619] It does not seem that the German courts should concern themselves with the cost of expert evidence, relative to the value of the dispute, when considering whether an opinion should be ordered. In a slightly surprising decision, the Federal Court of Justice ruled that the lower instance court was wrong[620] to refrain from instructing an expert opinion with a cost estimate of €3,500 to €4,000 in a case where €790 was in dispute.[621] The Federal Court of Justice commented:

> The fact that an expert opinion will cost many times the amount in dispute is not a reason alone to refrain from instructing one. [Translation by author][622]

The case is particularly interesting as the lower instance court had taken steps to determine the content of the applicable foreign law more cost-effectively, using the London Convention.[623] Perhaps less legal certainty should, in fact, be acceptable in cases of lower value, eg where the cost of a thorough investigation will exceed the value of the dispute by a factor of four.[624]

[617] Geimer (n 51), para 2627.

[618] Prütting, '§ 293' (n 6), para 70; Rühl (n 238), 573; Bacher (n 151), para 29. Bacher accepts that there may be an argument in extreme cases for the parties to be relieved of the costs of an expert opinion.

[619] Prütting, '§ 293' (n 6), para 72; Mankowski (n 238), 195.

[620] *Decision of the Federal Court of Justice from 14 January 2014* (BGH, II. Zivilsenat) II ZR 192/13, NJW 2014, 1244, 1246.

[621] *Decision of the Federal Court of Justice from 14 January 2014* (BGH, II. Zivilsenat) II ZR 192/13, NJW 2014, 1244, 1244.

[622] *Decision of the Federal Court of Justice from 14 January 2014* (BGH, II. Zivilsenat) II ZR 192/13, NJW 2014, 1244, 1246: 'Dass ein Gutachten ein Vielfaches des Streitwerts kosten wird, ist allein noch kein Grund, davon Abstand zu nehmen.'

[623] *Decision of the Federal Court of Justice from 14 January 2014* (BGH, II. Zivilsenat) II ZR 192/13, NJW 2014, 1244, 1244.

[624] In an interview reported in Stürner and Krauß (n 289), para 199, one judge compared the quoted cost of the expert opinion in a case with the cost of a small car (*Kleinwagen*), which appears to have led to the parties leaving the proceedings *in stasis* and potentially leading to the denial of justice in the case. Such outcomes can scarcely be seen as desirable. It can be easy to forget the often immense and sometimes unbearable costs involved for parties in litigating.

V. Failure to Prove the Content of the Applicable Foreign Law

A. Causes

This section addresses the situation where the content of the applicable foreign law has not been successfully proven to the court's satisfaction. The point at which there will be a failure of proof will occur at the determinative stage of the process. Thus, in such circumstances, based on any investigation carried out and any evidence presented to the court, the judge will feel unable to draw conclusions as to the content of the applicable foreign law. Such a situation is to be separated from issues that may arise at the application stage, for example, where the application of the *lex causae* breaches the public policy of the forum (*ordre public*).

The situation where there is a failure of proof may arise for several reasons. There may be insufficient materials available on the content of the *lex causae*, or it may be impossible to find someone with the requisite knowledge to provide an opinion and give evidence to the court, although this seems increasingly unlikely in the modern day with its wealth of information and communication possibilities.[625] More realistic is that the cost of obtaining an expert opinion is in no way proportionate to the value of the case – although, as stated previously, this does not appear to be a relevant consideration as far as the German Federal Court of Justice currently views matters[626] – or, alternatively, that the relevant foreign country is in a state of flux or instability.[627] Moreover, as considered previously, the situation where there has been a failure of proof should be strictly separated from the situation where foreign law has not been placed at issue in the case, despite there being a foreign element in its factual matrix. There is also a clear difference between a failure to prove the content of the applicable foreign law and the absence of a foreign rule addressing the matter requiring resolution. Thus, in a case from 1960, the German court was entitled to conclude that Afghan law did not recognise bills of exchange as,[628] in 1937, no law had yet been enacted to address their existence.[629] In such circumstances, it would not have been appropriate for the

[625] C Thole, 'Anwendung und Revisibilität ausländischen Gesellschaftsrechts in Verfahren vor deutschen Gerichten' (2012) 176 *Zeitschrift für das gesamte Handelsrecht und Wirtschaftsrecht* 15, 47.

[626] *Decision of the Federal Court of Justice from 14 January 2014* (BGH, II. Zivilsenat) II ZR 192/13, NJW 2014, 1244, 1246.

[627] Nonetheless, caution must be exercised before giving up too easily. The author of this work was able to source an expert opinion from Syria, despite its current political situation, as certain parts of the country are relatively stable.

[628] *Decision of the Federal Court of Justice from 24 November 1960* (BGH, II. Zivilsenat) II ZR 9/60, NJW 1961, 410, 412.

[629] *Decision of the Federal Court of Justice from 24 November 1960* (BGH, II. Zivilsenat) II ZR 9/60, NJW 1961, 410, 410.

court, despite the protestations of the claimant,[630] to apply an alternative law, as the law – or rather the lack thereof – in Afghanistan had been demonstrated to the court's satisfaction. Where, as discussed previously, the court is faced with a situation as yet unresolved by the *lex causae*, it is necessary for the court to solve the case on the basis of what the foreign court is likely to decide if presented with the same factual matrix.[631]

At what point can there be said to be a failure of proof, aside from obvious cases where no serious attempt has been made to prove the content of the applicable foreign law,[632] or the quality of the evidence provided is manifestly defective?[633] In Great Britain, a party in civil proceedings is required to adduce evidence that satisfies the court on the balance of probabilities,[634] which is the test that applies in all civil proceedings.[635] As with many yardsticks, the test gives rise to significant difficulties in definition and application. There can be a temptation to place an unnecessary gloss on the words. In *Rehman* (2003), Lord Hoffmann set out the correct approach:

> The civil standard of proof always means more likely than not. The only higher degree of probability required by the law is the criminal standard.[636]

However, despite making clear that the question always turns on whether a court considers, on the basis of the evidence available, a fact's existence to be more probable than not, Lord Hoffmann went on to point out that some things are inherently more probable than others:

> It would need more cogent evidence to satisfy one that the creature seen walking in Regent's Park was more likely than not to have been a lioness than to be satisfied to the same standard of probability that it was an Alsatian.[637]

[630] *Decision of the Federal Court of Justice from 24 November 1960* (BGH, II. Zivilsenat) II ZR 9/60, NJW 1961, 410, 411–12.

[631] See section II.B.(i), text to nn 227–232 and II.B.(vi), text to nn 461–466.

[632] See, for example, *R v R* [2015] EWCA Civ 1138, [46], with regard to the failure to prove the law of Slovenia.

[633] In *Callwood v Callwood* [1960] AC 659, a case involving the US Virgin Islands, which had previously been owned by Denmark, a party had provided an opinion from a US attorney as to the content of Danish community property law. The English court, at 676, found the opinion to be wholly unsatisfactory. The opinion referred to a judgment of the US Court of Appeals for the Third Circuit, which, according to the Judicial Committee of the Privy Council, 'expressed no opinion upon, the rights of spouses subject to the Danish system of community as regards the enjoyment or disposal of the joint property during the continuance of the marriage.' Their Lordships held that they 'strongly deprecate this mode of providing evidence of foreign law.'

[634] Zuckerman, *Zuckerman on Civil Procedure* (n 293), para 22.55.

[635] ibid, para 22.59.

[636] *Secretary of State for the Home Department v Rehman* [2003] 1 AC 153, 194. See also, in respect of Scots law, E Keane and F Davidson (eds), *Raitt on Evidence: Principles, Policy and Practice*, 3rd edn (W Green, 2018), paras 6-20 to 6-24, which note some historic evidence of a notion of a third or intermediate standard of proof in Scottish authorities, but that any ambiguity was settled by Lord Morison in the five-judge decision in *Mullan v Anderson* [1993] SLT 835.

[637] *Secretary of State for the Home Department v Rehman* [2003] 1 AC 153, 194.

Thus, in the context of proving foreign law in the British courts, which, as a question of fact, is measured against the balance of probabilities yardstick,[638] it is likely that a British court would require particularly cogent evidence before accepting as proven that contracts entered into in Germany require, for formal validity, to be written on parchment paper, but less cogent evidence that contracts for the sale of land require to be in writing.

Strictly speaking, the German courts do not apply a burden of proof when determining the content of foreign law, ie the parties are not required to prove a rule of foreign law to a particular standard, not least because the responsibility for investigating the content of the applicable foreign law lies squarely in the German judge's hands. Nonetheless, it appears that the German judge seeks more certainty than his British counterpart. A foreign rule's existence merely being more likely than not would not be enough for the German judge to apply it,[639] although there is no necessity for absolute or irrefutable certainty.[640]

Where difficulties arise in the investigation, it is the German judge's decision as to whether to continue the investigation or to accept that it is not possible to ascertain the content of the applicable foreign law.[641] This represents an important difference between the British and German approaches in so far that the German judge has an additional decision to make: whether to continue the investigation or not? This carries with it the objection that it always ought to be possible, if enough effort is made and money spent, to ascertain the content of the applicable foreign law, even if the conclusion is that the matter is highly controversial or there is no rule governing the matter. There appears to be no agreement in the case law and academic materials as to exactly how much effort must be exerted by the German judge before it can be concluded that the content of the foreign law cannot reasonably be determined (*Nichtfeststellbarkeit*).[642] However, there is some authority suggesting that the investigation may be stopped by the German judge where it would require disproportionate effort, and where

[638] *Yukos Capital Sarl v OJSC Oil Company Rosneft* [2014] EWHC 2188 (Comm), [25]: 'the Court is required to determine the foreign law as a question of fact on the basis of the evidence deployed by the parties, according to the usual civil standard'.

[639] It appears that a broadly similar standard of proof applies to foreign law as to facts, although it is difficult to find concrete evidence. See, for example, Thole (n 625), 47, who suggests that the judge must be able to make a sure conclusion as to the content of the applicable foreign law, and Prütting, '§ 293' (n 6), para 59, who argues that the judge, in principle, should not be left in doubt as to the content of the applicable foreign law. See also Saenger (n 274), § 293 para 12, who requires that the judge be '*überzeugt*' (convinced).

[640] Samtleben (n 561), 3061.

[641] Junker (n 51), § 11 para 12.

[642] ibid, § 11 para 12; Thole (n 625) 46.

investigation (or further investigation) would require a substantial and unacceptable delay.[643]

B. Outcomes

(i) Recourse to the Lex Fori *and the Presumption of Similarity*

In the absence of successful proof of the content of the applicable foreign law, all relevant jurisdictions consider the application of the *lex fori* a possible solution. In Great Britain, the application of the *lex fori* in this context appears to have been justified, first, by the evidential implications of the fact approach,[644] and, second, through the presumption of similarity (or identity)[645] that, unless the contrary is proved, the *lex causae* is presumed to be the same as the *lex fori*.[646] If there is a difference between the application of the *lex fori* and the presumption of similarity, both leading practically to the same result, it can only be in so far as the presumption of similarity gives recognition to the existence of the relevant choice of law rule, ie it acknowledges that the relevant foreign law is nominally applicable, but then introduces the positive, evidential fiction that the terms of the *lex causae* are presumed to be the same as the *lex fori* unless the contrary is proved.[647]

[643] *Decision of the Federal Court of Justice from 26 October 1977* (BGH, IV. Zivilsenat) IV ZB 7/77, BGHZ 69, 387, 393. See also Junker (n 51) § 11 para 14.

[644] *Global Multimedia International Limited v ARA Media Services* [2006] EWHC 3612 (Ch), [38]: 'The true proposition, I believe, is that as foreign law is in most cases a question of fact to be proved by evidence, in the absence of such evidence the court has no option but to apply English law.' This is the approach taken in the relevant rule in Collins (Lord Collins of Mapesbury) and Harris (eds) (n 112): 'In the absence of satisfactory evidence of foreign law, the court will apply English law to such a case.'

[645] This term occasionally appears in the literature, eg AR Miller, 'Federal Rule 44.1 and the Fact Approach to Determining Foreign Law: Death Knell for a Die-Hard Doctrine' (1967) 65 *Michigan Law Review* 613 and R Fentiman, 'Foreign Law as Local Law: a Case of Mistaken Identity?' in M Pfeiffer and others (eds), *Liber Amicorum Monika Pauknerová* (Wolters Kluwer, 2021). According to the Oxford Dictionary, in addition to its usual meaning, ie the identity of a person or a thing, identity can mean a close similarity or affinity. But it also appears to have a more antiquated meaning of identicalness. See Oxford Dictionaries, 'English Oxford Living Dictionaries: Definition of Identity', en.oxforddictionaries.com/definition/identity.

[646] See, for example, *Royal Boskalis Westminster NV v Mountain* [1999] QB 674, 724: 'Where foreign law is applicable a presumption will usually arise in an English action that the foreign law is the same as English law.' See also *Ertel Bieber & Co v Rio Tinto Co Ltd* [1918] AC 260, 301, and, for Scottish authority, *Rodden v Whatlings Limited* 1961 SC 132, 133: 'Where, however, a pursuer is not expressly founding on some specialty of foreign law, the presumption for him, and against him, is that the law applicable to the case does not differ from Scots law.'

[647] This justification for the presumption was given by Lord Leggett in *FS Cairo (Nile Plaza) LLC v Lady Brownlie* [2021] UKSC 45, [116] and [118]: 'If either party pleads that under the relevant rules of English private international law foreign law is applicable to an obligation, and that case is well founded, it is the duty of the court to apply foreign law. To apply English domestic law in that situation would ex hypothesi be unlawful … if English law has any role to play, it can only be on the basis of a presumption that the content of the applicable foreign law is materially similar to the English law on the matter in question.'

The presumption probably finds its roots in US procedural law,[648] and it has been criticised both in the case law[649] and in the literature:[650]

> To speak of such a presumption at all, rather than admitting that English law applies as the *lex causae* where no other is proved, may rest on a conceptual mistake … It is unclear therefore that it is ever appropriate to speak of a presumption of similarity between English and foreign law.[651]

In seeking to counter criticisms directed against the presumption of similarity, in *FS Cario (Nile Plaza) LLC* (2021), Lord Leggett justified the presumption in the following terms:

> These arguments, in my view, would have force if the presumption were inflexible and applied in circumstances where there is good reason to think that the applicable foreign law is different in a material respect from English law. However, that is not and has never been the effect of the presumption. The common law has never required unrealistic or unreasonable assumptions to be made about the content of foreign law.[652]

Lord Leggett then set out detailed justification as to why criticisms of the presumption are misplaced. In summary, first, he argued that

> while there are of course many differences between the laws of different countries, there are also often similarities.[653]

He noted that this would be more likely between common law countries, but he considered that there was

[648] The practice of US courts dismissing cases on the basis of the vested rights doctrine, where the applicable foreign law was not proven, ie a given right only existed in the applicable foreign law, appears to have subsequently led to the creation of the presumption fiction to avoid this outcome. See, in the context of US law, Sprankling and Lanyi (n 106), 24: 'The harshness of the sanction for noncompliance prompted courts to create exceptions to the basic rule. These exceptions took the form of presumptions that the law of the foreign jurisdiction and the law of the forum were similar.' It appears that federal courts adhered to the vested rights approach up until the introduction of Rule 44.1 of the Federal Rules of Procedure, the terms of which are considered in due course. See Sprankling and Lanyi (n 106), 26. Lord Leggett noted in *FS Cairo (Nile Plaza) LLC v Lady Brownlie* [2021] UKSC 45, [109], that the first edition of AV Dicey's text on the *Conflict of Laws* referred only to US authority when stating the proposition that: 'in the absence of proof of the foreign law, it will be presumed to be the same as that of the forum.'

[649] *Al Misnad v Azzaman Ltd* [2003] EWHC 1783 (QB), [37]. Although the judge appears to have been attacking the implications of the presumption as well when he cited, also at [37], a 1991 report which described the presumption as 'quite unrealistic and curiously egocentric in the post-imperial age.'

[650] See also Collins (Lord Collins of Mapesbury) and Harris (eds) (n 112), para 9-025; A Nussbaum, 'The Problem of Proving Foreign Law' (1941) 50 *Yale Law Journal* 1018, 1035ff; Hood, 'Drawing Inspiration?' (n 70), 191.

[651] Fentiman, *Foreign Law in English Courts* (n 70) 147. Fentiman recently argued 'the presumption superficially represents the most egregious and unlikely of fictions. It is factually counter-intuitive, and has echoes of chauvinism.' Although he noted that it is 'on inspection, neither indefensible, nor without a role' and later concluded 'Easily misunderstood as it is, it has a basis in principle; clumsy as it may be, it has a role.' See Fentiman, 'Foreign Law as Local Law: a Case of Mistaken Identity?' (n 645), although this article was published prior to the UK Supreme Court's decision in *FS Cairo (Nile Plaza) LLC v Lady Brownlie* [2021] UKSC 45.

[652] *FS Cairo (Nile Plaza) LLC v Lady Brownlie* [2021] UKSC 45, [122].

[653] *FS Cairo (Nile Plaza) LLC v Lady Brownlie* [2021] UKSC 45, [123].

> often good reason to expect that the foreign law will provide the same answer to a legal question, even if the result is reached by a different legal route,

also noting the harmonisation of laws through international conventions, particularly in the commercial sphere.[654] Second, he noted the requirement of materiality, ie unless there is a 'real likelihood' of a different outcome, there is no good reason to put a party to the trouble and expense of adducing evidence of foreign law.[655] Third, he noted that

> the presumption of similarity does not itself determine any legal issue … It only ever operates unless and until evidence of foreign law is adduced.[656]

He then went on to note that:

> There is no warrant for applying the presumption of similarity unless it is a fair and reasonable assumption to make in the particular case. The question is one of fact: in the circumstances is it reasonable to expect that the applicable foreign law is likely to be materially similar to English law on the matter in issue (meaning that any differences between the two systems are unlikely to lead to a different substantive outcome)?[657]

Following detailed discussion of several domestic and foreign cases where the presumption had been considered,[658] Lord Leggett set out what he described as general guidance, noting that it

> is impossible to state any hard and fast rules as to when it may properly be employed.[659]

In summary, his four general observations were as follows. First, the presumption is more likely to be appropriate where the applicable foreign law is another common law system rather than a system based on Roman law.[660] Second, the presumption is less likely to be appropriate where the relevant domestic law is contained in a statute.[661] Third, the presumption's application may often be uncertain, so that it is difficult to predict whether a judge will consider that the presumption can be relied on in a particular case.[662] Fourth, the procedural context in which the presumption is relied on matters. Accordingly, it will be more acceptable to rely on it at an earlier stage of proceedings, with reliance on the presumption at trial a riskier course of action.[663]

[654] *FS Cairo (Nile Plaza) LLC v Lady Brownlie* [2021] UKSC 45, [123].
[655] *FS Cairo (Nile Plaza) LLC v Lady Brownlie* [2021] UKSC 45, [124].
[656] *FS Cairo (Nile Plaza) LLC v Lady Brownlie* [2021] UKSC 45, [125].
[657] *FS Cairo (Nile Plaza) LLC v Lady Brownlie* [2021] UKSC 45, [126].
[658] *FS Cairo (Nile Plaza) LLC v Lady Brownlie* [2021] UKSC 45, [127]–[142]. Lord Leggett was particularly complimentary of a 'very thorough survey of the relevant case law' in the decision of the New South Wales Court of Appeal in *Damberg v Damberg* [2001] NSWCA 87.
[659] *FS Cairo (Nile Plaza) LLC v Lady Brownlie* [2021] UKSC 45, [143].
[660] *FS Cairo (Nile Plaza) LLC v Lady Brownlie* [2021] UKSC 45, [144].
[661] *FS Cairo (Nile Plaza) LLC v Lady Brownlie* [2021] UKSC 45, [145].
[662] *FS Cairo (Nile Plaza) LLC v Lady Brownlie* [2021] UKSC 45, [146].
[663] *FS Cairo (Nile Plaza) LLC v Lady Brownlie* [2021] UKSC 45, [147].

In terms of whether the presumption of similarity may be used to fill gaps, where satisfactory evidence of the content of foreign law is produced in some respects, but the evidence is lacking in other respects,[664] Lord Leggett noted:

> adducing direct evidence of foreign law narrows the potential for relying on the presumption; but whether it eliminates the potential for doing so altogether must depend on the circumstances.[665]

While Lord Leggett's approach in *FS Cairo (Nile Plaza) LLC* (2021) makes sense, it is submitted that the presumption of similarity ought to be approached with a fair degree of caution. The fact is that while there are similarities between the various jurisdictions of the world, there are many complicated and technical differences, even amongst jurisdictions with similar legal traditions, and the absurdity of assuming, for example, that Californian law offers the same remedies as exist under the Defamation Act 2013 and has the same costs regime as in England has been justifiably pointed out.[666]

Nonetheless, if Lord Leggett's approach is correctly applied to the extent that it is clearly acknowledged that the presumption of similarity

> is only ever a basis for drawing inferences about the probable content of foreign law in the absence of better evidence,[667]

then the presumption, as essentially a rebuttable presumption of law,[668] has the attraction of providing a reasonable starting point, particularly at the interlocutory or interim stage of proceedings.[669] Nonetheless, it should be clear that application of the presumption ought to quickly become untenable as the complexity of the law involved increases, and courts should not allow parties to rely on the presumption where there is credible evidence that the applicable foreign law leads to a different result, or application of the presumption would be absurd in the circumstances.[670]

[664] Lord Leggett gave the example of providing the text of a foreign statute, but no evidence as to how that statute would be interpreted by the relevant foreign court. In this situation, the court is entitled to 'apply similar principles of statutory interpretation to an English court.' *FS Cairo (Nile Plaza) LLC v Lady Brownlie* [2021] UKSC 45, [151].

[665] *FS Cairo (Nile Plaza) LLC v Lady Brownlie* [2021] UKSC 45, [151].

[666] *Soriano v Forensic News LLC* [2021] EWHC 56 (QB), [151], which was cited approvingly by the Court of Appeal in *Soriano v Forensic News LLC* [2021] EWCA Civ 1952, [63].

[667] *FS Cairo (Nile Plaza) LLC v Lady Brownlie* [2021] UKSC 45, [149].

[668] See Keane and Davidson (eds) (n 636), para 7-15: 'a rebuttable presumption may be countered by evidence to show that in the particular case it is unsafe to arrive at conclusion B purely on the basis of fact A. However, unless some rebutting evidence is produced, the conclusion almost certainly will be drawn. The effect of a presumption *juris tantum* is therefore to place a burden of proof on the party against whom it operates to lead evidence to prevent the operation of the presumption.' Examples of rebuttable presumptions of law include the presumption of regularity of legal acts (*omnia praesumuntur rite esse acta*) and the presumption of continuation of a domicile of origin. Keane and Davidson (eds) (n 636), paras 7-18 and 7-23. See also Malek, Auburn and Bagshaw (eds) (n 243), para 6-18.

[669] See *PT Pan Indonesia Bank Limited TBK v Marconi Communications International Limited* [2005] EWCA Civ 422, [70].

[670] In addition to the example given above in *Soriano v Forensic News LLC* [2021] EWCA Civ 1952, [63], there are several other examples where courts have expressed reservations about applying the presumption of similarity. Two examples are *Österreichische Länderbank v S'Elite Ltd* [1981] QB 565, 569,

It must also be questioned whether allowing parties to lead evidence of the relevant foreign law on particular points, whilst allowing them to fall back on the presumption in others, is wholly satisfactory, particularly from the point of view of avoiding tactical game-playing.[671] While Lord Leggett's approach in this respect does have the advantage of offering logical coherence – ie the judge is simply taking the best evidence available on each relevant point – it could result in mind-boggling complexity where the judge is required to piece together a solution from two different legal systems, depending on the extent to which the presumption is successfully relied on, with an outcome that would derive from the individual provisions of neither.

In Germany, where the content of the applicable foreign law is not satisfactorily established, the application of the *lex fori* appears to result from a choice of the court to apply its own law, rather than, as in Great Britain, from the evidential implications of the fact approach or the presumption of similarity, which is a concept unknown in Germany. In other words, the German court determines that the *lex fori* should be applied rather than the nominally applicable foreign law, although there is no statutory basis for this in German law.[672] Austrian law, by way of comparison, mandates in statute the default application of the *lex fori*, where the content of the *lex causae* cannot be determined within a reasonable space of time.[673]

The lack of statutory regulation in Germany seems to have given rise to the alternative law theory, which is considered below. Thus, Schack is sceptical as to the application of the *lex fori* in cases where choice of law rules determine that a foreign law is applicable. In his view, the possibility for the application of the *lex fori* will be taken too eagerly by domestic courts, who are driven by a homeward trend towards applying their own law.[674] Thus, he strongly advocates recourse to an alternative law.[675] Kropholler sensibly measures the acceptability of recourse to the *lex fori* against whether there is a sufficiently strong connection with the forum

in respect of provisions of Austrian statute law, and *Shaker v Al-Bedrawi* [2003] Ch 350, 373, in respect of provisions of Pennsylvanian company law.

[671] There is evidence of this in *FS Cairo (Nile Plaza) LLC v Lady Brownlie* [2021] UKSC 45. In a different context see, *GDE LLC and Goffe v Anglia Autoflow Ltd* [2020] EWHC 105 (Comm), where the English court was faced with a stand-off, with both parties resistant to the court applying a law that was not their preference. While the court accepted that the Rome Convention must be invoked by the parties for the court to apply it, thus countenancing voluntary choice of law, the court considered it, at [31], to be 'parting company with all common sense' to suggest that pleading rules prevent the court from considering a law that is not pleaded by the parties.

[672] Prütting, '§ 293' (n 6), para 60.

[673] See the Austrian Federal Law on Private International Law of 15 June 1978, as at 12 May 2020 (n 63), Art 4(2). See also Swiss law, which also mandates the application of the *lex fori* where the content of the *lex causae* cannot be determined: 'Swiss Federal Law on Private International Law of 18 December 1987, as at 1 January 2022 (Bundesgesetz über das Internationale Privatrecht vom 18 Dezember 1987, Fassung vom 01.01.2022)', www.admin.ch/opc/de/classified-compilation/19870312/index.html, Art 16(2).

[674] Schack, *Internationales Zivilverfahrensrecht* (n 7), para 771.

[675] ibid, para 770ff.

itself; only where there is a sufficiently weak connection should recourse potentially be had to an alternative foreign law.[676]

(ii) Recourse to an Alternative Foreign Law

In circumstances where the *lex causae* cannot be satisfactorily investigated, there is suggestion that the German court may opt to apply an alternative foreign law.[677] This is an approach that is completely unknown in Great Britain. Which alternative law ought to be chosen in such circumstances is the subject of effervescent academic debate in Germany.[678] Several different possibilities have been suggested. The German court could draw on another closely related legal system.[679] The court could draw on international principles, for example, those principles which have been developed in the Principles of European Contract Law (PECL) or the Draft Common Frame of Reference (DCFR).[680] The court could choose the alternative law with reference to the choice of law rules,[681] eg the place of the accident (*lex loci delicti*),[682] rather than the law of the habitual residence of the parties, which 'shall' apply where it is their shared habitual residence at the time of the accident.[683] Perhaps the strongest argument for the choice of an alternative law can be made where legal systems are very closely related or based directly upon one another.[684] For example, a German court might apply Swiss law as a possible alternative to Turkish law,[685] in view of the fact that Turkey adopted the Swiss Civil Code in 1926.[686]

[676] Kropholler (n 5), 216–17.
[677] Junker (n 51), § 11 para 11.
[678] ibid, § 11 para 15ff; Schack, *Internationales Zivilverfahrensrecht* (n 7), para 772ff; Saenger (n 274), § 293 para 22; Thole (n 625), 32–33; Prütting, '§ 293' (n 6), para 59ff.
[679] Junker (n 51), § 11 para 16, which is described as the preferred solution.
[680] See Schack, *Internationales Zivilverfahrensrecht* (n 7), para 773. A prominent advocate of the theory was Hein Kötz. See H Kötz, 'Allgemeine Rechtsgrundsätze als Ersatzrecht' (1970) 34 *Rabels Zeitschrift für Ausländisches und Internationales Privatrecht* 663. The Scottish courts have referred to the DCFR when considering unclear points of Scots law. See *Wills v Strategic Procurement (UK) Ltd* [2013] CSOH 26, [10], and related commentary L Richardson, 'The DCFR, anyone?' (2014) *The Journal of the Law Society of Scotland*, www.journalonline.co.uk/magazine/59-1/1013494.aspx#.XLH3SMRCS70. There are demonstrated similarities between Scots law and the DCFR. See L Macgregor, 'Report on the Draft Common Frame of Reference: A report prepared for the Scottish Government' (2008) *Scottish Government*, www.webarchive.org.uk/wayback/archive/3000/https://www.gov.scot/Resource/Doc/262952/0078639.pdf.
[681] Junker (n 51), § 11 para 17.
[682] Rome II Regulation (n 79), Art 4(1).
[683] ibid, Art 4(2).
[684] Schack, *Internationales Zivilverfahrensrecht* (n 7), para 772. In an English appeal to the House of Lords, *Compagnie d'Armement Maritime SA v Compagnie Tunisienne de Navigation SA* [1971] AC 572, 583–84, Lord Reid expressed scepticism about treating the law of a recently independent country in the same terms as its former colonial power: in the case, Tunisian law in the same terms as France law.
[685] Although it seems unlikely that any points of Turkish law will be impossible for a German court to investigate.
[686] See YM Atamer, 'Rezeption und Weiterentwicklung des schweizerischen Zivilgesetzbuches in der Türkei' (2008) 72 *Rabels Zeitschrift für Ausländisches und Internationales Privatrecht* 723, 730ff.

An investigation of Swiss law will be significantly easier for the German court simply on the basis that German is an official language of Switzerland.

However, the approach of applying an alternative law has some major drawbacks. First, an alternative law can only be applied where there is a failure to prove the content of the *lex causae*. This means that there will be further significant cost and time incurred in seeking to investigate the content of at least two legal systems. Second, there is no authority in the choice of law rules for such an approach. Thus, the approach of applying an alternative law is essentially a procedural gadget with a substantive outcome, in the same way that the British fact approach can lead to an outcome that was not envisaged by the drafters of the relevant choice of law rule. Third, even where the law of a similar legal system is applied, eg Swiss instead of Turkish law, there is every possibility that the relevant Turkish statutory provisions will have changed since the transposition in 1926 (!) took place, and, in any case, the relevant case law may be very different. Particular caution must be exercised if the court is dealing with a state with different territorial units (*Mehrrechtsstaat*).[687] By way of example, Scottish family law[688] is very different[689] to English family law,[690] although a German court might be tempted to apply English law to a case where Scots law is the *lex causae*. Thus, the alternative law in such a case could deviate from the *lex causae* even more radically than the *lex fori*, leading to greater injustice than if the *lex fori* were simply applied in the case. Schack himself points to the differences between the legal systems of the various States of the US.[691] It seems that the tenor of a 1977 decision of the German Federal Court of Justice, with regard to the potential application of an alternative law, must be correct:

> It means making reference to an unknown law and leads to considerable complication of the decision-making process. [Translation by author][692]

The decision suggests that, in the absence of a successful investigation of the content of the *lex causae*, the German court should first consider applying the *lex fori*. Only where that provides a very unsatisfactory solution, should the possible application of another law be considered.[693]

[687] Kropholler (n 5), 201ff.

[688] J Thomson, *Family Law in Scotland*, 7th edn (Bloomsbury Professional, 2014).

[689] Some differences are discussed in *Re V* [2016] EWHC 668 (Fam), which cites Morton Fraser, 'A guide to matrimonial law in Scotland for family lawyers in England and Wales' (2014), www.morton-fraser.com/knowledge-hub/guide-matrimonial-law-scotland-family-lawyers-england-wales.

[690] S Gilmore and L Glennon, *Hayes & Williams' Family Law*, 7th edn (Oxford University Press, 2020).

[691] Schack, *Internationales Zivilverfahrensrecht* (n 7), para 772.

[692] *Decision of the Federal Court of Justice from 26 October 1977* (BGH, IV. Zivilsenat) IV ZB 7/77, BGHZ 69, 387, 394: 'Sie bedeutet die Verweisung auf ein Ungewisses Recht und führt zu einer erheblichen Komplizierung des Entscheidungsprozesses.'

[693] *Decision of the Federal Court of Justice from 26 October 1977* (BGH, IV. Zivilsenat) IV ZB 7/77, BGHZ 69, 387, 394.

(iii) Dismissal

Conceptually speaking, it might be thought that a failure to prove the content of the *lex causae* should lead to dismissal of a case.[694] In Germany, however, it has been argued that the dismissal of a case on the basis that the content of the *lex causae* cannot be proved would breach a claimant's right to access justice (*Justizgewährungsanspruch*).[695] As considered above, there are several options open to the German court, eg to further investigate the content of the *lex causae*, to apply the *lex fori*, or, even, to apply an alternative law. There is no recent authority that an action may be dismissed due to a failure to determine the content of the *lex causae*.

In Great Britain, there was suggestion from Lord Leggett in *FS Cairo (Nile Plaza) LLC* (2021) that where a party has introduced a choice of law rule but fails to prove the content of the applicable foreign law:

> the ordinary consequence must follow that, if a party fails to prove its claim or defence, the claim is dismissed or the defence rejected.[696]

However, Lord Leggett was clear that where the applicable foreign law has not been properly evidenced, the presumption of similarity will usually apply, at least as a starting point.[697] Therefore, where foreign law is applicable and foreign law has not been proven to the satisfaction of the court, it is essentially only where the application of the presumption of similarity would lead to absurdity or injustice that a case may be dismissed by, at least, an English court on the basis that the court cannot conduct its own investigation,[698] and it may be uncomfortable applying the presumption of similarity in the circumstances.[699] However, the circumstances where a case will be dismissed or a defence rejected, rather than the presumption of similarity applied, are likely to be limited, particularly as there are then other options available, such as leading further evidence on the *lex causae*.

Considering the procedural background of *FS Cairo (Nile Plaza) LLC* (2021), it is unclear whether the case offers any guidance for the Scottish courts on this point. It is suggested that the Scottish court might ultimately dismiss an action in

[694] It seems that this approach was previously taken in the US because of the implications of the vested rights doctrine. Thus, an action only existed under the foreign law which gave rise to it. See Sprankling and Lanyi (n 106), 23ff.

[695] Junker (n 51), § 11 para 11. See also Schack, *Internationales Zivilverfahrensrecht* (n 7), para 770 and Geimer (n 51), para 2594.

[696] *FS Cairo (Nile Plaza) LLC v Lady Brownlie* [2021] UKSC 45 [117].

[697] *FS Cairo (Nile Plaza) LLC v Lady Brownlie* [2021] UKSC 45 [118].

[698] As noted, in England in status cases, there is the possibility of making a reference to the Queen's Proctor. For example, *H v H (Queen's Proctor Intervening) (Validity of Japanese Divorce)* [2006] EWHC 2989 (Fam).

[699] In considering the general suitability of applying the presumption, Lord Leggett considers a number of authorities from various jurisdictions in *FS Cairo (Nile Plaza) LLC v Lady Brownlie* [2021] UKSC 45 [127]–[142], although it is difficult to draw any firm conclusions from these cases other than that the presumption will not always be applied.

that small number of cases where absurdity or injustice would result if the *lex fori* or the presumption of similarity were applied, but such a course of action seems extremely unlikely in most cases.

VI. Appeals

In Germany, there are two stages of appeal in ordinary civil proceedings. The first is the *Berufung*, which is heard by a *Berufungsgericht*, eg a Court of Appeal (OLG). This is an appeal on both points of fact and law, which allows the appeal court to reconsider the case and, if necessary, seek further evidence.[700] The second is the *Revision*. A *Revision* is an appeal on points of law only.[701] A *Revision* must be heard by the Federal Court of Justice (BGH) in Karlsruhe,[702] which is known in this context as the *Revisionsgericht*. The following analysis concentrates mainly on those cases which go to *Revision*; however, for reasons that will become clear, it is important to bear the difference between the *Berufung* and the *Revision* in mind.

The Scottish Court of Session, which sits in Edinburgh, is divided into the Outer and Inner Houses. It is only the Inner House which hears appeals on questions of law, with the Outer House essentially being a court of first instance for complicated and high value cases.[703] The recently introduced Sheriff Appeal Court also hears appeals on points of law from the sheriff courts, which have privative (exclusive) jurisdiction in civil matters of a value up to £100,000.[704] In all relevant jurisdictions, the procedural specifics of appeals are complicated. For example, although the English Court of Appeal hears almost all appeals from the High Court, questions of law of general public importance can potentially 'leapfrog' from the High Court to the UK Supreme Court.[705] A detailed account would exceed the scope of this work; however, there are many such accounts available.[706]

A. Incorrect Application of the Relevant Choice of Law Rule

To what extent can a failure to apply, or a failure to correctly apply, the relevant choice of law rule be subject to successful appeal in the relevant jurisdictions?

[700] Grunsky and Jacoby (n 60), para 671ff.

[701] ZPO § 545 I.

[702] § 133 of the Gerichtsverfassungsgesetz (GVG); Saenger (n 274), Vorbemerkung zu §§ 511–577, para 5.

[703] C Hennessy, *Civil Procedure and Practice*, 5th edn (W Green, 2018), para 9-01ff.

[704] Courts Reform (Scotland) Act 2014, s 46ff.

[705] Administration of Justice Act 1969, s 12ff. A well-known case, which leapfrogged the Court of Appeal, is *R (Miller) v Secretary of State for Exiting the European Union* [2017] UKSC 5.

[706] See, regarding German law, H-J Musielak and W Voit, *Zivilprozessordnung*, 17th edn (Franz Vahlen, 2020), Book 3; regarding English law, J Leabeater and others, *Civil Appeals: Principle and Procedure*, 2nd edn (Sweet & Maxwell, 2014); and, regarding Scots law, although comparatively brief, Hennessy (n 703), para 18.01ff.

In Germany, it has been made clear on many occasions that,[707] as the appeal court is obligated to consider whether domestic law has been applied correctly, and, as choice of law rules are an integral part of German law, the duty of the appeal court extends to consideration of whether choice of law rules have been correctly applied in the lower instance proceedings:

> The correct application of German private international and procedural law is subject to review during appellate proceedings. [Translation by author][708]

This means that even if the question of foreign law is only first considered at the appeal stage then, assuming that a choice of law rule is applicable designating a foreign applicable law, the failure to have applied that rule is grounds for the decision of the lower instance court to be reversed by the appeal court and returned to the lower instance court for further consideration.[709]

The procedural consequences that follow from a failure to apply, or a failure to correctly apply, choice of law rules in British court proceedings, in so far as civil appeals are concerned, is a matter that appears to have received little dedicated academic consideration. There is no doubt that the incorrect application of a choice of law rule is grounds for appeal, eg the first instance judge's determination that Scots law, rather than English law, is applicable to the facts of the case.[710] Moreover, where a party has pleaded the content of a foreign law, but the first instance judge has taken the view that foreign law is not applicable to the facts of the case then that is also clearly subject to possible appeal.[711] However, there is no authority suggesting that a British appeal court can take issue *ex proprio motu* with a complete failure, by both parties, to rely on the applicable choice of law rule. The lack of any general requirement on first instance British courts to intervene in this situation has been previously considered.[712]

More controversial, on a number of levels, is the position where there is an initial failure to mention foreign law, but a party who realises that they have a better right available under the *lex causae* than the *lex fori*, seeks to introduce foreign law at a later stage.[713] While this situation arguably involves prima facie

[707] *Decision of the Federal Court of Justice from 7 April 1993* (BGH, XII. Zivilsenat) XII ZR 266/91, NJW 1993, 2305, 2306; *Decision of the Federal Court of Justice from 6 March 1995* (BGH, II. Zivilsenat) II ZR 84/94, NJW 1995, 2097; *Decision of the Federal Court of Justice from 15 July 2008* (BGH, VI. Zivilsenat) VI ZR 105/07, BGHZ 177, 237, 239; *Decision of the Federal Labour Court from 7 May 2020* (BAG, II. Senat) 2 AZR 692/19, NZA 2021, 225, 231.

[708] *Decision of the Federal Court of Justice from 30 April 2013* (BGH, VII. Zivilsenat) VII ZB 22/12, NZI 2013, 763, 765: 'Die richtige Anwendung des deutschen internationalen Privat- und Zivilverfahrensrechts ist im Rechtsbeschwerdeverfahren von Amts wegen zu prüfen.'

[709] *Decision of the Federal Court of Justice from 21 September 1995* (BGH, VII. Zivilsenat) VII ZR 248/94, NJW 1996, 54, 54.

[710] See, for example, *Ennstone Building Products Ltd v Stanger Ltd* [2002] 1 WLR 3059.

[711] See, for example, *Sophocleous v Secretary of State for Foreign and Commonwealth Affairs* [2019] QB 949, which was an appeal of the decision of Lord Justice Kerr in *Sophocleous v Secretary of State for the Foreign and Commonwealth Office* [2018] EWHC 19 (QB).

[712] See section II.A.(i)(b).

[713] An example of a case where a party sought to introduce, by means of an amendment, a right available under a foreign law was *Red Sea Insurance Co Ltd v Bouygues SA* [1995] 1 AC 190.

an error of law, in so far that the choice of law rule was applicable in the lower instance proceedings, the only established way to introduce an applicable foreign law rule in British civil proceedings at any stage, in terms of the fact approach, is for the relevant party to seek to introduce an amendment to their pleadings setting out the averred position under the *lex causae*.[714]

In Scots law, a minute of amendment containing the necessary averments as to the content of the *lex causae* can be introduced at any point during the proceedings.[715] Thus, a party is technically competent to introduce a minute of amendment both while an appeal is pending and while the appeal is being heard.[716] However, this does not mean that the amendment will be allowed. The court will be mindful of the interests of justice, and the potential prejudice that may be caused to the opposing party through a substantial late-stage change in the pleadings,[717] and criticism has been levied against parties who attempt to do so:

> These and similar considerations bear out how undesirable it is to have amendments put forward at a late stage … It is a bad habit and one which reflects no credit on those responsible for the initial preparation of the case or for the state of the pleadings. The present Rules of Court as to amendment were intended to get rid of rigidity and formality. They were not intended as a cloak for laziness, ignorance and incompetence.[718]

Despite procedural differences, the fundamental position regarding amendment is essentially the same in England.[719] However, there is evidence that the English court is even less likely to allow the amendment, especially at a later stage of proceedings,[720] although there are cases where the 'heavy onus' has been met.[721]

Thus, in practical terms, the question as to whether foreign law can be introduced at any stage of ongoing proceedings turns on the potential for the introduction of an amendment and the fairness of such an amendment being allowed,[722] rather than whether choice of law rules are substantively applicable

[714] An example of where this was sought to be done during ongoing proceedings was *Ascherberg, Hopwood & Crew v Casa Musicale Sonzogno* [1971] 1 WLR 173.

[715] OCR 18.2(1); RCS 24.1(1).

[716] Cubie (ed) (n 120), paras 10.23–10.24.

[717] *Thomson v Glasgow Corp* 1962 SC (HL) 36, 51–52.

[718] *Thomson v Glasgow Corp* 1962 SC (HL) 36, 54.

[719] See, for a concise summary, R Parkes, A Mullis and G Busuttil, *Gatley on Libel and Slander*, 12th edn & 2nd supp (Sweet & Maxwell, 2017), para 26.46ff.

[720] The test in England was expressed in the following terms in *Worldwide Corp Ltd v GPT Ltd* [1998] EWCA Civ 1894, 1998 WL 1120764, 12: 'Where a party has had many months to consider how he wants to put his case and where it is not by virtue of some new factor appearing from some disclosure only recently made, why, one asks rhetorically, should he be entitled to cause the trial to be delayed so far as his opponent is concerned and why should he be entitled to cause inconvenience to other litigants? The only answer which can be given … is that without the amendment a serious injustice may be done because the new case is the only way the case can be argued, and it raises the true issue between the parties which justice requires should be decided.' This approach was cited with approval in the Court of Appeal in *Swain Mason v Mills & Reeve* [2011] 1 WLR 2735, 2756.

[721] *JW Spear & Sons Ltd v Zynga Inc* [2013] EWHC 1640 (Ch), [75].

[722] See, for example, *Roberts v Soldiers, Sailors, Airmen and Families Association* [2020] EWHC 994 (QB), [103], where German law was introduced into the case by way of an amendment. The English court has noted that this option is open to parties in other cases. See *GDE LLC and Goffe v Anglia*

to the case.[723] Nonetheless, a decision allowing or refusing an amendment is appealable.[724] Where the amendment contains averments of foreign law, it is unclear whether the appeal court will place any emphasis on the choice of law dimension when weighing up whether to allow the amendment. If the amendment is allowed then the court, at that point, should order any necessary further procedure, eg a retrial.[725] In all likelihood, the party relying on the amendment will be held liable for the resultant expenses.[726]

B. Failure to Adequately Investigate the Content of the Applicable Foreign Law

At issue is whether failure of the lower instance court to adequately investigate the content of the *lex causae* can be grounds for a successful appeal. This implies a duty on the court to carry out an investigation; otherwise, it is obvious that there can be no breach of duty. Thus, there is little to be usefully said about British practice as the British judge has no investigative duty in so far as the content of the *lex causae* is concerned.[727] The question as to whether the *lex causae* has been correctly applied by the lower instance court is a different matter and is considered in detail below.

Long-standing German jurisprudence has made clear that a failure to carry out an adequate investigation into the content of the *lex causae* is a breach of German procedural law, and grounds for appeal to the Federal Court of Justice (BGH).[728] The yardstick which the Federal Court of Justice applies is whether the judge has correctly operated within his margin of discretion and has exhausted all sources available to him.[729] The investigative burden on the German court increases

Autoflow Limited [2020] EWHC 105 (Comm), [34], and *Iranian Offshore Engineering and Construction Co v Dean Investment Holdings SA* [2019] 1 WLR 82, 92.

[723] The necessity, in the past, to rely on amendments to introduce foreign law was criticised in the US, and this seems to have been a reason for its movement away from the fact approach. See Brown, '44.1 Ways to Prove Foreign Law' (n 262), 186.

[724] See, for example, *Red Sea Insurance Co Ltd v Bouygues SA* [1995] 1 AC 190, 196.

[725] *GL Baker Ltd v Medway Building and Supplies Ltd* [1958] 1 WLR 1216. In Scotland, known as an additional proof. See Cubie (ed) (n 120), para 10.25.

[726] Cubie (ed) (n 120), para 10.27; Parkes, Mullis and Busuttil (n 719), para 26.46.

[727] See section II.B.(iii).

[728] *Decision of the Federal Court of Justice from 29 June 1987* (BGH, II. Zivilsenat) II ZR 6/87, NJW 1988, 647, 647; *Decision of the Federal Court of Justice from 30 April 1992* (BGH, IX. Zivilsenat) IX ZR 233/90, BGHZ 118, 151, 162. *Decision of the Federal Court of Justice from 30 January 2001* (BGH, XI. Zivilsenat) XI ZR 357/99, NJOZ 2001, 1, 2; Junker (n 51), § 11 para 24. The Federal Court of Justice has made clear that the possibility of review of the lower instance court's investigation should not be used where, in reality, the purpose of the appeal is to achieve review of the conclusions made by the lower instance court as to the content of the applicable foreign law. See *Decision of the Federal Court of Justice from 30 April 1992* (BGH, IX. Zivilsenat) IX ZR 233/90, BGHZ 118, 151, 163.

[729] *Decision of the Federal Court of Justice from 23 April 2002* (BGH, XI. Zivilsenat) XI ZR 136/01, NJW-RR 2002, 1359, 1360; *Decision of the Federal Court of Justice from 30 January 2001* (BGH, XI. Zivilsenat) XI ZR 357/99, NJOZ 2001, 1, 2; and, in respect of the Federal Labour Court, *Decision of the Federal Labour Court from 7 May 2020* (BAG, II. Senat) 2 AZR 692/19, NZA 2021, 225, 231.

consonantly with both the complexity and the extent of the difference between German law and the *lex causae*.[730] There are numerous cases where the Federal Court of Justice has considered there to have been a failure of the lower instance court to adequately carry out its investigation into the content of the applicable foreign law. Examples are a failure to obtain an expert opinion;[731] a failure to adequately explain the basis for its conclusions;[732] and a failure to investigate the foreign case law in its interpretation of the foreign statutory authority.[733] Where there is insufficient evidence that the lower instance court has properly investigated the content of the applicable foreign law, the assumption will be made that it has not done so.[734]

It is usually enough for the Federal Court of Justice that the lower instance court has instructed an expert, eg from a recognised academic institution.[735] Nonetheless, even where an opinion has been obtained, the court must be aware of its potential shortcomings. As previously discussed, the court had not discharged its responsibilities of investigation where the opinion had been written by someone who had never previously written an opinion on Venezuelan law and had no specific expertise in its legal system.[736] Even where the court had had the benefit of an expert opinion on Thai law, the fact that the opinion failed to adequately engage with academic discourse and case law in respect of the applicable statutory provisions meant that it was unacceptable for the court to rely solely on it.[737] This was especially so as the claimant appears to have insisted that the expert opinion's conclusions, with regard to Thai law on prescription, were not consonant with practice in that country.[738] There are cases where the extent of the investigation has been considered insufficient, despite the fact that the *lex causae* is that of a German-speaking country.[739]

[730] *Decision of the Federal Court of Justice from 23 April 2002* (BGH, XI. Zivilsenat) XI ZR 136/01, NJW-RR 2002, 1359, 1360; Junker (n 51), § 11 para 5.

[731] *Decision of the Federal Court of Justice from 14 January 2014* (BGH, II. Zivilsenat) II ZR 192/13, NJW 2014, 1244, 1245.

[732] *Decision of the Federal Court of Justice from 12 October 1993* (BGH, X. Zivilsenat) X ZR 25/92, IPRax 1995, 38–39.

[733] *Decision of the Federal Court of Justice from 24 March 1987* (BGH, VI. Zivilsenat) VI ZR 112/86, NJW 1988, 648.

[734] *Decision of the Federal Court of Justice from 30 April 2013* (BGH, VII. Zivilsenat) VII ZB 22/12, NZI 2013, 763, 765: *Decision of the Federal Court of Justice from 23 April 2002* (BGH, XI. Zivilsenat) XI ZR 136/01, NJW-RR 2002, 1359, 1360; and, in respect of the Federal Labour Court, *Decision of the Federal Labour Court from 7 May 2020* (BAG, II. Senat) 2 AZR 692/19, NZA 2021, 225, 231.

[735] *Decision of the Federal Court of Justice from 21 January 1991* (BGH, II. Zivilsenat) II ZR 49/90, NJW-RR 1991, 1211, 1212.

[736] *Decision of the Federal Court of Justice from 21 January 1991* (BGH, II. Zivilsenat) II ZR 49/90, NJW-RR 1991, 1211.

[737] *Decision of the Federal Court of Justice from 23 June 2003* (BGH, II. Zivilsenat) II ZR 305/01, NJW 2003, 2685, 2686.

[738] *Decision of the Federal Court of Justice from 23 June 2003* (BGH, II. Zivilsenat) II ZR 305/01, NJW 2003, 2685.

[739] *Decision of the Federal Court of Justice from 12 October 1993* (BGH, X. Zivilsenat) X ZR 25/92, IPRax 1995, 38-39; *Decision of the Federal Court of Justice from 24 March 1987* (BGH, VI. Zivilsenat) VI ZR 112/86, NJW 1988, 648, 648.

Despite the very onerous obligations placed on the German judge to thoroughly investigate the content of the applicable foreign law, there are cases where the Federal Court of Justice has found the lower instance court to have fully satisfied its duty to investigate the content of the applicable foreign law. Thus, where an exhaustive investigation had been undertaken to establish the law of Afghanistan on bills of exchange, the lower instance court had done all that it could and it was unreasonable to expect more.[740] For example, the German embassy in Kabul had taken steps to obtain information,[741] and, further to a request from the German court, had obtained an expert opinion from a former legal adviser to the Afghan government.[742] The Federal Court of Justice emphasised that the duty to investigate extends only to accessible sources of foreign law.[743]

C. Incorrect Determination of the Content of the Applicable Foreign Law

In Germany, the long-standing principle is that the Federal Court of Justice (BGH), as *Revisionsgericht*, may not revisit the conclusions of the lower instance court regarding the content of the applicable foreign law.[744] This self-imposed prohibition applies even if the lower instance court's conclusions are wrong.[745] The prohibition is said to apply even where the rule of foreign law is the same as German law on the point or is based on international uniform law.[746] The Federal Court of Justice has held that terms and conditions governed by foreign law are caught by the prohibition.[747] However, this does not mean that the first instance court's decision is not subject to review in an appeal. The *Berufungsgericht*, ie the first level of appeal, which addresses points of both fact and law, *may* review the first instance court's conclusions as to the content of foreign law, which includes the power to obtain further evidence.[748]

[740] *Decision of the Federal Court of Justice from 24 November 1960* (BGH, II. Zivilsenat) II ZR 9/60, NJW 1961, 410, 411.
[741] *Decision of the Federal Court of Justice from 24 November 1960* (BGH, II. Zivilsenat) II ZR 9/60, NJW 1961, 410.
[742] *Decision of the Federal Court of Justice from 24 November 1960* (BGH, II. Zivilsenat) II ZR 9/60, NJW 1961, 410.
[743] *Decision of the Federal Court of Justice from 24 November 1960* (BGH, II. Zivilsenat) II ZR 9/60, NJW 1961, 410.
[744] *Decision of the Federal Court of Justice from 30 March 1976* (BGH, VI. Zivilsenat) VI ZR 143/74, NJW 1976, 1581, 1582; *Decision of the Federal Court of Justice from 24 November 1960* (BGH, II. Zivilsenat) II ZR 9/60, NJW 1961, 410, 411.
[745] *Decision of the Federal Court of Justice from 29 June 1987* (BGH, II. Zivilsenat) II ZR 6/87, NJW 1988, 647, 647; *Decision of the Federal Court of Justice from 23 June 2003* (BGH, II. Zivilsenat) II ZR 305/01, NJW 2003, 2685, 2868.
[746] Schack, *Internationales Zivilverfahrensrecht* (n 7), para 777.
[747] *Decision of the Federal Court of Justice from 19 September 1990* (BGH, VIII. Zivilsenat) VIII ZR 239/89, BGHZ 112, 204, 210.
[748] Saenger (n 274), § 293 para 26.

Moreover, there are several exceptions to the general, self-imposed restriction on the Federal Court of Justice reviewing the lower instance courts' conclusions. Indeed, viewed in their totality, they appear to fundamentally undermine it. The first exception is where the matter concerns the enforceability of a foreign judgment in Germany, and there is a potential lack of the necessary reciprocity between Germany and the state from which the judgment originates (*Verbürgung der Gegenseitigkeit*).[749] The second is where the applicable law in terms of a (non-EU)[750] German choice of law rule, of which there are few remaining, is thought to send the reference back to Germany (*renvoi*).[751] Third is where the law of the *lex causae* has changed since the lower instance court's decision was made.[752] Fourth is where the lower instance court was not aware that the relevant provision of foreign law exists.[753]

The self-imposed prohibition appears to be justified by the Federal Court of Justice on the basis that foreign law is not law within the meaning of § 545(1) of the German Code of Civil Procedure, which states:

> An appeal on points of law may only be based on the reason that the contested decision is based on a violation of the law.[754]

Similar wording appears in § 72 of the Act on Proceedings in Family Matters and in Matters of Non-contentious Jurisdiction (FamFG). It does seem a little peculiar that while German law is said to approach foreign law as law, rather than fact, the Federal Court of Justice has not extended this approach to allow an appeal based on the incorrect determination of the content of the *lex causae* in the lower

[749] *Decision of the Imperial Court of Justice from 10 December 1926* (RG) VI 344/25, RGZ 115, 103, 105; A more recent example is given in the *Decision of the Federal Court of Justice from 29 April 1999* (BGH, IX. Zivilsenat) IX ZR 263/97, BGHZ 141, 286; Schack, *Internationales Zivilverfahrensrecht* (n 7), para 778.

[750] In general, the application of *renvoi* is excluded by the EU regulations on private international law. See Art 20 of the Rome I Regulation (n 1) and Art 24 of the Rome II Regulation (n 79). A notable exception is provided for by Art 34 of the Regulation (EU) No 650/2012 of 4 July 2012 on jurisdiction, applicable law, recognition and enforcement of decisions and acceptance and enforcement of authentic instruments in matters of succession and on the creation of a European Certificate of Succession [2012] OJ L 201/107 (EU Succession Regulation).

[751] *Decision of the Federal Court of Justice from 21 November 1958* (BGH, IV. Zivilsenat) IV ZR 107/58, BGHZ 28, 375, 381; Junker (n 51), § 11 para 25; Schack, *Internationales Zivilverfahrensrecht* (n 7), para 778.

[752] *Decision of the Federal Court of Justice from 21 February 1962* (BGH, V. Zivilsenat) V ZR 144/60, BGHZ 36, 348, 350.

[753] *Decision of the Federal Court of Justice from 23 October 1963* (BGH, V. Zivilsenat) V ZR 146/57, BGHZ 40, 197, 200. However, the Federal Court of Justice may proceed on the basis that the lower instance court considered that the provision was not applicable. Although not a case involving the application of foreign law, see a relevant discussion in *Decision of the Federal Court of Justice from 9 July 1956* (BGH, III. Zivilsenat) III ZR 320/54, BGHZ 21, 214, 217. Nonetheless, a failure of the lower instance court to discuss the basis for its conclusions is likely, in and of itself, to render the decision subject to review. See *Decision of the Federal Court of Justice from 30 April 2013* (BGH, VII. Zivilsenat) VII ZB 22/12, NZI 2013, 763, 765 and *Decision of the Federal Court of Justice from 30 April 1992* (BGH, IX. Zivilsenat) IX ZR 233/90, BGHZ 118, 151, 163.

[754] Translation by Schöning (n 243), § 545.

instance courts. The question as to whether the Federal Court of Justice should be entitled to revisit the conclusions of the lower instance courts regarding the content of the *lex causae* is fiercely contested.[755] A 2009 revision[756] of the definition of law that is subject to appeal to the Federal Court of Justice appears to have fuelled the debate.[757] Fritz Sturm, in a 2011 article, argued strongly against such a possibility. Sturm argued that a decision of the Federal Court of Justice can only ever offer a snapshot of the relevant foreign law, and that the risk of error, even in decisions of the Federal Court of Justice, is too great to justify definitive judgments.[758] The Federal Court of Justice decided in 2013 that the revisions made in 2009 were not intended by the legislator to alter the existing position.[759] With reference to Sturm's 2011 article, the Federal Court of Justice considered that its decisions should never form the basis of future decisions concerning points of foreign law. Accordingly, the lower instance court must always independently investigate the current position in terms of the applicable foreign law.[760]

However, those seeing merit in the possibility of the Federal Court of Justice reviewing the lower instance courts' conclusions argue that essentially pragmatic considerations should not trump the interests of justice in individual cases,[761] with the current approach discriminating against foreigners and undermining the credibility of the German civil justice system.[762] An argument which supports the possibility for review is a literal interpretation of the modified wording; however, a previously convincing argument that similarly worded provisions in the Employment Courts Act (ArbGG) had been interpreted by the Federal Labour

[755] The various positions are discussed by the court in *Decision of the Federal Court of Justice from 4 July 2013* (BGH, V. Zivilsenat) V ZB 197/12, BGHZ 198, 14, 18–19.

[756] T Riehm, 'Vom Gesetz, das klüger ist als seine Verfasser – Zur Revisibilität ausländischen Rechts' (2014) *Juristenzeitung* 73, 74. The previous wording referred, inter alia, to '*Bundesrecht*' (Federal Law), however, the wording since 2009 only refers to '*Recht*' (law). Thus, the argument is that, as foreign law is considered law, not fact, in Germany, foreign law should now be treated as law for appeal purposes.

[757] The two sides of the argument are best represented, on one hand, by F Sturm, 'Wegen Verletzung fremden Rechts sind weder Revision noch Rechtsbeschwerde zulässig' (2011) *Juristenzeitung* 74, who argues that no change was brought about by the revision, and, on the other, Geimer (n 51), para 2610, who argues that foreign law should be examined by the Federal Court of Justice to the fullest extent. Geimer acknowledges the fact that the Federal Court of Justice has refused to take this position. See also W Hau, 'Ein Rückzugsgefecht des BGH gegen die Revisibilität ausländischen Rechts' (2014) *Praxis des Internationalen Privat- und Verfahrensrechts* 397.

[758] Sturm, 'Wegen Verletzung fremden Rechts sind weder Revision noch Rechtsbeschwerde zulässig' (n 757), 77.

[759] *Decision of the Federal Court of Justice from 4 July 2013* (BGH, V. Zivilsenat) V ZB 197/12, BGHZ 198, 14, 20. See critical commentary, in this regard, by Riehm (n 756), 77–78.

[760] *Decision of the Federal Court of Justice from 4 July 2013* (BGH, V. Zivilsenat) V ZB 197/12, BGHZ 198, 14, 20–21; Junker (n 51), § 11 para 20.

[761] Riehm (n 756), 75–77. Geimer, who is particularly critical, asks who is better placed than the Federal Court of Justice, with its especially qualified lawyers and the best library, to determine difficult issues of foreign law? Geimer (n 51), para 2613.

[762] Schack, *Internationales Zivilverfahrensrecht* (n 7), para 777.

Court as allowing it to review conclusions made regarding the content of foreign law is now no longer valid.[763] In a decision from 7 May 2020,[764] the Federal Labour Court reversed its previous approach and determined that it may not review the lower instance courts' conclusions regarding the content of foreign law,[765] while nonetheless acknowledging that there is nothing in the wording of the relevant legislation preventing such a review on the basis that German law treats foreign law as law.[766]

The fact that the Federal Court of Justice does not revisit the conclusions of the lower instance courts regarding the content of the *lex causae* is of fundamental significance when considering the overall treatment of foreign law in Germany, ie it undermines the argument that foreign law is strictly a matter of law in German civil procedure. Nonetheless, there can be little doubt that the jurisprudence of the Federal Court of Justice has sought to mitigate the impact of this restriction, essentially through the backdoor.[767] Thus, when reversing decisions of the lower instance courts, the Federal Court of Justice justifies the reversal by determining that the investigation by the lower instance court was flawed as there is, after all, a fine line between a flawed investigation and an error in the determination of the content of the *lex causae*.[768] In approaching the problem in this way, injustice is generally prevented in individual cases, as an incorrect decision can usually, but not always, be attributed to a failure to properly carry out the investigation.

Despite foreign law being considered a question of fact in British civil procedure, which would normally render it subject to very limited review in the appeal

[763] Thole (n 625), 55; J Gruber, 'Die Anwendung ausländischen Rechts durch deutsche Gerichte' (1992) *Zeitschrift für Rechtspolitik* 6, 7. See *Decision of the Federal Labour Court from 10 April 1975* (BAG, II. Senat) 2 AZR 128/74, BAGE 27, 99 for the court's reasoning as to why determinations as to the content of foreign law should be subject to appeal in the Federal Labour Court.

[764] *Decision of the Federal Labour Court from 7 May 2020* (BAG, II. Senat) 2 AZR 692/19, NZA 2021, 225, 232.

[765] Schack, *Internationales Zivilverfahrensrecht* (n 7), para 778; M Benecke, 'Eingriffsnormen und Revisibilität ausländischen Rechts – Bekanntes und Neues zum Internationalen Arbeitsrecht und Arbeitsprozessrecht in BAG 7.5.2020 – 2 AZR 692/19' (2020) *Recht der Arbeit* 366, 368. The decision of the Federal Labour Court could be described as *obiter*, as the decision of the lower instance court was obviously insufficient in so far that there appears to have been no investigation of the applicable Indian law, and so the appeal could have been allowed due to the failure to investigate its content. See the *Decision of the Hessen Higher Labour Court from 13 June 2019* (LAG Hessen, XI. Berufungskammer) 11 Sa 812/18, BeckRS 2019, 42174, where it is merely said 'Tatsachen, die die Unwirksamkeit der Kündigung nach indischem Recht begründen könnten, hat der Kläger nicht vorgetragen' ('The applicant has not presented any facts that could justify the invalidity of the dismissal under Indian law.') [Translation by author]. The Federal Labour Court was highly critical. *Decision of the Federal Labour Court from 7 May 2020* (BAG, II. Senat) 2 AZR 692/19, NZA 2021, 225, 231.

[766] *Decision of the Federal Labour Court from 7 May 2020* (BAG, II. Senat) 2 AZR 692/19, NZA 2021, 225, 232. The court drew on the well-rehearsed reasoning of the Federal Court of Justice that lower instance courts must always review the content of foreign law, as justification not to allow determinations as to the content of foreign law to be made in the Federal Labour Court.

[767] The Federal Labour Court appears to have adopted the same approach in *Decision of the Federal Labour Court from 7 May 2020* (BAG, II. Senat) 2 AZR 692/19, NZA 2021, 225. See Benecke (n 765), 369.

[768] Junker (n 51), § 11 para 24.

courts,[769] there is an established willingness of British appeal courts to consider determinations made by lower instance courts regarding the content of the *lex causae*.[770] This means that the high threshold, ie that the trial judge has 'gone plainly wrong' in his assessment of the evidence,[771] normally required for an appeal court to interfere with findings of fact made by trial judges, does not need to be met, although the English Court of Appeal has nonetheless stressed a general reluctance to interfere when reviewing findings in respect of foreign law.[772]

The fundamental willingness of appeal courts to interfere in respect of foreign law is because, first, the British courts have long recognised that foreign law is a 'peculiar kind'[773] of fact, and, second, expert evidence is treated in British appeals differently from findings regarding primary facts.[774] Thus, when considering determinations made on the content of the *lex causae*, the British appeal court may review the cited authorities.[775] It may consider the qualifications of the respective experts and determine that one speaks with more authority than the other.[776] It may consider expert opinions and oral evidence given, including points raised in cross-examination, potentially reaching a different conclusion from the first

[769] The general position, as regards determinations of fact, is that an appeal court must consider that the first instance judge's conclusions are plainly wrong. See *Clarke v Edinburgh & District Tramways Co Ltd* 1919 SC (HL) 35, 36: 'It is quite true that a Judge who hears the witnesses has a great advantage in determining upon the question of their credibility, but when you have to deal with the inference which he draws from the evidence given before him, I think, before his finding is disturbed, it is absolutely necessary that the Court of appeal should be clear that he has drawn a wrong conclusion from the evidence.'

[770] *DNO Oman Ltd v Clouston* 2019 SLT 395, 407, and *Parkasho v Singh* [1968] P 233, 250. An appeal regarding a determination of the content of foreign law may be considered at all levels, including the UK Supreme Court. See, for example, *Lazard Bros & Co v Midland Bank Ltd* [1933] AC 289, where the House of Lords considered Soviet law.

[771] See *McGraddie v McGraddie* [2013] 1 WLR 2477, 2487–89. and *Royal Bank of Scotland Plc v Carlyle* 2015 SC (UKSC) 93, 99–100, citing the well-known case of *Thomas v Thomas* 1947 SC (HL) 45.

[772] See *Dexia Crediop SPA v Comune di Prato* [2017] EWCA Civ 428, which stresses, at [42], the English appeal courts' general 'reluctance to intervene in cases involving findings of foreign law.' The court goes on to state, also at [42]: 'The trial judge not only has the advantage of asking questions of the experts, but also reads all the expert evidence and sees and hears the experts being cross-examined on it. He will see the extent to which the experts were able to justify their opinions and will be able to evaluate their reasoning. This is not solely, or even primarily, a question of assessing their "demeanour". This court is in no position to recreate the judge's experience from a reading of the transcript and by "island hopping" (to use Lewison LJ's vivid metaphor) in the sea of relevant evidence available to the judge.' The Scottish Inner House of the Court of Session was comparatively more enthusiastic in *DNO Oman Ltd v Clouston* 2019 SLT 395, 407: 'The same considerations as apply to a review of fact, and the advantages which a first instance judge has from having heard and seen the witnesses testify, do not apply with quite the same force … The appellate court is at no disadvantage in carrying out the same exercise to see if the judge has correctly understood their import.'

[773] *Parkasho v Singh* [1968] P 233, 250.

[774] *Ted Jacob Engineering Group Inc v Morrison* 2019 SC 487, 491, citing *W v Greater Glasgow Health Board* [2017] CSIH 58: 'Expert evidence is not evidence of primary facts, but is rather an expression of opinion about the analysis of those facts according to the specialist knowledge and skill of the expert; as such, it should be treated as inferential in nature, and an appellate court is fully entitled to assess such evidence and if so advised to come to a different conclusion from the judge at first instance.'

[775] *Ted Jacob Engineering Group Inc v Morrison* 2019 SC 487, 492.

[776] See, for example, *Lazard Bros & Co v Midland Bank Ltd* [1933] AC 289, 298–99.

instance court on the basis of that evidence.[777] Where the conclusions of the lower instance court are found to be wrong, the appeal court can, inter alia, revise the judgment made by the lower instance court.[778]

When comparing the British and German approaches to appeals, it is clear that both struggle to frame foreign law in terms of traditional notions, with both recognising that foreign law presents unique challenges. On one hand, the British approach, which essentially allows a review at all levels of appeal, recognises that incorrect decisions of lower instance courts regarding the content of foreign law should not be allowed to stand. The usual test which applies in relation to findings of fact is too high a threshold in this context. On the other hand, the German approach also recognises that foreign and domestic law are not equals. While a Court of Appeal, as *Berufungsgericht*, may review the determination of the first instance court, the Federal Court of Justice, as *Revisionsgericht*, refuses to do so in most circumstances. As a result, the Federal Court of Justice is not required to give determinative rulings as to the content of foreign law. However, where the lower instance court's investigation was flawed, the opportunity remains for a case to be returned by the Federal Court of Justice to the lower instance court for further review to mitigate the risk of injustice in individual cases.[779]

[777] *DNO Oman Ltd v Clouston* 2019 SLT 395, 407; *Parkasho v Singh* [1968] P 233, 250.

[778] For the position in England, see Zuckerman, *Zuckerman on Civil Procedure* (n 293), para 25.191ff and, in Scotland, at least as far as the Sheriff Appeal Court is concerned, Cubie (ed) (n 120), para 18.140. Appeal procedure differs substantially between Scotland and England. Detailed consideration would be beyond the scope of this work.

[779] *Decision of the Federal Court of Justice from 29 June 1987* (BGH, II. Zivilsenat) II ZR 6/87, NJW 1988, 647, 647; *Decision of the Federal Court of Justice from 30 January 2001* (BGH, XI. Zivilsenat) XI ZR 357/99, NJOZ 2001, 1, 3.

4

Future

I. Domestic Reform

A. Voluntary Choice of Law

As a rule, the German court introduces and applies choice of law rules *ex proprio motu.*[1] There is neither judicial nor broad academic support for the voluntary choice of law approach in Germany. As matters stand, it is inconceivable that the voluntary choice of law approach would be adopted in that jurisdiction. Indeed, the voluntary choice of law approach, in so far as EU choice of law rules are concerned, has, in principle, been criticised in Germany as being of questionable conformity with the terms and spirit of EU law.[2] Even Fritz Sturm, once a prominent advocate of voluntary choice of law in Germany, did not support the voluntary approach where the applicable rules derive from international conventions:

> Whoever accedes to choice of law conventions also assumes the obligation to apply these rules in cases with foreign elements, regardless of whether the parties want this or not. [Translation by author][3]

It is equally clear that the general effect of choice of law rules in Great Britain is, and traditionally has been, that it is essentially the choice of the parties as to whether to draw on them in British court proceedings.[4] As a rule, the British court will not *ex proprio motu* introduce and apply choice of law rules, an approach which was confirmed by Lord Leggett in *FS Cairo Nile Plaza LLC* (2021), even in

[1] See Chapter three, section II.A.(i)(a).

[2] For a particularly critical viewpoint, see H Schack, *Internationales Zivilverfahrensrecht*, 8th edn (CH Beck, 2021), para 752. Wagner, with reference to French case law, doubted that international choice of law conventions require the application of choice of law rules by the court *ex proprio motu.* G Wagner, 'Fakultatives Kollisionsrecht und prozessuale Parteiautonomie' (1999) *Zeitschrift für Europäisches Privatrecht* 6, 38–40.

[3] F Sturm, 'Fakultatives Kollisionsrecht: Notwendigkeit und Grenzen' in H Bernstein, U Drobnig and H Kötz (eds), *Festschrift für Konrad Zweigert zum 70. Geburtstag* (JCB Mohr (Paul Siebeck), 1981), 342: 'Wer kollisionsrechtlichen Abkommen beitritt, übernimmt auch die Verpflichtung, diese Normen in Fällen mit Auslandsberührung anzuwenden, und zwar ohne Rücksicht darauf, ob die Parteien dies wollen oder nicht.'

[4] See Chapter three, section III.A. Possible professional negligence in a lawyer failing to raise the applicability of a choice of law rule with their client was considered Chapter three, section III.A., text to fns 487–488.

the context of the Rome I and II Regulations, when he concisely set out the terms of what he referred to as the 'default rule':

> the English court is not obliged to apply the choice of law rules contained in the Rome I and Rome II Regulations if neither party chooses to assert in its statement of case that foreign law is applicable.[5]

As previously discussed, Lord Leggett reasoned that the parties' failure to refer to a foreign rule of law can be considered a tacit choice in favour of the *lex fori* and, where relevant, can usually be subsumed within the scope of the party autonomy granted by the EU instruments.[6] He also noted that, under their own terms, those instruments never intended to impact on domestic rules of evidence and procedure.[7]

British academics are generally favourable towards the voluntary choice of law approach, even if not described in these terms.[8] The most powerful argument supporting the voluntary approach is undoubtedly party choice, ie it should be a matter for the parties to decide whether they wish to expend the money and time required to prove the content of the *lex causae*.[9] Beaumont has argued:

> The applicable law rules which the parties are ignoring were primarily designed to meet the legitimate expectations of private parties. If these particular parties do not want to

[5] *FS Cairo (Nile Plaza) LLC v Lady Brownlie* [2021] UKSC 45 [114]. There is nothing to suggest that the Scottish courts would not take the same approach as the English courts on this point.

[6] *FS Cairo (Nile Plaza) LLC v Lady Brownlie* [2021] UKSC 45 [114]. See also, for similar analysis, PR Beaumont, 'When should EU private international law require that foreign law be applied?' in J von Hein, E-M Kieninger and G Rühl (eds), *How European is European Private International Law?* (Intersentia, 2019) 179.

[7] See the Convention on the law applicable to contractual obligations opened for signature in Rome on 19 June 1980 (Consolidated Version) (80/934/EEC) (Rome Convention), Art 1(2)(h), and, in the same terms, Regulation (EC) No 593/2008 of the European Parliament and of the Council of 17 June 2008 on the law applicable to contractual obligations [2008] OJ L 177/6 (Rome I Regulation), Art 1(3): 'This Regulation shall not apply to evidence and procedure, without prejudice to Article 18'. See also Regulation (EC) No 864/2007 of the European Parliament and of the Council of 11 July 2007 on the law applicable to non-contractual obligations [2007] OJ L 199/40 (Rome II Regulation), Art 1(3). For similar provision in UK law, see the Private International Law (Miscellaneous Provisions) Act 1995, s 14(3)(b), although this provision goes further in so far that it specifically refers to rules of 'pleading'.

[8] TC Hartley, 'Pleading and Proof of Foreign Law: The Major European Systems Compared' (1996) 45 *ICLQ* 271, 285, which Hartley also described as the 'default rule'; Beaumont, 'When should EU private international law require that foreign law be applied?' (n 6); R Fentiman, *Foreign Law in English Courts: Pleading, Proof and Choice of Law* (Oxford University Press, 1998), 293; A Briggs, *The Conflict of Laws*, 4th edn (Oxford University Press, 2019), 7ff.

[9] Lord Justice Underhill also drew attention to the 'trouble and expense of establishing' foreign law, and generally set out the case for voluntary choice of law in *FS Cairo (Nile Plaza) LLC v Brownlie* [2020] EWCA Civ 996, [175], particularly when he stated: 'In cases where it is applied the court is not wilfully shutting its eyes to the obvious fact that (say) the Egyptian law of contract does not look like anything in *Chitty*. Rather, it is proceeding, for good pragmatic reasons, on the assumed basis that Egyptian law will be, in the relevant respects, to substantially the same effect as English law, whatever the differences in its structure or formulation. That will sometimes be contrary to the actual facts, but to regard that as an objection misses the point that the whole object of the exercise is not to have to go to the trouble of finding out what the facts are. It is for the same reason no objection to say that the exercise is "artificial": in one sense artificiality is necessarily inherent in the default rule.'

> invest resources in using those applicable law rules, then why should the State compel them to do so or instead pay for it itself through legal aid or through the time of its judges.[10]

Despite the fact that the voluntary choice of law approach is clearly applicable in Great Britain and notwithstanding the arguments in favour of it, one difficulty is that its effect arguably runs contrary to the text of British statute law, particularly those residual EU choice of law regulations,[11] which were voluntarily adopted by the UK.[12] Indeed, both the Rome I and II Regulations set out what is required to reach a choice of law[13] – which is not necessarily complied with under the default rule[14] – and limit party autonomy in some respects,[15] the designated laws applicable under the regulations being designed to have substantive effect. Even amongst advocates of voluntary choice of law, there is a recognised difficulty when it comes to weaker parties,[16] who do not necessarily receive the full protection that may be envisaged in the relevant instruments, although this does not itself justify

[10] Beaumont, 'When should EU private international law require that foreign law be applied?' (n 6), 179.

[11] Under the Consolidated version of the Treaty on the Functioning of the European Union of 26 October 2012 [2012] OJ C 326/47 (TFEU), Art 288: 'A regulation shall have general application. It shall be binding in its entirety and directly applicable in all Member States.' This covered significant parts of private international law in Great Britain. See Chapter one at section I.C. Fentiman recognised that statutory choice of law rules, where based on international instruments, may have mandatory effect. See Fentiman, *Foreign Law in English Courts* (n 8), 270 and 298, when writing in the context of the Rome and Brussels Conventions. Kirsty Hood KC briefly alluded to the problem in a 2006 article: 'This is open to an objection of illogicality. Domestic law, including the system's conflict rules, falls within the judicial knowledge of a judge.' K Hood, 'Drawing Inspiration? Reconsidering the Procedural Treatment of Foreign Law' (2006) 2 *Journal of Private International Law* 181, 183. She also noted, at 184, the fact that the debate was brought even more sharply into focus by the increased use of EU regulations in British private international law.

[12] See, particularly in relation to the now defunct UK opt-in, Chapter one, section I.C., text to fns 132–144.

[13] Rome I Regulation (n 7), Art 3(1), which requires that a 'choice shall be made expressly or clearly demonstrated by the terms of the contract or the circumstances of the case.' See also Rome II Regulation (n 7), Art 14.

[14] It might be suggested, at least as far as Germany is concerned, that there are two relevant criteria if the regulations are to be applied properly. First, it should only be possible to rely entirely on the *lex fori* where the relevant regulation allows this choice of law to be made without reservation and, second, both parties should clearly make a choice of law in favour of the *lex fori*, ie they should be aware that another law is applicable to the case. Allowing the parties to tacitly make a choice of law in favour of the *lex fori* through failure to plead foreign law has been criticised in Germany, but appears to be accepted practice.

[15] See, particularly, the Rome II Regulation (n 7), Arts 6 and 8, in respect of unfair competition and intellectual property rights, which provide that 'The law applicable under this Article may not be derogated from by an agreement pursuant to Article 14.' See, for discussion, Beaumont, 'When should EU private international law require that foreign law be applied?' (n 6), 181, which describes such cases as 'highly exceptional' and the application of choice of law rules *ex proprio motu*, which would require an elaborate state-funded system, as not justified.

[16] Beaumont, 'When should EU private international law require that foreign law be applied?' (n 6), 180, which considers that cases where it could be necessary for the court to apply foreign law *ex proprio motu* for the benefit of a weaker party are 'relatively rare'; Hartley (n 8), 291.

movement away from the traditional approach taken to foreign law in British civil procedure.[17]

While it would be problematic and unrealistic to suggest that there should be any shift away from voluntary choice of law in Great Britain, it would be helpful to clarify the extent to which any interventions may legitimately be made by judges. British judges ought to have the right,[18] where the interests of justice require it, to discuss with the parties, with reference to any applicable rules, the choice of law dimension at a case management hearing, and, potentially, make orders in respect of it, although this is arguably already sufficiently clear in England.[19] As has been previously discussed, English civil procedure does allow the judge significant leeway to discuss elements of the case with the parties,[20] and the judge's case management role is now deeply ingrained in the English Civil Procedure Rules.[21]

While the British judge should not have to investigate *ex proprio motu* the content of any applicable foreign law – which would far overstep the judge's role throughout the British adversarial systems[22] – it would be desirable if judges were to have the right to order *ex proprio motu* that an expert opinion on foreign law be obtained in exceptional circumstances, eg where both parties are representing themselves, the opinion is required to properly resolve the case, and the interests of justice require it.[23]

[17] Beaumont, 'When should EU private international law require that foreign law be applied?' (n 6), 183.

[18] This is broadly the position that was advocated by the European Group for Private International Law (or Groupe européen de droit international privé) in 2013. See Groupe européen de droit international privé, '*Vingt-troisième réunion, Lausanne, 20–22 septembre 2013, Compte rendu des seances de travail: III. Le traitement du droit étranger en droit international privé européen*', gedip-egpil.eu/wp-content/uploads/2020/10/2013-Lausane.pdf: '*Lorsqu'au vu des éléments du litige le juge constate que celui-ci peut soulever une question de loi applicable en vertu du droit de l'Union européenne, il invite, dès que possible, les parties à prendre position sur cette question.*' Kirsty Hood KC in a brief 2006 article seemed to favour some movement in this direction: 'As the civil procedure of both jurisdictions sees increasing reform, changes often encourage a higher degree of judicial case-management, thus perhaps allowing more opportunity for judicial intervention to this end.' Hood (n 11), 190.

[19] This happened to a limited extent in *FS Cairo (Nile Plaza) LLC v Lady Brownlie* [2021] UKSC 45, where the claimant had served two reports from an expert on Egyptian law referring to rules of Egyptian law which were not pleaded, and there was uncertainty as to the extent to which the claimant was seeking to rely on the presumption of similarity. Lord Leggett held, at [166], that 'the defendant is entitled to know where the claimant stands on those matters.'

[20] Although this right is not nearly as extensive as the responsibilities given to German judges under § 139 of the Code of Civil Procedure (ZPO). See J Fritsche, '§ 139' in W Krüger and T Rauscher (eds), *Münchener Kommentar zur Zivilprozessordnung: Band 1 (§§ 1–354)*, 6th edn (CH Beck, 2020).

[21] See, for example, CPR, Part 3.

[22] Although the extent of the court's involvement requires consideration in the context of this work, it should not be forgotten that the ultimate right of the parties to choose how to frame and argue their cases is a tenet of most parts of both British and (albeit to a lesser extent) German procedural law. See, in respect of British law, *Iranian Offshore Engineering and Construction Co v Dean Investment Holdings SA* [2019] 1 WLR 82, 90, although some of the court's conclusions in the case are questionable. See Wagner (n 2), 18ff, for an analysis in respect of German law which considers that the scope for the parties to influence the application of German domestic law is greater than usually thought.

[23] Giving the British judge this right would help address the issues raised by cases such as *Padero-Mernagh v Mernagh* [2020] EWFC 27, which were discussed in the first and third chapters. See

Finally, perhaps Brexit affords the UK an opportunity to consider whether it still wishes to retain the EU choice of law instruments as part of its domestic law. It must be questioned whether these instruments truly sit well with British civil procedure, a fact which manifests itself particularly clearly when the impact of the voluntarily approach is considered. Moreover, the case law of the EU in respect of the relevant choice of law instruments, which have been transposed into UK domestic law, will continue to develop without the input of British courts and judges. It is questionable whether it is desirable to have two strands of jurisprudence developing should the British courts decide to go their own way on specific points.

In view of this and the other issues discussed in this work – for example, the absence of any implementing legislation to facilitate references under the London Convention and the questionable status of the British Law Ascertainment Act 1859 – there would be merit in the issues involved in the application of foreign law in the British courts, which are largely of a technical nature, being considered by the Law Commission of England and Wales and the Scottish Law Commission. Ideally this would be framed in a joint report, as has been done in the past in respect of other matters involving private international law,[24] and ideally as part of a wider review of private international law following Brexit. A joint law commission report, potentially leading to legislation, if required, would be an excellent way to also involve relevant expert academics, judges, and legal practitioners. Depending on the findings, a decision could be made as to whether any legislation ought to be UK-wide, with the necessary consents,[25] or dealt with as a devolved matter. As many of the matters involved would be procedural, there would also be an inevitable role for the Scottish Civil Justice Council[26] and its equivalents.

Chapter one, section II.E, fn 260 and Chapter three, Chapter three at section II.A.(ii)(b). The resultant costs would either fall on the parties or, if they are of insufficient means, the public purse. This is more likely to be necessary in the family law context, eg in cases involving status, as in *Padero-Mernagh* (2020), than commercial law. A careful balancing act will inevitably be required.

[24] See The Law Commission and The Scottish Law Commission, 'Private International Law: The Law of Domicile (Law Com No 168 and Scot Law Com No 107)' (1987), www.scotlawcom.gov.uk/files/3212/7989/6557/rep107.pdf and The Law Commission and The Scottish Law Commission, 'Private International Law: Choice of Law in Tort and Delict (Law Com No 193 and Scot Law Com No 129)' (1990), www.scotlawcom.gov.uk/files/5812/7989/6877/rep129.pdf.

[25] It is hoped that the UK and Scottish Parliaments can work more harmoniously together now that the Brexit process has been completed, so that the Sewel Convention can be properly upheld. See G Anthony, 'Devolution, Brexit, and the Sewel Convention' (2018), consoc.org.uk/wp-content/uploads/2018/04/Gordon-Anthony-Devolution-Brexit-and-the-Sewel-Convention-1.pdf, 2–5. See also, more recently, M Sandford and C Gormley-Heenan, '"Taking Back Control", the UK's Constitutional Narrative and Schrodinger's Devolution' (2020) 73 *Parliamentary Affairs* 108.

[26] See, for discussion of the role of the Scottish Civil Justice Council, which was established under the Scottish Civil Justice Council and Criminal Legal Assistance Act 2013, NR Whitty, 'Civil Procedure (Reissue) (2007): Introduction (paras 1–45)', *The Laws of Scotland: Stair Memorial Encyclopaedia* (LexisNexis), para 45A.

B. Conceptual Treatment of Foreign Law

A significant portion of this work is dedicated to the consideration of specifics, eg the various mechanisms by which foreign law can be investigated in both the British and German courts. This section takes a step back and considers the fundamental approach taken to foreign law in the relevant jurisdictions, ie its putative treatment as a question of fact in Great Britain or as law in Germany.

Before turning a more critical eye to the fact approach, it is important to be clear about its advantages at the investigative stage. To establish the content of foreign law it is necessary for an investigation to be carried out. British judges do not know, nor can they be expected to know, the content of (most) foreign laws. Where the parties are well-funded, the fact approach's implications are generally positive. There can be few more effective means of establishing the content of the *lex causae* than well-reasoned evidence provided by competing experts on that legal system.[27] Moreover, recent procedural innovations introduced by the English Civil Procedure Rules have reduced costs and improved the quality of expert evidence in that jurisdiction, for example, by increasing judicial control, and making provision for joint meetings to take place between the experts of opposing parties.[28] Conversely, unless the relevant point is simple, there can be few less effective means of establishing the content of the *lex causae* than the judge undertaking his own research when he may not understand the legal system he is researching, and may be using poor quality materials to undertake his research, for example, out-of-date textbooks.

A major problem with the fact approach, in the context of the investigation and determination of foreign law, is its rigidity, in so far that it traditionally applied unnecessary rules of evidence to the process of proving the content of foreign law.[29] US federal procedural law[30] provides an insightful guide as to possible reform that could be undertaken to both English and Scottish procedural law in this context, as significant reform[31] was undertaken, during the middle of the twentieth century, of the US federal procedural rules governing the proof of foreign law,[32] which previously treated foreign law as a question

[27] T Pfeiffer, 'Methoden der Ermittlung ausländischen Rechts' in R Stürner and others (eds), *Festschrift für Dieter Leipold zum 70. Geburtstag* (Mohr Siebeck, 2009), 291. Pfeiffer talks of *gegenseitiger Kontrolle* (or mutual control).

[28] CPR 35.12.

[29] For example, the rule that foreign materials lodged in the trial bundle are not admissible evidence, without expert evidence speaking to it, of the foreign law relied on in the choice of law context. *Bianco v Bennett* [2015] EWHC 626 (QB), [22].

[30] Although the US is a federal country, in this work reference is made almost exclusively to (1) its Federal Rules of Civil Procedure, and (2) the Restatement (Second) on the Conflict of Laws.

[31] The US Supreme Court recently commented in *Animal Science Products Inc v Hebei Welcome Pharmaceutical Co Ltd* (2018) 585 US ___ (Slip Opinion), 7: 'Federal Rule of Civil Procedure 44.1, adopted in 1966, fundamentally changed the mode of determining foreign law in federal courts.'

[32] AR Miller, 'Federal Rule 44.1 and the Fact Approach to Determining Foreign Law: Death Knell for a Die-Hard Doctrine' (1967) 65 *Michigan Law Review* 613, 638ff. This article was recently cited by the US Supreme Court in *Animal Science Products Inc v Hebei Welcome Pharmaceutical Co Ltd* (2018) 585

of fact.[33] These changes appear to have been driven, at least in part, by the erstwhile position that courts based in the various States of the US were being forced to prove the law of other States as facts, even though materials on these other States' laws were easily accessible and understandable.[34] Brown describes the fact approach in US procedure as having been 'inefficient, expensive, and highly constrictive.'[35] Under Rule 44.1 of the Federal Rules of Civil Procedure:

> A party who intends to raise an issue about a foreign country's law must give notice by a pleading or other writing. In determining foreign law, the court may consider any relevant material or source, including testimony, whether or not submitted by a party or admissible under the Federal Rules of Evidence. The court's determination must be treated as a ruling on a question of law.

In short, Rule 44.1 renders proof of the content of foreign law free from the normal rules of evidence,[36] with academic commentary suggesting that this approach has generally brought positive benefits to the process of proving foreign law in US courtrooms.[37] Certain implications would flow from this more flexible approach.[38] Parties would be permitted to lodge relevant materials in process, such as textbooks and cases. British courts would no longer refuse consideration of such materials merely because they have not been spoken to by an expert witness, ie the court could freely peruse any materials lodged.[39] Lawyers would be permitted to

US ___ (Slip Opinion), 7. MJ Wilson, 'Demystifying the Determination of Foreign Law in US Courts: Opening the Door to a Greater Global Understanding' (2011) 46 *Wake Forest Law Review* 887, 900ff; MJ Ahn, '44.1 Luftballons: The Communication Breakdown of Foreign Law in the Federal Courts' (2014) 89 *New York University Law Review* 1343, 1349ff.

[33] *Animal Science Products Inc v Hebei Welcome Pharmaceutical Co Ltd* (2018) 585 US ___ (Slip Opinion), 7.

[34] A Nussbaum, 'The Problem of Proving Foreign Law' (1941) 50 *Yale Law Journal* 1018, 1020.

[35] JR Brown, '44.1 Ways to Prove Foreign Law' (1984) 9 *Maritime Lawyer* 179, 181. See also the analysis of the US Supreme Court in *Animal Science Products Inc v Hebei Welcome Pharmaceutical Co Ltd* (2018) 585 US ___ (Slip Opinion), 8.

[36] Wilson, 'Demystifying the Determination of Foreign Law in US Courts' (n 32), 902, and by the same author, MJ Wilson, 'Improving the Process: Transnational Litigation and the Application of Private Foreign Law in US Courts' (2013) 45 *New York University Journal of International Law & Politics* 1111, 1122; Brown (n 35), 196: 'Rule 44.1 … has untied the hands of judges and has removed the blinders imposed by the somewhat xenophobic fact doctrine.'

[37] Although see for a detailed account of the difficulties that have arisen in practice: Ahn, '44.1 Luftballons' (n 32), 1363: 'courts have become confused about the scope of their authority and have read the rule more narrowly than intended.' US courts also seem to be highly reluctant to carry out independent research. See Brown (n 35), 182.

[38] There are some technical questions to consider; for example, whether the content of foreign law should still be laid out in the parties' pleadings or whether both notice of intention to seek the application of foreign law and notice of its specific content should be given separately to the pleadings, as is envisaged in US procedure. See Brown (n 35), 186. Fentiman has acknowledged the potential benefits of taking a more flexible approach to the proof of foreign law. See R Fentiman, 'Foreign Law in National Courts: A Common Law Perspective' in M Andenas and D Fairgrieve (eds), *Courts and Comparative Law* (Oxford University Press, 2015), 86.

[39] It is accepted that the procedural rules applicable in England and, to a lesser extent, Scotland, when proving foreign law are not quite as strict as they were in the US, when movement started taking place away from the fact approach. See, for an explanation of the then problem in the US, B Busch and

make submissions to the court based on documentary evidence alone. Whilst, in most cases, expert assistance would still be required to successfully determine the content of the *lex causae*, the actual mechanism by which it would be determined in individual cases would be a matter for consideration by individual judges at case management hearings. In a relatively small number of cases, ie where the Scottish court is applying English law and vice versa, it may be possible to avoid calling expert evidence altogether. Indeed, the current position is that, where foreign law is being applied through the conduit of a choice of law rule, dual-qualified lawyers are, in principle, not allowed to make submissions regarding English law in the Scottish courts, and vice versa, even though they may be eminently qualified to do so.[40] The revised approach would be more pragmatic than the current one by recognising, first, that rules for evidence of fact have no place in the context of foreign law, second, that some matters of foreign law are relatively straightforward, and, third, that in each case where foreign law is at issue, individual consideration ought to be given to how the content of the applicable foreign law can be proven efficiently and cost-effectively.[41]

In *FS Cairo (Nile Plaza) LLC* (2021), Lord Leggett appears to have taken a significant step in the direction of what is being suggested in this work when he noted that:

> The old notion that foreign legal materials can only ever be brought before the court as part of the evidence of an expert witness is outdated.[42]

He then went on to say:

> Whether the court will require evidence from an expert witness should depend on the nature of the issue and of the relevant foreign law. In an age when so much information

OC Sommerich, 'Expert Witness and the Proof of Foreign Law' (1952–1953) 38 *Cornell Law Quarterly* 125, 131 and Brown (n 35), 181.

[40] In practice, there is evidence that the requirement for (additional) expert evidence in such circumstances is not always followed. See *Re A (Children) (Adoption: Scottish Permanence Orders)* [2018] Fam 177, [35] and [38].

[41] See the critical analysis of the US Court of Appeals for the Seventh Circuit as regards the 'practice of trying to establish the meaning of a law of a foreign country by testimony or affidavits of expert witnesses, usually lawyers or law professors, often from the country in question' in *Bodum USA v La Cafetiere* 621 F 3d 624 (2010). At 633, Judge Posner comments: 'I cannot fathom why in dealing with the meaning of laws of English-speaking countries that share our legal origins judges should prefer paid affidavits and testimony to published materials.' With regard to the laws of non-English speaking countries, he comments: 'It is only a little less perverse for judges to rely on testimony to ascertain the law of a country whose official language is not English, at least if is a major country and has a modern legal system.' With regard to the fact that 'most judges' are monolingual, he argues: 'our linguistic provincialism does not excuse intellectual provincialism. It does not justify our judges in relying on paid witnesses to spoon feed them foreign law that can be found well explained in English-language treatises and articles. I do not criticize the district judge in this case, because he was following the common practice. But it is a bad practice, followed like so many legal practices out of habit rather than reflection. It is excusable only when the foreign law is the law of a country with such an obscure or poorly developed legal system that there are no secondary materials to which the judge could turn. The French legal system is obviously not of that character.'

[42] *FS Cairo (Nile Plaza) LLC v Lady Brownlie* [2021] UKSC 45 [148].

> is readily available through the internet, there may be no need to consult a foreign lawyer in order to find the text of a relevant foreign law. On some occasions the text may require skilled exegesis of a kind which only a lawyer expert in the foreign system of law can provide. But in other cases it may be sufficient to know what the text says.[43]

However, it is important to be precise as to what is being suggested, namely that foreign law requires specific treatment in procedural terms. In a 2006 article, when arguing that foreign law should potentially be subject to the concept of judicial notice, Fentiman suggested:

> To say that a court has judicial notice means that it has, or is deemed to have, knowledge of that matter … To say that a court has judicial notice of a matter does not merely refer to a court's actual or presumed knowledge. It means that the task of establishing that matter is within a court's province, and so does not depend upon rules of evidence.[44]

The idea that foreign law should be judicially noted by English courts has received support from the appeal courts:

> We may perhaps be permitted to add that we hope that the time may not be far off when it will be permissible for the English courts to take judicial notice of decisions of foreign courts, including those in the European Union, (and perhaps academic writings) in deciding what the relevant foreign law is in cases of this kind.[45]

The application of judicial notice to foreign law is also an approach that has been favoured in the United States.[46] The concept of judicial notice was previously considered in respect of imputed knowledge. It was identified as being a nebulous concept, which encompasses both questions of fact and domestic law.[47] While extending judicial notice to cover foreign law may prima facie appear to be a neat solution, ie bringing foreign law within existing, trusted concepts, the solution to improve the quality of the process underlying the investigation of the content of foreign law does not lie in the existing British concept of judicial notice. Although it is accepted that extending the scope of that concept to cover foreign law would be preferable to the current approach,[48] simply applying judicial notice to the

[43] *FS Cairo (Nile Plaza) LLC v Lady Brownlie* [2021] UKSC 45 [148]. In terms of the risk of materials going out of date, Lord Leggett noted that 'the presumption of continuity may be a more reliable foundation in the absence of contrary evidence than the presumption of similarity.'

[44] R Fentiman, 'Laws, Foreign Laws, and Facts' (2006) 59 *Current Legal Problems* 391, 402.

[45] *Morgan Grenfell & Co Limited v SACE – Istituto per i Servizi Assicurativi del Commercio* [2001] EWCA Civ 1932, [53].

[46] See, for an historical analysis of the somewhat piecemeal development of the application of judicial notice to foreign law in the US, Busch and Sommerich (n 39), 132ff and Nussbaum (n 34), 1020ff.

[47] See Chapter three at section II.B.(ii).

[48] There is existing precedent in the Hague Convention of 25 October 1980 on the Civil Aspects of International Child Abduction (Hague Child Abduction Convention) for this approach, which states at Art 14: 'In ascertaining whether there has been a wrongful removal or retention within the meaning of Article 3, the judicial or administrative authorities of the requested State may take notice directly of the law of, and of judicial or administrative decisions, formally recognised or not in the State of the habitual residence of the child, without recourse to the specific procedures for the proof of that law or for the recognition of foreign decisions which would otherwise be applicable.'

content of foreign law would be to impute knowledge of foreign law to the British judge that he cannot reasonably be expected to have to any meaningful extent.[49]

Where the parties make submissions regarding a point of domestic law, it can be assumed that the judge will understand the material, even if it may not be immediately familiar to him. Thus, he ought, at some stage, to have encountered the material, be it during academic study or in practice. His knowledge and understanding of the relevant point of domestic law is even likely to have been examined in an academic or professional context. The same cannot be said with regard to the content of foreign law. Extending judicial notice to encompass the content of foreign law would be failing to recognise the important distinction between domestic and foreign law, at least in so far as the difficulties involved in investigating and determining the content of the latter are concerned. The distinction is made clear when considering that experts are required in most cases to prove the content of foreign law. What is required is recognition that foreign law presents a unique procedural challenge warranting specific treatment.

There is clear precedent for a more flexible interaction with foreign law in the British courts. As discussed in Chapter one, while there is no doubt a difference between using foreign law as a source of comparison to improve domestic law, and applying foreign law as applicable law in the context of choice of law rules, it is not clear why the British courts have traditionally insisted on taking such radically different approaches to foreign law in each of these separate contexts.[50] On one hand, the British courts are extremely flexible in looking across jurisdictional borders to enhance domestic law. On the other, where the matter concerns the application of foreign law through the conduit of choice of law rules, the restrictions have traditionally been onerous, even somewhat parochial.[51]

[49] It is recognised that all foreign laws are not equal. Thus, a British judge will find it significantly easier to grasp concepts of US State law than of Thai law. In the US State of Maryland, judicial notice is applied to the 'common law and statutes of every state, territory, and other jurisdiction of the US, and of every other jurisdiction having a system of law based on the common law of England.' See Maryland Courts & Judicial Proceedings Code § 10-501 (2018). This rule appears to be of some vintage. See CT McCormick, 'Judicial Notice' (1952) 5 *Vanderbilt Law Review* 296, 307.

[50] M Wolff, *Private International Law*, 2nd edn (Clarendon Press, 1950), 220: 'The whole system of treating foreign law as if it were an extra-legal fact, in particular of not admitting judicial knowledge, would seem inconsistent with the court's frequent practice, when dealing with purely English law, of citing parallels from foreign laws, quoting American decisions, and basing its own decision on views expounded there.'

[51] The situation has given rise to confusion in Scotland. In *Roy v MR Pearlman Ltd* 1999 SC 459, 469, the defender resisted reference to French law by the court in its application of the Commercial Agents (Council Directive) Regulations 1993, which was said to be based on French law. The defender claimed that reference to French law would require expert evidence. Lord Hamilton rejected this approach and held: 'French law and practice is not being invoked because an issue in this court requires to be determined in accordance with French law but because, in the context of a directive which provides for a remedy drawn from French legal experience, assistance towards a harmonised approach may be obtained by having regard to the longer experience of the French courts in applying that remedy. That is more in the nature of a comparative law exercise, for the purposes of which a Scottish court is entitled to have direct regard to sources of foreign law.' The Inner House of the Court of Session recognised the difficulty which this state of affairs presents, in so far that it 'might be thought to be a paradoxical'

The focus so far has been practical, in so far that this work has sought to identify a means of enhancing the effectiveness of the investigative and determinative phases. But movement away from the fact approach in Great Britain would have the theoretical advantage of recognising that foreign law, which provides substantive rights, cannot be defined as a question of fact, even if evidence must be led to prove its terms. For example, whether the pursuer was hit by a car being driven by the defender at a particular speed at a particular time is clearly a question of fact, which can be proven by evidence. Thus, regardless of whether it can be proven, to the court's satisfaction, that a particular set of events took place, the fact is that the pursuer was driving a particular car at a particular speed at a particular time when it collided with the defender to his injury. However, such a past state of affairs does not exist in respect of questions of law.[52] Though the answer to some legal questions may be relatively clear cut, a good answer to a legal problem will often start with: it depends. Thereafter, an answer will follow backed up by argument and authority. Substantive foreign law is not 'a question of fact of a peculiar kind';[53] it simply is not fact at all.[54]

German procedural law recognises that foreign law is law,[55] but essentially law of a 'peculiar kind'. Thus, German procedural law does not treat foreign law as equivalent to domestic law.[56] Schack's analysis is correct in so far that foreign law is neither transformed into domestic law through choice of law rules, nor is it rendered fact.[57] If foreign law were the equivalent of German domestic law, the doctrine of *iura novit curia* would extend to the content of foreign law,[58] the Federal Court of Justice (BGH) would review determinations regarding the content of foreign law on appeal to that court,[59] and the costs of investigating the content of foreign law could not be passed onto the parties.[60] While the German judge may

situation, but then went on to reassert the principles of the fact approach in *McGowan v Summit at Lloyds* 2002 SC 638, 644.

[52] See the comments of Lord Robertson in *Scottish National Orchestra Society Ltd v Thomson's Executor* 1969 SLT 325, 333, when he was confronted with a controversial issue of Swedish law: 'It is difficult to come to a definite conclusion on the Swedish law applying to the situation. In a Scottish court it is a question of fact. But the questions at issue are theoretical, indeed hypothetical …'.

[53] *Parkasho v Singh* [1968] P 233, 250.

[54] Wolff (n 50), 217: 'What the court applies to the facts laid before it is "law", not mere fact. It is meaningless to say that a judge applies a "fact" to facts. Every judicial decision constitutes a syllogism; its major premise is a legal rule and cannot be anything else, its minor is a set of facts.'

[55] Otto considers this to be beyond question in the German literature and case law. G Otto, 'Der verunglückte § 293 ZPO und die Ermittlung ausländischen Rechts durch "Beweiserhebung"' (1995) *Praxis des Internationalen Privat- und Verfahrensrechts* 299, 301. The point was briefly considered, with further references, in the Introduction to this work. In is notable that the Federal Labour Court has recently reaffirmed this principle in the *Decision of the Federal Labour Court from 7 May 2020* (BAG, II. Senat) 2 AZR 692/19, NZA 2021, 225, 231: 'Ausländische Rechtsnormen sind Rechtssätze und keine Tatsachen.' ('Foreign laws are law and not facts.') [Translation by author].

[56] See also Wagner (n 2), 17, which argues that foreign law is treated by the German court as if it were fact.

[57] Schack (n 2), para 755.

[58] See Chapter three at section II.B.(ii).

[59] See Chapter three at section VI.C.

[60] See Chapter three at section IV.E.

attempt his own internal investigation, in many cases he is required to draw on external expert assistance.[61] Where he does so, the matter becomes essentially an evidential matter,[62] and, by extension, essentially a factual matter. In short, foreign law in Germany has and deserves its own category and treatment. While lawyers understandably prefer binary solutions, eg proven or not proven, fact or law, this should be recognised as a false dichotomy in this context.[63] Thus, foreign law will continue to present idiosyncratic difficulties which make it impossible to frame comfortably in terms of the usual concepts found in domestic law.

C. Specialist Courts

The allocation of disputes to the various courts of the relevant jurisdictions is generally a question determined solely by the monetary value of the case.[64] However, where foreign law is at issue in a case, the value of the dispute is not necessarily indicative of its complexity.[65] Moreover, regardless of which court hears the case, judges may, in practice, rarely be confronted with the difficulties involved in applying foreign law.[66] There is much to support the proposition that resolving cases requiring the application of foreign law should be considered a specialist area.[67]

The approach of appointing experts with specialist knowledge of private international law to the appeal court bench in certain States in Germany is welcome.[68]

[61] See Chapter three at section II.B.(iii).

[62] A Junker, *Internationales Privatrecht*, 4th edn (CH Beck, 2021), § 11 para 3. There is, nonetheless, a desire of some German writers to avoid using the terminology associated with evidence. See Schack (n 2), para 755.

[63] Schlesinger argues that § 293 of the German Code of Civil Procedure places the emphasis correctly in so far that it avoids the necessity to categorise foreign law into law or fact. Schlesinger considers the fundamental question to be: How can the necessary knowledge of foreign law be provided quickly and cheaply to the court, but still in a way that guarantees thorough and impartial results? RB Schlesinger, 'Die Behandlung des Fremdrechts im Amerikanischen Zivilprozess' (1962) 27 *Rabels Zeitschrift für Ausländisches und Internationales Privatrecht* 54, 71.

[64] In ordinary German civil proceedings, the local court (*Amtsgericht*) has exclusive jurisdiction to the extent of €5,000, see § 23 *Gerichtsverfassungsgesetz* (GVG). In England, proceedings should be started in the county court, unless the value of the case is more than £100,000, see CPR, Practice Direction 7A, a rule that is essentially mirrored in Scotland, see the Courts Reform (Scotland) Act 2014, s 39.

[65] This point assumes that the higher instance courts of the relevant jurisdictions, eg the Scottish Court of Session, are better equipped to deal with complicated cases.

[66] There is evidence from Germany that most lower and higher first instance courts seldom hear cases requiring the application of foreign law. M Stürner and F Krauß, *Ausländisches Recht in deutschen Zivilverfahren: Eine rechtstatsächliche Untersuchung* (Nomos, 2018), paras 173 and 336ff.

[67] For a sceptical viewpoint on creating specialist courts, see O Remien, 'Die Anwendung und Ermittlung ausländischen Rechts im System des Europäischen Internationalen Privatrechts' (2016) 115 *Zeitschrift für vergleichende Rechtswissenschaft* 570, 581. A more optimistic viewpoint can be found in Schack (n 2), para 764. For a thoughtful analysis of the benefits of specialist courts in general, see RA Posner, 'The Role of the Judge in the Twenty-First Century' (2006) 86 *Boston University Law Review* 1049.

[68] R Hüßtege, 'Zur Ermittlung ausländischen Rechts: Wie man in den Wald hineinruft, so hallt es auch zurück' (2002) *Praxis des Internationalen Privat- und Verfahrensrechts* 292, 294.

This appears to have been done in at least two instances, ie in the Stuttgart[69] and Munich Courts of Appeal.[70] This reflects the desirability for judicial specialism to deal effectively with matters of foreign law at the appeal level. However, thought must also be given to supporting first instance courts to deal with cases involving a foreign law dimension. Value must not be the only relevant factor. While there is some recognition in the relevant jurisdictions that cases involving international family law,[71] especially international child abduction,[72] constitute a specialist area, and should be dealt with by specialist first instance courts, it is unclear why such an approach could not be taken more widely in cases with an international dimension,[73] although it is accepted that, first, whether a case is sufficiently

[69] Faculty of Law of the University of Tübingen, 'Martin Gebauer zum Richter auf Lebenszeit am Oberlandesgericht Stuttgart ernannt', uni-tuebingen.de/einrichtungen/universitaetsbibliothek/home/newsfullview-home/article/martin-gebauer-zum-richter-auf-lebenszeit-am-oberlandesgericht-stuttgart-ernannt/#:~:text=Dr.er%20nun%20im%20Nebenamt%20verst%C3%A4rkt. According to the organisation of business of the Stuttgart Court of Appeal for the year 2022, Professor Gebauer sits in the fifth chamber of that court, which is responsible for appeals relating, inter alia, to legal disputes concerning obligations deriving from a law other than German law, obligations deriving from the CISG, and questions relating to the international jurisdiction of German courts: Oberlandesgericht Stuttgart, 'Geschäftsverteilungsplan für das Jahr 2022', oberlandesgericht-stuttgart.justiz-bw.de/pb/site/pbs-bw-rebrush-jum/get/documents_E-1009728032/jum1/JuM/OLG%20Stuttgart/GVP/GVP%202022%20-%20Stand%2001.03.2022.pdf.

[70] *Passauer Neue Presse*, 'Jura-Professor Wolfgang Hau ist Richter am Oberlandesgericht', www.pnp.de/lokales/stadt_und_landkreis_passau/passau_stadt/1928002_Jura-Professor-Wolfgang-Hau-ist-Richter-am-Oberlandesgericht.html. According to the organisation of business for the Munich Court of Appeal for the year 2022, Professor Hau-Faymonville sits in the twenty-fifth chamber of that court, which is responsible for appeals relating, inter alia, to legal disputes concerning the recognition and enforcement of international judgments: Oberlandesgericht München, 'Geschäftsverteilungsplan für das Jahr 2022', www.justiz.bayern.de/media/images/behoerden-und-gerichte/oberlandesgerichte/muenchen/gvp_2022.pdf.

[71] This has long been the case in Hamburg. See G Luther, 'Kollisions- und Fremdrechtsanwendung in der Gerichtspraxis' (1973) 37 *Rabels Zeitschrift für Ausländisches und Internationales Privatrecht* 660, 669ff. The organisation of business for the year 2022 for the Hamburg local courts specifically identifies two judges who are responsible for cases involving international child law. See Amtsgericht Hamburg, 'Geschäftsverteilungsplan für das Jahr 2022', justiz.hamburg.de/contentblob/4426938/792a3e7c0df580eb93f8abafcdeddf1a/data/hamburg-mitte.pdf, para 3.9.4.1.

[72] In Germany, only 22 of its 600 family courts have jurisdiction in these cases. See Bundesamt für Justiz, 'Zuständige deutsche Gerichte', www.bundesjustizamt.de/DE/Themen/Buergerdienste/HKUE/Gerichte/Gerichte_node.html.

In Scotland, these cases must be heard by the Court of Session in Edinburgh, whereas, in England, it is the High Court that has jurisdiction in these cases, see the Child Abduction and Custody Act 1985, s 4. There are no specialist British appeal courts for cases of child abduction. However, some appeal courts in Germany, for example, the Munich Court of Appeal, appear to have specialist chambers to hear such appeals. See Oberlandesgericht München (n 70), 56, in respect of the twelfth chamber of that court.

[73] It should be noted that there are examples of courts in the relevant jurisdictions regularly dealing with complicated, high-value litigation, often involving a foreign element, with the Commercial Court in London being a prime example. See HM Courts & Tribunals Service, 'Commercial Court', www.gov.uk/courts-tribunals/commercial-court. The recent introduction of Commercial Courts in the State of Baden-Württemberg is to be welcomed. There is a dedicated website setting out the advantages of using these courts, for example, that its judges can conduct proceedings in English and that its decisions are automatically recognised throughout the EU and Lugano Convention signatory states. See Der Commercial Court, 'The advantages of the Commercial Court', www.commercial-court.de/en/commercial-court.

complicated is not always clear, and, second, cases involving foreign law can cover numerous areas of law including employment, commercial, and succession. Moreover, the foreign connection in a case may be trivial or straightforward to resolve. Accordingly, even if more specialist courts were set up, it ought ultimately to be a question for the local judge to decide whether a case should be transferred there. Careful thought would have to be given to which judges would sit in these courts, based on their backgrounds and judicial experience. Such specialist courts could be given additional resources, eg an enhanced library provision, to deal with cases requiring the application of foreign law, rather than spreading precious resources more thinly throughout the jurisdiction.

II. Multilateral Reform

A. Aiding the Investigation of the Content of the *Lex Causae*

This work has discussed several ways that foreign law can be investigated in the relevant jurisdictions. It should be clear that there is potential to improve the effectiveness of the choice of law process by aiding parties and courts with their investigations. The following analysis briefly considers some mechanisms that could potentially achieve this at the multilateral level.

It should be noted that both the EU and the HCCH have invested time, with limited degrees of success, over the last two decades in attempting to deal with the difficulties faced by domestic courts in ascertaining the content of foreign law.[74] Unfortunately, it seems that no formal work has been done on the issue by the HCCH since its Council decided to remove the topic of accessing foreign law from its agenda in March 2015.[75] A joint conference[76] organised jointly by the European Commission and HCCH took place in February 2012. The conference unanimously reached several promising conclusions including highlighting the importance of the issue and stressing 'the need for, and the advantages of,

[74] An excellent analysis of the work done in this area by both the EU and the HCCH is to be found in MR Isidro, 'The Application of European Private International Law and the Ascertainment of Foreign law' in J von Hein, E-M Kieninger and G Rühl (eds), *How European is European Private International Law?* (Intersentia, 2019).

[75] See para 11 of HCCH, 'Council on General Affairs and Policy of the Conference (24–26 March 2015): Conclusions and Recommendations adopted by the Council' (2015), assets.hcch.net/upload/wop/gap2015concl_en.pdf. No documents have been uploaded to the relevant page since 2014. See HCCH, 'Access to Foreign Law', www.hcch.net/en/publications-and-studies/studies/access-to-foreign-law1.

[76] It seems particularly sensible that both the European Commission and the HCCH work jointly together in this area, not only because both the Rome I Regulation (n 7), Art 2, and Rome II Regulation (n 7), Art 3, provide that the applicable law under both regulations may or may not be the law of a Member State.

co-operative mechanisms to be developed at the global level to facilitate access to foreign law', and confirmed:

> that any global instrument in this field should focus on the facilitation of access to foreign law and should not attempt to harmonise the status of foreign law in national procedures.[77]

While the issue is recognised as being an important one, finding a solution has thus far proven elusive. One possibility is that judges should be able to draw on some form of multilateral database to more efficiently investigate the content of the *lex causae*.[78] Despite potential benefits in theory, such a database would be scarcely workable in practice, regardless of whether it were an initiative of the EU or the HCCH.[79] Who would be responsible for the task of creating and maintaining it? Would the database seek to provide answers to legal problems,[80] or would it simply provide access, without commentary, to legislation and cases? If so, at least in all the relevant jurisdictions, this need is already largely catered for,[81] and many other countries already provide publicly available information, sometimes with significant detail, on their legal systems, including with non-official translations.[82] If the database sought to provide detailed analysis, would it cover complicated

[77] European Commission and the HCCH, 'Access to Foreign Law in Civil and Commercial Matters: Conclusions and Recommendations' (2012), assets.hcch.net/docs/b093f152-a4b3-4530-949e-65c1bfc9cda1.pdf.

[78] This is implied in the argumentation of Marta Requejo Isidro in Isidro (n 74), 167. In advocating the involvement of the public sector in the creation of a database she writes: 'It would seem appropriate that the public institutions should be in charge of facilitating access to the applicable law for all those who engage in such transactions, assuming thereby the risks and costs of internationality.'

[79] As discussed previously, the EU's European Judicial Network already seeks to provide information on the domestic laws of EU Member States, but it is not yet nearly comprehensive enough to be relied on for professional purposes.

[80] The legal systems of Great Britain are covered by Practical Law, which describes itself as an 'online legal know how service. It provides rigorous peer-reviewed resources, such as practice notes, current awareness and standard documents to help you work smarter and advise with confidence.' This commercial website thus seeks to provide legal practitioners with solutions to legal problems in a far more targeted way than more academic sources. See What is Practical Law?, 'Practical Law', uk.practicallaw.thomsonreuters.com/Browse/Home/About/AboutUsAboutPracticalLaw?transitionType=Default&contextData=%28sc.Default%29.

[81] In Great Britain, see, for free access to case law, BAILII, 'British and Irish Legal Information Institute', www.bailii.org/, and for free access to legislation, The National Archives, 'legislation.gov.uk', www.legislation.gov.uk/. It should be noted that legislation.gov.uk is not always kept fully up to date and making reference to statutory instruments can be particularly difficult. In Germany, for free access to legislation (with some important legislation available in English), see Bundesministerium der Justiz und für Verbraucherschutz und das Bundesamt für Justiz, 'Gesetze im Internet', www.gesetze-im-internet.de/. It is said that decisions of the German Constitutional Court, the highest federal courts, as well as the federal patent courts, have been provided on the internet for free since 2010. See Bundesministerium der Justiz und für Verbraucherschutz und das Bundesamt für Justiz, 'Rechtsprechung im Internet', www.rechtsprechung-im-internet.de/jportal/portal/page/bsjrsprod.psml.

[82] See the HCCH, 'Accessing the Content of Foreign Law: Report of the Meeting of Experts on Global Co-operation on the Provision of Online Legal Information on National Laws (19–21 October 2008)' (2009), assets.hcch.net/docs/d9c58909-e39e-45b1-aa82-a9b13a00ad19.pdf. The report is over 10 years old and so the situation will have improved even further.

areas of law, and if so, would it properly reflect conflicting viewpoints? Would the database only be available in English, or would it also be available in several other languages? Would the database seek to supplant existing commercial electronic databases, eg beck-online[83] and Westlaw?[84] It is submitted that if such a database were created to aid the processes involved in applying foreign law, it would not be enough just to provide access to materials in electronic form, eg textbooks and cases, as, without experience in the given legal system, it is difficult to solve legal problems of any complexity. If the database sought to be all-encompassing, then it is unlikely that it would ever be complete, and even if it were, it would no doubt be a source of significant, ongoing controversy amongst lawyers, requiring to be constantly updated at significant cost. As Beaumont noted in the context of possible expansion by the EU of the European Judicial Network, most taxpayers might regard this as disproportionate to the potential benefits.[85] And even if such a database could be created and maintained, a justifiable scepticism would remain regarding its effectiveness for use in professional practice. Indeed, it is easy to forget how complex even domestic law can be, and the value that experience, both academic and professional, in a given legal system contributes to the ability to resolve legal problems arising in respect of it. In other words, it is likely that even if a database could be created and maintained, experts would still be required in many cases. This is not to suggest that encyclopaedias of law are not desirable academic exercises, with, for example, the Scottish *Stair Memorial Encyclopaedia*[86] being an excellent contribution to the field of jurisprudence in that jurisdiction.

It is submitted that much more effective sources of information on foreign law than any form of pan-European database are specialist practising and academic lawyers qualified in that legal system – both in terms of their knowledge and experience – failing which, a locally-based academic lawyer with specialist knowledge of the relevant legal system. It follows that a far more sensible approach than creation of any form of all-encompassing database would be to provide infrastructure for a swifter exchange of opinions between experts based in different legal jurisdictions.[87] Thus, rather than parties or courts being left to source experts themselves, requests for opinions could pass through central authorities, a mechanism which could operate in a similar way to requests made under the Hague

[83] Verlag CH BECK, 'beck-online', beck-online.beck.de/Home.

[84] Thomson Reuters, 'Westlaw UK', legalsolutions.thomsonreuters.co.uk/en/products-services/westlaw-uk.html.

[85] Beaumont, 'When should EU private international law require that foreign law be applied?' (n 6), 178.

[86] 'The Laws of Scotland: Stair Memorial Encyclopaedia', www.lexisnexis.co.uk/store/products/the-laws-of-scotland-stair-memorial-encyclopaedia-skuuksku9780406048493LSVMW29800/details. The *Stair Memorial Encyclopaedia* describes itself as 'the only comprehensive narrative statement of the law of Scotland.' As at 29 June 2020, it was retailing in paper form for £11,204.00, rendering its purchase potentially uneconomical for any foreign jurisdiction.

[87] This is essentially what was recommended by the HCCH in 2009. See HCCH, 'Accessing the content of foreign law and the need for the development of a global instrument in this area – A possible way ahead' (2009), assets.hcch.net/docs/ec2804c3-f55c-427d-9761-e0fa4eac41a7.pdf.

Child Abduction Convention.[88] The system would work most effectively if there were some legal aid provision available in the foreign state, as is the position under the Hague Child Abduction Convention.[89] Perhaps the most sensible criterion for whether legal aid should be granted in the foreign state is whether the party is eligible for legal aid in the domestic court, a matter that could be certified as part of the request.

While a system of coordinated referrals may be thought to offer questionable benefits in the internet age,[90] where it is possible to look up potential foreign lawyers to instruct very easily, there are numerous risks when sourcing experts abroad, including receiving a poor-quality service and being overcharged. On this basis, it is understandable why the Max Planck Institute for Comparative and International Private Law,[91] which offers a service in the court's language, is so popular in Germany.[92] The author of this work has already spent a relatively large amount of time in a relatively short career sourcing foreign experts. It is clearly very difficult, even with access to the internet, to find reliable experts in foreign jurisdictions charging a reasonable price. An important objective of any coordinated system of referrals would be to mitigate the risks of instructing experts based furth (outside) of the jurisdiction. A centrally organised system with a table of fees and a list of expert lawyers working to those rates could operate more transparently than picking names out of a directory. In Great Britain, there might be

[88] See for an excellent, albeit slightly outdated, account of the value of central authorities in the operation of the Hague Child Abduction Convention (n 48): CS Bruch, 'The Central Authority's Role under the Hague Child Abduction Convention: A Friend in Deed' (1994) 28 *Family Law Quarterly* 35.

[89] Bruch (n 88), 45.

[90] A cursory glance at Legal 500 ('The Legal 500', www.legal500.de/) or Chambers and Partners ('Chambers and Partners', chambers.com/), which cover many of the world's jurisdictions, can give a swift indication of who is considered an expert in their respective field.

[91] Max Planck Institute for Comparative and International Private Law, 'About Us', www.mpipriv.de/1040131/ueber-uns.

[92] While it is unquestionably well-respected, its work in producing opinions on foreign law has been questioned. For example, see K Arndt and G Kegel, 'Zur Verbesserung der Deutschen Zivilrechtsprechung in internationalen Sachen: Denkschrift vom 26 August 1970' (1971) 35 *Rabels Zeitschrift für Ausländisches und Internationales Privatrecht* 323, 326, where the author observed that the opinions are often drafted by junior staff, under limited supervision, and that the Institute suffers under the sheer volume of work sent to it. Although Remien observes that the volume of opinions produced has lessened in recent decades in Remien (n 67), 576, there is little to suggest that the overall pressure of work has significantly lessened, with the complexity of cases likely to have increased. Judges have reported waiting months for a response from the Institute. Stürner and Krauß (n 66), para 198. As previously stated, expert opinions produced by the Institute are regularly published, allowing for the quality of its work to be scrutinised. Fritz Sturm was notably critical of the some of the work produced. See, for example, F Sturm, 'Buchbesprechung: Gutachten zum internationalen und ausländischen Privatrecht 1977 bzw. 1978, veröff. im Auftrage des Deutschen Rates für IPR von Murad Ferid, Gerhard Kegel, Konrad Zweigert. Redaktion: Hilmar Krüger. Frankfurt a. M.: Metzner 1979 bzw. 1980 X, 434 S and X, 504 S' (1983) 47 *Rabels Zeitschrift für Ausländisches und Internationales Privatrecht* 386, 391ff, and F Sturm, 'Buchbesprechung: Gutachten zum internationalen und ausländischen Privatrecht. Veröffentlicht im Auftrag des Deutschen Rates für Internationales Privatrecht von Jürgen Basedow, Gerhard Kegel, Heinz-Peter Mansel. Redaktion 1999: Karsten Otte (2000/01: Christine Budzikiewicz) (Part II)' (2008) 72 *Rabels Zeitschrift für Ausländisches und Internationales Privatrecht* 831, 841ff.

an opportunity for sufficiently experienced junior counsel to gain experience of complex, cross-border cases by placing themselves on a list. Equally possible would be a competitive public tender with a small number of firms ultimately being passed the work through a central authority to manage. It might be that some lawyers would not seek membership of any list because they would not be prepared to work for the rates offered, but the prestige of being on the list, and the professional experience that would be gained from it would no doubt provide an incentive for many. A central database of foreign experts compiled and provided by each of the relevant jurisdictions for use primarily in that jurisdiction is another option,[93] although it would be better if reform were undertaken as a multilateral exercise. It is recognised that well-resourced parties, for example those commencing proceedings in the Commercial Court in London, may simply prefer to find and instruct their own experts. Such a system would be no bar to this.

Finally, there remains the possibility of providing a mechanism in order that the domestic court can refer a case to a foreign court for an opinion to be given.[94] There can be no better source of knowledge on foreign law than foreign courts,[95] with their opinions constituting the Rolls-Royce mechanism of investigating the content of foreign law. Such a procedure would have the benefit of providing rulings on discrete issues that could potentially be drawn on in future disputes, both by domestic and foreign courts. There is precedent for courts giving opinions that are not necessary to solve a pending case in that jurisdiction but are necessary or useful for ongoing cases in other jurisdictions,[96] or for cases that might arise in that jurisdiction in the future.[97] Such a mechanism would have the potential

[93] See Wilson, 'Demystifying the Determination of Foreign Law in US Courts' (n 32), 930.

[94] Contemporary examples involving New South Wales, New York, and Singapore were previously considered. See Chapter three, section II.B.(v). It should be noted that Regulation (EU) No 1215/2012 of the European Parliament and of the Council of 12 December 2012 on jurisdiction and the recognition and enforcement of judgment in civil and commercial matters (recast) [2012] OJ L 351/1 (Brussels I bis Regulation) provides, at Art 29(2), a limited mechanism allowing an EU Member State court seised of a dispute to request that any other EU Member State court also seised inform the former without delay of the date on which it was seised. There is an English–German example of the procedure working effectively in practice in respect of proceedings commenced before Brexit in *Jamieson v Wurttembergische Versicherung AG* [2021] EWHC 1111 (QB), where the English judge refused 'to question the reasoning that [lay] behind the response' of the German court. Fentiman, in a 2015 article, opposes a reference mechanism arguing: 'Here too, however, it is unlikely that such an approach offers a realistic solution, or a preferable alternative to resolving the matter before the court seised of the substantive dispute.' Fentiman, 'Foreign Law in National Courts' (n 38), 88. He later states, at 89, that such a mechanism is 'impractical'. See Wilson, 'Demystifying the Determination of Foreign Law in US Courts' (n 32), 915–16, for a much more enthusiastic viewpoint.

[95] Spigelman draws particular attention to those cases where discretion must be exercised, a discretion that is very difficult to replicate in a foreign jurisdiction. JJ Spigelman, 'Proof of foreign law by reference to the foreign court' (2011) 127 *LQR* 208, 214.

[96] See analysis of the case of *Westacre Investments Inc v The State-Owned Company Yugoimport SDPR* [2008] EWHC 801 (Comm) at Chapter three, section III.B.(iii).

[97] In the context of Scottish criminal law, under the Criminal Procedure (Scotland) Act 1995, s 123(1), where a person tried on indictment is acquitted or convicted of a charge, the Lord Advocate may refer a point of law which has arisen in relation to that charge to the High Court for its opinion. Under the Criminal Procedure (Scotland) Act 1995, s 123(5), the opinion on the point referred under subsection (1) above shall not affect the acquittal or, as the case may be, conviction in the trial.

to enhance legal certainty in cross-border cases, and to strengthen the relationship between the courts of different states. The mechanism could take the form of a preliminary reference system akin to that offered by the Court of Justice of the European Union (CJEU).[98] However, the risk is that busy national appeal courts could face a flurry of references from foreign courts, placing an excessive burden upon them. Considering that English law is often the law of choice in international contracts,[99] a preliminary reference system could burden courts in that jurisdiction disproportionately. Also potentially problematic would be where the foreign appeal court has misunderstood the facts of the case or takes an unacceptably long time to respond, both of which are liable to both undermine the efficient operation of any reference mechanism, and potentially damage relations between states. Careful thought would accordingly have to be given to the mechanism's implementation and restrictions.

B. Reducing the Need to Apply Foreign Law

It should follow from the analysis undertaken in this work that the investigation and determination of the content of foreign law is both time- and cost-intensive, with especially uncertain outcomes in complicated cases. Nonetheless, this work recognises the crucial importance of the principles highlighted by it in Chapter one, eg the principles of party autonomy and the closest connection, both of which can justify the application of foreign law through the conduit of choice of law rules.[100] However, the importance of such principles must be balanced against the economics of cases, and the value in the swift, effective administration of justice. Legal disputes do not take place in a vacuum, often being stressful and expensive for those involved. It is easy to forget that the parties, even in a purely domestic case, can quickly find themselves spending more in legal fees than the value of the dispute itself.[101] The overriding objective of the English Civil Procedure Rules, ie that cases ought to be dealt with justly and at proportionate cost,[102] is an excellent guiding principle.

The courts best placed to apply a law are the courts of that respective jurisdiction. It is absurd to suggest otherwise.[103] The drafters of any choice of law

[98] This model is favoured by Remien (n 67), 582.

[99] G Cuniberti, 'The International Market for Contracts: The Most Attractive Contract Laws' (2014) 34 *Northwestern Journal of International Law & Business* 455.

[100] See Chapter one at section II.D.

[101] There are many examples from the English courts. A particularly egregious example is provided by *J v J* [2015] 1 Costs LO 31, where costs in a seemingly straightforward matrimonial finance action reached £920,000. See also *M v M* [2020] EWFC 41, [98]: 'This self-defeating litigation is now over. It is scarcely credible that at the end of it all, they emerge with about £5,000 each of liquid assets, having incurred nearly £600,000 of costs, but such is the reality.'

[102] CPR, Part 1.

[103] Wagner accepts that the loss of quality of adjudication when a court applies foreign law cannot seriously be questioned. Wagner (n 2), 7–8.

instrument should ask themselves whether, considering the backdrop of the applicable jurisdiction rules,[104] the interests of justice are best served by a choice of law rule that is likely to require the application of a foreign law. This may militate against some of the existing rules and presumptions applicable in the absence of choice, such as those found in the Rome I and II Regulations[105] (eg that a contract for the sale of goods shall be governed by the law of the country where the seller has his habitual residence[106]) and operate in favour of choice of law rules leading to the application of the *lex fori* in the majority of cases, excepting those situations where the case is manifestly more closely connected with another law.[107] In other words, even if the choice of law rule does not theoretically lead, on balance, to quite as just an outcome in some cases, such an approach may nonetheless be more economical and certain at the substantive stage by reducing the need to investigate, determine, and apply foreign law. Any changes must be carefully considered against the potential risk of injustice and forum shopping, something that is more likely to be attempted in high-value litigation.

The difficulties involved in investigating the content of foreign law must be taken particularly seriously in low-value actions, where forum shopping is less likely to be attempted.[108] An insightful example of the complexity involved in the application of some private international law instruments, and their individual provisions, is Article 6(2) of the Rome I Regulation, which seeks to regulate choice of law in consumer contracts:

> Notwithstanding paragraph 1, the parties may choose the law applicable to a contract which fulfils the requirements of paragraph 1, in accordance with Article 3. Such a

[104] J Basedow, 'Kohärenz im Internationalen Privat- und Verfahrensrecht der Europäischen Union – Eine einleitende Orientierung' in J von Hein and G Rühl (eds), *Kohärenz im Internationalen Privat- und Verfahrensrecht der Europäischen Union* (Mohr Siebeck, 2016), 15. Basedow talks of the '*Gleichlauf*' (synchronisation) of jurisdiction and applicable law.

[105] Rome I Regulation (n 7) and Rome II Regulation (n 7). Basedow draws on the example of direct actions brought against foreign insurance firms, which are often brought in Germany in relation to accidents having taken place abroad. Basedow argues that foreign insurance firms often initially take a highly defensive attitude, requiring an exchange of expert opinions on foreign law in a case that is worth significantly less than the cost of investigating it. See Basedow (n 104), 17–18.

[106] Rome I Regulation (n 7), Art 4(1)(a). The problem is caused by the fact that, under the Brussels I bis Regulation (n 94), Art 7(1)(b), and *Car Trim GmbH v KeySafety Systems Srl*, Case C-381/08, [2010] ECR I-1255, the courts of the Member State where the goods have reached their final destination have jurisdiction, in addition to the courts of the defender's habitual residence. Where the buyer seeks to sue the seller, they may raise their action either in their state or in the state of the seller's domicile. However, in either case, the law applicable is the law of the seller's habitual residence, under the Rome I Regulation (n 7), Art 4(1)(a). It is accepted that the CJEU's interpretation of Art 7 may not have been anticipated by its drafters.

[107] Such 'exceptionality' provisions are well-known in the EU choice of law regulations, for example Rome I Regulation (n 7), Art 4(3): 'Where it is clear from all the circumstances of the case that the contract is manifestly more closely connected with a country other than that indicated in paragraphs 1 or 2, the law of that other country shall apply.'

[108] The possibility for consumers to sue at the seller's domicile, for example, under Brussels I bis Regulation (n 94), Art 4, should not be forgotten. The possibility for forum shopping therefore also exists in such cases.

> choice may not, however, have the result of depriving the consumer of the protection afforded to him by provisions that cannot be derogated from by agreement by virtue of the law which, in the absence of choice, would have been applicable on the basis of paragraph 1.

The effect of Article 6(2) of the Rome I Regulation is, in principle, generous and favourable to the consumer. Where there is a choice of law in favour of a law that is not the law of the consumer's habitual residence, the consumer benefits from the most favourable mandatory provisions of the two. Thus, where an Amazon purchase is at issue,[109] courts in the relevant jurisdictions are required to afford more protection to the consumer than would otherwise be the case if the applicable law were simply decided by the consumer's place of residence.[110] However, while the wording of Article 6(2) of the Rome I Regulation is undoubtedly a masterpiece of legal drafting, it is unintelligible to the average consumer, and is difficult for the court to apply effectively in the majority of cases. The laws of Luxembourg appear only to be publicly available in the French language.[111] Thus, to determine the law of Luxembourg, a Scottish sheriff would require, as a minimum, a translation of the applicable provisions of that legal system, and an expert opinion explaining their operation in practice. The sheriff would then be required to apply his mind to the question of which law is more favourable to the consumer, and whether the relevant provisions may not be derogated from. With many consumer disputes being of low value,[112] and with parties often representing themselves,[113] it is questionable what is really gained by requiring such a complicated exercise to be undertaken.

It is unacceptable for legislators to provide rules that are essentially unworkable in practice. Choice of law rules should be effective, understandable, and serve the interests of justice. When all factors are taken into consideration, the best option in consumer cases is to apply the *lex fori*, failing which, the law of the consumer's habitual residence, as the substantive law.[114] As a rule, there should only be

[109] Amazon's terms and conditions state a choice of law in favour of laws of the Grand Duchy of Luxembourg. See 'Conditions of Use & Sale for Amazon UK', www.amazon.co.uk/gp/help/customer/display.html/ref=footer_cou?ie=UTF8&nodeId=201909000, and the German language equivalent for Amazon DE, 'Amazon.DE Allgemeine Geschäftsbedingungen', www.amazon.de/gp/help/customer/display.html?ie=UTF8&nodeId=201909000&ref_=footer_cou.

[110] See PR Beaumont and PE McEleavy, *Anton's Private International Law*, 3rd edn (W Green, 2011), para 10.332. It appears that a small number of Member States were concerned that cross-border commerce would be impaired by a mandatory *lex fori* provision in consumer contracts, in so far that sellers would have to deal with the different substantive contract laws of the Member States.

[111] Le Gouvernment du Grand-Duché de Luxembourg, 'Journal officiel du Grand-Duché de Luxembourg', legilux.public.lu/.

[112] Department for Business, Energy & Industrial Strategy, 'Resolving Consumer Disputes: Alternative Dispute Resolution and the Court System' (2018), assets.publishing.service.gov.uk/government/uploads/system/uploads/attachment_data/file/698442/Final_report_-_Resolving_consumer_disputes.pdf, 54.

[113] P Lewis, 'Litigants in person and their difficulties in adducing evidence: a study of small claims in an English county court' (2007) 11 *International Journal of Evidence & Proof* 24.

[114] The application of the law of the consumer's habitual residence is essentially the approach taken by Swiss law, although subject to conditions, eg that an offer or advertisement must have been directed to the state of the consumer's habitual residence. See Art 120 of the Swiss Federal Law on Private

a disconnect between the court and the substantive applicable law where there is compelling justification. This justification is absent in most consumer cases.

The European legislator appears to have recognised the difficulties involved in investigating and determining the content of foreign law, and has taken welcome steps in recent instruments to reduce the number of situations where foreign law must be applied through choice of law rules.[115] There is evidence that the rules of the Rome III Regulation,[116] regulating, inter alia, choice of law in divorce, have significantly reduced the number of situations where foreign law must be applied in German court proceedings.[117] Moreover, the EU Succession Regulation[118] specifically states, as an objective of the instrument, that:

> The rules of this Regulation are devised so as to ensure that the authority dealing with the succession will, in most situations, be applying its own law.[119]

Finally, while it is recognised that courts in all of the relevant jurisdictions are capable of applying foreign law to resolve disputes, it is unfortunate that European jurisdictional rules,[120] together with the jurisprudence of the Court of Justice of the European Union (CJEU), have rejected any residual role for the doctrine of *forum non conveniens*.[121] The doctrine of *forum non conveniens*, which finds

International Law of 18 December 1987, as at 1 January 2022 (Bundesgesetz über das Internationale Privatrecht vom 18 Dezember 1987, Fassung vom 01.01.2022), www.admin.ch/opc/de/classified-compilation/19870312/index.html. It should be noted that the Swiss approach can lead to the application of a foreign law. If a mandatory *lex fori* approach is taken, the jurisdiction rules should be such that businesses cannot be sued by consumers who they never, objectively speaking, could have envisaged trading with. See the Brussels I bis Regulation (n 94), Art 17, which seeks to achieve this aim.

[115] Basedow argues that steps were already taken in the drafting of the Rome I Regulation (n 7), although it appears that efforts have intensified in more recent instruments. Basedow (n 104), 16.

[116] Council Regulation (EU) No 1259/2010 of 20 December 2010 implementing enhanced cooperation in the area of the law applicable to divorce and legal separation [2010] OJ L 343/10 (Rome III Regulation). This instrument was not adopted by the UK.

[117] Stürner and Krauß (n 66), para 283ff.

[118] Regulation (EU) No 650/2012 of 4 July 2012 on jurisdiction, applicable law, recognition and enforcement of decisions and acceptance and enforcement of authentic instruments in matters of succession and on the creation of a European Certificate of Succession [2012] OJ L 201/107 (EU Succession Regulation). This instrument was not adopted by the UK.

[119] Rome III Regulation (n 116), Recital (27).

[120] The possibility of modifying the Brussels Convention of 1968 was considered in 1978 when the UK acceded to the European Community, but this was rejected on the grounds, first, that *forum non conveniens* was unknown in continental European jurisprudence, and, second, that the need for the doctrine in British procedural law would be lessened because of a reduction in the scope of application of the existing British exorbitant jurisdiction rules, eg jurisdiction based on service of a writ. The German author of the report on the matter succinctly summarised the purpose of the doctrine of *forum non conveniens*: 'Exceptionally, the courts may refuse to hear or decide a case, if they believe it would be better for the case to be heard before a court having equivalent jurisdiction in another State (or another judicial area) because this would increase the likelihood of an efficient and impartial hearing of the particular case.' P Schlosser, 'Report on the Convention of 9 October 1978 on the Association of the Kingdom of Denmark, Ireland and the United Kingdom of Great Britain and Northern Ireland to the Convention on jurisdiction and the enforcement of judgments in civil and commercial matters and to the Protocol on its interpretation by the Court of Justice' (1978), eur-lex.europa.eu/legal-content/EN/TXT/PDF/?uri=OJ:C:1979:059:FULL&from=en, paras 76–78.

[121] See *Owusu v Jackson* C-281/02, [2005] ECR I-1383, which is considered to be a controversial decision. See Beaumont and McEleavy (n 110), para 8.401. But see below in respect of Council Regulation

its origins in Scottish case law,[122] and has an established tradition in British jurisprudence,[123] allows a court to sist (stay) an action on the basis that another court is more appropriate to hear the dispute. In respect of its potential application in cases where foreign law is applicable, it has been argued:

> This in turn may point to the real truth, that a court should have the power to decline to hear certain cases if it is persuaded that a court elsewhere would be better placed to give the parties the adjudication they deserve.[124]

To give one example of a case where the doctrine of *forum non conveniens* was applied, in *Société du Gaz de Paris* (1925) it was noted by the Lord Justice Clerk:

> It will be the duty of the Sheriff-substitute to apply the law of France to the case. But then it must not be forgotten that the parties are at issue regarding that law. Is it to be said that the Sheriff-substitute must proceed, after, I suppose, hearing the evidence of French barristers *hinc inde*, to decide this purely Gallic controversy? I should think there can be no dissent from the view that such a result would be subversive of convenience, comity, and, I had almost added, common sense.[125]

The question is whether the European legislator[126] should allow the doctrine, or a form of it, to be applied in exceptional cases,[127] where it is obvious at an early stage of proceedings that the case involves a complex and controversial issue of foreign law,[128] which will, inter alia, require extensive expert evidence to resolve. Though

(EC) No 2201/2003 of 27 November 2003 concerning jurisdiction and the recognition and enforcement of judgments in matrimonial matters and the matters of parental responsibility [2003] OJ L 338/1 (Brussels II bis Regulation), Art 15.

[122] One of the earliest references to the doctrine appears to have been made by the Scottish court in *Longworth v Hope* (1865) 3 M 1049, 1053. In *Sim v Robinow* (1892) 19 R 665, 670, Lord M'Laren recognised that the complexities of proving the content of a foreign law could justify the invocation of the doctrine.

[123] The doctrine essentially crystallised in English procedure in the case of *Spiliada Maritime Corp v Cansulex Ltd (The Spiliada)* [1987] AC 460, especially 476ff, which drew 'in particular' on the existing Scottish authorities.

[124] A Briggs, *The Conflict of Laws*, 2nd edn (Oxford University Press, 2008), 7. The point is also made, albeit perhaps a little less succinctly, in the most recent edition of Briggs' text. See Briggs, *The Conflict of Laws* (n 8), 11.

[125] *Société du Gaz de Paris v Armateurs français* 1925 SC 332, 349.

[126] It may be that the UK will remain permanently outwith the European jurisdictional apparatus after Brexit, but there remains the possibility of the Lugano Convention being adopted in the future. See M Sonnentag, *Die Konsequenzen des Brexits für das Internationale Privat- und Zivilverfahrensrecht* (Mohr Siebeck, 2017), 85ff. If so, the *Owusu v Jackson*, C-281/02, [2005] ECR I-1383 jurisprudence would apply to prevent *forum non conveniens* being applied in most cases. See JJ Fawcett and P Torremans (eds), *Cheshire, North & Fawcett: Private International Law*, 15th edn (Oxford University Press, 2017), 460ff. In any case, the question remains of interest for Germany, and other Member States, as it does for the UK considering whether to reform its domestic law.

[127] For a writer who is strongly opposed, see Schack (n 2), para 610ff. The author argues, inter alia, that *forum non conveniens* abrogates the responsibility of courts to apply choice of law rules, which, as discussed, is a clear responsibility of courts under German procedural law. Moreover, at para 614, he criticises the idea of using *forum non conveniens* to achieve synchronisation (*Gleichlauf*) between the court hearing the case and the applicable law, citing the interest that claimants have, as judgments are not enforceable in all jurisdictions, in having the option of various forums to raise their claims.

[128] Many difficult and complicated cases will involve both domestic and foreign law. *Forum non conveniens* would carry the risk, which must be acknowledged, of difficult cases being transferred

the difficulties involved in investigating and determining the content of foreign law are by no means insurmountable, even in complex cases,[129] and have not always justified the application of *forum non conveniens*,[130] the consequences where difficult and controversial issues of foreign law arise in proceedings, potentially requiring multiple expert witnesses,[131] with no guarantee of a certain determination, means that some form of *forum non conveniens* in European jurisdictional rules warrants consideration. This all must, of course, be weighed up against justified concerns that the doctrine of *forum non conveniens* can create uncertainty, cause injustice, and increase costs, where its potential application is disputed,[132] with the doctrine even potentially leading to a denial of justice in cases.[133] While the risks may simply be judged as being too great, some concerns can potentially be addressed. First, the threshold for the application of the doctrine, or a form of it, ought to be a high one, and higher than the threshold previously applied under the

elsewhere, only for the foreign court to be faced with the same difficulties of investigation and determination of foreign law, though in reverse, ie in respect of the law of the court from which the transfer came.

[129] The Scottish appeal court was recently broadly dismissive of the difficulties involved. See *Ted Jacob Engineering Group Inc v Morrison* 2019 SC 487, 493–94: 'It is not difficult for a Scots lawyer to understand the legal concepts and rules of another civilian system. Expert evidence is obviously important in directing the court to the existing state of the law, and in particular any relevant case law. Interpreting the law, however, and most importantly determining how the law applies to a particular factual situation, are not matters that a Scottish court should find difficult.'

[130] In *Credit Chimique v James Scott Engineering Group Ltd* 1979 SC 406, 414–15, the plea was sustained partly on the basis that the case would require complex consideration of French law, which was also the case in *Société du Gaz de Paris v Armateurs français* 1925 SC 332. However, in *Parken v Royal Exchange Assurance Co* (1846) 8 D 365, 371, the court was firmly of the view that it could establish the content of English law without difficulty.

[131] See *Scottish National Orchestra Society Ltd v Thomson's Executor* 1969 SLT 325. In that case, four experts on Swedish law were required. A particularly striking example of the complexity that can be involved in proving foreign law is *Macmillan Inc v Bishopsgate Investment Trust Plc (No 3)* [1995] 1 WLR 978, during which 12 experts gave evidence on foreign law, all of whom were cross-examined at length. See 1013ff of the judgment.

[132] Fentiman's concern that *forum non conveniens* could lead to 'lengthy, costly and unsatisfactory' interlocutory hearings is justified. Fentiman, 'Foreign Law in National Courts' (n 38), 89.

[133] The classic example of the injustice that can be caused by the doctrine of *forum non conveniens* is the case of *Piper Aircraft Co v Reyno* 454 US 235, 102 S Ct 252 (1981). In the case, the US Supreme Court ruled the US courts *forum non conveniens* in relation to an action brought against the US manufacturer of a plane that crashed in Scotland. For a particularly critical view of the doctrine of *forum non conveniens*, as applied in this case, see Schack (n 2), para 612. Its application by US judges to 'dismiss difficult and time-consuming cases' on the basis of 'vague and amorphous' factors demonstrates the potential dangers of the doctrine. DW Robertson, 'Federal Doctrine of Forum Non Conveniens: "An Object Lesson in Uncontrolled Discretion"' (1994) 29 *Texas International Law Journal* 353, 358–59. It is argued elsewhere in the article, at 354, 'I have found the federal doctrine of forum non conveniens to be a serious mess ever since I came to understand it', and, at 358: 'It is worth noting that forum non conveniens seems to be the only area of the law in which it is considered legitimate for a court to base a decision on the condition of its docket.' Wilson attributes the difficulties in ascertaining foreign law to the increase in the application of *forum non conveniens* to cases: 'Accordingly, courts are increasingly receptive to motions to dismiss based on forum non conveniens grounds when dealing with international cases that involve foreign law.' Wilson, 'Demystifying the Determination of Foreign Law in US Courts' (n 32), 898.

common law doctrine.[134] Second, it should only be possible to apply the doctrine where another court has jurisdiction, and has indicated a willingness to hear the case.[135]

A form of what is being proposed here is found in Articles 8 and 9 of the 1996 Hague Convention,[136] as well as Article 15 of the Brussels II bis Regulation,[137] with the latter being modelled on the former[138] and both drawing on the principles underlying the doctrine of *forum non conveniens*,[139] in so far that the instruments

[134] The threshold which has traditionally been attributed to *forum non conveniens* is that as was set out by Lord Kinnear in *Sim v Robinow* (1892) 19 R 665, 668: 'And therefore the plea can never be sustained unless the Court is satisfied that there is some other tribunal, having competent jurisdiction, in which the case may be tried more suitably for the interests of all the parties and for the ends of justice.' The common law threshold has been described as requiring a clearly or distinctly more appropriate forum, with a mere balance of convenience in favour of the foreign forum being insufficient. See Fawcett and Torremans (eds) (n 126), 397.

[135] It must be ensured that litigants' rights under Article 6 of the European Convention of Human Rights are not denied. See Fawcett and Torremans (eds) (n 126), 395.

[136] Convention of 19 October 1996 on Jurisdiction, Applicable Law, Recognition, Enforcement and Co-operation in Respect of Parental Responsibility and Measures for the Protection of Children (1996 Hague Convention).

[137] It should be noted that the Brussels II bis Regulation (n 121) is being replaced by Council Regulation (EU) 2019/1111 of 25 June 2019 on jurisdiction, the recognition and enforcement of decisions in matrimonial matters and the matters of parental responsibility, and on international child abduction. The relevant provisions of the new instrument are to be found in Arts 12 and 13. There are some differences, for example, in so far that an EU Member State court without jurisdiction can request a transfer under Art 13, and Art 12(1) of the new instrument requires 'exceptional circumstances' for the provision to be engaged, whereas Art 15(1) of Brussels II bis Regulation (n 121) is more loosely worded in so far that it applies 'by way of exception'. A relevant change from the point of view of the UK is that, under Art 97(2)(b) of the new instrument, a case may now be transferred from an EU Member State to a UK court under the 1996 Hague Convention (n 136), ie Arts 8 and 9 of the 1996 Hague Convention shall apply, whereas this is not possible under the current Brussels II bis Regulation (n 121). See PR Beaumont, L Walker and J Holliday, 'Parental Responsibility and International Child Abduction in the proposed recast of Brussels IIa Regulation and the effect of Brexit on future child abduction proceedings' (2016) *CPIL Working Paper* No 2016/6, www.abdn.ac.uk/law/documents/CPIL_Working_Paper_No_2016_6_revised.pdf, although the relevant article numbers have changed somewhat since this paper was published.

[138] PR Beaumont, 'Private international law concerning children in the UK after Brexit: comparing Hague Treaty law with EU Regulations' *CPIL Working Paper No 2017/2*, www.abdn.ac.uk/law/documents/CPIL%20Working%20Paper%20No%202017_2.pdf 5.

[139] See para 52 of P Legarde, 'Explanatory Report on the Convention of 19 October 1996 on Jurisdiction, Applicable Law, Recognition, Enforcement and Co-operation in Respect of Parental Responsibility and Measures for the Protection of Children' (1996), assets.hcch.net/upload/expl34.pdf: 'These Articles introduce into the Convention a reversible mechanism for *forum non conveniens* and *forum conveniens*, where it appears that the child's best interest is that his or her protection be ensured by authorities other than those of the State of the habitual residence.' See detailed discussion in Beaumont, 'Private international law concerning children in the UK after Brexit' (n 138), who respectfully suggests revised wording: 'These Articles introduce into the Convention a reversible mechanism for *forum non conveniens* and *forum conveniens*, where it appears that authorities other than those of the State of the habitual residence are better placed to determine what measures of protection are needed in the child's best interests.' See comments in respect of Art 15 of the Brussels II bis Regulation (n 121) in *Re EC (A Child)* [2006] EWCA Civ 1115, [18]: 'That is an import into the regulation of the forum conveniens concept, which has more resonance for common law jurisdictions than for civil law States. It is a provision negotiated for the comfort of those jurisdictions who have reservations about the introduction of a strict lis alibi pendens rule into family litigation.'

allow the transfer of a case to the authorities of a country better placed to determine what measures of protection are needed in the child's best interests. In terms of Article 15 of the Brussels II bis Regulation, there has been recognition from the English courts of the dangers inherent to a discretionary system of transfer,[140] with examples both of cases being transferred[141] and refusals to transfer.[142] There is evidence that English courts have sought to approach the provision in the proper spirit:

> The construction of article 15 must be uniform throughout the courts of the member states. It cannot be dominated by a domestic law approach in cases brought under the domestic jurisdiction, whether it be statutory or inherent.[143]

In *Re M and L* (2016),[144] Mr Justice Baker considered an application to seek transfer of a case from Norway to England under Article 9 of the 1996 Hague Convention, which he considered to be the first case of its kind in England. In determining which court would be better placed to assess the child's best interests, he carefully weighed up the various factors involved in deciding whether to seek to transfer, considering that:

> the English and Norwegian courts are equally competent in general terms to determine issues about children. Each court operates in a sophisticated and advanced legal system manned by experienced judges who are manifestly capable of making decisions in this type of case. Although there are some differences in the respective processes, and each court has advantages which the other does not, overall there is no substantial difference. Comparisons are odious.[145]

More British case law in respect of the relevant provisions of the 1996 Hague Convention will no doubt follow in the next few years, particularly as the number of cases rise in the wake of Brexit, although it can be expected that a similar approach will be taken to Articles 8 and 9 of the 1996 Hague Convention as has been taken to Article 15 of the Brussels II bis Regulation.[146]

[140] *Re M (A Child)* [2014] EWCA Civ 152, [54]: 'Article 15 contemplates a relatively simple and straightforward process. Unnecessary satellite litigation in such cases is a great evil. Proper regard for the requirements of B2R and a proper adherence to the essential philosophy underlying it, requires an appropriately summary process.'

[141] *FE v MR* [2017] EWHC 2298 (Fam).

[142] *Re S (A Child)* [2018] EWHC 3054 (Fam).

[143] *Re T (A Child) (Care Proceedings: Request to Assume Jurisdiction)* [2013] EWCA Civ 895, [19]. The point is echoed by a further judge at [30].

[144] *Re M and L* [2016] EWHC 2535 (Fam).

[145] *Re M and L* [2016] EWHC 2535 (Fam) [33]. He noted favourably Mr Justice Mostyn's comment in *Re T (A Child) (Care Proceedings: Request to Assume Jurisdiction)* [2013] EWHC 521 (Fam) [37]: 'The analysis of best interests only goes to inform the question of forum and should not descend to some kind of divisive value judgement about the laws and procedures of our European neighbours.'

[146] See *Re D (Care Proceedings: 1996 Hague Convention: Article 9 Request)* [2021] EWHC 1970 (Fam), although that case involved Switzerland and would have been decided under the 1996 Hague Convention (n 136) regardless of Brexit. The court approvingly, at [41], cited the CJEU case of *Child and Family Agency v D*, C-428/15, [2017] 2 WLR 949, which considered the approach to be taken to Art 15 of the Brussels II bis Regulation.

It is submitted that the practice of the English courts in respect of both Articles 8 and 9 of the 1996 Hague Convention, as well as Article 15 of the Brussels II bis Regulation, ought to alleviate concerns that cases will be transferred inappropriately by legal systems which have traditionally been receptive to discretionary stays. Indeed, if courts can be trusted to issue judgments that cannot be subject to substantive review in other states, eg under the Brussels / Lugano regime[147] or under relevant Hague instruments,[148] courts ought to be trusted to determine whether they are, in fact, the best forum for the resolution of a dispute. It seems unlikely that courts will naturally be keen to relinquish jurisdiction in most cases, but where courts voluntarily choose to do so, the hope is that the case can then be resolved by a court better placed to adjudicate the dispute, eg a court applying its own substantive law.

[147] See, for example, the Convention on jurisdiction and the recognition and enforcement of judgments in civil and commercial matters of 21 December 2007 [2007] OJ L 339 (Lugano Convention), Art 36: 'Under no circumstances may a foreign judgment be reviewed as to its substance.'

[148] See, for example, the 1996 Hague Convention (n 136), Art 27: 'Without prejudice to such review as is necessary in the application of the preceding Articles, there shall be no review of the merits of the measure taken.'

Summary and Primary Conclusions

In the first chapter of this work, the application of foreign law by means of choice of law rules was distinguished from the use of foreign law as a means of comparison, and the scene was set for the subsequent substantive discussion. The importance of the delimitation between substance and procedure was highlighted, with a discussion then following regarding the transformation of the applicable choice of law rules in the relevant jurisdictions and the impact of Brexit. Thereafter, five prerequisites were identified for the application of foreign law through the conduit of choice of law rules. First, a foreign element in the factual matrix of the case is required. Second, the domestic court must be willing to apply foreign law. Third, there must exist a general norm compelling the court to apply domestic law, as opposed to any other law. Fourth, there must exist a relevant choice of law rule, which provides the conduit through which foreign law is applied by the court. Fifth, there must be a mechanism to facilitate the investigation and determination of the content of the *lex causae*. It is with the fifth point that this work is most concerned.

In the historical chapter of this work (Chapter two), the origins of the current approach taken towards foreign law in each of the relevant jurisdictions were identified, as well as how foreign law was investigated in the early cases. The fact approach mainly developed in Scotland during the seventeenth century through a combination of case law and the contribution of the Scottish institutional writer Stair. There is evidence that Scottish practice then influenced, especially through Lord Mansfield, the later development of the fact approach in England during the eighteenth century. In terms of how foreign law was proven in Scottish courts during the seventeenth century, the preference appears to have been remits to foreign judges for them to give a ruling on their law, with preference subsequently shifting in favour of remits to foreign lawyers during the eighteenth century. In England, there was initial preference in favour of authenticated, written foreign law, if available, with less emphasis on expert witness evidence, though practice developed in favour of requiring expert witness evidence in all cases during the mid-nineteenth century. In terms of the procedural law of the pre-unification German States, it was shown that legislative, judicial, and academic sources demonstrate a tendency towards treating foreign law as fact in the late eighteenth and early nineteenth centuries. The current approach, under § 293 of the Code of Civil Procedure, developed during the nineteenth century. There is limited evidence of how foreign law was investigated by eighteenth- and nineteenth-century German courts.

Today, the German judge has an obligation to introduce and effectively apply choice of law rules *ex proprio motu*. Choice of law rules can only be left out of account by the German court in limited circumstances. In the British courts, the introduction of choice of law rules is essentially voluntary, with the court having no obligation to introduce and apply choice of law rules where the parties do not rely on an applicable rule of foreign law, and indeed the court should refrain from doing so in such circumstances. It appears that foreign illegality and the sphere of criminal law are the only areas where it can be said that the voluntary approach is inapplicable, although the role of the King's (or Queen's) Proctor in England in cases involving status should not be ignored. The voluntary approach is potentially questionable in undefended cases with doubtful jurisdiction, and, in Scotland, where prescription is in play.

The objective of courts in the relevant jurisdictions is to apply foreign law as the foreign court would. To achieve this objective, the German court has an onerous duty to investigate the content of foreign law, a duty which can likely only be fulfilled in most cases through the instruction of an expert opinion. Such an investigative duty is unknown in the British courts.

To investigate the content of foreign law, there are only limited mechanisms available to courts in the relevant jurisdictions, other than expert opinions and, in Germany, independent research by the court. The London Convention has been ratified by both Germany and the UK. Although German courts occasionally avail themselves of its terms, there is authority that any answer provided by a foreign authority is often considered insufficient on its own. The British courts do not, and probably cannot, make requests under the London Convention as there is regrettably no mechanism available in either English or Scottish procedural law facilitating them. The database provided by the European Judicial Network is insufficient on its own for any serious investigation. The British Law Ascertainment Act 1859, which provided a reference procedure, was, in practice, only ever used amongst the Scottish and English courts. It is no longer good law and ought to be repealed. The procedure that allowed remit of a case by a Scottish court to a foreign lawyer is also defunct, and ought to be recognised in the literature as being so.

When determining the content of foreign law, the fact approach creates fundamental tension for the British court, as between the objective of the court to apply foreign law as the foreign court would and the restrictions imposed by the law of evidence. In other words, British judges should be careful not to stray too far from the expert witness evidence when reaching their determinations, which hinders their ability to meet the stated objective, especially if the expert evidence is of poor quality. German judges have significantly more flexibility when reaching their determinations. They are not bound by the parties' or experts' evidence and have a duty to look beyond it.

Parties in British civil proceedings have responsibility for introducing foreign law as an issue, managing the investigation of its content, and leading evidence on it through experts, though, in most cases, they may decide whether they wish to avail themselves of the opportunity of doing so. Parties in German civil proceedings do not have a comparable role, though the German court must take account of any relevant evidence produced and submissions made by them.

Experts appear to have a similar role in all the relevant jurisdictions. However, the preference in Great Britain is for sourcing experts from the relevant foreign jurisdiction. The preference in Germany is for sourcing opinions from German academic institutions providing expertise in comparative law. Traditionally, English courts were very reluctant to allow the use of academic, non-practising experts to prove the content of foreign law; however, there is growing flexibility in this regard. An important difference is that British courts require demonstrable, specialist expertise on the relevant foreign legal system, whereas the German courts appear to be more flexible as to the expert's specialist background. While British procedure generally requires that parties instruct their own experts, the expert's duty is ultimately to the court. The German court generally instructs experts directly, meaning that there is no doubt as to whom a duty is owed.

The consequence of the failure to prove the content of the *lex causae* is, as a rule, that the *lex fori* will be applied by the court, with the exception that, in Germany, recourse to an alternative law remains a possibility. In the British courts, a rebuttable presumption applies that the content of the *lex causae* does not materially differ from the *lex fori*, although the presumption should not be applied where it would lead to absurdity on the specific facts of the case.

The incorrect application of a choice of law rule clearly gives grounds for appeal in all relevant jurisdictions. However, a complete failure by the British court to apply a choice of law rule is not grounds for appeal because of the voluntary approach and because it is questionable who would even take the point. Where a party seeks to introduce foreign law at a later stage of British civil proceedings, they are entitled to seek to do so, but must do so by means of an amendment to their pleadings.

Failure by a German court to adequately investigate the content of the applicable foreign law is grounds for appeal. A particular justification for this becomes clear when considering that the Federal Court of Justice will only rule that the investigation conducted by the lower instance court was insufficient, not that the court's determination of the content of the applicable foreign law was wrong. Ruling the investigation as insufficient is essentially a backdoor way of asking the lower instance court to think again, thus preventing injustice in individual cases but avoiding the Federal Court of Justice having to give determinative rulings on foreign law. The position is almost entirely reversed in the British courts, which do not hold the lower instance courts to any investigative standard but do allow determinations on the content of foreign law to be reviewed in appeals as a 'peculiar kind' of fact.

Looking forward, while the UK Supreme Court recently clarified the scope and effect of the voluntary choice of law approach, which leaves the introduction of choice of law rules in the hands of the parties, British judges ought to have the right, to the extent that this is not already the case, to discuss the choice of law aspects of the case with the parties as part of their case management role, with parties having to make their intentions clear. Special considerations arise, for example, in some undefended litigation and cases involving status, which potentially warrant a more interventionist role for British judges in certain circumstances.

Movement away from the treatment of foreign law as fact in British procedure is desirable. However, the solution is not to frame foreign and domestic law as one and the same; nor does the solution lie in judicial notice of foreign law, which is a nebulous concept. Rather, foreign law requires its own separate procedural treatment, which recognises its unique characteristics. This point applies to a lesser extent to German procedure, which correctly identifies foreign law as law, but sometimes struggles with the reality that foreign and domestic law can never be true equivalents.

At the multilateral level, action should be taken to help improve the effectiveness of the investigative process in domestic courts. However, the solution does not lie in the provision of a comprehensive electronic database seeking to provide solutions to substantive legal questions; rather it lies in drawing on existing expertise available in the various jurisdictions of the world through the streamlined exchange of opinions. While, in some circumstances, the application of foreign law through the conduit of choice of law rules is both necessary and justified, the focus should be on those cases which genuinely require this complicated process to be undertaken. Thought ought to be given to reducing the need to apply foreign law when drafting choice of law rules, and whether there is a residual role for the doctrine of *forum non conveniens* in the context of rules regulating cross-border jurisdiction. Both would help to have disputes heard where they can best be adjudicated; that is, by a court applying its own substantive law.

BIBLIOGRAPHY

Ahn MJ, '44.1 Luftballons: The Communication Breakdown of Foreign Law in the Federal Courts' (2014) 89 *New York University Law Review* 1343.

Alpa G and Zeno-Zencovich Vincenzo, *Italian Private Law* (Routledge-Cavendish, 2007).

Anton AE, 'The Introduction into English Practice of Continental Theories on the Conflict of Laws' (1956) 5 *ICLQ* 534.

Arndt K and Kegel G, 'Zur Verbesserung der Deutschen Zivilrechtsprechung in internationalen Sachen: Denkschrift vom 26 August 1970' (1971) 35 *Rabels Zeitschrift für Ausländisches und Internationales Privatrecht* 323.

Arnold W, 'The Supreme Court of the United Kingdom (UKSC), an Exploration of the Roles of Judicial Officers and Court Administrators and how the Relationship between them may be improved and enhanced: a Case Study' (2014) 6 *International Journal for Court Administration* 19.

Atamer YM, 'Rezeption und Weiterentwicklung des schweizerischen Zivilgesetzbuches in der Türkei' (2008) 72 *Rabels Zeitschrift für Ausländisches und Internationales Privatrecht* 723.

Austin J, *The Province of Jurisprudence Determined and The Uses of the Study of Jurisprudence: with an Introduction by HLA Hart* (Hackett Publishing Company, 1998).

Bacher K, '§ 293' in V Vorwerk and C Wolf (eds), *BeckOK ZPO*, 43rd edn (CH Beck, 2022).

Baker TE, 'The Impropriety of Expert Witness Testimony on the Law' (1992) 40 *University of Kansas Law Review* 325.

Balfour (Lord Pettindreich) SJ, *Practicks: Or, a System of the more ancient Law of Scotland* (A Kincaid and A Donaldson, 1754).

Bankton AM, *An Institute of the Laws of Scotland in Civil Rights* vol 1 (A Kincaid and A Donaldson, 1751).

—— *An Institute of the Laws of Scotland in Civil Rights* vol 2 (A Kincaid and A Donaldson, 1752).

Bar C von (ed), See Von Bar

Barak A, 'A Judge on Judging: The Role of a Supreme Court in a Democracy' (2002) 116 *Harvard Law Review* 19.

Basedow J, 'Kohärenz im Internationalen Privat- und Verfahrensrecht der Europäischen Union – Eine einleitende Orientierung' in J von Hein and G Rühl (eds), *Kohärenz im Internationalen Privat- und Verfahrensrecht der Europäischen Union* (Mohr Siebeck, 2016), 4.

Bean D, Parry I and Burns A, *Injunctions*, 13th edn (Sweet & Maxwell, 2018).

Beaumont PR, 'Private international law concerning children in the UK after Brexit: comparing Hague Treaty law with EU Regulations' (2017) *CPIL Working Paper* No 2017/2, www.abdn.ac.uk/law/documents/CPIL%20Working%20Paper%20No%202017_2.pdf.

—— 'When should EU private international law require that foreign law be applied?' in J von Hein, E-M Kieninger and G Rühl (eds), *How European is European Private International Law?* (Intersentia, 2019).

—— 'Some reflections on the way ahead for UK private international law after Brexit' [2021] *Journal of Private International Law* 1.

Beaumont PR and Bremner P, 'Inter-regional conflicts within the United Kingdom relating to Private International Law of Succession – The development of the applicable law rule' (2010) 54 *Revista Valenciana d'Estudis Autonòmics* 238.

Beaumont PR and Holliday J, 'Habitual Residence in Child Abduction Cases: The Hybrid Approach Is Now the Norm but How Much Weight Should Be Given to Parental Intention?' in M Pfeiffer and others (eds), *Liber Amicorum Monika Pauknerová* (Wolters Kluwer, 2021).

Beaumont PR and McEleavy PE, *The Hague Convention on International Child Abduction* (Oxford University Press, 1999).
—— *Anton's Private International Law*, 3rd edn (W Green, 2011).
Beaumont PR, Walker L and Holliday J, 'Parental Responsibility and International Child Abduction in the proposed recast of Brussels IIa Regulation and the effect of Brexit on future child abduction proceedings' (2016) *CPIL Working Paper* No 2016/6.
Bell J, 'Sources of Law' (2018) 77 *CLJ* 40.
Benecke M, 'Eingriffsnormen und Revisibilität ausländischen Rechts – Bekanntes und Neues zum Internationalen Arbeitsrecht und Arbeitsprozessrecht in BAG 7.5.2020 – 2 AZR 692/19' [2020] *Recht der Arbeit* 366.
Bergmann A, Ferid M and Henrich D (eds), *Internationales Ehe- und Kindschaftsrecht* (Loose-leaf-collection of approximately 18,000 pages in 23 folders, 2021).
Berman F and Bentley D, 'Treaties and other International Instruments: Ratification, Accession, Acceptance and Approval, Treaty Succession' in I Roberts (ed), *Satow's Diplomatic Practice*, 7th edn (Oxford University Press, 2016).
Berner F, *Kollisionsrecht im Spannungsfeld von Kollisionsnormen, Hoheitsinteressen und wohlerworbenen Rechten* (Mohr Siebeck, 2017).
Bernstein H, 'Kollisionsrechtliche Fragen der Culpa in Contrahendo' (1977) 41 *Rabels Zeitschrift für Ausländisches und Internationales Privatrecht* 281.
Bingham TH, '"There is a world elsewhere": The Changing Perspectives of English Law' (1992) 41 *ICLQ* 513.
Black AC, 'The Institutional Writers: 1600–1826' in The Stair Society (ed), *An Introductory Survey of the Sources and Literature of Scots Law* (Robert Maclehose & Co Ltd, 1936).
Borth H and Grandel M, *Familiengerichtliches Verfahren*, Hans-Joachim Musielak (ed), 6th edn (Franz Vahlen, 2018).
Boylan-Kemp J, *English Legal System: The Fundamentals*, 4th edn (Sweet & Maxwell, 2018).
Brand O, *Das* Internationale Zinsrecht Englands (JCB Mohr (Paul Siebeck), 2002).
Briggs A, 'What did Boys v Chaplin decide?' (1983) 12 *Anglo-American Law Review* 237.
—— *The Conflict of Laws*, 2nd edn (Oxford University Press, 2008).
—— *The Conflict of Laws*, 4th edn (Oxford University Press, 2019).
Brown JR, '44.1 Ways to Prove Foreign Law' (1984) 9 *Maritime Lawyer* 179.
Brown SM, 'Review: The Concept of Law by HLA Hart' (1963) 72 *The Philosophical Review* 250.
Bruch CS, 'The Central Authority's Role under the Hague Child Abduction Convention: A Friend in Deed' (1994) 28 *Family Law Quarterly* 35.
Brutscher A-M, *Zivilrechtsakzessorietät des Strafrechts bei Sachverhalten mit Auslandsbezug – am Beispiel des § 242 StGB* (Mohr Siebeck, 2014).
Busch B and Sommerich OC, 'Expert Witness and the Proof of Foreign Law' (1952–1953) 38 *Cornell Law Quarterly* 125.
Buxbaum HL, 'Territory, Territoriality, and the Resolution of Jurisdictional Conflict' (2009) 57 *The American Journal of Comparative Law* 631.
Cairns JW, 'Institutional Writings in Scotland Reconsidered' (1984) 4 *Journal of Legal History* 76.
—— 'Historical Introduction' in K Reid and R Zimmermann (eds), *A History of Private Law in Scotland: Introduction and Property* (Oxford University Press, 2000) 14.
—— 'Ius Civile in Scotland, ca. 1600' (2004) 2 *Roman Legal Tradition* 136.
—— 'Attitudes to Codification and the Scottish Science of Legislation, 1600–1830' (2007) 22 *Tulane European and Civil Law Forum* 1.
Cannon M, Evans H and Stewart R (eds), *Jackson and Powell on Professional Liability*, 9th edn (Sweet & Maxwell, 2021).
Carruthers JM, 'Substance and Procedure in the Conflict of Laws: A continuing debate in relation to damages' (2004) 53 *ICLQ* 691.
Carswell RD, 'The Doctrine of Vested Rights in Private International Law' (1959) 8 *ICLQ* 268.
Cartwright J and Hesselink M, 'Introduction' in J Cartwright and M Hesselink (eds), *Precontractual Liability in European Private Law* (Cambridge University Press, 2008).

Cavers DF and others, '*Babcock v Jackson*, 12 NY 2d 473, 191 NE 2d 279, 240 NYS 2d 743 (1963)' (1963) 63 *Columbia Law Review* 1212.
Chalmers J and Leverick F, *The Criminal Law of Scotland*, 4th edn (W Green, 2016).
Clark DS, 'The Use of Comparative Law by American Courts (I)' (1994) 42 *The American Journal of Comparative Law Supplement* 23.
Collins L (ed), *Dicey and Morris on the Conflict of Laws* vol 1, 13th edn (Sweet & Maxwell, 1999).
Collins (Lord Collins of Mapesbury) L and Harris J (eds), *Dicey, Morris & Collins on the Conflict of Laws*, 15th edn & 5th supp (Sweet & Maxwell, 2018).
Coyle JF, 'The Canons of Construction for Choice-of-Law Clauses' (2017) 92 *Washington Law Review* 631.
Craig PP, 'The Process: Brexit and the Anatomy of Article 50' in F Fabbrini (ed), *The Law & Politics of Brexit* (Oxford University Press, 2017).
Craig PP and Búrca G de, *EU Law: Text, Cases, and Materials*, 7th edn (Oxford University Press, 2020).
Crawford EB and Carruthers JM, *International Private Law: A Scots Perspective*, 4th edn (W Green, 2015).
Cretney S, *Family Law in the Twentieth Century: A History* (Oxford University Press, 2005).
Cubie AM (ed), *Macphail's Sheriff Court Practice*, 4th edn (W Green, 2022).
Cuniberti G, 'The International Market for Contracts: The Most Attractive Contract Laws' (2014) 34 *Northwestern Journal of International Law & Business* 455.
Cunningham-Hill S and Elder K, *Civil Litigation: 2018–2019*, 11th edn (Oxford University Press, 2018).
Dicey AV, 'On Private International Law as a Branch of the Law of England' (1890) 6 *LQR* 1.
—— *A Digest of the Law of England with reference to the Conflict of Laws*, 2nd edn (Stevens and Sons; Sweet & Maxwell, 1908).
Dickinson A, 'Realignment of the Planets – Brexit and European Private International Law' [2021] *Praxis des Internationalen Privat- und Verfahrensrechts* 213.
Dickson B, 'The Contribution of Lord Diplock to the General Law of Contract' (1989) 9 *Oxford Journal of Legal Studies* 441.
Donaldson A, 'Some Conflict Rules of Scots Law' (1953) 39 *Transactions Year* 145.
Drobnig U, 'Rechtsvergleichung in der deutschen Rechtsprechung' (1986) 50 *Rabels Zeitschrift für Ausländisches und Internationales Privatrecht* 610.
Endemann W, *Das Deutsche Civilprozeßrecht* vol 1 (Bangel & Schmitt, 1868).
—— *Das Deutsche Civilprozeßrecht* vol 2 (Bangel & Schmitt, 1868).
Erskine J, *An Institute of the Law of Scotland* vol 2, New edition by James Badenach Nicolson (Bell & Bradfute, 1871).
Fawcett JJ and Torremans P (eds), *Cheshire, North & Fawcett: Private International Law*, 15th edn (Oxford University Press, 2017).
Fentiman R, *Foreign Law in English Courts: Pleading, Proof and Choice of Law* (Oxford University Press, 1998).
—— 'Laws, Foreign Laws, and Facts' (2006) 59 *Current Legal Problems* 391.
—— 'Foreign Law in National Courts: A Common Law Perspective' in M Andenas and D Fairgrieve (eds), *Courts and Comparative Law* (Oxford University Press, 2015) 79.
—— 'Foreign Law as Local Law: a Case of Mistaken Identity?' in M Pfeiffer and others (eds), *Liber Amicorum Monika Pauknerová* (Wolters Kluwer, 2021), 143.
Fergus DT and Maher G, 'Sources of Law (General and Historical) (Volume 22) (Original Date of Publication: 30 November 1986)', *The Laws of Scotland: Stair Memorial Encyclopaedia* (LexisNexis).
Ferid M and others (eds), *Internationales Erbrecht*, 116th edn (Loose-leaf-collection of 21,550 pages in 9 folders), 2021).
Fiorini A, 'The Codification of Private International Law in Europe – Could the Community Learn from the Experience of Mixed Jurisdictions?' (2008) 23 *Tulane European and Civil Law Forum* 89.
Flessner A, 'Fakultatives Kollisionsrecht' (1970) 34 *Rabels Zeitschrift für Ausländisches und Internationales Privatrecht* 547.
Forsyth C, 'Characterisation revisited: an essay in the theory and practice of the English conflict of laws' (1998) 114 *LQR* 141.

Forte ADM, 'Opinions by "Eminent English Counsel": Their Use in Insurance Cases before the Court of Session in the Late Eighteenth and Early Nineteenth Centuries' [1995] *Juridical Review* 345.

Fortunato SF, 'Vom römisch-gemeinen Recht zum Bürgerlichen Gesetzbuch' [2009] *Zeitschrift für das Juristische Studium* 327.

Fritsche J, '§ 139' in W Krüger and T Rauscher (eds), *Münchener Kommentar zur Zivilprozessordnung: Band 1 (§§ 1–354)*, 6th edn (CH Beck, 2020).

Fuller LL, 'Positivism and Fidelity to Law – A Reply to Professor Hart' (1957) 71 *Harvard Law Review* 630.

Furmston M, 'Proof of Foreign Law' (1959) 22 *Modern Law Review* 317.

Gaupp L, *Die Civilprozeßordnung für das Deutsche Reich* vol 1, 2nd edn (Akademische Verlagsbuchhandlung von JCB Mohr (Paul Siebeck), 1890).

Gaupp (ed) L and Stein F, *Die Civilprozeßordnung für das Deutsche Reich*, 4th edn (JCB Mohr (Paul Siebeck), 1901).

Gebauer M, *Grundfragen der Europäisierung des Privatrechts: Eine Untersuchung nationaler Ansätze unter Berücksichtigung des italienischen und des deutschen Rechts* (Universitätsverlag C Winter, 1998).

—— 'Uniform Law, General Principles and Autonomous Interpretation' (2000) 5 *Uniform Law Review* 683.

Geimer R, *Internationales Zivilprozessrecht*, 8th edn (Otto Schmidt, 2020).

Genzmer E, 'A Civil Lawyer's Critical Views on Comparative Legal History' (1966) 15 *The American Journal of Comparative Law* 87.

Gesterding F, *Ausbeute von Nachforschungen über verschiedene Rechtsmaterien* (Koch, 1832).

Gibb AD, 'International Private Law in Scotland in the Sixteenth and Seventeenth Centuries' (1927) 39 *Juridical Review* 369.

Gilbert M, 'Social Rules: Some Problems for Hart's account, and an alternative Proposal' (1999) 18 *Law and Philosophy* 141.

Giliker P, 'The Consumer Rights Act 2015 – a bastion of European consumer rights?' (2017) 37 *Legal Studies* 78.

Gilmore S and Glennon L, *Hayes & Williams' Family Law*, 7th edn (Oxford University Press, 2020).

Giuliano M and Lagarde P, 'Report on the Convention on the law applicable to contractual obligations' [1980], eur-lex.europa.eu/legal-content/EN/TXT/PDF/?uri=CELEX:31980Y1031(01)&from=EN.

Godfrey AM, 'Ratio Decidendi and Foreign Law in the History of Scots Law' in S Dauchy, WH Bryson and MC Mirow (eds), *Ratio decidendi: Guiding Principles of Judicial Decisions* (Duncker & Humblot, 2010), 81.

Goette W, 'Dialog zwischen Rechtswissenschaft und Rechtsprechung in Deutschland am Beispiel des Gesellschaftsrechts' (2013) 77 *Rabels Zeitschrift für Ausländisches und Internationales Privatrecht* 309.

Gomille C, 'Beweiserhebung – Unterschiede zwischen ZPO- und FamFG Verfahren' [2014] *Neue Zeitschrift für Familienrecht* 100.

Goodhart AL, 'Determining the Ratio Decidendi of a Case' (1930) 40 *Yale Law Journal* 161.

Grävell, Maximilian Carl Friedrich Wilhelm, *Praktischer Kommentar zur allgemeinen Gerichts-Ordnung für die preußischen Staaten* vol 1 (Keyser'sche Buchhandlung, 1825).

—— *Praktischer Kommentar zur allgemeinen Gerichts-Ordnung für die preußischen Staaten* vol 2 (Keyser'sche Buchhandlung, 1826).

Graziano TK, 'Is it Legitimate and Beneficial for Judges to Compare?' in M Andenas and D Fairgrieve (eds), *Courts and Comparative Law* (Oxford University Press, 2015) 25.

Greger R, 'Die ZPO-Reform – 1000 Tage danach' (2004) 17(3) *Juristenzeitung* 805.

Grothe H, 'BGB § 194 Gegenstand der Verjährung' in C Schubert (ed), *Münchener Kommentar zum Bürgerlichen Gesetzbuch: Band 1 (Allgemeiner Teil §§ 1-240, AllgPersönlR, ProstG, AGG)*, 9th edn (CH Beck, 2021).

Gruber J, 'Die Anwendung ausländischen Rechts durch deutsche Gerichte' [1992] *Zeitschrift für Rechtspolitik* 6.

——'Rechtsprechung: Anwaltshaftung bei Anwendung ausländischen Rechts' (1997) 7(11) *Deutsche Zeitschrift für Wirtschafts- und Insolvenzrecht* 460.
Grunsky W and Jacoby F, *Zivilprozessrecht*, 16th edn (Franz Vahlen, 2018).
Hahn C, *Die gesammten Materialien zur Civilprozessordnung und dem Einführungsgesetz zu derselben vom 30 Januar 1877* (RV Decker, 1880).
Haimerl FX, 'Ueber den Beweis ausländischer Gesetze; als Beitrag zur Erklärung des § 104 der allgemeinen Gerichtsordnung' [1833] *Zeitschrift für österreichische Rechtsgelehrsamkeit und politische Gesetzkunde* 281.
Harrison F, *On Jurisprudence and the Conflict of Laws* (Clarendon Press, 1919).
Hart HLA, *The Concept of Law*, 3rd edn (Oxford University Press, 2012).
Hartley TC, 'Pleading and Proof of Foreign Law: The Major European Systems Compared' (1996) 45 *ICLQ* 271.
Hau W, 'Ein Rückzugsgefecht des BGH gegen die Revisibilität ausländischen Rechts' [2014] *Praxis des Internationalen Privat- und Verfahrensrechts* 397.
Hausleiter M and Schramm B, 'Beschwerde gegen Widerrechtlichkeitsbescheinigung nach dem HKÜ' [2021] *Neue Juristische Wochenschrift-Spezial* 549.
HCCH, 'Accessing the content of foreign law and the need for the development of a global instrument in this area – A possible way ahead' (2009), assets.hcch.net/docs/ec2804c3-f55c-427d-9761-e0fa4eac41a7.pdf.
Heaney B, 'International private law – the default rule and presumption of similarity' (2021) 162 *Civil Practice Bulletin* 6.
Heffter A, *System des römischen und deutschen Civil-Proceßrechts* (Adolph Marcus, 1843).
Hein. See Von Hein
Hennessy C, *Civil Procedure and Practice*, 5th edn (W Green, 2018).
Herdegen M, *Völkerrecht*, 20th edn (CH Beck, 2021).
Heward E, *Lord Mansfield* (Barry Rose (Publishers) Ltd, 1979).
Hodge (Lord Hodge) P, 'The Scope of Judicial Law-Making in the Common Law Tradition' (2020) 84 *Rabels Zeitschrift für Ausländisches und Internationales Privatrecht* 211.
Hodgkinson T and James M, *Expert Evidence: Law and Practice*, 5th edn (Thomson Reuters (Professional) UK Limited, 2020).
Hohmann O, '§ 246' in GM Sander (ed), *Münchener Kommentar zum StGB: Band 4 (§§ 185–262)*, 4th edn (CH Beck, 2021).
Holdsworth W, 'The Rules of Venue, and the Beginnings of the Commercial Jurisdiction of the Common Law Courts' (1914) 14 *Columbia Law Review* 551.
Home (Lord Kames) H, *Principles of Equity*, 4th edn (Bell & Bradfute, and W Creecii, 1800).
Hood K, 'Drawing Inspiration? Reconsidering the Procedural Treatment of Foreign Law' (2006) 2 *Journal of Private International Law* 181.
—— *Conflict of Laws within the UK* (Oxford University Press, 2007).
Hübner R, *Ausländisches Recht vor deutschen Gerichten* (Mohr Siebeck, 2014).
Hüßtege R, 'Zur Ermittlung ausländischen Rechts: Wie man in den Wald hineinruft, so hallt es auch zurück' [2002] *Praxis des Internationalen Privat- und Verfahrensrechts* 292.
—— 'Internetrecherche contra Sachverständigengutachten – Zur Ermittlung ausländischen Rechts durch deutsche Gerichte' [2021] *Praxis des Internationalen Privat- und Verfahrensrechts* 261.
Huzel E, 'Zur Zulässigkeit eines "Auflagenbeschlusses" im Rahmen des § 293 ZPO' [1990] *Praxis des Internationalen Privat- und Verfahrensrechts* 77.
Isidro MR, 'The Application of European Private International Law and the Ascertainment of Foreign law' in J von Hein, E-M Kieninger and G Rühl (eds), *How European is European Private International Law?* (Intersentia, 2019), 139.
Johnston D, *Prescription and Limitation of Actions*, 2nd edn (W Green, 2012).
Jolowicz JA, 'Adversarial and Inquisitorial Models of Civil Procedure' (2003) 52 *ICLQ* 281.
Jones HW, 'Our Uncommon Common Law' (1975) 42 *Tennessee Law Review* 443.
Junker A, *Internationales Privatrecht*, 3rd edn (CH Beck, 2019).

—— *Internationales Zivilprozessrecht*, 5th edn (CH Beck, 2020).
—— *Internationales Privatrecht*, 4th edn (CH Beck, 2021).
Kahn-Freund O, *General Problems of Private International Law* (Kluwer Academic Publishers, 1976).
Kau M, 'Der Staat und der Einzelne als Völkerrechtssubjekte' in W Vitzthum and A Proelß (eds), *Völkerrecht*, 7th edn (De Gruyter, 2016).
Keane E and Davidson F (eds), *Raitt on Evidence: Principles, Policy and Practice*, 3rd edn (W Green, 2018).
Kegel G and Schurig K, *Internationales Privatrecht*, 9th edn (CH Beck, 2004).
Kennedy TP, 'Ireland' in C Esplugues, JL Iglesias and G Palao (eds), *Application of Foreign Law* (Sellier European Law Publishers, 2011) 231.
Kischel U, *Rechtsvergleichung* (CH Beck, 2015).
Kitchen M, *A History of Modern Germany: 1800 to the Present*, 2nd edn (Wiley-Blackwell, 2012).
Klerman D, 'Nonpromotion and Judicial Independence' (1999) 72 *Southern California Law Review* 455.
Klugkist E, 'Die Aktenversendung an Juristenfakultäten: Ein gemeinsames Kapitel aus der Geschichte des deutschen Prozeßrechts und der deutschen Universitäten' (1967) 22 *Juristenzeitung* 155.
Knetsch J and Jacquemin Z, 'France' in E Karner and BC Steininger (eds), *European Tort Law 2020* (De Gruyter, 2021) 178.
Köhler H, *BGB Allgemeiner Teil*, 45th edn (CH Beck, 2021).
Koopmans T, 'Comparative Law and the Courts' (1996) 45 *ICLQ* 545.
Kötz H, 'Allgemeine Rechtsgrundsätze als Ersatzrecht' (1970) 34 *Rabels Zeitschrift für Ausländisches und Internationales Privatrecht* 663.
—— 'Alte und neue Aufgaben der Rechtsvergleichung' (2002) 6 *Juristenzeitung* 257.
Kropholler J, *Internationales Privatrecht*, 6th edn (Mohr Siebeck, 2006).
Kunig P, 'Völkerrecht und staatliches Recht' in W Vitzthum and A Proelß (eds), *Völkerrecht*, 7th edn (De Gruyter, 2016).
Lang A, 'Briefing Paper Number 5855: Parliament's role in ratifying treaties' [2017] *House of Commons Library*, researchbriefings.parliament.uk/ResearchBriefing/Summary/SN05855.
Langenbeck W, 'Beiträge zur Lehre von dem Beweise fremder Rechte vor inländischen Gerichten' (1858) 41 *Archiv für die civilistische Praxis* 129.
Lawson CM, 'The Family Affinities of Common-Law and Civil-Law Legal Systems' (1982) 6 *Hastings International and Comparative Law Review* 85.
Leabeater J and others, *Civil Appeals: Principle and Procedure*, 2nd edn (Sweet & Maxwell, 2014).
Leadbetter JS, 'The Printed Law Reports: 1540–1935' in The Stair Society (ed), *An Introductory Survey of the Sources and Literature of Scots Law* (Robert Maclehose & Co Ltd, 1936).
Legarde P, 'Explanatory Report on the Convention of 19 October 1996 on Jurisdiction, Applicable Law, Recognition, Enforcement and Co-operation in Respect of Parental Responsibility and Measures for the Protection of Children' (1996), assets.hcch.net/upload/expl34.pdf.
Levasseur AA, 'The Use of Comparative Law by Courts (II)' (1994) 42 *The American Journal of Comparative Law Supplement* 41.
Lewis P, 'Litigants in person and their difficulties in adducing evidence: a study of small claims in an English county court' (2007) 11 *International Journal of Evidence & Proof* 24.
L'Heureux-Dube C, 'The Importance of Dialogue: Globalization and the International Impact of the Rehnquist Court' (1998) 34 *Tulsa Law Journal* 15.
Llewelyn Davies DJ, 'The Influence of Huber's De Conflictu Legum on English Private International Law' (1937) 18 *British Yearbook of International Law* 49.
Lorenzen EG, 'Huber's De Conflictu Legum' (1919) Paper 4563 *Faculty Scholarship Series.*
—— 'Story's Commentaries on the Conflict of Laws: One Hundred Years after' (1934) 48 *Harvard Law Review* 15.
—— 'The Qualification, Classification, or Characterization Problem in the Conflict of Laws' (1941) 50 *Yale Law Journal* 743.
Lucraft M, *Archbold: Criminal Pleading, Evidence and Practice*, 2021 edn (Sweet & Maxwell, 2020).
Ludwig von Bar C, *Theorie und Praxis des internationalen Privatrechts* vol 1, 2nd edn (Hahn'sche Buchhandlung, 1889).

Lüke W, *Zivilprozessrecht*, 10th edn (CH Beck, 2011).
Luther G, 'Kollisions- und Fremdrechtsanwendung in der Gerichtspraxis' (1973) 37 *Rabels Zeitschrift für Ausländisches und Internationales Privatrecht* 660.
Lüttringhaus JD, 'Das internationale Privatrecht der culpa in contrahendo nach den EG-Verordnungen "Rom I" und "Rom II"' [2008] *Recht der Internationalen Wirtschaft* 193.
Macgregor L, 'Report on the Draft Common Frame of Reference: A report prepared for the Scottish Government' [2008] *Scottish Government*, www.webarchive.org.uk/wayback/archive/3000/https://www.gov.scot/Resource/Doc/262952/0078639.pdf.
Mackay ÆJG, 'Who Wrote "Balfour's Practicks"?' (1898) 13(49) *The Scottish Antiquary, or, Northern Notes and Queries* 1.
Mackie JD and Dickinson WC, 'Relation of the Manner of Judicatores of Scotland' (1922) 19 *The Scottish Historical Review* 245.
Macphail (Lord Macphail) ID, 'Research Paper on the Law of Evidence of Scotland' [1979] *Scottish Law Commission*, www.scotlawcom.gov.uk/files/1913/1463/2308/Macphail_ch_20-25.pdf.
MacQueen HL, 'Mixing It? Comparative Law In The Scottish Courts' (2003) 6 *European Review of Private Law* 735.
—— 'The Sophistication of Unjustified Enrichment: A Response to Nils Jansen' (2016) 20 *Edinburgh Law Review* 312.
Maher G, 'Judicial notice and statute law' (2001) 117 *LQR* 71.
Maitland FW, 'The Making of the German Civil Code' in HAL Fisher (ed), *The Collected Papers of Frederic William Maitland* vol 3 (Cambridge University Press, 1911).
Mak E, 'Comparative Law before the Supreme Courts of the UK and the Netherlands' in M Andenas and D Fairgrieve (eds), *Courts and Comparative Law* (Oxford University Press, 2015) 407.
Malek H, Auburn J and Bagshaw R (eds), *Phipson on Evidence*, 20th edn (Sweet & Maxwell, 2021).
Mankowski P, 'Privatgutachten über ausländisches Recht – Erstattungsfähigkeit der Kosten' [2001] *Monatsschrift für Deutsches Recht* 194.
—— 'Die Qualifikation der culpa in contrahendo – Nagelprobe für den Vertragsbegriff des europäischen IZPR und IPR' [2003] *Praxis des Internationalen Privat- und Verfahrensrechts* 127.
Mann FA, 'Fusion of the Legal Professions?' (1977) 93 *LQR* 367.
Mann G, *Deutsche Geschichte des 19. und 20. Jahrhunderts*, 13th edn (Fischer Taschenbuch Verlag, 2011).
Markesinis BS, *Comparative Law in the Courtroom and Classroom: The Story of the Last Thirty-Five Years* (Hart Publishing, 2004).
Maurer H, *Staatsrecht I*, 6th edn (CH Beck, 2010).
McComish J, 'Pleading and Proving Foreign Law in Australia' (2007) 31(2) *Melbourne University Law Review* 400.
McCormick CT, 'Judicial Notice' (1952) 5 *Vanderbilt Law Review* 296.
McEleavy PE, 'The Evolution of European Private International Law' (2008) 57 *ICLQ* 969.
McGee A, *Limitation Periods*, 8th edn (Sweet & Maxwell, 2018).
McParland M, *The Rome I Regulation on the Law Applicable to Contractual Obligations* (Oxford University Press, 2015).
Mead JW, 'Stare Decisis in the Inferior Courts of the United States' (2012) 12 *Nevada Law Journal* 787.
Meador DJ, 'Inherent Judicial Authority in the Conduct of Civil Litigation' (1995) 73 *Texas Law Review* 1805.
Menkel-Meadow C, 'The Trouble with the Adversary System in a Postmodern, Multicultural World' (1996) 38 *William and Mary Law Review* 5.
Meyer O, 'Die Belehrungspflichten des Notars bei Auslandssachverhalten' [2018] *Deutsche Notar-Zeitschrift* 726.
Millar RW, 'Civil Pleading in Scotland (I)' (1932) 30 *Michigan Law Review* 545.
Miller AR, 'Federal Rule 44.1 and the Fact Approach to Determining Foreign Law: Death Knell for a Die-Hard Doctrine' (1967) 65 *Michigan Law Review* 613.
Miller DC, 'Sibling Mixed Systems: Reviewing South African/Scottish Comparative Law' (2016) 20 *Edinburgh Law Review* 257.

Mills A, 'Rethinking Jurisdiction in International Law' (2014) 84 *The British Yearbook of International Law* 187.
—— *Party Autonomy in Private International Law* (Cambridge University Press, 2018).
Miner RJ, 'The Reception of Foreign Law in the US Federal Courts' (1995) 43 *The American Journal of Comparative Law* 581.
Mittermaier, 'Ueber den Beweis ausländischer Gesetze in Rechtsstreitigkeiten' (1835) 18 *Archiv für die civilistische Praxis* 67.
Mortensen R, 'Brexit and private international law in the Commonwealth' (2021) 17 *Journal of Private International Law* 18.
Musielak H-J, *Die Grundlagen der Beweislast im Zivilprozeß* (Walter de Gruyter GmbH & Co KG, 1975).
Musielak H-J and Voit W, *Grundkurs ZPO*, 15th edn (CH Beck, 2020).
—— *Zivilprozessordnung*, 17th edn (Franz Vahlen, 2020).
Neumayer KH, 'Fremdes Recht und Normenkontrolle' (1958) 23 *Rabels Zeitschrift für Ausländisches und Internationales Privatrecht (Festgabe für Alexander N Makarov)* 573.
Nokes GD, 'Irish Law in English Courts' (1960) 9 *ICLQ* 564.
Nussbaum A, 'The Problem of Proving Foreign Law' (1941) 50 *Yale Law Journal* 1018.
O'Hare J and Browne K, *O'Hare & Browne: Civil Litigation*, 20th edn (Sweet & Maxwell, 2021).
Oppenheim HB, *System des Völkerrechts* (Literarische Anstalt (J Rütten), 1845).
—— *System des Völkerrechts*, 2nd edn (A Kröner, 1867).
Otte K, 'Betrachtungen zur Interessenlehre' in H-P Mansel (ed), *Internationales Privatrecht im 20. Jahrhundert* (Mohr Siebeck, 2014), 27.
Otto G, 'Der verunglückte § 293 ZPO und die Ermittlung ausländischen Rechts durch "Beweiserhebung"' [1995] *Praxis des Internationalen Privat- und Verfahrensrechts* 299.
Parkes R, Mullis A and Busuttil G, *Gatley on Libel and Slander*, 12th edn & 2nd supp (Sweet & Maxwell, 2017).
Paterson A, 'Duties to the Court' (University of Strathclyde Glasgow, 2007) *Strathprints*, strathprints.strath.ac.uk/4793/, accessed 9 May 2022.
Paul JR, 'The Isolation of Private International Law' (1988) 7 *Wisconsin International Law Journal* 149.
Payandeh M, 'The Concept of International Law in the Jurisprudence of HLA Hart' (2010) 21 *European Journal of International Law* 967.
Payne M, 'Hart's Concept of a Legal System' (1976) 18 *William and Mary Law Review* 287.
Pennington D, *Europe in the Seventeenth Century* (2nd edn, Routledge, 1989).
Pérez-Vera E, 'Explanatory Report on the Convention on the Civil Aspects of International Child Abduction' (1982), assets.hcch.net/upload/expl28.pdf.
Pfeiffer T, 'Methoden der Ermittlung ausländischen Rechts' in R Stürner and others (eds), *Festschrift für Dieter Leipold zum 70. Geburtstag* (Mohr Siebeck, 2009) 283.
Phillipson G, 'Max Mosley goes to Strasbourg: Article 8, Claimant Notification and Interim Injunctions' (2009) 1(1) *Journal of Media Law* 73.
Pinsler JD, 'The Inherent Powers of the Court' [1997] *Singapore Journal of Legal Studies* 1.
Pohlmann P, *Zivilprozessrecht*, 4th edn (CH Beck, 2018).
Pope H, 'The English Common Law in the United States' (1910) 24 *Harvard Law Review* 6.
Posner RA, 'The Role of the Judge in the Twenty-First Century' (2006) 86 *Boston University Law Review* 1049.
Potacs M, 'Effet utile als Auslegungsgrundsatz' (2009) 44(4) *Zeitschrift Europarecht* 465.
Powles S, Waine L and May R, *May on Criminal Evidence*, 6th edn (Sweet & Maxwell, 2015).
Prime T and Scanlan G, 'Stare decisis and the Court of Appeal; judicial confusion and judicial reform?' (2004) 23 *CJQ* 212.
Prütting H, '§ 286' in W Krüger and T Rauscher (eds), *Münchener Kommentar zur Zivilprozessordnung: Band 1 (§§ 1–354)*, 6th edn (CH Beck, 2020).
—— '§ 291' in W Krüger and T Rauscher (eds), *Münchener Kommentar zur Zivilprozessordnung: Band 1 (§§ 1–354)*, 6th edn (CH Beck, 2020).
—— '§ 293' in W Krüger and T Rauscher (eds), *Münchener Kommentar zur Zivilprozessordnung: Band 1 (§§ 1–354)*, 6th edn (CH Beck, 2020).

—— '§ 331' in W Krüger and T Rauscher (eds), *Münchener Kommentar zur Zivilprozessordnung: Band 1 (§§ 1–354)*, 6th edn (CH Beck, 2020).
Puchta GF, *Das Gewohnheitsrecht* vol 2, book 3 (Palm'sche Buchhandlung, 1837).
Rauscher T, *Internationales Privatrecht: Mit internationalem Verfahrensrecht*, 5th edn (CF Müller, 2017).
Reed (Lord Reed) R, 'Comparative Law in the Supreme Court of the United Kingdom' (2018) 82 *Rabels Zeitschrift für Ausländisches und Internationales Privatrecht* 563.
Reid K and Zimmermann R (eds), *A History of Private Law in Scotland: Introduction and Property* vol 1 (Oxford University Press, 2000).
Remien O, 'Die Anwendung und Ermittlung ausländischen Rechts im System des Europäischen Internationalen Privatrechts' (2016) 115 *Zeitschrift für vergleichende Rechtswissenschaft* 570.
Richardson L, 'The DCFR, anyone?' (January 2014) *The Journal of the Law Society of Scotland*, www.journalonline.co.uk/magazine/59-1/1013494.aspx#.XLH3SMRCS70.
Riehm T, 'Vom Gesetz, das klüger ist als seine Verfasser – Zur Revisibilität ausländischen Rechts' (2014) 69(2) *Juristenzeitung* 73.
Robertson DW, 'Federal Doctrine of Forum Non Conveniens: "An Object Lesson in Uncontrolled Discretion"' (1994) 29 *Texas International Law Journal* 353.
Rogoz T, *Ausländisches Recht im deutschen und englischen Zivilprozess* (Mohr Siebeck, 2008).
Rosenberg L, Schwab KH and Gottwald P, *Zivilprozessrecht*, 18th edn (CH Beck, 2018).
Ross M, Chalmers J and Callander I, *Walker and Walker: The Law of Evidence in Scotland*, 5th edn (Bloomsbury Professional, 2020).
Roth H, 'Entwicklung und Reformen der ZPO' [2018] *Juristische Rundschau* 159.
Rühl G, 'Die Kosten der Rechtswahlfreiheit: Zur Anwendung ausländischen Rechts durch deutsche Gerichte' (2007) 71 *Rabels Zeitschrift für Ausländisches und Internationales Privatrecht* 559.
Rupp C, 'Die Verordnung zum europäischen internationalen Ehegüterrecht aus sachenrechtlicher Perspektive' [2016] *Zeitschrift für das Privatrecht der Europäischen Union* 295.
Sack AN, 'Conflicts of Laws in the History of the English Law' in New York University (ed), *Law: A Century of Progress (1835–1935)* (New York University Press, 1937).
Säcker FJ, 'Einleitung (Einl. BGB)' in C Schubert (ed), *Münchener Kommentar zum Bürgerlichen Gesetzbuch: Band 1 (Allgemeiner Teil §§ 1–240, AllgPersönlR, ProstG, AGG)*, 9th edn (CH Beck, 2021).
Saenger I, *Zivilprozessordnung*, 9th edn (Nomos, 2021).
Samtleben J, 'Der unfähige Gutachter und die ausländische Rechtspraxis' [1992] *Neue Juristische Wochenschrift* 3057.
Sandford M and Gormley-Heenan C, '"Taking Back Control", the UK's Constitutional Narrative and Schrodinger's Devolution' (2020) 73 *Parliamentary Affairs* 108.
Sartorius R, 'The Concept of Law' (1966) 52 *Archiv für Rechts- und Sozialphilosophie* 161.
Savigny, see Von Savigny
Schack H, 'Keine stillschweigende Rechtswahl im Prozeß!' [1986] *Praxis des Internationalen Privat- und Verfahrensrechts* 272.
—— *Internationales Zivilverfahrensrecht* (8th edn, CH Beck, 2021).
Schlesinger RB, 'Die Behandlung des Fremdrechts im Amerikanischen Zivilprozess' (1962) 27 *Rabels Zeitschrift für Ausländisches und Internationales Privatrecht* 54.
Schlosser P, 'Report on the Convention on the Association of the Kingdom of Denmark, Ireland and the United Kingdom of Great Britain and Northern Ireland to the Convention on jurisdiction and the enforcement of judgments in civil and commercial matters and to the Protocol on its interpretation by the Court of Justice of 9 October 1978' [1978], eur-lex.europa.eu/legal-content/EN/TXT/PDF/?uri=OJ:C:1979:059:FULL&from=en.
Schurig K, *Kollisionsnorm und Sachrecht* (Duncker & Humblot, 1981).
—— 'Das Fundament trägt noch' in H-P Mansel (ed), *Internationales Privatrecht im 20. Jahrhundert* (Mohr Siebeck, 2014) 5.
Schütze R, 'Der Abschied von der Nichtrevisibilität ausländischen Rechts?' [1991] *Europäisches Wirtschafts- und Steuerrecht* 372.
Schuz R, *The Hague Child Abduction Convention: A Critical Analysis* (Hart Publishing, 2013).

Scott FR, 'The End of Dominion Status' (1944) 38 *The American Journal of International Law* 34.

Scottish Law Commission, 'Report on Family Law: No 135' [1992], www.scotlawcom.gov.uk/files/5912/8015/2668/Report%20on%20family%20law%20Report%20135.pdf.

Seuffert JA, *Handbuch des deutschen Civilprozesses auf der Grundlage und nach der Ordnung der bayerischen Gesetzgebung* vol 1, 2nd edn (JJ Palm und Ernst Enke, 1853).

—— *Handbuch des deutschen Civilprozesses auf der Grundlage und nach der Ordnung der bayerischen Gesetzgebung* vol 3, 2nd edn (JJ Palm und Ernst Enke, 1856).

Sherwood AM, '*Babcock v Jackson*: The Transition from the *Lex Loci Delicti* Rule to the Dominant Contacts Approach' (1964) 62 *Michigan Law Review* 1358.

Smith TB, 'English Influences on the Law of Scotland' (1954) 3 *The American Journal of Comparative Law* 522.

Smits JM (ed), *Elgar Encyclopedia of Comparative Law*, 2nd edn (Edward Elgar, 2012).

Sonnentag M, *Die Konsequenzen des Brexits für das Internationale Privat- und Zivilverfahrensrecht* (Mohr Siebeck, 2017).

Spigelman JJ, 'Proof of foreign law by reference to the foreign court' (2011) 127 *LQR* 208.

Sprankling JG and Lanyi GR, 'Pleading and Proof of Foreign Law in American Courts' (1983) 19 *Stanford Journal of International Law* 3.

Stadler A, *Allgemeiner Teil des BGB*, 20th edn (CH Beck, 2020).

Stewart WJ and Brodie D (eds), *Reparation: Liability for Delict*, 33rd Release (W Green, 2020).

Stobbe O, *Handbuch des Deutschen Privatrechts* (Wilhelm Hertz, 1871).

Story J, *Commentaries on the Conflict of Laws* (Hilliard, Gray, and Company, 1834).

—— *Commentaries on the Conflict of Laws*, 3rd edn (Maxwell and Son, 1846).

Sturm F, 'Fakultatives Kollisionsrecht: Notwendigkeit und Grenzen' in H Bernstein, U Drobnig and H Kötz (eds), *Festschrift für Konrad Zweigert zum 70 Geburtstag* (JCB Mohr (Paul Siebeck), 1981).

—— 'Buchbesprechung: Gutachten zum internationalen und ausländischen Privatrecht 1977 bzw. 1978, veröff. im Auftrage des Deutschen Rates für IPR von Murad Ferid, Gerhard Kegel, Konrad Zweigert. Redaktion: Hilmar Krüger. Frankfurt a. M.: Metzner 1979 bzw. 1980 X, 434 S and X, 504 S' (1983) 47(2) *Rabels Zeitschrift für Ausländisches und Internationales Privatrecht* 386.

—— 'Buchbesprechung: Gutachten zum internationalen und ausländischen Privatrecht. Veröffentlicht im Auftrag des Deutschen Rates für Internationales Privatrecht von Jürgen Basedow, Gerhard Kegel, Heinz-Peter Mansel. Redaktion 1999: Karsten Otte (2000/01: Christine Budzikiewicz) (Part II)' (2008) 72 *Rabels Zeitschrift für Ausländisches und Internationales Privatrecht* 831.

—— 'Wegen Verletzung fremden Rechts sind weder Revision noch Rechtsbeschwerde zulässig' (2011) 66(2) *Juristenzeitung* 74.

Stürner M and Krauß F, *Ausländisches Recht in deutschen Zivilverfahren: Eine rechtstatsächliche Untersuchung* (Nomos, 2018).

Symeonides SC, 'The First Conflicts Restatement through the Eyes of Old: As Bad as Its Reputation' (2007) 32 *Southern Illinois University Law Journal* 39.

—— *Choice of Law* (Oxford University Press, 2016).

The Law Commission, 'Classification of Limitation in Private International Law: Working Paper No 75' [1980], s3-eu-west-2.amazonaws.com/lawcom-prod-storage-11jsxou24uy7q/uploads/2016/08/No.075-Classification-of-Limitation-in-Private-International-Law.pdf.

The Law Commission and The Scottish Law Commission, 'Private International Law: The Law of Domicile (Law Com No 168 and Scot Law Com No 107)' (1987), www.scotlawcom.gov.uk/files/3212/7989/6557/rep107.pdf.

—— 'Private International Law: Choice of Law in Tort and Delict (Law Com No 193 and Scot Law Com No 129)' (1990), www.scotlawcom.gov.uk/files/5812/7989/6877/rep129.pdf.

Thiessen J, 'Von der (Linoleum-)Rolle. Die heimliche Anerkennung der culpa in contrahendo im Streit der Reichsgerichtsräte' in HC Grigoleit, J Neuner and J Petersen (eds), *Privatrechtsdogmatik im 21. Jahrhundert: Festschrift für Claus-Wilhelm Canaris zum 80. Geburtstag* (De Gruyter, 2017) 51.

Thole C, 'Anwendung und Revisibilität ausländischen Gesellschaftsrechts in Verfahren vor deutschen Gerichten' (2012) 176 *Zeitschrift für das gesamte Handelsrecht und Wirtschaftsrecht* 15.

Thomson J, *Delictual Liability*, 5th edn (Bloomsbury Professional, 2014).
—— *Family Law in Scotland*, 7th edn (Bloomsbury Professional, 2014).
Trautmann C, *Europäisches Kollisionsrecht und ausländisches Recht im nationalen Zivilverfahren* (Mohr Siebeck, 2011).
Trinder L and others, 'Litigants in person in private family law cases' [2014] *Ministry of Justice*, assets.publishing.service.gov.uk/government/uploads/system/uploads/attachment_data/file/380479/litigants-in-person-in-private-family-law-cases.pdf.
Turner H, 'The party litigant in the Scottish civil courts' [2018] *University of Glasgow*, theses.gla.ac.uk/30665/.
Unknown Authors, *Anmerkungen über den Codicem Juris Bavarici Judiciarii* (Johann Jacob Vötter, 1755).
—— *Entwurf eines Handelsgesetzbuches für das Königreich Württemberg* (JB Meßler'schen Buchhandlung, 1839).
—— *Entwurf einer Prozeßordnung in bürgerlichen Rechtsstreitigkeiten für den Norddeutschen Bund* (Königlichen Geheimen Ober-Hofbuchdruckerei, 1870).
Veeder VV, 'The English Reports (I): 1292–1865' (1901) 15 *Harvard Law Review* 1.
—— 'The English Reports (II): 1292–1865' (1901) 15 *Harvard Law Review* 109.
Viscount of Stair JD, *The Institutions of the Law of Scotland* (Printed by the Heir of Andrew Anderson, 1693).
—— *The Institutions of the Law of Scotland* vol 2 (A new edition, with notes and illustrations; by John S More, Bell & Bradfute, 1832).
Vitzthum W, 'Begriff, Geschichte und Rechtsquellen des Völkerrechts' in W Vitzthum and A Proelß (eds), *Völkerrecht*, 7th edn (De Gruyter, 2016).
Vogenauer S, 'Vertrag zugunsten Dritter' in J Basedow, KJ Hopt and R Zimmermann (eds), *Handwörterbuch des Europäischen Privatrechts* (2009).
Von Bar C, *Ausländisches Privat- und Privatverfahrensrecht in deutscher Sprache*, 10th edn (Otto Schmidt, 2017).
Von Bar C and Mankowski P, *Internationales Privatrecht: Band I – Allgemeine Lehren*, 2nd edn (CH Beck, 2003).
Von Hein J, 'EU Competence to Legislate in the Area of Private International Law and Law Reforms at the EU Level' in PR Beaumont and others (eds), *Cross-Border Litigation in Europe* (Hart Publishing, 2017) 19.
—— 'Einleitung zum Internationalen Privatrecht' in J von Hein (ed), *Münchener Kommentar zum Bürgerlichen Gesetzbuch: Band 12 (Internationales Privatrecht I, Europäisches Kollisionsrecht, Einführungsgesetz zum Bürgerlichen Gesetzbuche (Art 1–26)*, 8th edn (CH Beck, 2020).
Von Savigny FC, *System des heutigen Römischen Rechts* vol 1 (Veit und Comp, 1840).
—— *A Treatise on the Conflict of Laws* (William Guthrie trans, T&T Clark, 1869).
Wagner G, 'Fakultatives Kollisionsrecht und prozessuale Parteiautonomie' [1999] *Zeitschrift für Europäisches Privatrecht* 6.
Walton C, Kramer P and Cooper R (eds), *Charlesworth & Percy on Negligence*, 14th edn (Sweet & Maxwell, 2018).
Weber AD, *Ueber die Verbindlichkeit zur Beweisführung im Civilprozeß* (Rengerische Buchhandlung, 1805).
—— *Ueber die Verbindlichkeit zur Beweisführung im Civilprozeß*, 2nd edn (Rengerische Buchhandlung, 1832).
Weber H, *Die Theorie der Qualifikation* (JCB Mohr (Paul Siebeck), 1986).
Weller M, 'Mutual trust: in search of the future of European Union private international law' (2015) 11 *Journal of Private International Law* 64.
Wesenberg G and Wesener G, *Neuere deutsche Privatrechtsgeschichte: im Rahmen der europäischen Rechtsentwicklung*, 3rd edn (Moritz Schauenburg, 1976).
Westlake J, *A Treatise on Private International Law or the Conflict of Laws* (W Maxwell, 1858).
—— *A Treatise on Private International Law*, 2nd edn (William Maxwell & Son, 1880).

Whitty NR, 'Civil Procedure (Reissue) (2007): Introduction (paras 1–45)', *The Laws of Scotland: Stair Memorial Encyclopaedia* (LexisNexis).

Williams GL, 'International Law and the Controversy Concerning the Word "Law"' (1945) 22 *British Yearbook of International Law* 146.

Williams K, 'Litigants in person: a literature review' [2011] *Ministry of Justice*, assets.publishing.service.gov.uk/government/uploads/system/uploads/attachment_data/file/217374/litigants-in-person-literature-review.pdf.

Wilson MJ, 'Demystifying the Determination of Foreign Law in US Courts: Opening the Door to a Greater Global Understanding' (2011) 46 *Wake Forest Law Review* 887.

——'Improving the Process: Transnational Litigation and the Application of Private Foreign Law in US Courts' (2013) 45 *New York University Journal of International Law & Politics* 1111.

Wolf C and Klein S, 'Die Wiege der ZPO' in T Freudenberg (ed), *70. Deutscher Juristentag in Hannover: 16. bis 19. September 2014* (Redaktionsbeilage zu NJW, CH Beck, 2014).

Wolff M, *Private International Law*, 2nd edn (Clarendon Press, 1950).

Wong S and Cain R, 'The impact of cuts in legal aid funding of private family law cases' (2019) 41 *Journal of Social Welfare and Family Law* 3.

Woolf (Lord Woolf) H, 'Access to Justice – Final Report' [1996], webarchive.nationalarchives.gov.uk/20060213223540/http://www.dca.gov.uk/civil/final/contents.htm.

Wortmann B, 'Choice of Law by Arbitrators: The Applicable Conflict of Laws System' (1998) 14 *Arbitration International* 97.

Xu D, 'Proving foreign law in domestic proceedings – the futility of the "expert" advocate and some more sensible procedural solutions: Re Harish Salve' (2018) 37 *CJQ* 319.

Young EA, 'Foreign Law and the Denominator Problem' (2005) 119 *Harvard Law Review* 148.

Zimmermann W, '§ 407a' in W Krüger and T Rauscher (eds), *Münchener Kommentar zur Zivilprozessordnung: Band 2 (§§ 355–945b)*, 6th edn (CH Beck, 2020).

Zuck R, 'Postulationsfähigkeit und Anwaltszwang: Die Rolle des Anwalts in einer sich wandelnden Welt' (1993) 48(10) *Juristenzeitung* 500.

Zuckerman A, 'The Undertaking in Damages: Substantive and Procedural Dimensions' (1994) 53 *CLJ* 546.

—— 'Lord Woolf's Access to Justice: Plus ça change …' (1996) 59 *Modern Law Review* 773.

—— *Zuckerman on Civil Procedure: Principles of Practice*, 4th edn (Sweet & Maxwell, 2021).

Zweigert K and Kötz H, *Einführung in die Rechtsvergleichung: auf dem Gebiete des Privatrechts*, 3rd edn (JCB Mohr (Paul Siebeck), 1996).

INDEX

www.ingramcontent.com/pod-product-compliance
Ingram Content Group UK Ltd.
Pitfield, Milton Keynes, MK11 3LW, UK
UKHW020248290926
15470UKWH00002B/814

9 781509 959587